The Writer's Ultimate Research Guide

Ellen Metter

WRITER'S DIGEST BOOKS
CINCINNATI, OHIO

About the Author

Ellen Metter is a reference librarian and bibliographer in business, criminal justice, law and physical education at the University of Colorado at Denver. Ms. Metter was also a librarian in New Jersey and Philadelphia, where she received her Masters in Information Studies from Drexel University. She received her undergraduate degree in theater/music from Rutgers University's Douglass College in New Brunswick, New Jersey. Born in Brooklyn, New York, and raised in beautiful northern New Jersey, Ms. Metter currently lives in the land of hiking, Colorado.

The Writer's Ultimate Research Guide. Copyright © 1995 by Ellen Metter. Printed and bound in the United States of America. All rights reserved. No part of this book may be reproduced in any form or by any electronic or mechanical means including information storage and retrieval systems without permission in writing from the publisher, except by a reviewer, who may quote brief passages in a review. Published by Writer's Digest Books, an imprint of F&W Publications, Inc., 1507 Dana Avenue, Cincinnati, Ohio 45207. (800) 289-0963. First edition.

This hardcover edition of *The Writer's Ultimate Research Guide* features a "self-jacket" that eliminates the need for a separate dust jacket. It provides sturdy protection for your book while it saves paper, trees and energy.

Other fine Writer's Digest Books are available from your local bookstore or direct from the publisher.

99   98   97   96   95   5   4   3   2   1

Library of Congress Cataloging-in-Publication Data

Metter, Ellen.
    The writer's ultimate research guide / Ellen Metter.
        p.   cm.
    Includes index.
    ISBN 0-89879-668-7 (alk. paper)
        1. Authorship—handbooks, manuals, etc. 2. Research—Methodology—
    Handbooks, manuals, etc. 3. Bibliography—Methodology—Handbooks, manuals,
    etc. 4. Reference books—Bibliography—Handbooks, manuals, etc.— I. Title.
PN146.M47   1995
001.4—dc20   95-31185
                                                                      CIP

Edited by Jack Heffron and Roseann Biederman
Designed by Angela Lennert

Contents

To Alvin A. Sasso
1915-1994

Acknowledgments

Thanks to—
    Chris Reinhart, for excellent research support.
    Lori Oling, for the writing and research on the appendices.
    Dene Clark, for his law expertise.
    Jay Schafer, for being supportive, upbeat, and a good dad to Ted.
    Mallery Delaney Sasso and Harriet Sasso, for life.

Also thanks to—
    Curt Allred and Char Mayo, for their technical expertise.
    Colleen Archambaut, Connie Whitson, Dina Gold and all the ILL laborers.
    Orlando Archibeque, Terry Leopold, Kerranne Rile, Bob Wick, Louise Treff, Eveline Yank, Diane Turner, and all of the Aurarians for being supportive colleagues.
    Elaine Jurries, for her sanity (usually).
    Rich Metter and Norman Sanford, for much needed phone calls and e-mail.
    The fabulous Denver Public Library system and especially the good-humored librarians at the Ross-Broadway branch.
    Ryann Hamilton, for assistance and uplifting lyrics.
    John and Cynthia—for everything.

Introduction

All writers, at some time or another, will benefit from increased expertise in information gathering:

- Being able to find facts quickly.
- Knowing where to begin.
- Being aware of the information that is out there waiting to be tapped.

Though there are dozens of useful books geared specifically to writers, the bulk of sources I recommend are not publications that are expressly directed to writers. Instead, this book points out general and specialized print and electronic materials, easily found in most larger libraries, that writers should be aware of.

Your imagination and critical thinking skills are the elements needed to get the most out of this book. For example, a guide to toxic chemicals and poisons may be thought of as either a handy book for an industrialist *or* a treasure trove of evil, filled with ideas on how to dispose of an incidental character. A travel source could help you plan your vacation *or* describe the resort your protagonist has jetted to this season!

This book has a bias toward information available at libraries. A few reasons why:

Browsing at a library is different from browsing at a bookstore.

Believe me, I'm not knocking bookstores. Ask the Tattered Cover Book Store in Denver what my current credit balance is, and you'll know I spend more time there than I should. A bookstore will generally carry the newest and most popular reference books. Once a book has lost its cachet for the buying public, however, it will usually not be in stock, and might even be out of print. But a library probably bought that book. Until someone spills a soda on it or steals it, it will be in stock. Alternately, of course, a bookstore will have the best selection of the newest books, popular titles and sources that slip through the cracks and are never purchased by most libraries.

Browsing at a library is also different from browsing commercial at-home online services.

This book recommends many wonderful online sources. But often, the resources available in the library provide you with just what you need. And you incur no online charges or high phone bills. Which brings us to the next point:

Libraries are free.

Well not really. Your tax dollars support them. And there will occasionally be a charge for services. And if you're like me, you'll find that looking at a book in a library or trying an electronic resource stimulates the desire to buy it! But many of the book sources I recommend are quick look-up sources, ones you'll spend time with at the library and then leave to be reshelved.

Libraries have the tools and personnel needed to make research more efficient.
Books with common elements may end up being placed in different areas of a bookstore or library. At a library, the catalog will help you identify those sources. Indexes are available to help you piece together articles and information from thousands of magazines and newspapers, both historic and modern. And if you need assistance or direction, the librarian, who is an information expert, is there to assist you.

Biggest drawback to libraries.
Many general library collections will overlook "fringe" publications such as materials written by new age publishers, or the extremely conservative or exceedingly liberal press. Whereas most very large bookstores will have this material well represented, many large libraries will not. Academic libraries may be especially guilty of this deficiency, since many university libraries insist that their material come from "reputable" publishers whose authors have the "proper" credentials (i.e., a Ph.D. or accepted western schooling).

The Arrangement of This Book

The first chapter, "Navigating the Library—the Basics," highlights types of departments and materials common to different types of libraries. This chapter includes specific pointers for conducting research in a library, teaches conventions of online searching (both in and out of libraries), and discusses some options for reaching libraries and information databases via a computer and modem. Chapter 2, "Exploring Articles," looks at the many types and ways of accessing magazine, journal and newspaper articles, where writers may find some of their most useful information.

The rest of the book is comprised of chapters dedicated to specific kinds of searches, such as choosing a good hairstyle for your character or pinpointing a U.S. law. Every chapter contains research advice along with titles and descriptions of many reference sources.

One warning: You will not find every single source I have recommended in every single library you enter! But don't yell at the librarians. Tell them the source you are interested in, and then let them tell you if they have another source that is nearly identical. The publishing world is nothing if not repetitive. If they don't have the source or something like it, they can probably recommend a local library that does.

How Were the Resources in This Book Selected?

I chose reference sources that were either standard sources that would be easily found, at the very least, at large libraries, like *Grzimek's Animal Life Encyclopedia*, or sources that were a bit odd, such as *American Funeral Cars and Ambulances Since 1900*, which you might need to request through interlibrary loan. There are tons of books that fall in between these criteria. I know you will stumble in to most of those while looking up the sources I recommend. All the books recommended are written in English, but whenever possible, sources that include international information are listed.

Using the Library Fully

As a librarian, I was motivated to write this book to simply alert writers to the incredible resources at libraries. Some people leave high school or college and never again return to a library. I am part of a "salon" wherein a group of thoughtful people choose subjects to discuss each month. One month I recommended that we all find an article on our topic. You should have seen the faces pale and the jaws drop. "How do you do that?" they asked. Of course the process is quite simple. Just one that many people have lost touch with.

When library-hopping, try to visit either a large public library or a nearby academic library. (Many academic libraries are open to the public at no charge; some charge a small fee. Some private academic libraries charge a *large* fee.) Still, I am often amazed at the treasures I find in my teeny, tiny little branch library a few blocks from my home. Often a writer needs just a little bit of information to be nudged in the right direction.

I would be a liar if I said that entering a library guarantees instantaneous access to precisely what you need. But it can be fast. Sometimes you'll find what you want quickly—say something like the population of Ghana, easily found in the *World Factbook* (Washington, DC: Central Intelligence Agency. Annual.) or the *Europa World Year Book* (London: Europa Publications Limited. Annual.). Other times you need a more obscure fact and have to hunt through five specialized encyclopedias before you get what you need. Occasionally you get an idea from a handbook, that leads you to a book, that alerts you to two articles, that make you decide to change your entire original concept! All of these scenarios may be experienced by the best researchers; it's simply the nature of finding information.

A General Research Warning

Any book recommending research sources must pass on this advice: Reader Beware. When possible, try to confirm something you have read either by checking another source or by other means. Librarians who select books for the library do not check each fact for veracity or each idea for its usefulness. Books go out of date, but they remain on the shelves as historical works. Studies are debunked, but the original study is still on the shelf. Celebrities lie about their age, scholars puff up their credentials, and all that information might appear in a reputable biography. So just keep in mind that the written word is not always the gospel truth.

Chapter One

Navigating the Library: The Basics

Your research strategy will vary depending upon:

- Your research needs.
- The type of writer you are.
- The kind of person you are.

Though individual approaches to research vary greatly, a general understanding of how libraries are set up, and the basic knowledge of common search techniques will help get you started no matter what your style or requirements.

Choosing the Right Library

There are three general types of libraries: special libraries, public libraries and academic libraries. These libraries have different aims with each type having something unique to offer.

Public Libraries

Public libraries are meant to serve the public! So a public library collects materials that reflect the interests of the community it is based in. For example, the Idaho Falls Public Library subscribes to the *Potato Grower of Idaho Magazine*, a publication that probably gets a decent amount of use in a part of the world renowned for its spuds. Needless to say, the L.A. Public Library does not carry that particular magazine.

Public libraries may also be repositories of local historical data. Who created the ghastly sculpture in your town square? The public library may have the

answer. (Check with the local art museum or historical society as well; someone will eventually confess.)

In more populated areas, there will be a central public library where the bulk of materials are held. "Branch" libraries are created to bring library access physically closer to different parts of the community. These branches will generally have relatively tiny collections compared to the central library. It is simply not economically feasible to duplicate in branch libraries all the materials found in a central library. (Reference books are routinely priced at hundreds of dollars apiece and libraries pay the "institutional" cost, i.e., a lot more than what an individual would pay, for magazine subscriptions.) Public libraries usually maintain a system allowing you to request that materials from the central library be shipped to your branch in a day or two.

Unfortunately, many sparsely populated communities can only support libraries with rather small collections. Luckily, with the proliferation of online systems, you or your library can usually determine who else in the country—or even the world—owns what you need. (See "Using The Library From Home," page 18.) You can borrow items from distant locations through your library's interlibrary loan service (usually low cost or no cost) or order items through a commercial fee-based service.

No matter what the needs of the

community, almost all large public libraries have similar core publications that include periodical indexes to lead you to articles found in popular magazines, volumes that contain general statistics, lists of associations and some good encyclopedias.

Academic Libraries

Academic libraries, like public libraries, serve their community—their college community. The materials they select are intended to support the curriculum of their institution, and in some cases, when funding permits, the research needs of the faculty. Thus, a community college that has some freelance writing classes should have a decent selection of books that tutor writers, and a university offering a music degree should have references that would describe a kazoo. ("An instrument which amplifies the human voice, while also imparting a buzzing rasping quality to it."—*The New Grove Dictionary of Music and Musicians.* New York: Macmillan, 1980.)

There will be some crossover between large public and academic libraries, but the academic libraries will generally specialize in materials of a "scholarly" nature, specialized materials written by educated experts in the field. Since writers are seeking specialized information, you can see that it is worthwhile to investigate academic libraries.

Some academic libraries, especially those at state-subsidized institutions, will allow public patrons to use the library at no charge. Others will charge a small annual fee, and some, like Princeton University Library, will charge a rather princely sum. (At the time of this writing the cost at Princeton was $125 a year for access to

the library, and a $320 annual fee for both access and borrowing privileges.) The reason for the higher cost at private schools? They have no obligation to taxpayers and want to keep materials accessible to the college patrons. Still it can't hurt to inquire. It may be well worth paying a fee to gain access to a fine collection.

Special Libraries and Special Collections

Special libraries are geared to serve the specialized clientele and workers in agencies, societies, businesses and associations. With their tight focus, they may end up being just the library you need for a particular project. For example, a library at a botanic gardens would certainly have some excellent horticultural materials, and the library of a large corporation might purchase directories that are too specialized and expensive for a local library to invest in.

Some special collections will be open for you to browse, some will only lend their materials through interlibrary loan, and some are completely closed to the public. Still, I recommend that you follow my mother's advice when it comes to those libraries that are closed to the general public: "Ask! What can it hurt?" A polite phone call or a succinct letter may gain you entry or at least advice.

Special collections of materials may also be found within academic and public libraries. This area may be referred to as the Archives. Libraries often receive gifts of special collections ranging from rare books, personal libraries and belongings of celebrities or scholars, or posters representing a political movement. For example, the Auraria Library in Denver, Colorado, has all of the papers, publications and works collected by the National Municipal League. They even have huge framed paintings of the League's past presidents.

Libraries often choose to create and maintain collections in areas they feel have not been properly archived. For example, the University of Maryland in Baltimore is home to the Azriel Rosenfeld Science Fiction Research Collection, ranked among the top science fiction collections in the country. It includes the Walter Coslet Collection of over 15,000 fanzines from 1937-1972, sporting such names as *Extrapolation*, *Amazing Stories* and *Spicy Space Tales*.

Examples of institutions that may house libraries or special collections include hospitals, museums of all ilks, historical societies, clubs, associations, public schools, corporations and government agencies, like the U.S. Department of Transportation.

Finding Libraries

There are a number of directories that lead you to libraries of all stripes:

American Library Directory. 2 Volumes. New Providence, NJ: Bowker. Annual.

A geographically arranged guide to all types of libraries in the U.S. and Canada, including armed forces, academic, government, law, medical, public and religious. In addition to the library's name, address, phone and fax, each entry identifies contacts, size of staff and holdings, subject interests and special collections. Since there is no cross reference to subject specialties, this directory is best used for finding out about a particular library or

identifying a variety of libraries in specific geographic areas. Almost all libraries own this set.

Directory of History Departments and Organizations in the United States and Canada. Roxanne Myers Spencer. Washington, DC: American Historical Association. Annual.

Part III of this publication is comprised of detailed descriptions of historical collections and societies throughout the U.S. A similar title is the *Directory of Historical Organizations in the United States and Canada.* Nashville: American Association for State and Local History. Biennial. (Formerly titled: *Directory of Historical Societies and Agencies in the United States and Canada.*)

Official Museum Directory. The American Association of Museums. New York: R.R. Bowker. Annual.

This directory profiles over 7,000 museums in the U.S. Many of them have specialized library collections, including the Museum of Tobacco Art and History in Nashville, Tennessee, which includes a library of books and articles relating to the tobacco industry, and the Fire Museum of Maryland, Inc., with a 480-volume library. You will find this volume in most midsize to large public and academic libraries.

Subject Collections. Lee Ash and William G. Miller. 7th edition. New York: Bowker, 1993.

Writing about Mark Twain? *Subject Collections* names eighteen states with collections brimming with Twain material. Investigating poultry breeding? There are libraries in Iowa and

Massachusetts that can help you out. Arranged alphabetically under subject heading (almost 19,000 of them), this two-volume directory assists you in finding North American libraries that specialize in your research area. This directory also makes mention of any printed collections of library catalogs, such as the *Dictionary Catalog of the Harris Collection of American Poetry and Plays* (Boston: G.K. Hall, 1972.) See also the annually produced *Directory of Special Libraries and Information Centers* (Detroit: Gale.) It lists over 21,000 specialized libraries. *Subject Collections* is another source commonly found in most libraries.

World Guide to Libraries. 11th edition. New York: K.G. Saur, 1993.

Think you can leave the country to avoid research? Forget it. This guide lists over 45,000 libraries in 181 countries. Libraries listed are general libraries with over 30,000 volumes and special libraries with more than 5,000 volumes (with exemptions of these guidelines for some third-world nations). For each country, libraries are presented in the following categories: The National Library, General Research, University and College, School, Government, Ecclesiastical, Corporate, Public and Other Special Libraries. Libraries in non-English-speaking countries will of course have collections filled with non-English-language materials.

The World of Learning. London: Europa Publications Limited. Annual.

Learned Societies, Research Institutes, Libraries and Archives, Museums and Universities and Colleges,

are listed for countries worldwide. You'll find this one in most larger libraries and some smaller ones.

Your library may also have a locally produced listing of libraries in your area; for example, Colorado has the *Directory of Colorado Libraries*, which is produced by the State Library.

How Libraries Are Arranged

Each library has its unique points. Most libraries keep periodicals in a separate department, others intermingle them with book sources. Some loan out videos, others allow viewing in the library only. Libraries usually provide in-house guides, maps and help sheets to assist you in navigating that particular library. Grab those when you walk in the door. In this section, I will highlight the elements that are universal in almost all libraries to give you a solid background in the basics.

Library Materials Are Usually Arranged by Subject

Most library sources, whether slides, pamphlets, books or videos, are arranged by subject. One exception may be for magazines and journals, which libraries sometimes choose to merely alphabetize.

There are two major subject classification systems used by the majority of libraries: Dewey Decimal and Library of Congress. Both systems use letter/number combinations to create a unique "address" for each book; this is what is referred to as the call number. Though I will fill you in on a few details of each of the systems, the best thing you can remember is: The items in a library *are* filed in a logical order.

The good old Dewey Decimal System is the system that your grade school librarian probably taught you. Dewey is most often found in school libraries and public libraries. The Dewey call number assigned to each library item starts with a three-digit number. Each number grouping represents a particular subject area. Here's the general meaning of each grouping in the Dewey System:

000 General Works, including bibliographies, encyclopedias, library science, journalism and publishing materials

100 Philosophy and psychology, including metaphysics, epistemology, logic and ethics

200 Religion

300 Social sciences, including statistics, political science, economics, law, commerce, education and customs

400 Language and linguistics

500 Natural sciences and mathematics, including physics, astronomy, chemistry, earth and life sciences and zoology

600 Applied sciences, including engineering, medicine, home economics, agriculture and manufacturing

700 The Arts, including architecture, drawing, painting, photography and performing arts

800 Literature and rhetoric

900 History, biography and geography

Most academic and research libraries use the Library of Congress Classification System, also referred to as the LC System. A series of one to three letters (not numbers) begins each call number (yes, we still call it a call number . . . what can I say?) and represents different subject areas:

A General works, including encyclopedias

B Philosophy, psychology and religion, including logic, parapsychology, aesthetics and ethics

C Auxiliary sciences of history, including archaeology, numismatics, epigraphy, heraldry, genealogy and biography

D History: general and Old World

E History: United States (general)

F Local U.S. history and history of Canada, Latin America, South America, Central American and West Indies

G Anthropology, geography and recreation, including cartography, oceanography, folklore, customs, sports and dancing

H Social sciences, including statistics, economics, finance, transportation and communication, commerce and sociology

J Political science and public administration

K Law

L Education

M Music

N Fine arts, including architecture, sculpture, drawing, painting, printmaking and engraving and woodwork

P Language and literature, including how-to books on writing

Q Science, including mathematics, astronomy, physics, chemistry, geology, natural history, botany, zoology, anatomy, physiology and microbiology

R Medicine

S Agriculture

T Technology, including industrial engineering, mining, building construction, photography, handicrafts and home economics

U Military science
V Naval science
Z Bibliography and library science

Each call letter expands further with different combinations of letters and numbers designating specialized subjects.

Here's an example of a book's call number in both the Dewey and LC systems: The LC call number for the wonderful book *On Writing Well*, by William Zinsser (New York: HarperPerennial, 1990), is: PE1429.Z5 1990, while in Dewey it's 808.042Z66on. By the way, call numbers may vary slightly from library to library, since the catalogers have some leeway in each cataloging system. Usually, however, call numbers are quite consistent from library to library.

You will be doing yourself and your research a disservice if you rely solely on librarians. (What am I saying? I should be thinking of my job security!) Frankly, as a librarian, there are times when I know that I could recommend at least fifteen sources to answer a particular question, but I know that it would be ridiculous and confusing for me to suggest all fifteen. I end up recommending the ones I believe will be the most useful and advise the person to come back if they need additional help. I simply don't have the time to spend hours with each patron. If I did hover over the researcher, it would probably only serve to rush them, not allowing them to look carefully, making new mental connections and discoveries. Allow yourself the time and privacy to locate additional sources on your own.

Librarians

Librarians are information experts. Most have a master's degree in "information studies," "information systems" or "library science" and are generally devoted (i.e., forced) to keeping up with cutting-edge information sources and technology.

I absolutely encourage you to consult with a librarian whenever you feel unsure. A librarian may have a tip or two that you hadn't thought of. (There have been many times that subject-passionate researchers have introduced *me*, as a librarian, to a new source or research strategy.) Going back to a librarian more than once is also fine, since you may need assistance in bridging certain steps of your search. To give yourself a measure of independence in your research, also work on helping yourself.

Library Catalogs

Libraries that actually have real card catalogs, with real cards in them are a fast-dying breed. In the card catalog, each card represented one book. The catalog usually allowed you to look up books by author, title or subject. Most "card catalogs" are now online.

Online Catalogs

Your library may refer to the catalog as a PAC (Public Access Catalog) or an OPAC (Online Public Access Catalog). Many libraries refer to their system by using an acronym. My library uses CARL which stands for Colorado Alliance of Research Libraries; the library at Brown University calls its catalog Josiah, named after Josiah Carberry, a mythical professor of "psychoceramics" who appears only on Friday the 13th!

Unlike card catalogs, which generally guided you to only one format of information (for example, only books or only films), the modern online catalog may identify most or all of a library's holdings in one database: Books, Films, Magazines, Government Documents and Media. The basic library catalog will not usually access the articles within magazines, but there are other databases that will; See chapter 2, "Exploring Articles."

Generally, online catalogs are quite easy to use. Library users often walk up to the Reference Desk and say: "I don't know how to use a computer!" No problem. Once you know the basic conventions of searching, it's simple.

Searchable Elements in Online Catalogs

Just like the old card catalogs, you can still usually search by author, subject or title. Different systems use different terminology. In one catalog the term AUTHOR may be preferred, while in another you would use the word NAME to perform the same search. Subject searching might be called TOPIC or WORD searching. Take a moment to read the on-screen instructions. These catalogs are (theoretically!) designed to be simple to master. Generally, it's just a matter of using them a few times. If you think you will be using a system often, do try to learn the advanced techniques for using it. Such methods will usually allow you to dump the easy menus and work faster.

Each source in an online catalog is represented by a RECORD. Common elements in a record for a book, for example, may include:

—Title

—Author(s), Editor(s) or Illustrator (remember that the author might actually be an organization). The author's name is usually followed by his or her birth date (and death date if applicable).

—Publisher city

—Publisher

—Year published

—Number of pages

—Whether or not there are any illustrations (ill.)

—Sometimes, a summary of the topic of the book or, a practice that is becoming more common, a list of the titles of each chapter of the book

—Call number

—A listing of words that describe the contents of the book. This section will usually be labeled: Subject Headings, Entries, Descriptors or Terms. (See below under "What Words Should You Feed Into the Online Catalog?")

Online Catalog Advantages

The bad news about searching for information online: There is no computing miracle like the one shown in the Hepburn/Tracey film classic *Desk Set*. In this fanciful flick, Spencer Tracey, as the computer programmer, creates "Emerac," a.k.a. "Emmy," a computer that will answer natural language questions, that is, queries formulated the way we speak naturally. Of course there were some problems with Emmy, and Katherine Hepburn, as the librarian, prevails. (Yay!)

The good news: Searching for information using computer systems and personal computers can vastly improve the efficiency and reduce the time needed to perform certain searches.

At this time, we generally cannot "ask" an online information system a question in natural language, for example: "What's the political situation in Nicaragua?" However, we can feed the system the **key words** in our request, such as POLITICS and NICARAGUA. The system will then search for all occurrences of those words in the database records and show you the ones that contain both those words.

One of the great pluses of searching an online catalog is the ability to quickly link two or more concepts. Most online systems allow you to do "boolean" searching, that is, combining words in ways that exclude some terms and add others so that you can come up with the perfect brew for finding information on your subject. This is associated with Boolean algebra, which expresses logical relationships between truth values. It is associated with the logical operators AND, OR and NOT.

Common boolean searching strategies may be illustrated by using the terms AND, OR and NOT. The best way to explain these operations is with examples:

Subject: You need some quotes from baseball players. In the online catalog you type in:

Baseball and Quotes

The AND guarantees that you will pull up all records that have both the word baseball AND the word quotes in it. The computer will reject any record that does not have BOTH concepts in it. Illustrated, here's what that search

looks like:

The shaded area represents the sources you want, those containing both concepts you selected.

Subject: You realize that some baseball quotes might also show up in general sports quote books. So you do a more encompassing OR search by typing in:

(Baseball or Sports) and Quotes

Now the system will perform your request in the parentheses first, and create a set of all records that mention SPORTS or BASEBALL. It then combines that new set with the word QUOTES, finding only those sports or baseball books that have quotes in them. Visually, that search would look like this:

Subject: You want information about Paul Simon the politician, not Paul Simon the musician. So you might try this NOT search:

Paul Simon not music

Be careful with doing NOT searches. They may be useful in narrowing down a search if you get too many records, but they might also get rid of records you really want.

Some databases "assume" an AND. That is, if you type in two words next to each other, say POVERTY CITIES, it will search for all records that have both those words occurring in the record, no matter where in the record they occur. Other systems will *not* assume an AND and will instead check for the exact phrase POVERTY CITIES, which is not what you want at all! If it doesn't find those two words in the exact order they appear, right next to each other, it will say you got zero results. Always check the directions for the database you are working on.

A warning concerning AND, OR and NOT: Unfortunately, there is no widespread standard insisting that all publishers of search software use the same terms for boolean searching. Thus, there are any number of commands that will perform the operations I describe above! I have seen the term ANY used for OR, and COMBINE for AND. As long as you understand the boolean searching concepts, it doesn't really matter what they're called and you will be able to do a precise search for what you need. Read the instructions for the system you are using.

What Words Should You Feed Into the Online Catalog?

You can use any words you like when using an online catalog. That's called *free searching*. You throw in a word and hope that the word shows up somewhere in the record. Once you get a few

good records using the free search method, look at the part of the record that lists "subject headings" (which may also be called "terms," "entries" or "descriptors"). Those are the words that describe the source you found. You may want to use one of the words listed for your second search. For example:

Let's say you are looking for books dealing with training pets. You try a subject search in your library's online catalog; you type in PET TRAINING. You get a record for a book called *The Tellington Touch: A Breakthrough Technique and Care for Your Favorite Animal*. Though that sounds interesting, you would really like to find some more books on the subject. Looking at the part of the record for the *Tellington Touch* that designates the subject descriptors, you see these words and phrases:

PETS TRAINING
ANIMALS, TRAINING OF
HUMAN ANIMAL COMMUNICATION
PETS BEHAVIOR

So you can go back and try one or more subject searches with these new word combinations. (Note that your first "guess," PET TRAINING, was only one letter off of the official phrase: PETS TRAINING. But one letter can make quite a difference! Using the standard terminology will often assist you in finding the most sources.

The above is an example of a search using "controlled vocabulary," that is, referring to listings of standardized terminology that you will use to search with. The "subject headings" listed on each online catalog record come from such a standardized list. You can refer to these standard lists before you begin your search. Most libraries pull their subject headings from a set of books called *Library of Congress Subject Headings*. This multivolume collection is just a big list of the words that are used in card and online catalogs throughout the U.S. Some very small collections may use the *Sears List of Subject Headings* (13th edition. New York: Wilson, 1986).

Below are some of the standard Library of Congress Headings that deal with the art and craft of writing:

Authorship
Book Proposals
Children's Literature--Technique
Creative Writing
Crime Writing
Drama--Technique
Fashion Writing
Feature Writing
Fiction--Technique
Journalism--Authorship
Motion Picture Authorship
One-Act Plays--Technique
Playwriting
Plots
Poetry--Authorship
Popular Music--Writing Publishing
Queries Authorship
Radio Authorship
Technical Writing
Television Authorship
Travel Writing

And you can try searches combining a word or phrase describing the type of writing you are most interested in with the word authorship; for example:

ROMANCE AUTHORSHIP
SCIENCE FICTION AUTHOR-
SHIP

Note: When you see a double dash (--) between words, it is just a way to identify a heading and subheading. Don't type in the dashes when you do your subject search.

Hints on Searching by Subject on an Online Catalog

Be Sure That You Are Searching the Right Database.

A library's online system may consist of more than the catalog to that library's holdings. There may be a number of databases accessible through the system. For example, at the library I work for, any one of our in-house CARL terminals connects to a full-text encyclopedia, a directory of companies nationwide, several article indexes and the catalogs of dozens of other libraries . . . in addition to the catalog for our library!

Also, be certain you know the scope of the library catalog database you are looking in. For example, some library catalogs may include records for all the materials the library receives from the federal government. Other libraries will have an entirely different database or print source for locating items from the government. Some libraries may maintain a separate catalog of all their video holdings. Be sure the items you are looking for are included in the catalog you are looking at. The opening screen of each database should offer information on the contents of that database. If not, there is usually a "help" key to push that will bring the description into view.

Try a narrow topic, but if you can't find it— think of the broad topic.

You may be more familiar with the advice: Narrow your subject! And indeed that is good advice. But sometimes, on an online catalog, broad searching can unearth items others have left on the shelf.

For example, let's say you're writing an article about a vote coming up on a town ballot: the legalization of marijuana. You want to read articles or books discussing the pros and cons. You try a search on the online catalog using the words MARIJUANA and LEGALIZATION. You come up with two books, both checked out. At this point you could curse the writer from the town's other paper who has the books, or you could try a broader search, using the words DRUGS and LEGALIZATION. Books you find under the broader heading might have a chapter on marijuana, or at least provide some insight into the pros and cons of legalizing any currently unlawful narcotic. Though trends are changing, many books are still cataloged with only a limited number of subject headings, that is, the record in the catalog may not thoroughly describe the contents of the book. So be prepared to "think broad" sometimes.

Be a walking thesaurus.
It is often wise to do more than one search in an online catalog, trying a variety of terms that describe your subject. Even if you're consulting the *Library of Congress Subject Headings*, you'll find that there are still similar terms with different headings. For example, if you are writing an article advocating shorter or more flexible work weeks, and want to find books on the subject, all of the following are valid subject headings you might search with: FLEXIBLE HOURS OF LABOR, THIRTY-FIVE HOUR WORK WEEK, FOUR-DAY WORK WEEK, and FLEXIBLE WORK HOURS.

Browse the Collections of Libraries Worldwide.

Another advantage to online information systems is that they offer the capability of searching library holdings across the country or even around the world. Some services that offer such connections include WorldCat, OCLC and RLIN. Also, the holdings of the Library of Congress are accessible through the Internet. Ask your library if they have a connection to any of these systems. (Though most libraries do subscribe to OCLC, many use it exclusively for interlibrary loan use and limit or refuse public use.) Try the largest public and academic libraries for access to one of these services.

Also be aware of a few highly effective low-tech (print) methods of browsing huge numbers of sources by subject:

Subject Guide to Books in Print. R.R. Bowker.

Arranged by subject, the *SGBIP* is easy to flip through to see what is currently in print on particular subjects. This source will provide you with the author and publisher of the book, which you will need if you wish to order it through interlibrary loan or request it at a bookstore. Also listed are the price and the International Standard Book Number (ISBN), which can also be helpful when ordering a book from a bookstore.

The *SGBIP* and the bimonthly *Forthcoming Books* directory are also the perfect places to check to see if someone else has already written the book you've been contemplating. For example, the 1993 *SGBIP* lists eight books still in print on the subject of Clipper Ships. So, a book on clipper ships may or may not be welcome, depending on what your slant is. However, there were NO books written on the love lives of chickens, so that possibility is still wide open. If you do spot a title that looks frighteningly close to your idea, you can either buy or borrow the book or look up a review of the book. The book may seem similar to yours based on the title, but turn out, upon inspection, to be quite different.

Reference Books

The majority of the resources I recommend in this book are reference books, the kind of books you refer to for things like definitions, statistics, overviews of a subject, concise biographical information, addresses, facts, laws, court cases and chronologies of events. Reference sources include encyclopedias, almanacs, dictionaries, handbooks, chronologies, directories, yearbooks, atlases and gazetteers.

The right reference book can save you hours of time by synthesizing related information in one place. They may help to uncover "hidden" information that might be difficult to identify through a catalog or index. A tip on reference books: Read the instructions on how to use the book that usually appear in the first few pages. Though the arrangement of a reference book is rarely difficult, it is often, shall we say, obscure. Because these books are often jam-packed with fairly repetitive information, the editors will often use codes, abbreviations and different font styles to convey different

meanings. Below is an example from the *Martindale-Hubbell Law Directory*. The example below shows a typical listing describing a lawyer:

> *Smith,Oscar Q.(AV)* . . . *'55 '80 C.681 B.S.L, 1066 J.D. [Smith & Sons]*

The above tells you about the lawyer Oscar Q. Smith. After you look up the meaning of the various codes that appear on the first few pages, you decipher his "rating," year of birth, year of bar admission, college attended, first degree received, law school attended and where Oscar practices law. So you see that there is quite a bit of information you can glean from the few letters and numbers presented. (Most reference books are not quite so cryptic.)

Another hint on the use of reference books that extends to all books: Use the index in the back of the book, don't just rely on the table of contents in the front. If you need to find a tiny bit of information hidden away in a 400-page book, the table of contents will only get you into the shallow end of the pool. Dive in after that little detail by using the index. The same goes for multivolume reference sets. Though the major subjects are in alphabetic order in the set, small facts are hidden within each subject area. Use the index, which will usually be the last volume of the collection, to zero in on that idea. For example, a student of mine was looking up the concept of "heart rate." I couldn't understand why she wasn't finding what she needed in the encyclopedia I recommended to her, *The Encyclopedia of Human Biology* (8 Volumes. New York: Academic Press, 1991). Then I realized that she was just looking under "H" for Heart in the main volumes. Once we looked under "heart rate" in the index volume, it led us to several substantial mentions of heart rate in the sections titled "Exercise and Cardiovascular Function" and "Caffeine." She got the information she was looking for.

Electronic Reference

Just as library catalogs are now commonly automated, many standard library reference sources, such as encyclopedias, directories, law and business sources, are now available on disc or online. The information may be stored on a CD-ROM disc, a floppy disc, on tape or on a mainframe computer that is one hundred or one thousand miles away. No matter where the information is stored, you will be accessing it by looking at a monitor and using a keyboard, and perhaps a "mouse" (a remote control device that looks like a little, rolling, toy mouse, which can be hand-guided to move the cursor on the screen). Patrons often come to me, after looking at one of these terminals, and report: "I don't know how to use a computer." If that sounds like you, don't worry. Here's the tip: When you are using a terminal that is dedicated to a reference source, you are simply learning how to use the reference source. No need for you to be a computer expert. (Though more and more of you are.)

Just as you would need to familiarize yourself with the setup of a reference book, you need to learn the basic keystrokes needed to get to information stored electronically. The computer or dumb terminal that you are using is purely a means to an end. Generally, sources available through online and CD-ROM systems are fairly simple to learn. There are usually on-screen instructions located at the bottom or top of each screen, and most systems will provide a context-sensitive "help" button you can press at any point in your search to see what your options are. Most databases also offer a "tutorial" that takes you through a practice search. These tutorials are invaluable for becoming familiar with the basics.

A fair number of the reference sources recommended throughout this book will also be available in electronic format. At this time, few libraries will own all of them, though moderate-sized libraries will have some. Whenever a library purchases or subscribes to new online or electronic sources, they must have the personal computers or dumb terminals to run them on. This requires both space and money. As libraries continue to address the challenges of becoming "Virtual Libraries," access to sources in electronic format will increase.

Government Documents

Massive numbers of diverse publications are released each year by U.S. government agencies and other organizations whose services have been contracted by the government. Items issued from the U.S. government may come from one of dozens of departments and agencies and cover all subject fields. Examples of government documents include: a poster featuring the "Cats of North America" put out by the U.S. Department of the Interior, Fish and Wildlife Service, a 34-page guide titled *So You Have High Blood Pressure* published by the National Institute of Health, and a book from the Department of the Army, over three hundred pages long, called *Portugal: A Country Study.*

Government "documents" may be books, pamphlets, guides, hearings, transcripts, reports, journals, cookbooks, proceedings, laws, maps, posters, pamphlets, directories and more. At our library we have begun using the phrase government "publications," which we hope sounds somewhat less officious.

As you might suspect, a good number of government publications contain statistics, such as the Census publications. See chapter 10, "Fact and Statistics Books," for more examples of statistical documents issued by the U.S. government.

There are fifty-two full regional depository libraries in the United States that collect everything offered through the depository program. Depository publications are those seen as having educational value or interest for the public. There are a total of 1,400 libraries throughout the U.S. that are eligible to receive U.S. depository documents at no charge. Some of these libraries are full depositories, others are selective or partial depositories. For example, the library I work for selects only those documents most pertinent to the students on campus, which means we receive about 50 to 60 percent of the documents actually available. A document like "A Sampling System for Estimating the Cultivation of Wheat" is simply not useful to us because we don't have an agricultural program.

Even libraries that have no depository status most likely carry some of the more widely used government publications available for purchase. The first few pages of the *Monthly Catalog of United States Government Publications* supplies instructions for ordering government sources and lists the locations of the two dozen government bookstores located in major metropolitan areas across the United States.

Check the *Directory of Government Document Collections and Librarians* (6th Edition, Chicago: American Library Association, 1991), for collections in your area (or ask your librarian!).

Some useful guides for learning the breadth of government publications:

Guide to Popular U.S. Government Publications. 3d edition. William G. Bailey. Englewood, CO: Libraries Unlimited, 1993.

A listing of materials produced by departments and agencies of the federal government, arranged in subject order. For example, under SMOKING, in the Health and Medical Care section, there are a number of reports by the Department of Health and Human Services listed on the health consequences of smoking cigarettes and a report by the Department of Transportation on the risks of secondhand smoke to airplane passengers. This collection is just a listing; the two below offer additional instruction in finding government publications.

Tapping the Government Grapevine: The User-Friendly Guide to U.S. Government Information Sources. Judith Schiek Robinson. Phoenix: Oryx, 1988.

The author's goal is to "dispel the government information mystique."

Using Government Information Sources: Print and Electronic. 2d edition. Jean L. Sears and Marilyn K. Moody, Phoenix: Oryx, 1993.

This volume suggests strategies for finding U.S. government sources and lists many of them.

Full and partial depository libraries normally house their government publications in a separate section of the library and catalog them by yet *another* system of classification called The Superintendent of Documents Classification System. The number/letter combination assigned to each source is commonly referred to as the SuDocs Number.

The SuDoc classification is different than both LC and Dewey in that instead of arranging items by strict subject order, items are arranged by the agency that issued them! As you might guess, this plays havoc with librarians' desire to place sources covering the same subject together in order to assist browsing researchers. Many agencies publish in diverse areas. For example, the publications *Documents on Germany, 1944-1985* and *Cocaine 1980: Proceedings of the InterAmerican Seminar on Medical and Sociological Aspects of Coca and Cocaine* both show up within a few books of each other on the shelf because they are both published by The State Department.

If government items are very popular, a library may choose to recatalog the item under a Dewey or LC call number, so that the item will be in subject order with other highly used materials.

A number of indexes will assist you in tracking down government publications. *The Monthly Catalog to Government Publications*, mentioned above, is one. The items listed in the *Monthly Catalog* are indexed by Author, Subject, Series/Report, Contract Number, Stock

Number and Title/Keyword. The record for each item will include its unique SuDoc number. Unless the item has been reclassified in Dewey or LC, you will find it under that number at any full depository library. (All sources in the *Monthly Catalog* marked with a big black dot should have been sent to full depositories.) There is also a *Periodicals Supplement* to the *Monthly Catalog* that contains records for sources that are issued three or more times a year (i.e., magazines, reports, newsletters, etc.).

For additional indexes that access government documents, check Appendix A.

Using the Library from Home

If your library has an online catalog, there is a good possibility you can dial in to it from home using a personal computer, modem and communications software. Ask someone at your library what your dial-in options are.

Also you should feel free to telephone any library and ask a question. Just be aware that some libraries will only answer very brief questions over the phone. But ask! Who knows?

Who Else Can You Dial-In To?

Once you have your handy dandy personal computer, modem, communications software, and the proper accounts or subscriptions, you have several options:

- You can sign up with companies that will allow you to access that part of the information highway known as the Internet.
- You can dial-in to the databases created and controlled by information vendors.

- You can dial-in to services that offer access to information databases, entertainment options and connection to the Internet.

So, What About the Internet?

Ah, the Internet. This portion of the information superhighway, touted as the new miracle in information retrieval, is slowly beginning to live up to its reputation. The Internet is a collection of information and communication services accessible via worldwide interconnected computer networks. These computers communicate with each other through a data transport protocol called TCP/IP. Anyone with an account can tap into these services.

You can use the Internet and libraries hand in hand. Often you will find citations or references via the Internet that you will want to follow up on at a library. Sometimes you will access libraries themselves through an Internet connection. In the future, more and more libraries will probably provide direct connection to the Internet from terminals within the library. I'd like to go over a few of the questions I get about the Internet when I am working at the reference desk.

Is Internet access free?

Usually not. Some folks may be fortunate enough to have access to the Internet through their place of business—especially academic, government and research environments. Generally, an individual will need to pay a monthly fee to gain access to the Internet, just like a phone or cable bill. Opportunities for gaining access to Internet vary from state to state. Ask a librarian at one of the larger libraries, or the staff at a nearby computer store, for advice on local ways of connecting to Internet. Or check one of the many constantly evolving guides to the Internet. Subscribing to a state-sponsored service will usually cost less than a commercial service. However, a commercial service may supply more database enhancements and, more importantly, provide you with reliably available assistance. (See chapter 9, "Identifying Experts," for more about connecting to the Internet; see Appendix B for listings of vendors that can connect you to the Internet and to other interactive online services.)

Can I access the same databases on Internet that I am seeing more and more in libraries? Are those databases free?

Some government databases and those that are subsidized in some fashion may be free. For example, you can access the holdings of the largest library in America, the Library of Congress, in Washington, D.C., for no fee! (Those dialing in directly from a modem will pay the cost of the call . . . which can add up.) The most popular, commercially produced databases are not free. You may pay a subscription fee, telecommunications costs, per-minute charges, royalty fees and downloading or printing fees.

How can I try everything on the Internet?

Well, that would be a little like trying to phone every single person in the U.S. or reading every book in a really big library. Over time, and as the Internet becomes more easily accessible to more people, the elements of most interest to each of us will become apparent.

Is it hard to find what you need on the Internet?
At this point, I would have to say: somewhat! However, new methods are being refined daily, and books on both the use of the Internet and addresses for databases on it are multiplying quickly. Many Internet users agree: The best way to learn Internet is to get on and try it.

Is everything full-text on the Internet?
Again, this is evolving. Many databases still provide only citations, and often the "full-text" is full-text conversation, people chatting with each other.

In my opinion, the three most wonderful things about the Internet and other interactive online services at this time for the casual user are: e-mail, discussion groups/lists and library catalogs.

E-mail. E-mail, or electronic mail, allows you to send and receive written messages on your computer with individuals worldwide, sort of phoning people in writing.

Discussion groups/lists. These groups go under a number of different monikers, including ListServs, Bulletin Boards (BBS), Mailing Lists and Newsgroups, and are generally devoted to one particular topic. They provide a forum for opinion and discussion on that topic. These groups allow you to schmooze easily with others from all around the world about career topics, such as writing, scholarly topics, such as Business Law, or lighter topics, like Star Trek. (For more on avenues to explore in this area, and methods for getting started, see chapter 7, "Identifying Experts.")

Quick access to library catalogs around the world. Using the Internet can be a simple way of seeing what other, distant libraries own.

Other Internet options include accessing electronic journals (E-journals) and newsletters (full-text magazines and journals online), and the ability to retrieve full-text documents and software programs (using a process called File Transfer Protocol—FTP). Daniel P. Dern, editor of *Internet World* magazine, theorizes there is probably "one new major Internet service or site appearing roughly every hour."

Where do I sign up?
There are many different avenues for accessing the Internet. If you are part of a large educational or governmental agency, they might already have an Internet connection you may use. Ask your in-house library or computing staff. If you are not linked to the Internet, you'll need to use a personal computer, modem and communications software to dial up to a computer that is. You can achieve full or partial access through joining a number of commercial online services. (See below under "Other Online 'Libraries.'") If you just want e-mail, there are services such as MCI Mail, (800) 444-6245, that will sign you up for a fee depending on the services you want.

In some communities, services called "Freenets" have been established. They 1) offer community-based information databases, and 2) serve as a gateway to Internet options. There will sometimes be a (usually very reasonable) fee for accessing a freenet.

Though you can connect with a freenet that is *not* in your community, remember that you will be incurring long distance calling charges if you do. For locating freenets, ask at the library, check books about the Internet, or contact the National Public Telecomputing Network, Box 1987, Cleveland, OH 44106.

There are many companies popping up who would be happy, for a fee, to provide you with access to the Internet. Check Appendix B for some names and prices.

Some recommended titles for learning more about the Internet include:

The Internet Companion: A Beginner's Guide to Global Networks. Tracy LaQuey with Jeanne C. Ryer. Forward by Al Gore. Reading, MA: Addison-Wesley, 1994.

Pocket Guides to the Internet. Mark Veljkov and George Hartnell. Westport, CT: Mecklermedia, 1993.

V.1—Telneting

V.2—Transferring Files with File Transfer Protocol

V.3—Using and Navigating Usenet

V.4—The Internet E-Mail System

V.5—Basic Internet Utilities

V.6—Terminal Connections

The Whole Internet: Users Guide and Catalog. Ed Krol. Sebastopol, CA: O'Reilly & Associates, 1992.

Other Online "Libraries"

There are a number of online services, including *CompuServe, America Online, GEnie, Prodigy* and *DELPHI Internet,* that allow you a limited or full gateway to the Internet and also maintain specialized databases and services you can dial-in to. For example, *CompuServe Information Service,* with almost two million users worldwide, provides its users with avenues for learning, entertainment, buying, selling and chatting. *CompuServe* subscribers can access reviews from *Consumer Reports,* check the *Academic American Encyclopedia,* join one of dozens of discussion forums (including the *Journalism Forum*), place or read classified ads, read restaurant reviews and look up stock quotations. See Appendix B for a description of what *CompuServe's* competitors have to offer.

Chapter Two

Exploring Articles

Articles cover every subject and then some. Even if you could never look at a book again, you would have no problem finding all the written information you need through articles.

Since articles are truly indispensable, I recommend that you master the simple research concepts in this chapter. Writers use articles for both historical and contemporary research. Historical articles may show how an event was perceived at the time it occurred, as opposed to the way history now presents it. Contemporary articles may contain information that is timelier than anything you could find in a book. Both old and new articles are gold mines of quotation, biographical information, specialized topics, subject overviews and statistics. And of course articles contain recipes, always useful for your post-publication party.

In addition to reading research articles to assist in a particular project, you will also want to study articles to improve your own writing technique. For example, if you want to write a how-to article it would be wise to examine a few that are already published. It's also a good idea to browse the articles of a magazine or journal you will be submitting work to in order to get a feel for the type of work they accept. And of course there will be times when you simply want to read articles geared to writers dealing with the art and business of writing.

Articles are also a great source of ideas. Browsing through articles in national magazines may give you an idea for a regional slant—or vice versa.

Where to Find Different Types of Articles

Articles appear in periodicals: newspapers, magazines, journals and newsletters. The type of project you're working on will in part dictate the type of article that will help you most. Below are some of the unique qualities of different types of periodicals.

Journals

A type of periodical that contains news or information of current interest in a particular field. The *Journal of the American Medical Association* is an example. Authors of journal articles usually have a sophisticated level of understanding of the topic they are writing on, and claims and opinions are often backed up with the results of studies or surveys. Journals are often published by academic or association presses.

Just to clear up a common misconception I run into with college students I work with, I'll let you know that a journal does not have to have the word "journal" in the title to be a journal. Some examples of no-journal-in-the-title-journals would be *Phi Delta Kappan*, which publishes articles concerned with educational research, service and leadership, and *The Lancet*, a journal of medical science and practice.

One way to distinguish between a magazine and a journal is by the inclusion of a bibliography at the end of each article. Journals almost always provide a listing of the references the authors used in their research. That is not something you would find at the end of a story in *People Weekly*.

Journal submissions are usually "peer reviewed," meaning that a panel of experts in the field evaluated the article for accuracy. Articles that don't pass the peer review process might be rejected outright or the editor might request substantial revisions. This doesn't mean that no inaccuracies ever slip through!

When you read a journal article, the writer or writers will often expect a certain level of reader expertise. The writing may contain more "jargon" words. For example, I just read an article on how librarians might better integrate use of the Internet into library work, but nowhere in the article was the word *Internet* defined! When you are reading a journal article, be ready to grab a specialized dictionary for that subject area. (See chapter 13, "Language and Speech.")

Magazines

Magazines contain popular articles that are usually shorter and less authoritative than journal articles. These are the kind of periodicals you see in supermarkets, like *GQ*, *Good Housekeeping* or *Reader's Digest*. (But not the ones with pregnant aliens on the cover; those are tabloids.) Articles in popular magazines tend to be written by journalists, as opposed to experts on the subject of the article.

Since many magazine articles are written by nonexperts, they are easy to understand. Writers take the time to learn an unfamiliar subject, and they pass on to the reader what they have learned. Therefore, magazine articles might be just the place to start when you want to familiarize yourself with a topic. Since journalists are expert writers, the article will probably be written more clearly and smoothly than one written by a non-professional writer.

Newspapers

One of the most wonderful things about your average newspaper is it covers all subjects. Think about your hometown daily paper. In the last year they probably wrote some comprehensive articles on health, lifestyle and political issues, at the very least. They undoubtedly painted a few intimate portraits of some hometown heroes (who may be worth interviewing in the future).

Of course there are specialized publications produced in the newspaper format, such as *The Financial Times*, covering company and industry information, and *The Chronicle of Higher Education*, which covers academic educational concerns.

Newsletters

A newsletter is only a few pages in length and pinpoints very specialized topics. A newsletter may be produced for the employees of a certain firm, members of an association or people in a particular industry.

Some examples of newsletters include: The *Ghost Trackers Newsletter*, (Ghost Research Society, P.O. Box 205, Oaklawn, IL 60454-0205), which investigates paranormal phenomena, with an emphasis on ghosts, poltergeists and hauntings; the *Ice Cream Reporter: The Newsletter for Ice Cream Executives* (FIND/SVP, Inc., 625 Ave. of the Americas, New York, NY 10011), and *The Organizer* (National Alliance Against Racist and Political Repression, 11 John St. Rm. 702, New York, NY 10038), reporting on such issues as labor rights, repressive legislation and political prisoners. An excellent source for finding names, addresses, phone numbers and descriptions of newsletters in the U.S. and Canada is the directory *Newsletters in Print* (Detroit: Gale. Annual.).

There are thousands of magazines, journals, newspapers and newsletters published every year: all potential markets for your writing and research. The magazines you see at bookstores and in the supermarkets represent a small percentage of the specialized and niche periodicals that exist.

How to Find Articles on Particular Subjects or Written by Certain People: Using Periodical Indexes and Abstracts

Just as the index to a book leads you to the specific sections of a book, a *periodical index* leads you to the contents of hundreds of magazines. This makes life easier. Instead of browsing through hundreds of issues of the *Journal of the American Dietetic Association* in an effort to find an article on bulimia, you simply look in a periodical index such as *The General Science Index*. You look under the subject heading "bulimia" to find pertinent articles. The index will list specific articles in a variety of science, health and medical journals that talk

about bulimia.

In a nutshell: Indexes list subjects alphabetically. When you look up a subject in an index you'll find citations to articles in different magazines that wrote about that subject. The citation gives you all the information you need to actually go find that article: the title of the article, author, name of the periodical, volume, issue, pages and date.

Here is an example of a citation that appeared under the subject heading DNA Fingerprinting in the March 1994 volume of the *Social Sciences Index*, an index that helps you find articles on topics in the social sciences (i.e., sociology, crime, psychology, economics, etc.):

Legal criticisms of DNA typing: where's the beef? R.P. Harmon. J Crim Law Criminol v84 p178-88 Spr. '93.

First the title (*Legal Criticisms of DNA Typing: Where's the Beef?*) is listed, then the author (R.P. Harmon). Notice that the name of the journal is abbreviated: J Crim Law Criminol. Print indexes often use abbreviations to save space. The key-to-the-abbreviations page, either in the front or the back of the index, tells you the full name of the journal. In this case it is *The Journal of Criminal Law and Criminology*, Volume 84. Note that journal articles can be rather long; the one above, on pages 178-188, is eleven pages.

Abstracts are basically the same as indexes, except their citations include a summary (which is called an abstract) of the article. Abstracts usually lead you to scholarly journal sources. Some examples of abstracts include the *Criminal*

Justice Abstracts, International Political Science Abstracts and *Psychological Abstracts*. Most periodical indexes and abstracts also enable you to look up articles by author name in addition to subject.

Types of Periodical Indexes and Abstracts: General, Specialized and Newspaper

General Indexes.

There are hundreds of indexes and abstracts available. See Appendix A for examples. Some are general indexes, like the *Readers' Guide to Periodical Literature*, which leads you to articles found in popular magazines like *Newsweek, Psychology Today* and *Ebony*. Because popular magazines touch on almost all topics, the *Readers' Guide* covers all subject areas.

Specialized Indexes.

Other indexes lead you to journals in specialized areas, such as the *Art Index* and the *Applied Science and Technology Index*. Some are extremely specialized, including *Aerospace Medicine and Biology* and the *Lodging and Restaurant Index*.

Newspaper Indexes.

Major newspapers such as *The Wall Street Journal* and *The Washington Post* have their own indexes. So there is a *Wall Street Journal Index* and a *Washington Post Index*. Again, remember that newspapers cover all topics in an extremely timely way, so when you use an index to a major newspaper, such as the *New York Times Index*, there are hundreds of topics you might find.

Though indexes to local newspapers do exist, they may only be available at local libraries. For example, the index to the *Denver Post* may not be in demand in New York, but in my home state of Colorado almost every library owns the index. In fact my library subscribes to the full-text version of the *Post* on CD-ROM! The moral: If you need information you think would show up in the pages of a small newspaper, check with a public library for that area. They probably have the index.

Though very small community newspapers may be retained by their local library, they will probably not be indexed anywhere. But write or call the publication if you're trying to locate an article only half-remembered. Even small newspapers may maintain small subject-access files to back issues or, at the very least, a long-time editor with a great memory.

There is a dated but still useful index to newspaper indexes called *Newspaper Indexes: A Location and Subject Guide for Researchers* (Anita Cheek Milner. Metuchen, NJ: Scarecrow Press. Vol.1, 1977. Vol.2, 1979. Vol.3, 1982). This source identifies academic and public libraries, historical societies, museums and newspaper libraries that either maintain indexes for or actually do the indexing of all or part of local newspapers. Addresses are provided and photocopying/research services (circa 1977-1982) are described.

If you want to gather information by checking articles, choose the kind of index that best fits your needs. For example, if you want to find out just a little bit about plastic surgery, don't bother checking the professionally oriented medical index *Index Medicus* where you will get an article with a title like "Cosmetic Mastoidectomy for the Combined Supra/infratentorial Transtemporal Approach," from the September 1993 volume of the *Journal of Neurosurgery!* Just check an index to more general magazines where you would find the article "Questions about Cosmetic Surgery," from the March 1992 volume of the magazine *American Health*. And vice versa if you need a very detailed, technical article.

Check Appendix A for the names and descriptions of dozens of indexes and abstracts covering all subject areas.

Index Formats

Indexes are available in both print and electronic format. There are some advantages to both.

Print

Print indexes are typically published monthly or quarterly and cumulated annually. They are usually shelved in a special "Index" section of the library; sometimes they are shelved among the reference books. Since indexes are updated fairly often, a set of indexes might be comprised of dozens of volumes. If you were researching a topic such as "the rise of white supremacy groups over the last five years," you would need to look through at least five printed indexes to cover articles for that span of time.

Most indexes available in hardcopy (print) are now also available in electronic format. But there are still times when you will see both formats in a library. There are three reasons for this. First, when an electronic index goes "down" it is not accessible. The print copy is always available. Second, there

are a few instances when looking through a print index will be more efficient than searching an electronic one. For example, students often have a broad subject in mind but are not sure how to narrow it. It can be more time consuming to run through an online index scanning for ideas than it would be to glance over a page of citations. Third, some publishers are still offering special, lower pricing for electronic products if the library retains the hard-copy duplicate. Despite these reasons, print indexes are fast going the way of the card catalog.

Indexes in Electronic Format

As discussed in chapter 1, electronic sources, including indexes, may be found stored in a variety of ways: on CD-ROM, at a distant computer that you dial-in to, on tape or on floppy disc. CD-ROMs, which can hold the equivalent of 250,000 pages per disc, are especially popular in libraries and for use on home computers.

There are several advantages to using indexes in electronic format (which I will refer to below as online indexes for simplicity sake).

Searching large time periods quickly. An online index usually covers a minimum of five years of information. So instead of needing to search at least five print indexes, I type in my term once to cover the same period of time. I have to admit that I often end up doing a number of searches on online indexes simply to try out a variety of word combinations. For example, in the above topic on hate groups, I might do one search under White Supremacy Groups, and then do separate searches under the formal names of such groups, such as the Aryan Nation, Ku Klux Klan and so on.

Boolean Search Possibilities. Most online indexes allow boolean search options, enabling the searcher to link synonyms and to search two or more terms at one time. For a refresher on this technique, see chapter 1 under the section "Library Catalogs: Online Catalog Advantages" (page 10).

Lingo. Searching an online index can be especially handy when you are looking under a subject that is best defined with a modern slang word or phrase. For example, "Generation X" has become a popular term for describing people in their twenties. Generation X has not yet, and may not ever, become an "official" LC subject heading. But if you type the phrase "Generation X" into an online catalog, you will retrieve articles containing that phrase.

Dial-In Databases

In chapter 1, I mentioned such dial-in services as *CompuServe*. There are other online search services, such as *DIALOG*, that are generally found in businesses, institutions or libraries. These online services are commonly called database vendors, and like *CompuServe* and *GEnie*, they allow the user to tap into huge, subject-specific databases. The difference: They may enable the searcher to use more sophisticated searching techniques (though this distinction is rapidly disappearing over time), and most of the databases they offer contain either citations to periodicals or the full text of different periodicals. Very few databases are geared to home use for entertainment purposes.

(For a fuller description of each of these services and information for subscribing, see Appendix B.)

Vendors like *DIALOG* offer access to hundreds of databases from all disciplines. Some examples of databases you might reach if you were to subscribe to DIALOG include:

• *NewSearch*, a database containing 2,000 recent stories, articles and book reviews from 1,700 periodicals. This database only retains data no more than a month old; it is updated daily.

• *Sport*. Access to journal, book and theses citations for practical and research literature pertaining to sports and physical fitness.

• *Computer Database*. Citations to articles from computer, electronics and telecommunications journals, with the full text of seventy of the journals available online.

• *Magill's Survey of Cinema*. Comprehensive, full-text articles written on more than 3,500 films, from 1929 to the present.

Many databases that used to be exclusively available through such services as DIALOG are now routinely available on CD-ROM. Still, frequently the information on a CD-ROM disc will not go back as far as the dial-in *DIALOG* version of the database. (Not enough room on the disc!)

Quite often, libraries will carry subscriptions to such online services as *DIALOG*. Occasionally the service will be available in the public area where patrons pay to do the search themselves. More often, a librarian acts as an expert intermediary and performs the search for a fee with the patron close at hand.

Such searches can be valuable since some dial-in databases are more up-to-date than the CD-ROM or print versions, and there are some very specialized databases available.

When searching indexes on CD-ROMs within libraries, there will usually be no fee. There usually will be a fee when the database you are accessing is truly "online"; that is, a connection over phone lines or via Internet is made to a distant computer that contains the files you are reading. The money you pay for such searches may include costs for the searcher's time and the cost of accessing the online database.

An excellent directory that lists the availability of thousands of databases in a variety of formats for all topic areas is the *Gale Directory of Databases* (Kathleen Young, editor).

Periodical Directories

Let's say you read a marvelous article on Kelpie "cow dogs" in a magazine called *The Western Horseman*. Only you read it many years ago and just can't remember which issue it was. You can use an index to find out the exact citation of that article—once you find out what index you should use. Some directories that will tell you where individual magazines are indexed include:

Ulrich's International Periodicals Directory

Magazines for Libraries

The Serials Directory: An International Reference Book

Example: You would look up the magazine *Western Horseman* in any of those directories. In the entry for that magazine it would tell you that *Western Horseman* is indexed in ACCESS, Bio-

logical & Agricultural Index, Magazine Article Summaries, the Sports Periodical Index and SportSearch.

Annual Indexes

Some periodicals include an annual index to their publication, usually in the December or January issue. Libraries put these in a variety of places; they may be shelved, bound or filmed with the periodical itself, or placed in an index or reference section. Sometimes (rarely) these indexes will be cumulated over a five- or ten-year period. Generally, I don't tend to use these indexes. I prefer to use print or electronic periodical indexes that lead you to dozens of periodicals.

Still, single-issue indexes may be helpful when 1) you remember reading an article in a particular magazine and know about what year it was, 2) the topic you are looking for is the kind you expect to show up in a particular magazine, or 3) you want to be certain the magazine did not print an article on a subject.

Historic Periodicals Collections

Unfortunately, there will be times when there simply is no index to the items you want. This is particularly true of historical sources. But many of those sources are available, waiting for you to pick a time period and start browsing. *The New York Times* is commonly available, on microfilm, back to 1851 in most larger libraries. The *London Times* microfilm may go back to 1790! Thousands of older newspapers and periodicals have been collected by subject or time period and stored on microfilm or microfiche; some indexed, some not.

Some examples include:

Radical Periodicals in the United States. Westport, CT: Greenwood Press, 1970-1975.

A collection of over one hundred periodicals from the late nineteenth century through the mid twentieth century representing such groups as communists, socialists, anarchists and feminists.

English Literary Periodicals. (ELPS), 1681-1914. Ann Arbor, MI: University Microfilms International 1951-1976.

Comprised of 233 periodicals reflecting British life and culture.

History of Women. Woodbridge, CT: Research Publications, International.

A compilation on microform of books, pamphlets, periodicals, manuscripts and photographs concerning the history of women worldwide from the late eighteenth century through 1920.

Negro Newspapers, 1837-1910. New York: Datamics.

Covers over two hundred black U.S. newspapers.

Underground Press Collection. Bell & Howell, 1965-present.

Includes articles from over 500 titles of what the publishers call the "radical press . . . reflecting the deep-seated mistrust and alienation felt by a significant element of our society."

Find the titles of more microfilm collections by checking the *Guide to Micro-*

forms in Print. Munich: K.G. Saur. Annual.

How Periodicals Are Stored: Film, Fiche and Bound

If you've ever been to a library, you have probably used microform: filmed copies of periodicals or other materials that are either in a roll, called microfilm, or flat, called microfiche. Items are stored in microform for two major reasons: 1) To save space. Libraries would simply not be able to own as much as they do if they could not store it on a more compact medium than the printed page, and 2) To preserve the material. Pages of periodicals are often torn out or simply turn yellow because of inferior paper. Microform lives on. Although it does get scratchy with overuse, it can usually be replaced relatively inexpensively.

Full-Text Availability of Periodicals Online

It is becoming common to find the full text of items such as newspapers available and searchable on CD-ROM or through online access at larger libraries. Searching the full text of an item can be great, since the subject words you put in might "match" words found in the full text, that would not have matched words in the title or summary of a citation in a citation-only index. Since this is still an expensive option, it will be a little longer until all libraries offer such systems.

Periodicals for Writers

There will be times when you want to read articles purely for your own growth as a writer. There are a number of magazines and many newsletters dedicated to the art and craft of writing. You may choose to subscribe to a writing magazine, seeing what they have to offer each month. You can also use indexes to look up particular topics you want to read more about.

Two of the best-known writing magazines, *Writer's Digest* and *The Writer*, are easily found in bookstores and libraries. *Writer's Digest* is indexed in *Access, Index to How to Do It Information, Magazine Index, Popular Periodical Index, Reader's Guide* and *UnCover*. *The Writer* is indexed in *Children's Literature Abstracts, Magazine Index, Magazine Article Summaries, Reader's Guide* and *Uncover*.

Many of the publications for writers listed below may be in only very select libraries, or available only through personal subscription. I have included current (at the time of this writing) subscription addresses for all the publications:

America's Censored Newsletter, % Censored Publications, P.O. Box 310, Cotati, CA 94911.

Offers information and encouragement for aspiring writers. Founded 1992. Monthly, $20/year.

Authorship, % The National Writer's Club, 1450 S. Havana, Suite 620, Aurora, CO 80012. Phone (303) 751-7844, Fax (303) 751-8593.

Discusses creative and compositional techniques. Founded 1943. Bimonthly, $18/year.

The Bookwoman, % Women's National Book Association, 160 Fifth Avenue, New York, NY 10010. Phone (212) 675-7805.

Covers major topics of interest to publishers, librarians, educators, writers and agents in the book world. 3/year. Price included in membership.

Canadian Author & Bookman, % Canadian Authors Association, 275 Slater Street, Suite 500, Ottawa, ON, Canada K1P 5H9. Phone (613) 237-0143, Fax (613) 235-8237.

Canada's national writer magazine. Quarterly. $15/year Canada, $20/year U.S. and foreign.

Children's Book Insider, P.O. Box 1030, Fairplay, CO 80440-1030. Phone (719) 836-0394.

Geared to aspiring and working writers of children's fiction and nonfiction. Includes "how-to" articles on developing stories, writing styles and approaching publishers. Also has interviews with some top children's writers. Monthly. $34/year U.S., $38 U.S./year Canada, $40 foreign.

Comedy Writer's Association Newsletter, % Robert Makinson, Box 023304, Brooklyn, NY 11202-0066. Phone (718) 855-5057.

Looks at the creation and marketing of jokes, humorous scripts and stories. Quarterly. $5/issue; $18/year.

Easy Writer, % Arizona Writer's Network, P.O. Box 4004, Sedona, AZ 86340. Phone (602) 872-8806.

Provides members with regular group news and announcements. Quarterly. Price included in membership.

The Editorial Eye, % EEI, 66 Canal Center Plaza, Suite 200, Alexandria, VA

22314-1538. Phone (703) 683-0683, Fax (703) 683-4915.

Focuses on standards and practices for editors, writers and publication managers. Monthly. $87/year.

EFA Newsletter, % Editorial Freelancers Association, Inc. Box 2050, Madison Square Station, New York, NY, 10159. Phone (212) 677-3357.

News of the concerns and activities of the EFA, whose members "provide freelance editorial services to the publishing and communications industries." Bimonthly. Included in membership or $20/year for nonmembers.

Freelance, % Saskatchewan Writers Guild, P.O. Box 3986, Regina, SK, Canada S4P 3R9. Phone (306) 757-6310.

Covers news of the Guild. Price included in membership, $40/year for Canada nonmembers; $20 for students and senior citizens.

Hollywood Scriptwriter, % Hollywood Scriptwriter, 1626 N. Wilcox Avenue, Suite 385, Hollywood, CA 90028. Phone/Fax (805) 495-5447.

Practical answers, advice and guidance from working professionals. Monthly. $44/year U.S. and Canada. $25/half-year U.S. and Canada. $50/year foreign.

Locus: The Newspaper of the Science Field, % Locus Publications, P.O. Box 13305, Oakland, CA 94611. Phone (510) 339-9196, Fax (510) 339-8144.

Science fiction news, people and issues of interest to publishers, writers and others. Founded 1968. Monthly. $38/year.

Network, % International Women's Writing Guild, P.O. Box 810, Gracie Station, New York, NY 10028.

News of and by women writers. Founded 1980. Bimonthly, $35/year U.S., $45/year foreign.

Ohio Writer, % The Poets' League of Greater Cleveland, c/o Linda Rome, P.O. Box 528, Willoughby, OH 44094-0528. Phone (216) 257-6410.

Items of interest to writers living in Ohio. Bimonthly, $12/year individuals, $18/year institutions.

On Second Thought, % Center for Professional Writing, 200 University Ave. West, Waterloo, ON, Canada, N2L 3G1. Phone (519) 725-0279, Fax (519) 884-8995.

Presents information on professional writing. Quarterly. Free.

Our Write Mind, % Julian Associates, 6831 Spencer Hwy. Suite 203, Pasadena, TX 77505.

Articles, short stories, poems, fillers and cartoons on the subject of the art and business of writing. This publication is currently "on hold." The editors say that it will resume publication in the future.

Poets and Writers Magazine, 72 Spring Street, New York, NY 10012. Phone (212) 226-3586, Fax (212) 226-3963.

Discusses topics of interest to established and beginning writers. Includes commentary on publishing and political issues, interviews with authors and information on grants and awards. Bimonthly. $3.95/issue; $18/year; $32/2 years.

The Quill, % The Society of Professional Journalists, 16 S. Jackson St., P.O. Box 77, Greencastle, IN 46135. Phone (317) 653-3333.

National magazine for professional journalists and students and teachers of journalism. Founded 1909. 9 times/year, $27 U.S., $32 foreign.

Quill and Quire, % Key Publishers, 70 The Esplanade, 4th Floor, Toronto, Ontario, Canada M5E 1R2. Phone (416) 360-0044, Fax (416) 360-8745.

Articles and features on book selling, publishing and Canadian libraries for writers, booksellers, publishers and librarians. Monthly. $45/year Canada; $55/year U.S.

Registered Writer's Communique-Contacts and Assignments, % Gibbs Publishing Co., Box 600927, N. Miami Beach, FL 33160.

Directed to professional freelance writers. Founded 1986. Monthly. $18/year.

Romance Writers Report, % Romance Writers of America, Inc., 13700 Veterans Memorial Drive, No. 315, Houston, TX 77014. Phone (713) 440-6885.

Provides romance writers with information, assistance, knowledge and support by publishing agents' special reports, author profiles and how-to articles. Price included in membership.

Science Writers, % National Association of Science Writers, Inc., 7310 Broxburn Ct., Bethesda, MD 20817. Phone (301) 229-6770.

Covers the preparation and interpretation of science news for the public.

Quarterly. Price included in membership: $60/year U.S., $65/year Canada, $70/year foreign.

Screenwrite NOW! % Forum-Screenwrite NOW! P.O. Box 7, Long Green Pike, Baldwin, MD 21013-0007. Phone (410) 592-3466.

Oscar award-winning screenwriter William Kelley calls *ScreenWrite NOW* the "best kept secret in Hollywood." Presents articles on screenwriting by known writers, offers products at a discount, features successful members of the forum and lists screenwriting contests. 6/year. $38/year U.S., $68/year foreign.

SFWA Bulletin, % Science-Fiction & Fantasy Writers of America, P.O. Box 1277, Eugene, OR 97440. Phone (503) 935-6322, Fax (503) 935-6324.

Articles about the business of science fiction and fantasy writing from professionals in the field. Founded 1965. Quarterly. $15/year.

Speechwriter's Newsletter, % Lawrence Ragan Communications, Inc., 407 S. Dearborn St., Suite 1360, Chicago, IL 60605. Phone (312) 922-8245.

Offers practical information on speech writing and delivery. Weekly. $287/year.

A View From the Loft, % The Loft, 66 Malcolm, S.E., Minneapolis, MN 55414. Phone (612) 379-8999.

Provides a forum for the exchange of opinions and information about writing. Accepts unsolicited articles about writing. Monthly, except July. $30/year, $16/year low income.

The Writer, % The Writer, Inc., 120 Boyleston St., Boston, MA 02116. Phone (617) 423-3157.

Magazine for aspiring professional writers. Each issue features articles by experts in the publishing and writing fields, up-to-date market information and tips on manuscript submission. Monthly. $2/issue, $27/year.

Writer's Digest, % F&W Publications, 1507 Dana Ave., Cincinnati, OH 45207. Phone (513) 531-2222.

Contributed articles on writing techniques, success stories and profiles and interviews of authors. Covers nonfiction, fiction, poetry, playwriting, TV, radio, photography and word processing. Monthly. $2.75/issue, $24/year.

Writer's Journal, % Minnesota Ink, Inc., 27 Empire Drive, North, St. Paul, MN 55103. Phone (612) 225-1306.

Information, news and practical advice for freelance writers, communicators and consultants. Bimonthly. $3/issue, $18/year.

Writer's Lifeline, Box 32, Cornwall, Ontario, Canada K6H 5R9. Phone (613) 932-2135.

Literary, poem, book reviews, how-to articles, marketing. 4 issues/year. $4/issue; $18/year.

The Writer's Yearbook, % F&W Publications, 1507 Dana Ave, Cincinnati, OH 45207. Phone (513) 531-2222.

An annual magazine for freelance writers. Features advice on writing short stories, novels, articles, plays and TV and movie scripts. Covers trends in writing fields. Annual. $3.95.

Writers Connection—Newsletter, % Writers Connection, P.O. Box 1601 Saratoga/Sunnyvale Rd., Suite 180, Cupertino, CA 95014. Phone (408) 973-0227.

Provides how-to information on writing for publications, companies and businesses. Monthly. Price included in membership or $18 for U.S. nonmembers and $24 for Canadian nonmembers.

Writers Guild of America, East—Newsletter, % Writers Guild of America, East, 555 W. 57th St., New York, NY, 10019. Phone (212) 245-6180.

News of importance to members of this guild, a union representing writers in the motion picture, television and radio industries. 11/year. Price included in the membership or $22/year for nonmembers.

Writers Guild of America, West—Newsletter. Formerly called *The Forum, The Bulletin, The Screen Writer, Writer's Guild Bulletin,* % Writers Guild of America, West, Inc., 8955 Beverly Blvd., Los Angeles, CA 90048. Phone (213) 550-1000.

Same as above, for the West. $40/year for U.S. nonmembers; $45 for Canadian nonmembers; $50 elsewhere.

Chapter Three

Geography, Climate and Local Customs

Traveling to India to interview natives of the country? The 1992 *Culturgrams: The Nations Around Us*, reports that a host in India will sometimes adorn a guest with a garland of flowers. The guest should immediately remove the necklace and hold it in his hand as an expression of humility. Your host will no doubt be more happily interviewed if he is not offended. This chapter will introduce you to many books, like *Culturgrams*, which will help both you and your character conduct yourselves appropriately.

The geography, climate, local customs, myths, regional interests and superstitions of an area may all influence the behavior of your character. The references in this chapter will assist you in pinpointing factual data and population idiosyncrasies of areas all over the globe.

Where Does Your Character Live?

It may not be advisable to set your novel in a city you've never seen. If you do, you'll probably receive letters from the people who live there, all happy to detail your every descriptive inconsistency.

But novels use settings in a variety of ways. In some cases, a little information about an area could be stretched to accommodate your needs. Some of the traits of your characters may stem from

where they grew up or spent time. Perhaps your character, Louise, the exceedingly shy aunt, comes to visit from Sarasota. Is there something about that part of Florida that made her so reticent?

Statistics, figures and brief descriptions of areas may also be used in nonfiction works where the geography is not the main point of the story, but can add an interesting backdrop to the subject.

Many public libraries do purchase wonderful tour books; many of the same ones you'll find in bookstores, like *Access Visitors Guides*, *APA Insight Guides*, *Baedeker's*, *Blue Guides*, *Fodor's*, *Harvard Student Agencies*, *Moon Handbooks*, *Passport Guides*, *Sierra Club Adventure Travel Guides* and *Travel Survival Kits*.

You'll find that the latest library copies of these books are quickly snapped up, where they then travel with the library borrower to Aruba or wherever. Fortunately, several reference sources exist that, with a little imagination, paint a clear picture of where shy Aunt Louise comes from.

The books below will give you the details you need to describe a brief visit, or to see the influence a certain geographic area might have had on a character. Just remember that times change suddenly, so the 1990 statistic showing that River City was down and out may not reflect the economic boom of 1993.

Area Overviews

American Small City Profiles. Milpitas, CA: Toucan Valley Publications, 1993.

The word "small" in the title is slightly misleading. The cities included are those with populations over 25,000 that are located outside of major metropolitan areas. One page is devoted to each of the 324 cities and contains facts such as the percentages of different ethnicities in the area, the average weather, the name(s) of the major newspaper, hospital and college, the phone number for city hall, and the median household income.

American Suburbs Rating Guide and Fact Book. Alan Willis, Text Writer; Bennett Jacobstein, Statistical Data Compiler. Milpitas, CA: Toucan Valley Publications, 1993.

Suburbs surrounding the 50 largest metropolitan areas in the U.S. are rated on Economics, Affordable Housing, Crime, Open Spaces, Education, the Commute, and Community/Stability. A short blurb is also provided for each metropolitan area, supplying the general location of each suburban neighborhood in relation to the city, and looking at population growth, climate, types of industry and public transportation availability. Perhaps your angry character was born in one of the lowest-ranked suburbs?

America's Top Rated Cities: A Statistical Handbook. Rhoda Garoogian, editor. Boca Raton, FL: Universal Reference Publications, 1992.

Five regional guides are available in this collection: Southern, Central, Western, Eastern and Northeastern. The original source of information is provided for each group of statistics, making it simple to backtrack, if desired, to the source document. Some handy statistics: Average cost of rent and utilities (to be sure your character is living in a town they can afford) and average SAT scores (to see if your character is much smarter than the average citizen).

American Cost of Living Survey. Arsen J. Darnay and Helen S. Fisher. Detroit: Gale, 1993.

Can the college student in your novella afford to live in the city she's run away to? Check this survey. It's a compilation of reported prices for about six hundred products and services in over four hundred U.S. cities.

Americans Traveling Abroad: What You Should Know Before You Go. Gladson I. Nwanna. Baltimore, MD: World Travel Institute Press, 1994.

Geared to familiarizing travelers with conditions, laws, rules, regulations and requirements, both U.S. and foreign, that will affect a trip. Some areas covered: How to Search for a Child Abducted Abroad (terrible when true but interesting fiction), Tips on Bringing Food, Plant and Animal Products into the U.S. (what interesting fictional creature might be smuggled?), and Travel Tips for the Disabled (how does your one-legged heroine get around?).

Cities of the United States: A Compilation of Current Information on Economic,

Cultural, Geographic and Social Conditions. Peggy Saari and Diane L. Dupuis, editors. 4 Volumes. Detroit: Gale, 1990.

The title just about says it all. This encyclopedic set dedicates about a dozen pages to each of 130 cities in the United States, covering history of the area, major industries, types of art and cultural activities, names of local newspapers, information on local taxes and other particulars of interest to someone moving to, or writing about, an area. Each city section includes a (rather undetailed) map of the city, a photograph of the skyline and another photograph of a local point of interest.

Cities of the World: A Compilation of Current Information on Cultural, Geographical and Political Conditions in the Countries and Cities of Six Continents. Detroit: Gale, 1993.

Wondering how the golfing is in Antananarivo, Madagascar? Or how the hunting is in Tel Aviv? These four volumes have the answers. (By the way, the golfing is good, just fifteen miles out of the city, and hunters in Israel's second-largest city can expect to find partridge and wild boar.)

CQ's State Fact Finder: Rankings Across America. Victoria Van Son. Washington, DC: Congressional Quarterly, 1993.

Which state spent the most on highways? (In 1991 it was Alaska.) The most reported cases of rabies? (In 1992, Delaware.) Dozens of statistics on business, agriculture, crime, defense, education, energy, environment, health, population, recreation, government and transportation are reported and ranked within the states of the U.S. Be aware that some tables report figures a number of years out of date.

The Encyclopedia of Historic Places. Courtlandt Canby. 2 Volumes. New York: Facts on File Publications, 1984.

Name a place and this encyclopedic set will tell you why it's historically well known. This set provides coverage on all locations of historical significance: towns, cities, countries, provinces, regions, empires, deserts, forts, battle sites, lakes, mountains, rivers, shrines and archaeological sites. Could stimulate thoughts of some interesting settings.

The (Year) Geographic Reference Report: Annual Report of Costs, Wages, Salaries and Human Resource Statistics—U.S. and Canada. Redmond, WA: BTA Economic Research Institute. Annual.

For each metropolitan area highlighted, this report lists wage/salary and cost-of-living information. Median salaries for specific jobs are listed (sorry, nothing for writers), as well as median costs for renting an apartment or purchasing a house.

The Green Index: A State-by-State Guide to the Nation's Environmental Health. Bob Hall and Mary Lee Kerr. Washington, DC: Island Press, 1991.

The *Green Index* provides a ranking for each state based on 256 indicators of environmental health, things like percentage of farmland in the state, number of Superfund sites and sewage systems in noncompliance.

If one of your characters is an environmental activist with a yen to clear up air pollution, what's the state he should go picket for awhile? According to the Green Index, Connecticut is a candidate. In 1991, it ranked 50th (out of 50) for producing the most ozone-depleting emissions and violating air standards for carbon monoxide, and 48th for highest density of motor vehicle traffic. Yes, Connecticut.

The Lifestyle Market Analyst. Wilmette, IL: Standard Rate and Data Service. Annual.

LMA shows what percentage of people in a given area enjoy different types of activities, falling under the headings Good Life, such as gourmet cooking and travel, High-Tech Activities, including photography and watching (yes, watching) cable TV, Sports/Leisure, Outdoor, and Domestic, such as entering sweepstakes and owning a cat or dog.

This book convinced me to move to Denver, sight unseen! Just by browsing, I was able to get a good idea of what to expect when I hit the Rockies. Using the answers from millions of surveys, LMA tallies, by percentage, the relative likes and dislikes of citizens in 209 areas of the country. For each area, the top ten Lifestyles are listed. For example, the number one lifestyle activity for Bowling Green, Kentucky, is Bible/Devotional Reading, while the top choice for Washington, D.C. residents is Foreign Travel. Demographic figures let you determine who are the cities' minority citizens, how well-schooled the population is, and what the age and occupation breakdowns are.

The Livable Cities Almanac: How Over 100 Metropolitan Areas Compare in Economic Health, Air Quality, Water Quality, Crime Rates, Life Expectancy, Health Services, Recreational Opportunities and More. John Tepper Marlin. New York: HarperPerennial, 1992.

This almanac focuses on how healthy major U.S. metropolitan areas are. For each city, there is brief information supplied for all the factors listed in the book's title. Other factors examined include the Healthy Workplace (occupational hazards) and the safety of particular interstate highways (based on number of fatalities).

Moving and Relocation Sourcebook: A Reference Guide to the 100 Largest Metropolitan Areas in the United States. Diane Barlow and Steven Wasserman, compilers. 1st edition. Detroit: Omnigraphics, Inc, 1992.

This book names names. In addition to the statistics found in other sources (though some of these tend to be a few years out of date), the *Sourcebook* lists, by name, the largest employers, local colleges and libraries, shopping centers, newspapers, TV and radio stations and libraries for each metro area. Surely the Lonesome Pine Regional Library in Scott County, Virginia, held a good childhood memory for some little waif. And some story, somewhere, should include the Plaza Palomino in Tuscon, Arizona.

100 Best Small Towns in America. Norman Crampton. New York: Prentice Hall, 1993.

"Small Town" was defined, for this source, as places with between 5,000 and 15,000 inhabitants. The "best" ones were selected based on a number of criteria: communities with their own economic base, towns that are growing, per capita income, percentage of nonwhite population (racial diversity was desirable, though not all communities met this criteria very well), large 25-34 age groups, number of physicians, crime rate, percentage of highly educated people, and local government expenditures for public education. The author used many sources to gather his information, including over five hundred phone interviews with residents of each town! He says "my small-town contacts cheerfully tolerated long interviews."

Places Rated Almanac: Your Guide to Finding the Best Places to Live in North America. David Savageau and Richard Boyer. New York: Prentice Hall Travel, 1993. Updated irregularly.

This is the rating book that makes it to the national news whenever a new edition is published. Over three hundred metropolitan areas are ranked on factors that influence both the quality of the area and the people who live there. The 1993 edition proclaimed Cincinnati the overall most liveable city in the U.S., with especially high marks for jobs, transportation, education and the arts.

Retirement Places Rated: All You Need to Plan Your Retirement or Select Your Second Home. David Savageau. 3d Edition. New York: Prentice Hall, 1990.

In this source, areas are rated for items of particular interest to retirees, including climate evaluations, number of health practitioners (is there a doctah in the town?) and availability

of good restaurants. Specific figures are provided for number of golf courses, bowling centers and movie theaters. *Retirement Places Rated* will help you decide where to settle down after your book hits the half million in sales mark.

World Chamber of Commerce Directory. Loveland, CO: Worldwide Chamber of Commerce Directory, Inc. Annual.

This directory lists addresses and phone numbers for U.S. and foreign Chambers of Commerce, plus listings for convention and tourist information. These organizations will generally send you an information packet that includes maps, cost-of-living statistics and other glossy pages to tempt you to include the more attractive aspects of a town in your writings.

World Encyclopedia of Cities. George Kurian. 6 Volumes. 1993-97.

Eighty elements are covered for each city, and statistics are put in easy-to-read boxes, though the year the statistic refers to is not always noted. So far, only the first three volumes of this collection are out. Volumes 4, 5 and 6 are due in 1995, 1996 and 1997 respectively. Over six hundred cities will be surveyed in this collection. The writing is a little less dry than some books of this genre (what with Denver being noted for its "salubrious mild and dry climate").

How's the Weather?

Climatological Data. Asheville, NC: National Oceanic and Atmospheric Administration, Environmental Data and Information Service, National

Climatic Center, 1976-Present.

These monthly reports cover each state of the U.S. An annual summary for each area is also produced. These reports should be available in libraries that are full or partial government depositories.

The Times Books World Weather Guide: A City-by-City Guide for Forecasting the Weather in Any Part of the World at Any Time of the Year. Updated Edition. New York: Times Books, 1990.

The tables for each city in this guide list the average daily temperature (in both Fahrenheit and centigrade), the highest and lowest recorded temperatures for each month, the relative humidity and average monthly precipitation. The Comfort Index shows how to calculate the impact of an area's combined temperature and humidity on one's comfort. Quite a few public and academic libraries will own this volume or one of the two volumes listed directly below.

The Weather Almanac: A Reference Guide to Weather, Climate and Air Quality in the United States and Its Key Cities, Comprising Statistics, Principles and Terminology. Frank Bair, editor. 6th edition. Detroit: Gale, 1992.

The *Almanac* duplicates some of the weather narrative and statistics found in *Weather of U.S. Cities* (see below), but has more of a variety of additional information, including descriptions of phenomena such as hurricanes, lightening and floods, and a listing of record "highs" and "lows." A notable high: Overton, Nevada had a warmish day in June 1954—it hit 122 degrees.

Weather of U.S. Cities: A Guide to the Weather Histories of 270 Key Cities and Weather Observation Stations in the United States and Its Island Territories. Frank E. Bair, editor. 4th edition. Detroit: Gale, 1992.

For each city in this guide there's about a page of narrative just talking about the area's weather, and then tables showing the city's average temperatures and precipitation for each month, generally ranging from 1961 to 1990. Would you like to place a particularly chilling scene of your novel in a particularly chilly place? How about Valentine, Nebraska, where the average January temperature refuses to rise above freezing?

Gazetteers

A gazetteer is basically a geographic dictionary. A gazetteer covering, for example, the United States, will list named mountains, lakes, cities, towns and the like and provide such information as date founded, height (in the case of mountains), population, etc. This type of easily found geographical statistical information may come in handy, especially if you want to choose an especially high mountain for your characters to climb. For more on gazetteers, see chapter 14, "Choosing and Researching Names."

Maps and Atlases

Does your character need to give directions? Is one of your characters taking even a small trip in a place you've never seen? Do you want to create your own fictitious countries and make believable-looking maps, like the elaborate ones Robert Silverberg used in his *Lord Valentine's Castle* series? You need maps.

When searching for maps using an online catalog you will usually combine the name of the place you're looking for with the word ATLAS or MAPS. An example would be: ZAMBIA MAPS. If the library has no maps of just Zambia, try a broader search:

AFRICA MAPS or
AFRICA ATLAS

If the library has a map or atlas of Africa, Zambia will be in it. But don't hesitate to try that more specific search first. What the heck? It only takes a second to try. Maps can be found in a number of places.

Atlases that cover only one country, state or province. An example would be *The China Atlas*. Chicago: Rand McNally, 1990.

Atlases that cover many countries, a part of the world or the world. A sample title: *Cambridge Atlas of the Middle East and North Africa*. Gerald Blake, et al. New York: Cambridge University Press, 1988.

Fold-out, single maps. Some libraries now have these available for checkout.

Historical maps and atlases. Sources exist that show cities, travel routes, borders and the like as they existed for past time periods, or during historic events, worldwide. Some examples:

A Battlefield Atlas of the Civil War. Craig L. Symonds. Baltimore, MD: Nautical and Aviation Publishing Company of America, 1993.

Atlas of Russian History. New York: Oxford University Press, 1993.

Atlas of the Crusades. Jonathan Riley-Smith, editor. New York: Facts on File, 1990.

To search for maps of different eras try putting in the word HISTORY with your search, or the name of the time period, for example:

GERMANY HISTORY ATLAS
GERMANY MEDIEVAL MAPS

Maps that show up in books. Almost any book could contain a drawing of a map in it. To see if a book has a map in it when looking at the record on an online catalog, just look for the word "maps."

For more information on the statistical uses of atlases, see chapter 10, "Facts and Statistics Books."

Culture, Customs and Etiquette

It's time to become an amateur anthropologist and seek more information on the types of people either you or your characters will be mingling with.

The American Culture Series: 1493-1875. Ann Arbor, MI: University Microfilms, 1941-1974.

The ACS contains 5,750 titles of American books, pamphlets, memoirs and diaries, stored on 642 microfilm reels, all revealing glimpses of American culture of the past. The subject index, which is in hard copy, is arranged by author, title, subject and reel number. Samples of titles in this collection are *Life on the Plains Among Indians* and *The Practical Shepherd*.

The Cambridge Encyclopedia of Latin America and the Caribbean. Simon Collier, Thomas E. Skidmore and Harold Blakemore, general editors. 2d edition. New York: Cambridge University Press, 1992.

A one-volume overview of the geography, economy, peoples, history, politics and culture of the Latin American and Caribbean countries. Other *Cambridge Encyclopedias* cover:
Africa (1981).
China (1991).
India/Pakistan/Bangladesh/Sri Lanka/Nepal/Bhutan and the Maldives (1989).
Japan (1993).
Middle East and North Africa (1988).

Craighead's International Business, Travel and Relocation Guide to 81 Countries. 7th edition. Detroit: Gale, 1994-95.

The headings for each country report are Living in the Country, Health and Safety, Preparing for Your Trip, Getting Around the Country, Lodging, Dining, Nightlife, Leisure Activities, and Bibliography and Suggested Reading. Some useful subheadings include How to Find Housing, Telephone Installation, Sports and Fitness, and Tipping. Some items under business customs in Hong Kong include "bring a good appetite" and "never send white flowers;" while advice for Qatar says "patience is the key to success."

Cultural Atlas of Islam. Isma'īl R. al Fārūqī. New York: MacMillan Publishing Co., 1986.

This book opens with an examination of the historical reality from which Islam was born, proceeds to a definition of the essence of Islamic civilization, and goes on to survey the manifestations of Islam in action, thought and expression.

Culturgrams: The Nations Around Us. David M. Kennedy Center for International Studies. Brigham Young University, 1992.

Each *Culturgram* in this collection concisely describes cultural assumptions, values and customs for a specific nation. This popular and respected series covers Greetings, Visiting, Eating, Gestures, Personal Appearance, Dating and Marriage and more.

The Dictionary of Cultural Literacy: What Every American Needs to Know. E.D. Hirsch, Jr., Joseph F. Kett and James Trefil. Boston: Houghton Mifflin Co., 1993.

Comprised of twenty-three sections covering major areas of knowledge, including World Literature, Philosophy, Religion, Idioms, and Medicine and Health, the *Dictionary of Cultural Biography* briefly identifies ideas, events and individuals, explaining their significance in American culture and placing them in context. For example, the major section covering Anthropology, Psychology and Sociology lists the following entries: Brainwashing, Encounter Group, Girl Scouts of America, Margaret Mead, Old Boy Network and Woodstock.

A Dictionary of Indian Culture. M.L. Varadpande, New Delhi, India: Arnold Publishers, 1991.

This work, in alphabetic dictionary

fashion, looks at the culture of the peoples of India. An index would have been helpful in this source, cross-referencing back to words that fit certain categories. But, if you've heard mention of an Indian cultural belief that you don't know of, you can certainly look it up here. Some entries: Sinhasana Dwatrinshika—a collection of thirty-two stories about the valor and intellect of legendary King Vikramaditya, and SixtyFour Arts—the number of arts and crafts that Indian girls were expected to master in ancient India; these arts included the art of making ear ornaments, writing, drawing, tattooing and carpentry.

The Encyclopedia of Bad Taste. Jane Stern and Michael Stern. New York: HarperCollins Publishers, 1990.

As the authors say in the introduction, this is a guide to the "tacky, outré, and the outlandish" in the U.S. Some might ask, does this truly represent the tacky or some of the quintessential examples of objects that were a natural outgrowth of the culture of the time? Ample photographs dot these essays on such activities and items as "Enormous Breasts" (including Jane Russell's), "Children's Names" (Tiffany, Sioux and Ashley are all discussed), and "Mood Rings" (which, this book reveals, can be warmed in a toaster oven to produce the "happy" blue color).

Encyclopedia of Southern Culture. Charles Reagan Wilson and William Ferris, co-editors. Chapel Hill, NC: University of North Carolina Press, 1989.

Focusing primarily on the eleven states of the former Confederacy, this work looks at the region's music, literature, manners, myths, life, thought and the impact of its history and politics. There are twenty-four major topic headings, including Black Life, Folklife, Language, Religion, Urbanization, Violence and Women's Life.

The Encyclopedia of World Cultures. 10 Volumes. Boston: G.K. Hall, 1991.

This wonderful collection, produced under the auspices of the Human Relations Area Files (HRAF), is comprised of nine volumes covering different geographic areas: North America, Oceania, South Asia, Europe and the Middle East, East and Southeast Asia, the Soviet Union and China, South America, Middle America and the Caribbean, and Africa. The tenth volume contains cumulative lists of the cultures of the world, their alternate names and a bibliography of publications related to the listed groups. Each volume also has a map that pinpoints the location of each group described.

The longer essays in this collection contain some or most of the following: name, alternate names, origins, location of culture and description of the physical environment, language, population trends, economy, kin groups, rules and practices related to marriage, family, inheritance, socialization, death and the afterlife, ceremonies, arts and religion. This set records fascinating practices of both the present and past. Just a few afterlife beliefs: the Mimika of Indonesia believe that the spirits of the dead live in a beautiful underworld of sand and gardens; the Mennonites feel that access to Heaven is not predetermined and will only be awarded after having lived a life as a disciplined member of the Mennonite community; the Yakan, of the island of Basilan in the southern Philippines, believe that their dead have a one-hundred-day journey to the next world.

Gestures: The Do's and Taboos of Body Language Around the World. Roger E. Axtell. New York: John Wiley and Sons, 1991.

Body language to avoid and use is the subject of this book. Though the cartoons depicting the gestures are humorous, they're also accurate. Some advice from the author: In France, good friends will kiss each other on the cheeks, but be aware that "it is really touching cheeks and 'kissing the air' "; in Paraguay, the "O.K." gesture, of thumb and forefinger together, forming a circle, is seen as rude.

Handbook of American Popular Culture. Thomas Inge, editor. 2d edition. 3 Volumes. Westport, CT: Greenwood Press, 1989.

This set contains informed essays, with many pointers to further reading, on aspects of popular culture unique to the United States. Arranged in alphabetic order, the headings are wide-ranging, including The Automobile, Death, Games and Toys, Physical Fitness, the Self-Help Tradition and Popular Religion. This useful collection is due for an update since Beavis and Butthead aren't mentioned at all.

Hispanic American Almanac: A Reference Work on Hispanics in the United States. Nicolás Kanellos. Detroit: Gale Research, 1993.

Facts, dates, biographies and essays cover the facets of Hispanic life in the United States. Some areas covered include historic landmarks, education, literature, film and religion. Other, similar works from Gale Research: *The African American Almanac.* 1994. *The Native North American Almanac.* 1994.

Historical and Cultural Atlas of African Americans. Molefi K. Asante and Mark T. Mattson. New York: Macmillan Publishing Co., 1991.

With its many maps, the authors wanted to give the reader a "spatial representation of some of the most important events, personalities and facts about African Americans." Each section has been given the name of a spiritual (song). For example, section 1, titled "I Got My Religion from Out of the Sun," examines the ancient origins of African Americans, and section four, "I Know de Udder Worl' Is Not Like Dis," looks at the nature of African American slavery.

Illustrated Encyclopedia of Mankind. 22 Volumes. Richard Carlisle, editor-in-chief. New York: Marshall Cavendish, 1990.

These volumes cover over five hundred cultures and other general topics. The numerous color photographs, maps and illustrations are marvelous; simply reading about the neck rings of the Padaung women, for example, those they call the "giraffe-necked women," is much more effectively understood with the before (wearing the neck rings) and after (showing the woman after she takes them off) photographs.

Jewish-American History and Culture: An Encyclopedia. Jack Fischel and Sanford Pinsker, editors. New York: Garland Publishing, 1992.

A broad survey of the Jewish experience in the United States, encompassing historical events and figures, literature, art, popular entertainment and religious life. Some of the headings are Colonial American Jewry, Jewish Education and Yiddish Poetry. Perfect for those non-Jewish people who want to date a Jewish person (or write about them).

LAC: The Microbook Library of American Civilization. Chicago: Library Resources, 1971-72.

Stored on "ultrafiche," the LAC is 6,500,000 pages worth of pamphlets, periodicals, biographies, autobiographies, poetry, rare books and foreign material relating to America from the country's settlement through the beginning of World War I. There is a four-volume print index to this collection accessible by author, title, subject and "biblioguide." The subject index only indexes titles of books (no contents), but the biblioguide is a classified index with 29 subject headings broken down into 565 topics. Some of the topic headings include Amerindians, Religion, Manners and Customs, and Afro-Americans. Under the last heading are such dated entries as "Race Adjustment," "The New Negro: An Interpretation," "Our Brother in Black" and "Negro A Menace." (By the way, ultrafiche, which this collection is stored on, is no longer produced; it is a predecessor to microfiche. But libraries that have this collection will usually keep an old ul-

trafiche reader on hand to read this material.)

Letitia Baldrige's New Complete Guide to Executive Manners. Letitia Baldrige. New York: Rawson Associates, 1993.

Ms. Baldrige covers the many business situations that require a knowledge of etiquette and proper behavior, with advice on such topics as "How Many Times a Day Should One Say Please," "The Art of Introducing People" and "How to Gracefully Get Someone to Leave Your Office." Also by this author: *Letitia Baldrige's Complete Guide to the New Manners for the Nineties.*

Miss Manners Guide for the Turn-of-the-Millennium. Judith Martin. New York: Pharos Books, 1989. (Also available on audiocassette.)

This book is arranged in correspondence format; letters from readers to Judith Martin . . . er . . . Miss Manners are presented, with a question regarding appropriate behavior. Miss Manners replies to the "gentle reader." Such situations as "who decides the color of the bridesmaids' gowns" and "what to do when your houseguest is asleep, naked in the living room and you must pass through" are presented. Though Miss Manners is a created persona for the author, the advice is solid. Entertaining, enlightening and instructive reading.

The New Emily Post's Etiquette. Elizabeth L. Post. New York: Funk & Wagnalls, 1975.

For many of us, the name "Emily Post" is still synonymous with Good Etiquette. In 1922, she published her first etiquette book—it went through ninety printings. Miss Post passed on in 1960, and this 1975 edition was actually written by her granddaughter-in-law.

Since some aspects of etiquette are timeless, this book will still, in part, be useful for contemporary purposes. And of course this, and even older editions, can help you decide how your early and midcentury characters should conduct themselves. At the risk of sounding rude, I must quote one of the more dubious recommendations in this tome. From the section on Circuses, Ice Shows and Rodeos: "Don't blow your cigarette smoke into your neighbor's face and don't let your enthusiasm get so out of hand that your voice may burst his eardrums. This is one time when it is perfectly all right to discard peanut shells, paper cups, wrappers, etc., on the floor, but be *sure* you don't discard them all over your neighbor's feet or shoulders."

The Writer's Guide to Everyday Life in the 1800's: For Writers of Historic Fiction, Westerns, Romance, Action/Adventure, Thrillers and Mysteries. Marc McCutcheon. Cincinnati, OH: Writer's Digest Books, 1993.

This guide is divided into useful sections, describing items and behaviors common to the eighteenth-century citizen. Some chapter headings are: Slang and Everyday Speech, Money and Coinage, and Common Food, Drinks and Tobacco. Another guide in this vein is *The Writer's Guide to Everyday Life in the Middle Ages: The British Isles from 500 to 1500* (Sherrilyn Denyon. 1994).

Apparel

Now that you know how your characters should act and how they should think, it's time to dress them up!

Fashions in Hair: The First Five Thousand Years. Richard Corson. London: Peter Owen, 1971.

This book looks at hair on the face and head (both real and created) as worn in ancient civilizations through the early 1960s. The author and illustrator (who hopes his book will be of interest "to all people with hair") has provided small but detailed and abundant black-and-white drawings.

An Illustrated Dictionary of Hairdressing and Wigmaking. Steven J. Cox. London: B.T. Batsford Ltd, 1984.

The first portion of this dictionary is dedicated to defining U.S. and British terms and phrases, both contemporary and obsolete, related to hairdressing and wigmaking. The second portion contains over 1,000 sketches and photographs of men and women from primarily the eighteenth and nineteenth centuries, displaying a wide array of U.S. and English hair, wig, mustache and beard styles, along with some of the implements of the trade.

The Mode in Hats and Headdress. Turner R. Wilcox. New York: Charles Scribner's Sons, 1948.

The black-and-white line drawings are clear and numerous for the hundreds of hats, turbans, bowlers, helmets, caps, veils, wigs, bonnets, crowns and hairstyles featured beginning with Ancient Egyptian styles through 1944. Nobility, ecclesiastics and regualr joes are all represented.

History of Shoe Fashions. Eunice Wilson. New York: Pitman Publishing, 1969. The author provides sketches and background for footwear worldwide, over time. Some are quite fancy and frivolous, like the men's boots and shoes often adorned with a bow in the late 1600s, others are spare, like the slip-on footwear of the Normans between 1066 and 1154.

The Costume Accessories Series. Aileen Ribeiro, general editor. New York: Drama Book Publishers.

A series of books highlighting fashion accessories, including:

Bags and Purses. Vanda Foster. 1982.
Fans. Helene Alexander. 1984.
Gloves. Valerie Cumming. 1982.
Hats. Fiona Clark. 1982.
Jewelry. Diana Scarisbrick. 1984.
Shawls, Stoles and Scarves. Alice Mackrell. 1986.
Shoes. June Swann. 1982.
Socks and Stockings. Jeremy Farrell. 1992.
Umbrellas and Parasols. Jeremy Farrell. 1985.

Military Uniforms in America. San Rafael, CA: The Company of Military Historians.

A series of volumes illustrating uniforms of not only American soldiers but of those who fought with and against them on U.S. soil. Titles in the series, all written by John R. Elting, Colonel U.S. Army, Retired:

Era of the American Revolution: 1755-1795. 1974.
Years of Growth: 1790-1851. 1977.
Long Endure—The Civil War Period: 1852-1867. 1982.
Modern Era: From 1868. 1988.

Ribbons and Medals: The World's Military and Civil Awards. Captain H. Taprell Dorling. Revised by Francis K. Mason. Garden City, NY: Doubleday & Co., Inc., 1974.

Each medal and ribbon featured is accompanied by a black-and-white photograph and details of its history and appearance. There are several color pages of ribbons as well.

Uniforms of the World: A Compendium of Army, Navy and Air Force Uniforms, 1700-1937. Richard Knötel and Herbert Sieg. New York: Charles Scribner's Sons, 1980.

The verbal descriptions of the uniforms are quite detailed; unfortunately the 1,600 black-and-white sketches are rather small. This is an updated version of the 1869 German reference, *Handbuch Der Uniformkunde.*

For more apparel resources, see page 141.

Mythology and Superstitions

Don't comb your hair after sunset—it will bring disaster! Or so says the *Dictionary of Superstitions.* (Perhaps this is the reason Michelle Pfeiffer doesn't neaten her hair. . . .) Many mystical tomes lurk in the average library collection. Although these works interest horror and mystery writers, I also see their appeal for humorists.

Of course, the study of mythology often has historic "backing" and is, in itself, a scholarly field. Though many myths are closely associated with religious beliefs, I have chosen, based on the types of references published, to place religious beliefs in the section following this one. Myths will also appear in the resources listed in that section.

Animal-Speak: The Spiritual and Magical Powers of Creatures Great and Small. Ted Andrews. St.Paul, MN: Llewellyn Publications, 1994.

Animal-Speak provides techniques for reading signs and omens in nature and recounts both mythical associations and physical realities of over one hundred animals, birds, insects and reptiles.

The Continuum Encyclopedia of Symbols. Udo Becker. New York: Continuum, 1994.

The symbolic significance of over fifteen hundred objects and concepts in different cultures. The items and ideas examined are quite varied; some sample entries include Butterflies (a symbol of women in Japan), a Lighthouse (a representation of the heavenly harbor the soul sails into) and the Veil (a symbol of concealment and of mystery). Unfortunately, many of the entries refer to symbolic meaning in "many" cultures, rather than naming the specific cultures.

A Dictionary of Angels Including the Fallen Angels. Gustav Davidson. New York: The Free Press, 1967.

The author has compiled an alphabetic listing of angels culled from religious and literary writings. Some sample entries from the books include "Ababaloy—an angel invoked in Solomonic incantation operations. Ababaloy is mentioned in the black-magic manual Grimorium Verum," and "Iabiel—an evil angel invoked in ceremonial magic for separating a husband

from his wife. Iabiel is mentioned in The Sword of Moses." About one hundred fascinating black-and-white reproductions of drawings and paintings of angels are included.

A Dictionary of Dream Symbols. Eric Ackroyd. London: Blandford, 1993.

This book opens with advice on how to interpret your dreams and an overview of the thoughts of both Sigmund Freud and Carl Jung on dreams. The bulk of the book is an A to Z listing of several possible meanings of dream images. Some entries: Hall—1) A hall, particularly if large and symmetrical, may symbolize the self. 2) If the hall is a mere antechamber (like a doctor's waiting room) it may mean a large part of your psyche still remains unexplored; and Swimming—swimming may symbolize a trustful and receptive attitude toward your unconscious, or your mother or Mother Nature.

The Dictionary of Imaginary Beings. Jorge Luis Borges. New York: E.P. Dutton and Co., 1969.

What is a Golem? A Zaratan? And what's all this about the Shaggy Beast of La Ferté-Bernard? The author provides some answers in his descriptions of these (allegedly) imaginary beings. The Shaggy Beast would be a particularly awesome animal to behold: the size of bull, with a snake's head, tortoiselike feet and a round body covered with long green fur, which hid its deadly stingers! Such fascinating creatures were simply meant to show up in lots of modern-day stories . . . including yours?

Dictionary of Native American Mythology. Sam D. Gill. Santa Barbara, CA: ABC-CLIO, 1992.

Descriptions and definitions of ritual and myth of the many tribes of North America. The *Dictionary* names a number of creatures to be wary of, including the Ganiagwaihegowa, a mythic, human-devouring, hairless bear, and Anal Snakes, which enter the bodies of sleeping people in order to kill them. There is a useful cross-reference index by tribe.

Dictionary of Satanism. Wade Baskin. New York: Philosophical Library, 1972.

This work embraces concepts, issues, people, places and events associated throughout history with the concept of Satan. Includes short but scary definitions, like Shedim, a type of demon that has the claws of a cock, and Hexen, the name for witches in Germanic folklore.

Dictionary of Superstitions. Iona Opie and Moira Tatem. New York: Oxford University Press, 1989.

The place to look to find divinations, spells, cures, charms, signs, omens, rituals and taboos, chiefly from Great Britain and Eire. Arranged alphabetically by the central idea or object, the "definitions" are actually quotations, listed chronologically, related to the superstition. In addition to the "Don't brush your hair after sunset!" warning mentioned above, another hair warning appears under HAIR: Keeping—"My grandmother said to my mother 'Don't you ever keep your own hair.' But she did, and she died when she was forty." (Perhaps there is some great luck, after all, in being bald.)

Encyclopedia of Archetypal Symbolism: The Archive for Research and Archetypal Symbolism. Beverly Moon, editor. Boston: Shambhala, 1991.

This book examines the psychological meaning, historical and cultural context, and cross-cultural symbolism of archetypes; illustrated in 120 color photographs of worldwide art works/ artifacts. These are arranged by archetypal theme, including Cosmos and Creation, Sacred Animals, Goddesses, Gods, Death and Transformation.

An Encyclopedia of Fairies: Hobgoblins, Brownies, Bogies and Other Supernatural Creatures. Katharine Briggs. New York: Pantheon Books, 1976.

The author recounts the myths and legends of many of the alleged supernatural creatures of Europe pulled from literature and fable. Many entries discuss particular beings, such as the shape-shifting goblins known as brags. Others discuss particular cultural habits of the creatures, such as Fairy Food, Fairy Funerals and Solitary Fairies.

Encyclopedia of Witches and Witchcraft. Rosemary Ellen Guiley. New York: Facts on File, 1989.

Information is provided pertaining to the history, beliefs, practices and adherents of witchcraft in Western civilization. The author also compiled the *Encyclopedia of Ghosts and Spirits* in 1992, a compendium of paranormal activity worldwide.

Faiths and Folklore of the British Isles: A Descriptive and Historical Dictionary.

W. Carew Hazlitt. 2 Volumes. New York: Benjamin Blom, 1965.

Covering Norman times to the end of the nineteenth century, this dictionary defines the superstitions, beliefs and popular customs of England, Scotland, Wales and Ireland. From these volumes I learned the tale of The Chin, an imp that resides in the chimneys of nurseries and can be called upon to take away misbehaving children, and the superstition that a baby born with a blue vein on the side of its nose is destined to be drowned!

Index to Fairy Tales: Including Folklore, Legends and Myths in Collections. (Original Author: Mary Huse Eastman.) Norma Olin Ireland. (Original publishers: Boston Books and F.W. Faxon.) Metuchen, NJ: Scarecrow Press, 1915-86.

This collection assists the reader in locating tales found in collections of stories. Examples of some of the collection titles: *100 Armenian Tales* (Detroit: Wayne State University, 1982), and *The Hungry Woman; Myths and Legends of the Aztecs* (New York: William Morrow, 1984). The first and second editions allow you to find stories by title only. The editions beginning with the 1949-1972 compilation are especially useful since a subject index to the writings is provided in addition to the title access. With subject access, you can specifically look under a place, like Turkey, to find tales that originate there, or a subject such as Darkness and find stories with the dark as their focus.

Library of the World's Myths and Legends. New York: Peter Bedrick Books.

This is a series of slim, well-illustrated books that look at myths and religious beliefs of different cultures. Books in this series include:

African Mythology. Edward George Parrinder. 1986.

Celtic Mythology. Prooinsias Mac-Cana. 1985.

Chinese Mythology. Anthony Christie. 1983.

Christian Mythology. George Every. 1987.

Egyptian Mythology. Veronica Ions. 1983.

European Mythology. Jaqueline Simpson. 1987.

Greek Mythology. John Pinsent. 1991.

Illustrated Dictionary of Greek and Roman Mythology. Michael Stapleton. 1986.

Indian Mythology. Veronica Ions. 1983.

Japanese Mythology. Juliet Piggott. 1982.

Jewish Legends. David Goldstein. 1987.

Mexican and Central American Mythology. Irene Nicholson. 1985.

Near Eastern Mythology. John Gray. 1985.

North American Indian Mythology. Cott C.A. Burland. 1985.

Persian Mythology (Iran). John R. Hinnels. 1985.

Roman Mythology. Stewart Perowne. 1984.

Scandinavian Mythology. Hilda Roder Davidson. 1986.

South American Mythology. Harold Osborne. 1986.

Man, Myth and Magic: The Illustrated Encyclopedia of Mythology, Religion and the Unknown. Richard Cavendish, editor. 12 Volumes. New York: Marshall

Cavendish, 1985.

This set is chock-full of illustration. Use the cumulative index (the last volume) to find what you need, since there may be several mentions of a myth or belief throughout this set.

Mythology of All Races. 13 Volumes. Boston: Archaeological Institute of America, Marshall Jones Co., 1916-1932.

A "standard" collection in most large libraries. The subjects for each volume: V.1—Greek and Roman, V.2—Eddic, V.3—Celtic and Slavic, V.4—Finno-Ugric, Siberian, V.5—Semitic, V.6—Indian, V.7—Armenian and African, V.8—Chinese and Japanese, V.9—Oceanic, V.10—North American, V.11—Latin-American, V.12—Egyptian and Indo-Chinese, and V.13—Index to the set.

Oxford Companion to Australian Folklore. Gwenda Beed Davey and Graham Seal, editors. Melbourne: Oxford University Press, 1993.

Arranged in dictionary fashion, this companion defines and describes folklife and folklore in historic and modern-day Australia. Both aboriginal and non-native peoples are included.

The Woman's Dictionary of Symbols and Sacred Objects. Barbara G. Walker. San Francisco: HarperSanFrancisco, 1988.

Objects covered include those commonly used in everyday life, like a broom, and sacred pieces such as the Mezuzah. The symbolism of nature's creatures, formations and occurrences is described, along with significant rituals and supernatural figures. Many

common religious symbols are included, which the author contends "were stolen from ancient woman-centered systems and reinterpreted in the contexts of patriarchy."

The Woman's Encyclopedia of Myths and Secrets. Barbara G. Walker. San Francisco: Harper and Row, 1983.

Author Walker looks at word origins, legends, superstitions and customs and examines their "patriarchal origins" in the history, mythology and folklore of many cultures. In A to Z arrangement.

Religious Beliefs

The Concise Encyclopedia of Islam. Cyril Glassé. San Francisco: Harper and Row, 1989.

One-volume coverage of the beliefs of Islam and its prominent persons. The author points out that the fundamental Western belief in separation of Church and State makes Islam a particularly difficult culture and religion for Westerners to understand. The author says the Islamic people do indeed "lodge religious belief not only at the center of their individual conduct, but also at the center of their politics." A chronology of Islam in maps and text is supplied at the end of this volume.

Encyclopedia Judaica. 16 Volumes. Jerusalem, Israel: Keter Publishing House, 1972.

A compendium of Jewish life, culture and beliefs. This set includes eight thousand illustrations, including maps, charts, diagrams and color photographs. Note that Volume 1 is the index to the collection.

Encyclopedia of African American Religions. Larry G. Murphy, J. Gordon Melton and Gary L. Ward, editors. New York: Garland Publishing, 1993.

This encyclopedia supplies biographical coverage of the founders of larger African American religious groups, and of selected bishops serving the black community. Also included are descriptions of African American denominations, and prominent religious groups and organizations.

Encyclopedia of the American Religious Experience: Studies of Traditions and Movements. Charles H. Lippy and Peter W. Williams, editors. 3 Volumes. New York: Scribner's Sons, 1988.

Whether founded in America, like The Church of Jesus Christ of Latter-Day Saints (a.k.a. the Mormons), or from other parts of the world, like the Buddhists, this encyclopedia tries to cover all religions that have been or are practiced in America. The substantive essays that make up this compilation fall under nine parts, including Religions Outside the Jewish and Christian Tradition, Movement in American Religion, and Religion and the Political and Social Orders.

The Encyclopedia of the Lutheran Church. Julius Bodensieck. 3 Volumes. Minneapolis: Augsburg Publishing House, 1965.

International in scope, this work describes the theology of the Lutheran faith, supplies biographical information on leaders in the church, examines the historical roots of the faith,

recounts specific tasks and actions of Lutherans, and elaborates on specific thoughts of the church on a variety of issues such as war and prostitution.

Encyclopedia of Mormonism: The History, Scripture, Doctrine and Procedure of the Church of Jesus Christ of Latter-day Saints. Daniel H. Ludlow. 5 Volumes. New York: Macmillan Publishing Co., 1992.

This set delves into the teachings, beliefs, cultural activities and roots of the 160-year old Church of Latter-day Saints (LDS), more widely known as the Mormons. The biographical entries cover those who were influential contemporaries of the founder of the Church, Joseph Smith, Presidents of the Church and some auxiliary founders. The last volume of the collection contains a copy of the *Book of Mormon* and the *Doctrine and Covenants* of the Mormons.

Encyclopedia of Native American Religions. Arlene Hirschfelder and Paulette Molin. New York: Facts on File, 1992.

This book looks at the spiritual traditions of the native peoples in the U.S. and Canada pre-European exposure. Sacred sites involved in public dispute are named, as are some Native American religious practitioners. Some Protestant and Catholic missionaries who had influence on the Native American religious tradition are also included. The authors state that they "include enough material for readers to gain an understanding and appreciation of spiritual traditions, but have also tried to avoid the specific descriptions that would offend Native peoples."

Encyclopedia of Religion. Mircea Eliade, editor-in-chief. 16 Volumes. New York: MacMillan Publishing Co., 1987.

An extensive and scholarly global survey of religious beliefs, concepts and practices. Using the index, Volume 16, it is simple to track specific beliefs. For example, the concept of Afterlife has several dozen entries in the index, representing the afterlife beliefs of different groups including Albanian, Caribbean Islamic, North American Indian and Turkic religions.

Encyclopedia of Unbelief. Gordon Stein, editor. 2 Volumes. Buffalo, New York: Prometheus Books, 1985.

"Unbelief," as addressed in this encyclopedia, is defined in the forward of this set as "the rejection of belief in miracles and divine revelation, in life after death, and in any supernatural beings—gods, devils, and surrogate deities." The *Encyclopedia of Unbelief* describes movements, ideas, and people who oppose traditional religious doctrines. Some essays examine unbelief within religious movements (i.e., Unbelief Within Christianity) or in geographic areas (such as Unbelief in Japan). The impact of unbelief is also scrutinized in relation to ideas such as evolution, evil, moral judgements and the origin of life. The existence of writings of unbelief in various world literatures is also investigated.

Encyclopedic Dictionary of Yoga. Georg Feuerstein. New York: Paragon House, 1990.

A dictionary on the elements of the religious/philosophical system known as Yoga, which the author has written to "inform rather than overwhelm the lay reader, while at the same time providing valuable references for the professional Yoga researcher and historian of religion." Both the metaphysical and practical dimensions of Yoga are addressed.

Guide to the Gods. Marjorie Leach. Santa Barbara, CA: ABC-CLIO, 1992.

A worldwide overview of deities. Each grouping in the book is based upon the function and attributes of the gods, thereby bringing together deities from all over the world, allowing easy comparison. Some examples of groupings include Celestial Deities, such as solar or lunar gods, and Terrestrial Deities, including animal/bird gods and fire gods. The entries are very brief, ranging from a phrase to a few sentences, but a citation pointing the reader to further recommended reading is included for each entry.

The Mennonite Encyclopedia: A Comprehensive Reference Work on the Anabaptist-Mennonite Movement. Cornelius Krahn, editor. Revised Edition. 4 Volumes. Scottdale, PA: The Mennonite Publishing House, 1969-73. Supplemental Volume 5: Cornelius J. Dyck and Dennis D. Martin, editors. Scottdale, PA: Herald Press, 1990.

The original four volumes survey the Mennonite history, life and theology worldwide from its inception in the sixteenth century through the twentieth century. The supplemental volume, in addition to supplying updated and new entries, also added more biographies of influential women Mennonites who the editors felt were underrepresented in the original set where they almost always were included because they were martyrs.

New Catholic Encyclopedia. William J. McDonald, editor-in-chief. 15 Volumes. New York: McGraw-Hill Book Co., 1967.

International in scope, this encyclopedia updates the *Catholic Encyclopedia*, issued between 1907 and 1914. The set looks at the doctrines, institutions and activities of the Catholic Church throughout the world. Thoughts of the Church on subjects as abortion and the Vietnam War are recorded.

The New Catholic Encyclopedia has had three supplement volumes added to the original fifteen, in 1974, 1979 and 1989. The latest volume, Volume 18, focuses on developments in the Catholic religion over the decade between the printing of volumes 17 and 18. More supplements are expected since, as it says in the Foreword of Volume 18, "renewal through supplements has been the plan from the outset for an encyclopedia centered on a Church always in renewal."

The New Schaff-Herzog Encyclopedia Of Religious Knowledge. Samuel Macauley Jackson, editor-in-chief. 15 Volumes. Grand Rapids, MI: Baker Book House, 1977, Reprint. (Original: Funk and Wagnalls, Co., 1908.)

Described in the subtitle as "Embracing Biblical, Historical, Doctrinal and Practical Theology and Biblical, Theological and Ecclesiastical Biography From the Earliest Times to the Present Day." Found in most academic and larger public libraries.

Chapter Four

Architecture and Decor

As you describe the haunts of your characters, there will be times when you want to describe a decorative object, piece of furniture or an entire room. You could opt to use pieces from your own home or the homes of friends. You might also visit stores that sell furniture and decorative pieces. Another option would be to browse museums and preserved homes of historical figures to see older, restored or rare pieces.

Books and magazines containing photographs of architecture and decor may be particularly handy for both the added descriptions of objects they provide and the chance they offer you to sit and stare at them for as long as you'd like! Browse the art and architecture collections in the circulating books area of your local library, especially a larger one that caters to art and/or architecture clientele. (Your local art museum may also maintain a specialized collection of art books.)

The recommended call number areas for browsing are:

Library of Congress:
NA Architecture, including architectural decoration.
NK Decorative Arts, including interior design, furniture and lighting.

Dewey Decimal:
700s Fine and decorative art, design, architecture.

Architecture and Decor Magazines and Journals

There are many magazines devoted exclusively to worldwide art and architecture of the present day and the past. Look for a school in your area with an architectural or interior design program to find the widest variety to browse through. Otherwise, many libraries may have the more popular titles.

Here are examples of popular, professional and scholarly design and architectural periodicals that would be useful to page through:

A&U: Architecture and Urbanism. Tokyo, Japan: A + U Publishing Co. Monthly. 1971-present.

In-depth coverage of modern architects and their work worldwide; includes full-page color photographs.

Abitare. Milan, Italy: Abitare Segestm SpA. 10/year. 1961-present.

An Italian periodical featuring contemporary residential architecture and design. The emphasis is on Europe. The colorful, detailed and plentiful Italian ads also provide insight into cutting-edge Italian decor.

Architectural Digest: The International Magazine of Fine Interior Design. New York: Condé Nast. Monthly. 1925-present.

The interiors displayed are full of very costly objects and art, but many enjoy paging through this magazine just to get ideas.

Architectural Record. New York: McGraw-Hill. Monthly. 1891-present. America's most influential architecture magazine.The main focus of the magazine is on recent architectural projects, most of them in the United States.

Architectural Review. London: MBC Architectural Press. Monthly. 1896-present.
Complementary to the *Architectural Record* in that it is quite similar in style and content, but focuses on British and other European architectural projects.

Casabella: International Architectural Review. Milan, Italy: Elemond Periodici. Monthly. 1928-present.
Casabella, published in Italy, focuses on public buildings and urban design worldwide.

Colonial Homes. New York: Hearst Corp. Bimonthly. 1974-present.
A magazine that provides decorating ideas for those interested in describing an authentic Early American decorative style.

Daidalos: Architektur, Kunst, Kultur. Gutersloh, Germany: Bertelsmann Fachzeitschriften. Quarterly. 1981-present.
A German quarterly with international coverage but an emphasis on Central European architecture and design.

Domus: Monthly Review of Architecture,

Interiors, Design, Art. Milan, Italy: Editoriale Domus SpA. 11/year. 1928-present.
Domus looks at modern architecture and design worldwide. It is known for its creative layout.

GA: Global Architecture. Tokyo: A.D.A. Edita Tokyo Co. Semiannual. 1977-present.
Each issue is devoted to only one or two buildings or projects, thoroughly photographed and discussed. This publisher also puts out *GA Document: A Serial Chronicle of Modern Architecture,* with each issue covering about ten buildings, and *GA Houses,* which looks at modern residential architecture around the world.

House and Garden: The Magazine of Creative Living. New York: Condé Nast Publications. Monthly. 1901-present.
House and Garden seeks to inspire by showing current trends in interior design in well-to-do, usually professionally designed homes. Geared to a younger audience and featuring many homes decorated by "everday" people is *House Beautiful* (Hearst Corp. Monthly. 1896-present).

ID (International Design): Magazine of International Design. New York: Design Publications, Bimonthly. 1954-present.
ID contains international examples of creative design of everyday objects used both in commercial and home settings. Each year the magazine also compiles a special publication, the *Annual Design Review,* which presents the works of the winners of *ID*'s annual competition.

Inland Architect: The Midwestern Building Arts Magazine. Chicago: Inland Architect Press. Bimonthly. 1957-present.

Inland Architect concentrates on projects in the United States and abroad by midwestern architectural firms.

Interior Design. 16/year. New York: Interior Design Division of Whitney Communications Corp., 1932-Present.

Aimed at design professionals, coverage includes design of homes, offices and other public spaces.

Landscape Architecture. Washington, DC: American Society of Landscape Architects. Monthly. 1910-present.

A look at the design of the grounds surrounding buildings; international and sometimes historical.

Metropolis: The Urban Magazine of Architecture and Design. New York: Bellerophon Publications. 10/year. 1981-present.

This is the oversized magazine you may have seen on newsstands. Known for its imaginative graphics and articles about the general goings-on in Manhattan (in addition to urban architecture and design).

Mimar: Architecture in Development. London: Concept Media Pte., Ltd. Quarterly. 1981-present.

The definition of Mimar is "master builder" in quite a few languages. Reviewed as the most "truly international architectural periodical available."

Process: Architecture. Tokyo: Process Architecture Publishing. Monthly. 1977-present.

The focus is on the work of Japanese architecture, with each issue devoted to a single subject.

Terrazzo: Architecture and Design. New York: Rizzoli International Publications. Semiannual. 1988-present.

A book-length periodical, amply illustrated, with a worldwide focus.

Victorian Homes. Millers Falls, MA: Vintage Publications. 1982-present.

The magazine of Victorian style, with advice on how to create the Victorian aura while allowing for modern conveniences. All of the advertisements in this magazine deal with products and services related to Victoriana.

World Architecture. London: Grosvenor Press International. Bimonthly. 1990-present.

The official magazine of the International Academy of Arts in London.

Zodiac. New York: Rizzoli International Publications. Semiannual. 1989-present.

International coverage with special attention to urban public buildings.

Cityscapes

How can you find out what a certain area or city looked like in the time period you are featuring it in? Well, there's usually no quick way in the reference collection, unfortunately. While books of landmarks and specific buildings show up in ready reference sections, you'll need to search for books examining cities and places of different time periods by conducting subject searches in a library catalog (or asking the bookstore owner what they have).

There are a variety of word combinations you should try if you're looking for illustration-heavy books on architecture for specific places. Try searching by the name of the area combined with the word HISTORY. For example:

NEW JERSEY HISTORY
CHICAGO HISTORY

Other words to match with place names are:

HISTORIC BUILDINGS
LANDMARKS
BUILDINGS STRUCTURES
DESCRIPTION TRAVEL

By conducting such searches you'll uncover books like:

150 Years of Chicago Architecture: 1833-1983. Ante Glibota and Frederic Edelmann. Paris: Paris Art Center, 1983.

An oversized volume containing photographs and illustrations of exteriors and some interiors of Chicago buildings. Many architectural plans are also displayed.

Cincinnati Observed. John Clubbe. Columbus, OH: Ohio State University Press, 1992.

This guide includes detailed descriptions of the sights of fifteen general areas in Cincinnati, including Fountain Square, Riverfront, Over-the-Rhine and Mount Adams. Twelve of the chapters are detailed walking tours, advising on exactly where to turn and recounting the historical and contemporary stories of each area.

The Street Book: An Encyclopedia of Manhattan's Street Names and Their Origins. Henry Moscow. New York: Fordham University Press, 1978.

An A-to-Z guide to the roadways and sections in New York City, with each entry listing the namesake and some history about its naming. Photographs and drawings of the streets complement the text.

The Victorian City: Images and Realities. Harold James Dyos. Boston MA: Routledge and Kegan Paul, 1973.

Provides black-and-white images from daily Victorian life along with detailed discussion of the Victorian existence.

Design and Architecture Reference Books

It wouldn't be quite true to say that all of the sources listed below are reference books. The titles I have chosen are books that are referencelike in nature; that is they tend to provide some quick overviews in particular areas of decor and construction. You may actually find some of these titles in the circulating collections of libraries.

Landmark Architecture and Design

Would you like your traveling character to comment on the facade of a famous structure as she strolls by it? The following books will help you describe and picture fabulous landmarks you have never seen (or perhaps just need a refresher in).

Landmarks of the World's Art: The Modern World. Norbert Lynton. New York: McGraw-Hill Book Co., 1965.

Part of a series of books that survey major artists, architects and their works, including paintings, sculptures and buildings. Other titles in the series include:
The Age of Baroque. Michael Kitson. 1966.
The Ancient World. Giovanni Garbini. 1966.
The Classical World. Donald Emrys Strong. 1965.
Man and the Renaissance. Andrew Martindale. 1966.
The Medieval World. Peter Kidson. 1967.
The Oriental World: India and Southeast Asia. Jeannine Auboyer. 1967.
Prehistoric and Primitive Man. Andreas Lommel. 1966.
The World of Islam. Ernst J. Grube. 1967.

World Architecture Index: A Guide to Illustrations. Edward H. Teague. New York: Greenwood Press, 1991.

An index that will assist you in tracking down photographs of specific architectural works. It indexes the contents of over one hundred books commonly found in libraries with architectural collections (with titles such as New Directions in African Architecture [New York: George Braziller, 1969] and Gold in Azure: One Thousand Years of Russian Architecture. [Boston: D.R. Godine, 1983]). Illustrations can be located by site, name of architect, type of structure or name of structure (i.e., the Tower of London). Also by this author: Index to Italian Architecture: A Guide to Key Monuments and Reproduction Sources (1992).

House and Building Design

Period Houses and Their Details. Colin Amery, editor. London: The Architectural Press, 1974.

A close look at elements of the interiors and exteriors of British homes. These photographs, matched with detailed drawings, are reprinted from early editions of The Architectural Review, part of a series the periodical ran called the Practical Exemplar of Architecture. No style pictured is earlier than Jacobean or later than Regency.

Primitive Architecture. Enrico Guidoni. New York: Harry N. Abrams, 1978.

Shelters of nonindustrialized societies are shown in photographs. The methods of building the homes are described, as are some of the beliefs and habits of the people who live(d) in them. Some of the areas where structures are shown include Mali, Nigeria, British Columbia, the United States (Arizona) and the Samoa Islands of Polynesia. This book is part of the History of World Architecture series. Some other titles in the series:
Byzantine Architecture. Cyril A. Mango. 1976.
Late Baroque and Rococo Architecture. Charles Schulz Norberg. 1974.
Oriental Architecture. Mario Bussagli. 1974.
Romanesque Architecture. Hans Erich Kubach. 1975.

World Atlas of Architecture. Boston: G.K. Hall & Co., 1984.

In part, based on Great Architecture of the World by Mitchell Beazley. An oversized book featuring photographs and drawings of public buildings and private dwellings around the world from the ancient world to the twentieth century.

Interior Design

Authentic Decor: The Domestic Interior—1620-1920. Peter Thornton. New York: Viking, 1984.

The author looks at fifty-year blocks of time in each chapter, examining Western World home decor. Most of the numerous illustrations are drawings and paintings of rooms (painted in the time period they represent, i.e., there are no illustrations of new "restored" homes).

Colonial Interiors: Federal and Greek Revival. Harold Donaldson Eberlein and Cortlandt Van Dyke Hubbard. 3d Series. New York: Bonanza Books, 1938.

This volume provides 153 black-and-white plates of the interior details of federal and greek revival homes in southeastern Pennsylvania, New Jersey, Delaware, New York, New Hampshire and Maryland. This is a series of three volumes.

Series I. Leigh French—[New England and Connecticut.] 1923.

Series II. Edith Tunis Sale—[Parts of the South in the U.S.] 1930.

The Elements of Style: A Practical Encyclopedia of Interior Architectural Details From 1485 to the Present. Stephen Calloway and Elizabeth Calloway, editors. New York: Simon & Schuster, 1991.

A period-by-period visual survey of styles throughout the ages evident in U.S. and British architecture, begin-

ning with Jacobean and Tudor styles and finishing up with "Beyond Modern," referring to the period from 1950 to 1990.

The Elements of Style is filled with hundreds of sketches and photographs covering every atom you can imagine wanting to design or decorate inside or outside a home, including doors, floors, woodwork, walls, fireplaces, built-in furniture, staircases and ceilings. Definitely an idea-generating volume.

Furniture and Rugs

Complete Illustrated Rugs and Carpets of the World. Ian Bennet. New York: A & W Publishers, 1977.

A pictorial guide, with detailed descriptions and background, of floor coverings of Africa, Asia, Europe and North America.

The Encyclopedia of Furniture. Joseph Aronson. 3d edition. New York: Crown Publishers, 1965.

This book is primarily comprised of black-and-white photographs and line drawings of examples of furniture from many nations. Definitions are also provided for types of furniture, furniture components and ornament. Also from this author is the *Book of Furniture and Decoration: Period and Modern* (New York: Crown Publishers, 1941).

New Mexican Furniture, 1600-1940: The Origins, Survival and Revival of Furniture Making in the Hispanic Southwest. Lonn Taylor and Dessa Bokides. Santa Fe, NM: Museum of New Mexico Press, 1987.

This book displays photographs of the beautiful carved furniture associated with the Southwest—shades of natural brown accented with pinks, blues, oranges, yellows and greens. (Okay, well, the majority of the shots are not in color, but I live in Colorado, so trust me on this one.)

Sotheby's Concise Encyclopedia of Furniture. Christopher Payne, general editor. New York: Harper & Row, 1989.
A compact volume showing international examples of furniture from different stylistic periods, including the Renaissance, Baroque, the Rococo Period and the Machine Age.

Twentieth Century Furniture. Philippe Garner. New York: Van Nostrand Reinhold Co., 1980.
Examples of art nouveau, art deco, modern, neomodern, pop and high tech. (Be sure to check out the gilt bronze serpent lamp designed by Edgar Brandt. Stunning!)

Lighting

Ancient Lamps. Tihamér Szentléleky. Amsterdam: Adolf M. Hakkert, Publisher, 1969.
Featured are simple black-and-white line drawings of clay and molded lamps in the style popularly associated with the story of Aladdin's lamp.

The Best of Lighting Design. Wanda Jankowski. New York: PBC International, 1987.
The way an area is lighted can make all the difference in the way an area looks, and you can certainly convey that concept in writing. This book features incredible examples of lighting design in homes, museums, churches, stores, showrooms, hotels, restaurants and out-of-doors.

Colonial Lighting. Arthur H. Hayward. Third Enlarged Edition. New York: Dover Publications, 1962.
Lighting devices used during the Colonial Period in America are described and pictured in black-and-white. The book shows samples of candlesticks, oil lamps, lanterns, wall sconces, brass, pewter, tin and glass lamps, astral lamps and chandeliers. The opening chapter surveys some of the Lamps of Ancient Days around the world.

Lanterns That Lit Our World: How to Identify, Date and Restore Old Railroad, Marine, Fire, Carriage, Farm and Other Lanterns. Anthony Hobson. Spencertown, NY: Golden Hill Press, 1991.
The lanterns are shown in detailed black-and-white drawings (with just a smattering of actual photographs).

The New Let There Be Neon. Rudi Stern. New York: Harry N. Abrams, Inc., Publishers, 1988. [First edition was released in 1979.]
Vivé la France, the discoverers of neon! Put on your shades before you open this volume. It features neon creations worldwide in advertisements, architecture, interior design and art. See also *The Best of Neon: Architecture, Interiors, Signs.* Vilma Barr. Cincinnati, OH: Rockport Publishers/ Allworth Press, 1992.

Oil Lamps II: Glass Kerosene Lamps. Catherine Thuro. Paducah, KY: Collector Books, 1983.

Over nine hundred oil lamps are featured in *Oil Lamps II*, with almost half shown in rich color. The earlier edition is titled *Oil Lamps: The Kerosene Era in North America.*

Practical Home Accessories and Decorative Objects

Dictionary of Silverware. Harold Newman. London: Thames and Hudson, 1987.

Don't make the mistake I did when I heard this title; I thought that this dictionary featured table utensils, i.e., knives, spoons and forks. No. This volume illustrates and describes British and North American wares made of silver, including pots, bowls, trophies, tureens, statuettes and even a dog collar. Coverage is from *c.* 1500 to the present.

The Encyclopedia of Decorative Arts: 1890-1940. Philippe Garner, editor. New York: Van Nostrand Reinhold, 1978.

Numerous examples of furniture, art and ornament throughout the United States and Europe from 1890 to 1940. The Surrealism section caught my eye, featuring, as it does, the enormous Lobster Chair, the Mae West Lips Sofa, and the stool supported by three lifelike human legs.

The Encyclopedia of Decorative Styles: 1850-1935. William Hardy. Secaucus, NJ: Well Fleet Press, 1988.

A guide to three major art movements: the Arts and Crafts Movement, Art Nouveau and Art Deco. Examples of three-dimensional objects, paintings, jewelry, room ornamenta-

tion, drawings, architecture and furniture are provided.

Glass Bottles, Lamps and Other Objects. Jane Shadel Spillman. New York: Alfred A. Knopf, 1983.

Three hundred forty-six examples of American glass, with photographs of glass flasks of various shades, and bottles of every shape, including some shaped as figures (including George Washington, a bear and a crying baby!). Glass lamps and candlesticks are also featured, along with some miscellaneous objects, such as flower-shaped glass picture hangers and blown glass hats (for decorative purposes, of course, not fashion). The companion volume to this title is the *Knopf Collectors' Guide to Glass Tableware, Bowls and Vases.*

Sotheby's Concise Encyclopedia of Glass. David Battle and Simon Cottle, editors. Boston: Little, Brown, 1991.

Perhaps you will be as surprised as I was at the many relics of glass work still in existence from centuries ago, here pictured and discussed. Present-day glass pieces are featured as well.

Antiques in General

The Complete Encyclopedia of Antiques. The Connoisseur, compiler. New York: Hawthorn Books, 1962.

International in scope, the *Encyclopedia* has illustrations and descriptions in seventeen sections, including Barometers, Clocks and Watches, Carpets and Rugs, Mirrors, and Scientific Instruments. Not every piece described is pictured; the illustrations are black-and-white photographs and drawings. This book is a compilation of material from *The Concise Encyclopedia of Antiques* and *The Concise Encyclopedia of American Antiques.*

The Encyclopedia of Collectibles. 16 Volumes. Alexandria, VA: Time-Life Books, 1978-1980.

The photographs are lustrous in this collection, allowing you to see detail of hundreds of collectibles of all types: cash registers of the 1800s and 1900s, carnival glass in the shape of a tobacco humidor, and musical instruments, including a Civil War cornet with a gorgeous carry case lined with patterned velvet. Descriptions are provided for each type of collectible; museums they may be admired in are named, as are organizations and publications pertinent to each.

Miller's World Encyclopedia of Antiques. Judith Miller and Martin Miller, general editors. New York: Viking Studio Books, 1989.

Miller's gives advice on how to look at antiques and what to look for in the twelve major areas of collecting: Furniture, Pottery and Porcelain, Glass, Clocks, Rugs and Carpets, Arms and Armor, Art Nouveau, Art Deco, Dolls, Toys, English and American Silver, and Barometers. Over one thousand photographs, with over half in color, are provided.

The What, Where, When of Theater Props: An Illustrated Chronology from Arrowheads to Video Games. Thurston James. Cincinnati, OH: Betterway Books, 1992.

Though geared to the theater crowd, this book supplies simple sketches and descriptions for objects and furniture that might adorn the set of a play or a scene in a novel. In addition to furniture and ornament pieces, this book goes over kitchen and household appliances, instruments of punishment, Catholic and Jewish ceremonial objects, pipes (tobacco), hearing aids and eyeglasses.

Searching for Books on Collectibles

There are hundreds, probably thousands, of books devoted to the description and history of very specialized collectibles. To search for these in an online library catalog, try the type of collectible, along with one of the following subject words:

COLLECTIBLES
COLLECTING (*In a card catalog, look under* COLLECTORS AND-COLLECTING.)
PRICES

For example:
COLLECTIBLES BASEBALL
COLLECTING MUSIC
PRICES ANTIQUES

Also try the name of the designer; for example:
WEDGEWOOD
TIFFANY
HUMMEL

Just a few examples of books devoted to specific collectibles:

Boxes. William C. Ketchum, Jr. Washington, DC: The Cooper-Hewitt Museum, 1982.

A volume examining mostly ornate

containers around the world of various shapes and sizes, including a box from China in the shape of a crab ("the Chinese delighted in creating delicate china boxes in unexpected forms such as shellfish, flowers and animals").

A Collector's Guide to Spoons Around the World. Dorothy T. Rainwater and Donna H. Felger. Hanover, PA: Everybody's Press, 1976.

The wealth and variety of spoons pictured in this collection is vast. The black-and-white photographs show spoons that are elegant and exotic (a Japanese spoon shaped like a geisha, with her parasol at the rounded end), and interesting (such as the American spoon with opera singer Lillian Russell's likeness carved into it). Also by these authors: *American Spoons* (1969).

Luckey's Hummel Figurines and Plates. Carl F. Luckey. 10th edition. Florence, AL: Books Americana, 1994.

A pricing and identification guide for Hummel figurines, bells, plates and other objects bearing the Hummel name, such as holy water fonts and thimbles.

Wedgewood. Robin Reilly. 2 Volumes. New York: Stockton Press, 1989.

Over eight hundred pages, celebrating the work of Josiah Wedgewood, with hundreds of examples of Wedgewood creations—vases, teapots, dishes, portrait medallions and figurines.

A book that will help direct you to collectible experts is *Maloney's Antiques and Collectibles Resource Directory.* (Radnor, PA: Wallace-Homestead

Book Co., 1993). It's a listing of buyers, dealers, experts, appraisers, auction houses, restorers, clubs, museums and periodicals related to thousands of collectibles. This book illustrates just how vast and varied the collector's market is. Would you have guessed the following had collectors: Menus, Smurfs, Tennis Rackets and Potato-Related Collectibles (requested by the Potato Museum in Great Falls, Virginia; their newsletter is called *Peelings*)?

Identifying Collectibles

The *mark,* or *backstamp,* on glassware, pottery, jewelry and the like, is often your key to identifying the value of an item. For example, older jewelry pieces created by Monet, and stamped with that name, are collectible. The mark may also just be a symbol. There are books that will assist you in identifying marks. (And somehow, it seems to me that a mark may somehow be part of an intriguing plot in a mystery story.) Some books that identify marks:

A Dictionary of Marks. Margaret MacDonald-Taylor, editor. 4th edition, Newly Revised. London: Barrie and Jenkins, 1992.

A guide to marks, signatures and labels on metalwork, tapestry, ceramics and furniture.

Kovels' New Dictionary of Marks: Pottery and Porcelain-1850 to the Present. Ralph and Terry Kovel, New York: Crown Publishers, 1986.

The first part of the book is comprised of marks that look like objects, i.e., crowns, birds, flowers; the second half is in alphabetical order for marks comprised of initials or names.

Glass Signatures, Trademarks and Trade-names: From the Seventeenth to the Twentieth Century. Anne Geffken Pullin. Radnor, PA: Wallace-Homestead Book Co., 1986.

The symbols, signatures and so on are for the most part just identified; very little additional information beyond the name of the creator/company is provided, since this is intended as a quick source to be used by glass dealers and collectors for preliminary dating and authenticating.

Appraising Collectibles

Do you want your rich character to own a particularly precious objet d'art? Or do you want your poor one to find one in the false bottom of Mom's old dresser? Pricing guides can help you put a price tag on collectibles.

Prices are also handy when you want to place outrageously expensive items in the homes of your characters or identify what you think was an outrageously priced item in the home of someone you've interviewed. The illustrations and photos normally found in pricing guides (though some list only prices and provide no illustrations) also help decorate the settings of your sets, stages and pages.

There are many, many pricing guides. Some supply volumes are devoted to a particular collectible (for example, one volume devoted to antique watches). Others, such as auction houses, provide price guides for a wide variety of collectibles.

As far as libraries go, a public library will probably be your best bet for finding the best selection of guides. For the most up-to-date information, you will probably do better at a bookstore.

Remember that *Maloney's*, described above, is an excellent referral source for finding the names of organizations and writings that will help you learn more about collectibles. Looking in the *Encyclopedia of Associations* is another excellent method of locating collector's associations.

Below are just a few sample titles of the many types of collectible price books available:

Kovels' Know Your Collectibles. Ralph and Terry Kovel. New York: Crown Publishers, 1992.

Kovels' guides are well known and widely available in bookstores and libraries. Some other *Kovels'* collections include:

Kovels' American Art Pottery: The Collector's Guide to Makers, Marks and Factory Histories. 1993.

Kovels' Depression Glass and American Dinnerware Price List. 1991.

Kovels' Know Your Antiques. 1990.

Other major collectibles pricing publishers (with a sample title listed for each):

The Antique Collectors' Club— (*Miller's Pocket Antiques Fact File: Essential Information for Dealers, Collectors and Enthusiasts.* 1993.)

Berkley Publishing Group—(*The Lyle Official Antiques Review: The Identification and Price Guide.* Annual.)

Books Americana—(*Three Hundred Years of Kitchen Collectibles.*)

Collector Books—(*Collectible Cats: An Identification & Value Guide.* 1993.)

Currency: What Should Your Character Pay With?

Don't be like the Michael J. Fox character in the movie *Back to the Future*—pulling out inappropriate money for the time period he was in. Money is different from nation to nation and era to era. You may also want to keep in mind that coins were not invented until late seventh century B.C. in Turkey. Some coin and currency compendiums that will help you fill your characters' pockets properly:

Coin Atlas: The World of Coinage from Its Origins to the Present Day. Joe Cribb, Barrie Cook and Ian Carradice. New York: Facts on File, 1989.

The book is arranged by continent, with each nation of the continent afforded its own entry. The coinage history of each country is recounted in chronological order. There are photographs of many of the coins discussed. Small maps are provided to help pinpoint the areas being examined. The arrangement of this book makes it simple to ascertain the type of coinage used in different areas and eras.

The Comprehensive Catalog of U.S. Paper Money. Gene Hustler. Chicago: Henry Regnery Co., 1974.

This volume contains descriptions and photographs of U.S. paper currency throughout the country's history. The first twelve sections of the catalog portion of the book are arranged by the bills' denominations, going from one-dollar to one-hundred-thousand-dollar bills. Other chapters of interest show Unissued and Rejected Designs, Error and Freak Notes and Counterfeit Notes.

Gold Coins of the World—Complete from 600 A.D. to the Present: An Illustrated Standard Catalog with Valuations. Robert Friedberg, editor. 6th Edition. New York: Coin and Currency Institute, 1992.

Gold coins from every coin-issuing country from 600 A.D. to 1960 are named, with over three thousand of them pictured, actual size. The book is arranged alphabetically by country, from Afghanistan to Zanzibar.

Paper Money of the United States: A Complete Illustrated Guide with Valuations. Robert Friedberg. Clifton, NJ: Coin and Currency Institute, Inc. 1964.

This slim guide has black-and-white reproductions of paper currency issued in the U.S. beginning in Colonial times through modern day.

Standard Catalog of World Paper Money. Volume 1: Specialized Issues. Volume 2: General Issues. Albert Pick. Iola, WI: Krause Publications, 1975-present.

The *Catalog* shows photographs of paper money from all over the world. Though the pictures are black-and-white, the colors are described, allowing the writer to describe a flash of color being withdrawn from the pocket of the protagonist.

World Coin Encyclopedia. Ewald Junge. New York: William Morrow and Co., 1984.

An A-to-Z numismatic encyclopedia containing descriptions of specific coins around the world, marks, mints, coinmakers, medalists and collectors. Mostly black-and-white photographs with some color plates. Not every coin discussed is pictured.

To find books about money in your library's online catalog, try searches that pair one of the following words

MONEY
COINS
COINAGE
NUMISMATICS

with the words of a place, an era or simply the word HISTORY. For example:

GREECE COINS
COINAGE HISTORY

The best call number areas to simply browse in the library:

Library of Congress: CJ
Dewey Decimal: 737

Here are some sample titles of specialized books about money.

Coins of the Roman Empire (Routledge, 1990).

A Handbook to the Coinage of Scotland (Argonaut, 1968).

Byzantine Coins (Putnam, 1973).

The Coinage of Switzerland: 1850 to Date (Malter-Westerfield, 1967).

Finally, if you find you're getting a bit of a cramped feeling looking at books of priceless collectibles and fine architecture, relax with a copy of *Fantastic Architecture: Personal and Eccentric Visions.* (New York: Harry N. Abrams, 1980). Some of the edifices examined: giant cowboy boots that are actually the restrooms for a Texas restaurant; a house with a roof shaped like a pineapple (built in 1761 by the Earl of Dunmore in Stirlingshire, Scotland), and homes, castles and models of landmarks constructed out of glass bottles by carpenter George Plumb. My favorite, however, is *The Rigid Digit*, an inflated finger, 12 meters high, which was created to point the way from the Nuremberg airport to the city. (This is my current temporary coffee-table book.)

Chapter Five

Modes of Travel

Whether floating by in a hot-air balloon or zooming past in a Maserati, your character may need transportation. Browse through some of the sources in this section to determine the apropos mode of transportation based on your character's temperament.

Automobiles

Automobiles of the World: The Story of the Development of the Automobile with Many Rare Illustrations from a Score of Nations. Joseph H. Wherry. Philadelphia: Chilton Book Co., 1968.

This volume supplies text and nine hundred black-and-white photographs of cars from twenty-one countries; from their inception through 1940.

Encyclopedia of the Car. London: Grange Books, 1993.

A worldwide guide, alphabetically arranged, to what the editors term the "great cars." For each car, specifications, performance detail and history are supplied. The realistic color drawings of the vehicles are barely distinguishable from the photographs also included.

The New Illustrated Encyclopedia of Automobiles. David Burgess Wise. Secaucus, NJ: Wellfleet Press, 1992.

From A to Z, this one-volume ency-

clopedia describes many of the world's automobiles throughout time, complemented by numerous (though at times tiny) photographs.

Sports Cars. Lincolnwood, IL: Publications International, Ltd., 1990.

Some of the autos pictured and described include different makes of the Austin-Healy (ca. 1953-1967), the Ferrari Testarossa (1985-1987) and the Triumph TR6 (1969-1976). The latest cars mentioned are from 1990. Dowdy car, dowdy character. The babies in this book would never be driven by Sgt. Columbo.

The World's Great Automobile Stylists. John Tipler. New York: Mallard Press, 1990.

Stylists are those men and women that design the look of the car; they must be both technician and creative artist. The automobiles of famous stylists such as Gordon Buehrig (Stutz le Mans cars of 1929), Marcello Gandini (Lamborghini Muira) and Alex Tremulis (the Thunderbolt) are featured in color photographs and drawings. Some of the drawings show prototypes and ideas for cars that never quite came to existence as imagined.

The World of Automobiles: An Illustrated Encyclopedia of the Motor Car. 22 Volumes. New York: Columbia House, 1974.

Each volume of this colorful twenty-two-volume set covers six to seven topics, including: descriptions of twentieth-century cars, a look at the notable car makes in history, concepts and workings of automobile parts and design, a who's who of race car drivers, and descriptions of racing competitions.

Rescue and Emergency Vehicles

American Funeral Cars and Ambulances Since 1900. Thomas A. McPherson. Glen Ellyn, IL: Crestline Publishing, 1973.

A black-and-white pictorial survey of hearses and ambulances, arranged by year, from 1900 through 1973.

The Fire Engine. T.A. Jacobs. New York: Smithmark Publishers, 1993.

Over one hundred photographs of bright and shiny red fire engines (only one or two are yellow) from the eighteenth century to the present.

Flight for Life: A Matter of Life and Death. Opal Cavitt. Golden, CO: Sanuk, 1991.

The history and workings of the Flight for Life program—the emergency medical service involving the use of helicopters equipped as mini-emergency rooms.

Police Cars: A Photographic History. Monty McCord. Iola, WI: Krause Publications, 1991.

A neatly laid-out book featuring black-and-white photos of U.S. police vehicles in chronological order from The Early Years (the 1890s) through the present.

Aircraft

Great Aircraft of the World: An Illustrated History of the Most Famous Civil and Military Planes. Secaucus, NJ: Chartwell Books, 1992.

A look at fifty-five of what the author refers to as "celebrities of the air." For each of the aircraft, information is supplied concerning the history of its development, its use and technical specifications (accompanied by photographs and diagrams).

The Illustrated History of Helicopters. Andy Lightbody and Joe Poyer. Lincolnwood, IL: Publications International, Ltd., 1990.

Helicopters of six nations, including the U.S., are pictured and described in war and peace. Most of the full-color photographs capture the helicopters of America, the Soviet Union, Great Britain, France, West Germany and Italy in flight.

Jane's All the World's Aircraft. Mark Lambert, editor. Alexandria, VA: Jane's Information Group. Annual.

An annual survey of the world's aircraft that are in continuing production or under development. (Since that standard would omit many planes still being used, short entries are often provided for these lame duck aircraft.) The types of aircraft covered include civil and military, airships and helicopters.

In addition to providing a photo of each craft, *Jane's* lists information about the manufacturer and a description of the aircraft including specifications.

Jane's Encyclopedia of Aviation. [Also available as originally published in 5 Volumes in 1980 by Jane's Publishing. This edition is one volume.] Michael J.H. Taylor, New York: Portland House, 1989.

This volume, compiled from the archives of aviation's premiere publishers, looks at the history of aircraft ranging from hot-air balloons to supersonic transports. There are both black-and-white and color photographs.

Riders of the Winds: The Story of Ballooning. Don Dwiggins. New York: Hawthorn Books, 1973.

An illustrated history of the first ballooning attempts in the late 1700s through contemporary times. The author investigates the use of hot-air balloons in scientific and military use, as well as just for fun.

Spacecraft

If you would like to base space vehicles in your fictional story upon real spacecraft, take a look through some of the following encyclopedias.

The Cambridge Encyclopedia of Space. Michael Rycroft, editor. New York: Cambridge University Press, 1990.

An oversized volume (allowing for more realistic viewing of the photographs of rockets included!) looking at all aspects of space technology and space science, including the uses of satellites and space stations.

The Dream Machines: A Pictorial History of the Spaceship in Art, Science and Literature. Ron Miller. Malabar, FL: Krieger Publishing Co., 1993.

A fascinating chronological look at humankind's imaginings, theories and actual development of spacecraft from 360 B.C. through 1992. The early excerpts are writings that muse about life away from earth, many with surprisingly accurate theories. Gradually, these musings turn into factual accounts and data concerning the reality of being able to rocket off the planet. This volume is illustrated with line drawings and photographs of air- and spaceships.

Trains

The American Railroad Passenger Car. John H. White, Jr. Baltimore: Johns Hopkins University Press, 1978.

Some glimpses inside trains of the U.S. are provided, ranging from lunch-counter service in the thirties and forties, to rattan chairs in the late 1800s (in the parlor car, of course). Along with many photographs of trains both inside and out are detailed design drawings, with attention to how the trains were constructed.

Rails Across America: A History of Railroads in North America. William L. Withuhn, consultant editor. New York: Smithmark Publishers, 1993.

A well-illustrated accounting of the history of rail transport in the United States and Canada, showing trains, the men who laid the tracks, and much of the paraphernalia of trains. Some of the more contemporary photos show the "double stack" container train from Conrail (like a double-decker bus, allowing more room for storage) and the X2000, which has radial axles, permitting greater speed on the curves of conventional tracks.

Railways of the World. Brian Hollingsworth. New York: Gallery Books, 1979.

A look at historic and contemporary (up to the 1970s) urban rapid transit systems the world over.

Trolleys and Streetcars on American Postcards. Ray D. Applegate. New York: Dover Publications, 1979.

This collection of almost two hundred postcards shows trolleys in cities and towns all over America in the late nineteenth and early twentieth centuries. Some are horse drawn. The caption to each card lists the town the trolley or streetcar is in, the name of the system or company it was a part of, and a few facts about it (such as how far it ran or how many cars were in the system). Unfortunately, exact dates to match the postcards are not always available. One interesting photograph shows an "automobile-less traffic jam" in Chicago—about fifty trolleys backed up. The caption on the postcard says, "A busy day on Dearborn and Randolph Streets, Chicago."

Boats

The History of Ships. Peter Kemp. London: Orbis Publishing Limited, 1981.

A history of ships from the times of "sweated labor" (oared ships) through sailing ships and those powered by engines. Though ships designed for many purposes are described, they are generally enormous ones. There are both color and black-and-white illustra-

tions. Gilligan's tiny sailing ship is not in here.

The Illustrated Encyclopedia of Ships, Boats, Vessels and Other Waterborne Craft. Graham Blackburn. Woodstock, NY: The Overlook Press, 1978.

Arranged A to Z, this book covers Egyptian craft of 4,000 B.C. through nuclear-powered vessels of the 1970s; both military and commercial ships are covered. A charming-looking book, with all of the illustrations and text seeming to be hand drawn. Charm aside, many of the entries neglect to associate a time period with the ship described.

Nautical Antiques with Value Guide. Robert W.D. Ball. Atglen, PA: Schiffer Publishing, Ltd., 1994.

Geared to collectors, this guide displays bits and pieces of seafaring vessels, including carved whales' teeth, (and many items fashioned from whalebone), an early twentieth-century diving suit and ships' clocks.

Ships. Enzo Angelucci and Attilio Cucari. New York: McGraw-Hill Book Co., 1975.

From animal skins sewn together and waterproofed through nuclear-powered vessels, *Ships* traces, through information and illustration, the use of ships throughout history. This is not just a generic look at ocean vessels; almost every one included has a name and a story.

Yachts, Sail Boats and Other Contemporary Pleasure Boats. To see many people with the wind in their hair and the sea over their shoulder, try browsing some of the magazines directed to boat owners (and potential boat owners) such as:

Boating. Focusing on power-boating.

Cruising World. Writes about sail-powered cruising.

Motor Boating & Sailing. A popular magazine, found in many public libraries.

Power and Motoryacht. Covers large powerboats and megayachts; directed to those who can easily afford such vessels.

Powerboat: The World's Leading Performance Boating Magazine. About high-powered, high-performance powerboats.

Sail. Dedicated to sail craft.

Trailer Boats. Aimed at the owners of the most purchased boats in the U.S.—boats that are 28-feet long or less.

Yachting. For the sail and motor yachtsman; a showcase for the world's most expensive and exotic yachts.

Motorcycles and Bicycles

The New Illustrated Encyclopedia of Motorcycles. Erwin Tragatsch, author of original edition; revised by Brian Wooley. Secaucus, NJ: Wellfleet Press, 1992.

A survey of all types of motorcycles from their inception to the present. Some of the early models looked more like manual bicycles, especially their tiny bicycle seats. Models are shown from America, Germany, Japan, Great Britain, Italy and Spain.

Richard's Ultimate Bicycle Book. Richard Ballantine and Richard Grant. New

York: Dorling Kindersley, 1992.

A beautifully illustrated volume containing information about bikes of all kinds (mountain, racing, touring, police use, family use), their construction and maintenance. Bicycle clothing is discussed, as is training and form. A section on the Future Bike shows bicycles that already exist (at least in prototype) but have not yet made it into widespread use. Some of these sci-fi looking pedal vehicles would fit very nicely into a future-novel.

The Ultimate Motorcycle Book. Hugo Wilson, in association with the Motorcycle Heritage Museum. New York: Dorling Kindersley, 1993.

Examples of over two hundred classic and contemporary motorcycles of the world are pictured, drawn from private collections and museums. Since the bikes shown are primarily from collections, they are in fabulous condition.

Early Modes of Transportation

Animal Transport

Before there were wheels and engines there were hooves and sinews; instead of Ford and Chevrolet there was horse and camel.

The Camel and the Wheel. Richard W. Bulliet. New York: Columbia University Press, 1990.

A scholarly book examining the use of the camel, for transportation and as a draft animal throughout history, chiefly in the Middle East and North Africa (though other areas, such as

Australia, are also touched upon). There are black-and-white photographs of camels with riders astride them, and of pieces of art depicting the dromedary.

The Encyclopedia of the Horse: Every Recognized Breed of Horse and Pony. Charles Evelyn Graham Hope and G.N. Jackson. New York: Viking Press, 1973.

The *Encyclopedia of the Horse* traces the evolution of the horse family, examines the development, distribution and characteristics of particular breeds, looks at their use throughout time in different regions of the world, and describes accoutrements both ancient and contemporary.

The Ultimate Horse Book. Elwyn Hartley Edwards. Bob Langrish, photographer. New York: Dorling Kindersley, 1991.

A great book for in-depth viewing of eighty breeds of horses. For each breed, there is one large photo, showing off the shape and coloring of the animal. Smaller color shots show different angles and features of these beauties. Information for each horse type includes both characteristics and origins.

Wheeled Vehicles and Ridden Animals in the Ancient Near East. M.A. Littauer and J.H. Crouwel. Leiden, The Netherlands: E.J. Brill, 1979.

A very scholarly treatment of the use of animals and wheeled vehicles for transportation from the later fourth millennium B.C. through the later first millennium B.C. The author covers Mesopotamia, Iran, the Levant and Anatolia. Some material for Trans-

caucasia, Egypt and Cyprus is also mentioned. There are eighty-five simple black-and-white drawings and reproductions of stone reliefs depicting animals, vehicles and accessories.

Carriages

American Horse-Drawn Carriages. Jack D. Rittenhouse. New York: Bonanza Books, 1948.

A collection of 218 drawings, with brief descriptions, reproduced from the fashion plates of the builders and photographs of 183 horse-drawn vehicles. Some featured include the Light Pony Wagon, which had a black body but usually brightly colored gear painted wine, yellow or carmine, the Twelve-Quarter Coach, so named for the number of panels (quarters) on each side, and the Drygoods Wagon, an enclosed commercial vehicle of the 1880s.

The History of the Carriage. László Tarr. New York: Arco Publishing, 1969.

A history of the origins and uses of horse-drawn carriages and chariots throughout the ages and the world, accented with black-and-white drawings of the vehicles and replicas of carriages as seen in art. Some of the groups surveyed include the Egyptians, Chinese, Greeks, Etruscans and the Europeans.

Looking at Carriages. Sallie Walrond. London: Pelham Books, 1980.

Looking at Carriages focuses on a representative cross-section of dozens of carriages from the eighteenth and nineteenth centuries, which are depicted in the many photographs. The author describes the origin and physical attributes of each vehicle. For some, useful historic notes are also supplied.

Plain Buggies: Amish, Mennonite and Brethren Horse-Drawn Transportation. Stephen Scott. Lancaster, PA: Good Books, 1981.

A survey of the buggies still used by those groups who, for religious beliefs, do not drive cars.

Western Wagon Wheels: A Pictorial Memorial to the Wheels That Won the West. Lambert Florin. Seattle: Superior Publishing Co., 1977.

The carts and carriages used for hauling people, belongings and food in the early American West are highlighted in this "pictorial memorial." The emphasis in the photographs really is on wheels, with some truly weather-beaten relics on display. Full vehicles, including some fancy-looking hearses, are also shown.

International Public Transportation

To find books that detail the type of public transportation available in a specific area, try a subject search in your library's online catalog using the phrase LOCAL TRANSIT combined with the area you are interested in. For example:

LOCAL TRANSIT ENGLAND
LOCAL TRANSIT INDIA

Chapter Six

Company, Product
and Industry Information

There are thousands of books, directories, articles and online systems geared to the business researcher. They describe how companies and industries are faring and discuss new product innovations. They list companies and offer background and financial information about them. They tell you about businessmen and women, describing the work they do and the range of salaries they earn. Some of this information comes with a premium price tag attached, while much can be found in larger libraries. This chapter will help you sift through these resources to find the business information you need.

Company Information

Whenever you are looking up information on a company, the first question to ask is:

Is it a public or private company?

Public Companies

A "public" corporation has issued securities (i.e., stocks), and the shares are traded in the open market. A private company may, on occasion, also have stockholders, but they are people who own, work for or are closely related to the company. Such firms may also be public, but their stocks are known as "closely held."

A public corporation offers its stocks beyond a small circle, to the public.

Thus you will see the phrases *publicly held* or *publicly owned* sometimes used to describe a public firm. Publicly held companies make life somewhat easier for information gatherers. These companies are required, by law, to file specific reports with the Securities and Exchange Commission (the SEC).

The material that public companies are required to report in SEC filings includes broad financial data and news of events that would influence those who are stockholders or considering investing. If the CEO has a torrid and embarrassing love affair with one of the junior executives, that does not have to be reported. Even public companies don't have to reveal everything! Some documents that public companies are required to file and that will be fairly simple for you to find at larger libraries:

Annual Report to Stockholders (ARS)—Annual reports are usually glossy and lovely. They will have full-color photographs depicting well-pleased consumers using the company's products or services. Though the information should be technically correct, it also serves as a kind of advertisement to the shareholders, to show them what a nifty firm they have their dollars invested in. It is mailed each year to the shareholders. The information in an annual report may be quite useful. Standard elements contained in annual reports:

• Letter to Shareholders—sometimes

called the President's Letter. In this letter, the company's president or chairman of the board reviews the company's past year and looks ahead to the next.

- Financial Data—including a Balance Sheet, Income Statement, Stockholder's Equity Statement and Cash Flow Statement.
- Auditor's Report—the verification from an independent CPA of the numbers put forth in the annual report. Sometimes the auditor will *not* be completely satisfied.
- Management Discussion—Specific comments on how the company's actions over the last three years affected its performance and financial position, and what the numbers mean.
- Social Responsibility Report—Occasionally the ARS will include discussion of the firm's contributions to the community, both in time and money.

10-Ks—Sometimes called Form 10-K. There are no lovely photographs or illustrations. Every 10-K Report follows the exact same format, insuring uniformity in every 10-K you look at. The 10-K is usually not automatically sent to shareholders. In addition to detailed financial information, the 10-K covers the following:

- How the Firm Does Business—including a description of the products it produces, where it sells and how it distributes. Some will also discuss competition in their market, research and development activities and patent ownership.
- What the Firm Owns—listings of subsidiaries, major properties and

foreign operations.
- Raw Materials—which ones the company uses and where they obtain them.

Proxy Statements—This notice is sent to all stockholders before their annual meeting with the company. The Proxy Statement looks at all matters that will be voted on, including proposals from shareholders, and provides background information on the proposal. Sometimes the shareholders will suggest a socially motivated change in policy for the company, such as changing packaging of a certain product. Or they might suggest that the CEO take a cut in pay. The Proxy Statement also includes salaries of top officers and directors.

Obtaining SEC Filings

Annual Reports, 10-Ks and Proxy Statements are eminently attainable. Some of the following methods are faster than others.

Call the Company. For little or no fee, the company will usually mail you a copy of the filing that you want.

Library Collections with Print Copies of Filings. It is rare that a library will maintain a substantial number of SEC filings in print version. There are too many of them and they are too difficult to control. Sometimes a library will make an effort to collect a segment of the filings in hard copy, for example, for companies in their state or the Fortune 500 companies.

Microfiche Collections. It is very common for large libraries catering to business clientele to subscribe to microfiche collections of SEC filings. Two suppliers of such collections are *Q-Data* (their product is called *SEC File*) and *Disclosure*.

Online and CD-ROM Options. There are several databases that contain either full or partial SEC filings (I have also listed databases that include the foreign equivalent of some of the elements that you would find in SEC filings):

Compact D/Canada. Toronto, Ontario: Micromedia Ltd. This CD-ROM database contains financial and management information extracted from corporate documents for all the major industrial and service companies in the ten provinces and two territories of Canada; over eight thousand in all. The online equivalent is *Canadian Corporations—CanCorp*, available on *DIALOG*, and *Data-Star*. (These online vendors are discussed below.)

Compact D/SEC. Bethesda, MD: Disclosure. Also known as *Compact Disclosure*, this database contains lengthy extracts from SEC documents. Versions of Compact D/SEC are available on CD-ROM and through a number of database vendors including *Data-Star*, *DIALOG*, *FirstSearch* and the *LEXIS/NEXIS* system.

Disclosure/Worldscope Database. Worldscope/Disclosure Partners—A Partnership of Wright Investor's Service and Disclosure. A compilation of comparative information on more than ten thousand companies in forty nations in six major industry classes: Industrials, Utilities, Transportation, Banks, Insurance and Other Financial Institutions. The data is extracted from documents

filed with stock exchanges in all countries and from other sources (for example, the Ministry of Finance in Japan). Available on *Dow Jones News Retrieval*, *FirstSearch*, *LEXIS* and others.

Electronic Data Gathering, Analysis and Retrieval (EDGAR). Companies that are required to file with the SEC now do so electronically, using *EDGARLINK* software. Basically, access to EDGAR is the result of a Ralph Nader-related consumer group (Jamie Love's Taxpayer Assets Project) demanding less expensive online access to SEC filings. The drawback to EDGAR: It doesn't have the software niceties of commercial online vendors. But it continues to improve. Available "free" on the Internet for the time-being; the funding status is currently being evaluated.

EXTEL Cards—London: Extel Financial, Ltd., Fitzroy House. This online system consists of international company news and financial data updated weekly. (On *Data-Star*, *DIALOG*, *LEXIS/NEXIS* and *FT-Profile*.)

ICC Full-Text Company Reports. Hampton, Middlesex, England: ICC Information Group, Ltd. Both financial and general information is supplied for over three thousand European firms on *ICC Full-Text*. (On *Data-Star*, *DIALOG*, *LEXIS/NEXIS* and *FT-Profile*.)

Laser D/SEC. Bethesda, MD: Disclosure. Updated annually, this CD-ROM product contains the full text of SEC documents filed by approximately eleven thousand publicly held corporations. It is quite pricey, so don't expect to find it in any but the most well-funded of libraries.

SEC Online. Hauppage, NY: SEC Online. A full-text database of the complete annual reports, 10-Ks, 10-Qs, Proxy Statements for all NYSE and AMEX companies and over two thousand NASDAQ companies. (On *DIALOG, Dow Jones News Retrieval, LEXIS, WESTLAW.*)

To determine whether your company is public or private, check the *Directory of Companies Required to File Annual Reports with the U.S. Securities and Exchange Commission* (Washington, DC: Securities and Exchange Commission, 1976-present), which lists firms required to file with the SEC both alphabetically and by industry. This book does not tell you what exchange the company's stocks are traded on (or what its ticker symbol is, which can also be useful when using some reference sources). There are several books that will help you discover a company's exchange and symbol:

Common Stock: Newspaper Abbreviations and Trading Symbols. Howard R. Jarrell. Metuchen, NJ: Scarecrow Press, 1989. *Supplement.* 1991.

Part One is an alphabetic list of the full names of companies, with the market listing (exchange), the common newspaper abbreviation and the trading symbol. For example, the Goodyear Tire and Rubber Company is listed as being on the New York Stock Exchange, its newspaper abbreviation is Goodyr and its symbol is GT. Part Two is arranged by newspaper abbreviation, and Part Three by trading symbol.

The McGraw-Hill Dictionary of Wall Street Acronyms, Initials and Abbreviations. Jerry M. Rosenberg. New York: McGraw-Hill, 1992.

The place to go when you see any investment-related abbreviation you can't figure out. This dictionary lists company symbols as well as the industry's lingo.

If none of the above directories are available at your library, you can also browse through some of the directories listed in this chapter under the heading "Business Directories." Usually, the directory will actually denote the company as *public* or *private*, listing which stock exchange the public company is listed on and giving its ticker symbol.

Stock, once purchased, is often traded from one owner to another. This is done at stock exchanges or through the Over-the-Counter (OTC) market. The two nationwide stock exchanges in this country, and the ones you will see many references to, are:

NYSE—The New York Stock Exchange

AMEX or ASE—The American Stock Exchange

Exchanges are actual, physical places where brokers buy and sell securities in an auction style on behalf of others. There are also many regional exchanges in large cities of the U.S., including Chicago, San Francisco, Philadelphia and Boston.

Alternately, the Over-the-Counter market is not a physical place. It is a network of dealers that belong to the National Association of Stock Dealers (NASD) and use a computerized trading system called NASDAQ. These brokers purchase stock that they specialize in, and then sell it for a markup.

NASDAQ—National Association

of Security Dealers Automated Quotations

Some OTC stocks are not part of the NASDAQ system because they don't trade often enough or are too small to meet SEC filing requirements. These are referred to as *unlisted* stocks.

Is Your Company a Parent?!

Often a company will be a subsidiary, division or affiliate of a "parent" company. For example, Avia Group International is a subsidiary of Reebok International. Unfortunately, the SEC filings deal primarily with the parent company. You will sometimes find information of decent length about the subsidiaries within SEC reports, but not always. However, here's a tip: If the company you are researching is a subsidiary that was at one point acquired or taken over by the parent company, go back and look at the SEC reports and articles from the year it was acquired. There should be more information available from that time period.

A multivolume source that may help you in determining whether the firm you are looking for is a parent is the *Who Owns Whom* series (London: Dun and Bradstreet Ltd. Annual). There are four editions of *Who Owns Whom* that cover different areas of the world: North America, Continental Europe, The United Kingdom and Ireland, and Australia and The Far East. All are available in print, on the *Data-Star* and *DIALOG* online services and on CD-ROM. Most larger libraries will have the print version. Other sources that list company affiliations are *America's Corporate Families* (Parsippany, NJ: Dun's Marketing Services) and *The Directory of Corporate*

Affiliations (National Register Co.). Also of related interest:

Worldwide Branch Locations of Multinational Companies. David S. Hoopes, editor. Detroit: Gale, 1994.
For five hundred of the world's principal multinational corporations, this directory identifies their approximately twenty-six thousand overseas subsidiaries, branches and offices. The main portion of the directory lists branch locations in order by country, with indexes also presenting the branches in SIC order and alphabetic order.

Private Companies

Researching private companies is a whole other ball game from that of public companies. They don't legally have to tell anybody anything if they don't want to. (And, of course, the majority of companies are indeed private.) But vee haf our vays of finding things out.

The main method of locating information on private companies, beyond directory-type information, is through articles. Of course, articles written about such small companies may only show up in newspapers that serve the area the companies are in. A database on CD-ROM called *Business Newsbank* can be useful in such a search.

Business Newsbank (New Canaan, CT: Newsbank) provides access to the full text of articles from the business sections of "local" newspapers around the United States, as well as regional newspapers that exclusively cover business issues. It does not cover papers like the *New York Times*; its roster is filled with titles like the *Sacramento Bee*, the *Cincinnati Enquirer* and the *Dallas Morning*

News. Larger public or academic libraries with substantial business collections may have *Business Newsbank*.

There are more tips on article searching further on in this chapter. Also consult chapter 2, "Exploring Articles." Be prepared: very often there are simply no fast and simple ways to access published information about private companies. Sometimes there is no way.

A few well-placed phone calls may help you find out something about a private company. Calling the company's local Chamber of Commerce may reveal, at the very least, how long the company has been in business in the town. The Better Business Bureau will let you know if they have had any complaints. And of course you can call the business itself and ask the owners and employees whatever you want!

SIC Codes

Just as the Library of Congress Classification System helps put books in order by subject, the Standard Industrial Classification (SIC) System organizes business information by product and industry. Developed by the U.S. Office of Management and Budget (OMB), the SIC codes are often used in many business publications as a way of organizing the information. So, if you are looking for information about a company or industry, you may want to find out what SIC code category it fits into.

To determine the SIC category for an industry, look at the *Standard Industrial Classification Manual*. Look in the back section, where types of industries are listed alphabetically. There you will see a number: the SIC code. Look up that code in the front of the directory where you will find that a more complete description of the industry is provided so that you can be sure you've made the right choice.

The longer the SIC code, the more specialized its meaning. For example: 22 is an industry grouping number that refers to Textile Mill Products, 225 designates Knitting Mills, and 2251 represents Women's Full-Length and Knee-Length Hosiery (Except Socks). (Really.) The SIC codes created by the OMB do not go beyond four digits.

For specificity, some publishers enhance the SIC codes used in their directories, indexes and databases. For example, in the *F&S Index*, which accesses articles by company name and enhanced SIC codes, the codes are lengthened to denote specific products; thus 225130 stands for Females' Seamless Hosiery. Don't worry about memorizing any of these numbers! After years of library reference work I haven't memorized a single one. (But I use the *SIC Manual* quite a bit.)

So how would you use the SIC code? Here's an example: You need to find the names of just a few companies in the women's clothing manufacturing business so that you can call them and ask about a new garment that's hot on the market, say rubber gloves for formal wear. When you look in a general business index, such as *Ward's Business Directory of U.S. Private and Public Companies*, the cross-reference index to companies by industry is in SIC order. You can't just look up CLOTHING, WOMEN, you need to know the SIC code. So you would look up the SIC code in the *SIC Manual*, and use that number in the index to see what companies are listed.

SIC frustrations: Because the *SIC Manual* is updated so infrequently, you may find you are looking up a business that has not yet been acknowledged. Also, you might find smaller industries lumped under one code with other industries that are only vaguely similar.

At the time of this writing, the OMB has proposed changing the SIC system to a revised system called The North American Industry Classification System (NAICS). They are forecasting that it will be put into practice by 1997.

Online Business Databases

A quick review here of the role of online database suppliers. As explained in chapter 1, there are a number of "vendors" of online databases who handle databases like video stores handle videos: They buy the right to distribute certain databases and customers can pick and choose which ones they want. At video stores you need to be a member; in the case of databases, you need to be a subscriber.

There are hundreds of business databases available through database vendors. These services are generally not available by dialing-in to libraries. Most are just too expensive. Though some large, usually academic, libraries may provide user access to online systems, it is not a widespread practice. (If there is access, it will usually be limited to students and faculty of the campus.)

Because of the high cost, there is generally a charge attached to using many of these services at a library. Many libraries have a professional searcher perform the search for you, for a fee, in order to do as efficient and inexpensive a search as possible.

The services most commonly offered in libraries (often with an intermediary searcher) are *DIALOG* and OCLC's *FirstSearch. LEXIS/NEXIS* may also be in some academic libraries, but use is *strictly limited* to students and faculty of the campus (because academic users receive a discount for this expensive but wide-ranging service for restricting its use). For an expanded overview of these vendors' databases, services and subscription arrangements, see Appendix B.

You would rarely find access to the more home-oriented services, such as *GEnie, America Online,* or *CompuServe,* at a library. But millions of people subscribe to these popular services and use them from their residences or offices.

All of the following services offer a substantial amount of information of interest to those conducting research in business. Some of the databases the vendors offer are unique to one service, but most can be found in more than one; there is a great deal of overlap these days. Be wary: Some databases are offered in a more complete format in some systems than in others. For example, the *Worldscope* database, which provides financial statements for companies worldwide, has more company records on the CD-ROM version than on the version offered through the *FirstSearch* system. Since vendors expand their services constantly, I would encourage you to contact them to confirm their current offerings.

Below, I have listed just a few of the business-oriented databases offered by each vendor:

America Online (*AOL*). Vienna, VA: American Online, (800) 827-6364.

Executive Desk Register. Descriptions of more than five thousand publicly held companies. (Also on Delphi.)

NewsBytes News Network. News and commentary on computers and technology. (Also on Delphi, GEnie, NewsNet and Prodigy.)

TradeassistantPlus. Market quotes on stocks, mutual funds, commodities, future options and indexes; securities information, analysis and statistics. (Also on *DIALOG* and *CompuServe.*)

USA Today *Decisionline.* Items from *USA Today* newspaper.

CompuServe. Columbus, OH: CompuServe Information Service. (800) 848-8199.

International Stocks Database. Financial and business information for companies traded on stock exchanges worldwide. (Also on *NEWSNET.*)

Investor's Guide and Mutual Fund Directory. An annually updated directory of information on mutual funds that do not charge sales commissions.

Small Business Reports. Ideas and guidelines on how to operate a small business.

Valueline Quarterly Reports. Quarterly financial data for over seventeen hundred public companies. (Also available in print at most libraries.)

DIALOG. Knight-Ridder Information. Mountain View, CA.

D&B—Dun's Market Identifiers. A directory database with information on over seven million U.S. companies. (Also on *CompuServe, Data-Star* and *DJNR.*)

Dun's International Market Identifiers. Provides access to almost three million non-U.S. firms.

PTS New Product Announcements/Plus. The full text of product-related press releases from all industries. Also supplies key details about new products and technologies, including technical specifications, availability, uses, licensing agreements, distribution channels and prices. (Also on *Data-Star.*)

Times/Sunday Times (London). The full text of the *Times* of London, from 1988 to present. (Also on *DJNR.*)

Data-Star. Knight-Ridder Information. Mountain View, CA.

Company Intelligence. Information on 140,000 public and private U.S. firms and 31,000 international companies, with an emphasis on hard-to-find privately held companies. (Also on *DIALOG, NEXIS* and CD-ROM.)

Harvard Business Review Online. From 1976 to present, the complete text of the *HBR.* From 1971 to 1975, citations are provided. (Also on *DIALOG, LEXIS/NEXIS.*)

Management and Marketing Abstracts (MMA). Abstracts and citations for thousands of articles, book sections, conference proceedings and government publications dealing with practical areas of marketing and management. (Also on *Data-Star.*)

Tradeline Securities Pricing. Historical and current securities market data for more than 150,000 issues traded on major North American Exchanges. (Also on *DJNR.*)

Dow Jones News/Retrieval (DJNR). Princeton, NJ: Dow Jones Information Services. (800) 815-5100.
Dow Jones News (DJN). Continuously updated business and financial news worldwide; from thirty seconds to ninety days old.
Dow Jones Real-Time Quotes (RTQ). Stock prices (with no delay) from major North American exchanges.
DowQuest. Full-text coverage of about four hundred national, regional and local trade journals and magazies, updated weekly.
Wall Street Journal. DJNR is the exclusive online provider of the full text of the *Wall Street Journal.*

FT-Profile. Sunbury-on-Thames, Middlesex, England: Information Access Company. +44 (0) 932 761444.
American Banker. The *Wall Street Journal* of the banking industry; full text online.
Euroscope. Contains the complete text and summaries of commentaries prepared by Coopers and Lybrand on EC policy and legislation and its effects on business. (Also on *LEXIS.*)
Mintel Retail Intelligence (MRI). Complete text of reports on retailing in United Kingdom and European Markets.

GEnie—General Electric Network for Information Exchange. Rockville, MD: GE Information Services. (800) 638-9636.
Dr. Job. A bulletin board featuring a question-and-answer column covering employment-related topics.
ExecuGrid. Full-text business and financial news. (Also on *CompuServe.*)

Investment ANALY$T. Current and historic stock price data, stock performance analysis and stock screening and selection. (Also on *NEWSNET.*)
Wall Street SOS. Recommendations on the sale and purchase of NYSE and AMEX common stocks. (Also on *Delphi.*)

MAID: Market Analysis and Information Database. London: MAID House. Phone—071-253-6900. (New York Phone—212-447-6900.)
Datamonitor. Full-text access to Datamonitor Market Research Reports, which supply analysis and forecasts for more than five hundred market sectors. (Also on *Data-Star, DIALOG* and *FT-Profile.*)
MAID supplies access to many research reports; see below under the heading MARKET RESEARCH REPORTS for more *MAID* databases.

LEXIS/NEXIS. See Appendix B.

OCLC FirstSearch Catalog. Dublin, Ohio: OCLC Online Computer Library Center. (800) 848-5878.
Business Dateline. Full-text articles from newspapers, city business magazines and wire services. (Also on *CompuServe, DIALOG, DJNR* and *NEXIS.*)
Business Periodicals Index. Citations to articles in over three hundred business magazines. (Also on *CDP.*)
Business Organizations, Agencies and Publications Directory. A directory to business contacts worldwide.
Wilson Business Abstracts. The same as the *Business Periodicals Index*, except that summaries of the articles are

included in addition to the citation. (Also on CD-ROM.)

Exports Goods
• Names of Company Officers
• Year established.

Business Directories

Business is a perfect field for online information. Business people often want timely information on stocks or corporate changes. Business directories online can save the user money; instead of paying several hundred dollars for a directory, the researcher only pays for the time that he or she accesses the databases. (Of course, a ride to the library to use print directories that the library owns *may* be even less expensive!)

In the following annotations, the various electronic formats the resources are available in will be noted in italics; online versions will be indicated by the name of the vendor or database. Versions on CD-ROM or floppy disc will be indicated with those generic labels. Unless specifically stated, all sources are also available in print.

Basic and Specialized Nuts-and-Bolts Company Directories

Below are examples of general business directories that libraries and businesses commonly purchase. Even the smallest library should own one of these titles. These directories provide similar data; most will have these elements:
• Company Name
• Address
• Whether the Firm is Public or Private
• Phone and Fax Numbers
• Line(s) of Business
• SIC Code or Codes
• Annual Sales
• Number of Employees
• Whether the Firm Imports or

Be aware that there are generally several SIC codes associated with each company since it is common for companies to produce more than one product or service. For example, the Beatrice Company, which produces, among many other things, Bonkers cat treats and Grandpa John's snack foods, is listed in one directory with four SIC codes: 2033—Canned Fruits and Vegetables, 2079—Edible Fats and Oils, 2011—Meat Packing Plants, and 2032—Canned Specialties.

The main part of these directories is arranged in alphabetic order by company name. Most provide separate index volumes or sections that are industry and geographic cross-references (meaning you can look under a certain state or type of business to find related businesses.) The industry index will usually be arranged by SIC code, so be ready to grab that *SIC Manual* to look up the code you need.

North American Business Directories—General

American Business Information. (Formerly called *Trinet U.S. Businesses.*) Omaha, NE: American Business Information.

Available on *DIALOG, LEXIS/ NEXIS* and some corporate information services, the *American Business Information* online database lists millions of company records, providing address, phone number, county, metropolitan area, primary and secondary SIC numbers (i.e., major and minor product types or services they dabble in), sales, number of employees, type of location (i.e., branch, headquarters, etc.) and, for some, an estimate of market share.

Hoover's Handbook of American Business. Austin, TX: Reference Press. 1991-present. Annual.

One-page profiles of five hundred U.S. enterprises. Another volume published by Reference Press is *Hoover's Handbook of Emerging Companies,* which reports on companies that are "growing rapidly." (On *America Online, LEXIS/NEXIS*).

Million Dollar Directory: America's Leading Public and Private Companies. New York: Dun and Bradstreet. Annual.

About 160,000 companies meeting one of the following criteria: 250 or more employees at one location, $250,000,000 or more in sales volume, or tangible net worth greater than $500,000. The *Million Dollar Directory* is sometimes referred to as *Dun's* or the *D&B Directory.* (On *DIALOG, CD-ROM.*)

Standard and Poor's Register of Corporations, Directors and Executives. New York: Standard and Poor's. 3 Volumes. 1928-present. Annual.

Volume 1 lists over 55,000 public and private corporations in the United States and some from Canada. Volume 2 is the biographical volume; see below under the heading "Business Biography." (On *DIALOG, LEXIS/ NEXIS,* CD-ROM and diskette.)

Ward's Business Directory of U.S. Private and Public Companies. 5 Volumes. Bel-

mont, CA: Information Access. Annual.

Lists over 140,000 public and private companies. Volume 5 ranks companies; see under the heading "Rankings," below. (On CD-ROM as part of the *Companies International* CD-ROM.)

Ward's Private Company Profiles. Detroit: Gale. Annual.

The basic company data in this directory is culled from *Ward's Business Directory,* but the information for the 150 companies in this volume is enhanced by articles and excerpts about each company from a variety of sources, including local, regional, national and trade journals, books, company brochures and investment reports. You may be surprised at how many well-known companies are private firms listed in this directory, including Levi Strauss and Co., Barnes and Noble, R.H. Macy and Company, and Publix Super Markets. (I would have thought some of these were public.)

The two sources below give far more information than the general directories listed above (but cover fewer companies.) Almost all libraries will have at least one of these services (or at least some of the *Moody's Manuals.*)

Moody's Manuals. New York: Moody's Investor's Service.

Moody's lists quite a bit of information for each company: corporate officers and directors, company history, subsidiaries, major plant locations, different lines of business the corporation deals in, capital structure and financial statements. There are different manuals for different sectors:

Bank and Finance Manual (Updated semiweekly.)

Industrial Manual (Updated semiweekly.)

Municipal & Government Manual (Updated semiweekly.)

OTC Industrial Manual (Updated semiweekly.)

OTC Unlisted Manual (Updated weekly.)

Public Utility Manual (Updated semiweekly.)

Transportation Manual (Updated weekly.)

Each set is bound annually with newer information stored in loose-leaf binders.

Standard and Poor's Corporation Records. Very similar to the *Moody's* manuals, listing about ten thousand publicly owned companies with detailed background descriptions and financial structure and securities information. In loose-leaf format. (On *DIALOG*, *LEXIS/NEXIS*, CD-ROM, Microfiche.)

Non-U.S. Directories—General

Asia's 7,500 Largest Companies. ELC International. Annual.

A listing of large corporations in Hong Kong, Japan, Malaysia, the Philippines, Taiwan, Indonesia, South Korea, Singapore and Thailand.

Companies International CD-ROM. Detroit: Gale.

This database on CD-ROM contains information on 250,000 U.S. and foreign businesses. Basically an address/ fax/phone directory, though some re-

cords give brief financial information. The U.S. firms are actually culled from *Ward's Business Directory of Private and Public Companies* (see above), and the foreign firms come from the *World Trade Center's Association World Business Directory.*

Directory of American Firms Operating in Foreign Countries. 12th edition. 3 Volumes. New York: World Trade Academy Press, 1994.

Volume 1 lists American firms that have operations overseas. Volumes 2 and 3 contain listings, by country, from Algeria to Zimbabwe, of the American firms' foreign operations.

Dun's Europa Directory. High Wycombe, England: D&B England, Ltd. Annual.

Short entries for 60,000 leading European companies. Dun's also publishes: *Dun's Asia Pacific Key Business Enterprises, Canadian Key Business Directory, Key British Enterprises, Brazil's Top 10,000 [Brazil Dez Mil]*, and *Jobson's Year Book of Public Companies* (for companies in Australia and New Zealand).

Financial Post Survey of Industrials. Toronto: Financial Post Information Services. 1949-present. Annual.

A guide to publicly traded Canadian firms. The companion publication is the *Financial Post Survey of Mines and Energy Resources.* Also available is the annual *Financial Post 500,* covering Canada's largest companies in industry and finance.

Global Company Handbook: An Analysis of the Financial Performance of the

World's Leading 10,000 Companies. 2d edition. 4 Volumes. Princeton, NJ: Center for International Financial Analysis and Research—CIFAR, 1993.

Volume 1 contains company rankings; Volumes 2-4 supply profiles of the ten thousand companies.

Hoover's Handbook of World Business: Profiles of Major European, Asian, Latin American and Canadian Companies. Austin: The Reference Press, 1991-present. Annual.

The 1993 edition had two-page profiles of 71 "significant" regions and nations and 191 corporations of "global importance." A nice feature: a listing of each company's key competitors.

Kompass Directories.

The publisher Kompass produces a number of directories to products and companies worldwide, with each directory devoted to a specific nation. Some titles in the series: Bahrain, Denmark, Iceland, Luxembourg, Malaysia, Malta, Morocco, Tunisia and the United Arab Emirates. A handy feature of the directories is their level of specificity when naming products produced by a company. Instead of saying that a company produces, for example, electronic equipment, it will name each type of electronic equipment.

Principal International Businesses: The World Marketing Directory. New York: Dun & Bradstreet. 1974-present. Annual.

Has brief listings for 53,000 corporations in 140 countries. Available on *DIALOG*.

Moody's International Manual. New York: Moody's Investors Service. Annual with weekly updates.

Lengthy entries provide history, description of business and property, and financial information for almost 6,700 companies in 107 countries. Available on *DIALOG* and on CD-ROM.

3W Register of Chinese Business. 3W International Digital Publishing. Annual.

A register of 30,000 companies in China. Available on CD-ROM.

Some directories specialize in highlighting the industries of a certain state or area. American Business Directories, a publisher, produces the *State Business Directory Series*, comprised of a company directory for each of the states in the U.S., such as the *Alabama State Business Directory* and the *Alaska State Business Directory*. Dun and Bradstreet publishes *Dun's Regional Marketing Directories* for all states.

There are most likely directories in your library that are put out by your Chamber of Commerce or a local publisher. (You can get the number for local chambers in the *World Chamber of Commerce Directory*, mentioned in chapter 3.) For example, in Colorado we have several regionally produced directories, including the *Rocky Mountain High Technology Directory*.

Specialized Company Directories

There are thousands of directories that provide basic information on companies in specific industries. So before you go look at a general directory, you may want to find out if there is one geared specifically to your needs. Do you want to call advertising agencies that specialize in promotions in the health industry? Check the *Standard Directory of Advertising Agencies*.

Advertising/Marketing.

Green Book: International Directory of Marketing Research Houses and Services. New York: New York Chapter, American Marketing Association, 1973-present. Annual.

An alphabetical listing of names, addresses and numbers, plus short statements about each firm. Two cross-reference indexes of interest: Company Services, makes it simple to find firms that perform certain marketing services like Interviewing or Test Market Simulation; and Market/Industry Specialties, such as the Aging/Mature Market or the Gay Market.

Standard Directory of Advertisers. Wilmette, IL: National Register Publishing Co., 1964-present.

Commonly called the "Advertiser Red Book" or just the "Red Book." For each of the over 27,000 companies listed, the Red Book lists the products the company spends advertising dollars on and where the money goes: to cable television, billboards, radio, newspapers, consumer magazines, posters or network television. Often the dollar amount spent in each medium is also disclosed. This is an excellent place to find out the names of the sales or marketing people in a company.

There are two versions of this directory that contain exactly the same information: the geographic edition and the classified edition. The geographic edition lists firms by area, making it simple to pinpoint those closest to you. The classified edition is arranged by product groupings, such as Beer, Ale and Soft Drinks, Fabrics, Yarns and Sewing Notions, and Recreational Vehicles. A companion volume is *The Standard Directory of Advertising Agencies*. There is also a worldwide edition called *The Standard Directory of International Advertisers and Agencies*.

Consultants.

Consultants and Consulting Organizations Directory. 2 Volumes. Detroit: Gale. 1973-present. Triennial.

Both consulting firms and individual consultants are listed, with a description of their consulting activities. The types of consultation available are incredibly varied; there are specializations in Computer Automation, the Selection and Purchase of Art, and Nuclear Engineering, just to name a few.

Directory of Management Consultants. Fitzwilliam, NH: Kennedy Publications.

This directory profiles about fifteen hundred management consulting firms, specifying what industries they might specialize in and what assistance they offer, including such services as Strategic and Long-Range Planning, Attitude Surveys, Employee Communication and Motivation, Personnel Recruitment and Project Management.

Franchises.

Franchise Annual. Lewiston, New York: Franchise News Inc., 1961-present. Annual.

Provides international coverage, listing over five thousand franchises. (A franchise is a series of outlets owned by independent managers, like Subway Sandwiches and Salads, Petland, and Fat Boys Bar-B-Q.)

Franchise Opportunities Guide: The Official Guide Published by the International Franchise Association. Washington, DC: International Franchise Association. Semi-annual.

In addition to listings, this guide also provides advice to would-be franchisers.

Worldwide Franchise Directory. Detroit: Gale Research. Annual.

Describes franchises in fifteen countries. Presented by industry or service.

Healthcare.

Dun's Healthcare Reference Book: America's Leading Healthcare Providers and Suppliers. Parsippany, NJ: Dun and Bradstreet, 1991-present. Annual.

A directory to manufacturers of healthcare suppliers as well as the healthcare providers themselves, including hospitals, long-term care facilities, outpatient rehabilitation facilities, hospices, laboratories and rural health clinics.

Hospital Blue Book. Atlanta, GA: Billian Publishing. Annual.

The greater portion of this directory is a state-by-state, county-by-county listing of U.S. hospitals, providing names of key physicians and staff, accreditation and training requirements, the total number of beds, the average number of patients in-house and those making outpatient visits, the number of employees and the type of hospital. Also listed are DRGs, HMOs, PPOs and Healthcare Systems. There is also a Canadian edition of this directory. For additional healthcare directories, see chapter 16, "Diseases and Mental Illnesses."

High Tech.

CorpTech: Corporate Technology Directory. Wellesley Hills, MA: Corporate Technology Services, 1986-present.

An excellent directory for locating companies in most high-tech fields, including computer hardware and software, photonics, robotics, artificial intelligence, biotechnology and defense systems. Beyond address/phone, the directory also lists the products each company makes, responsibilities of key executives, the number of employees, growth rate, average job creation since formation, and government contractor status. Since this is an expensive multivolume collection, smaller libraries may not own this one. Those libraries who can afford it, generally own it. (Also on CD-ROM, *Data-Star, ORBIT* and *QUESTEL.*)

High Technology Market Place Directory. Princeton Junction, NJ: Princeton Hightech Group, 1985-present.

A one-volume alternative to *CorpTech.* The arrangement of the subject index makes it almost impossible to simply look up a company by the type of work the firm does. The company entries, in alphabetic order, list the businesses the company is engaged in, some financial figures and names of some company executives. Other sections in the book include: Foreign Companies Operating in the U.S., and the Top 1000 Companies Arranged by Research and Development Spending and Percentage of Net Sales.

Financial Institutions.

Moody's Bank and Finance Manual. See above, under the heading "North American Business Directories— General," Moody's Manuals.

Polk Financial Institutions Directory, North America. Nashville: R.L. Polk & Co. Semiannual.

This listing includes financial institutions that are active as well as those that have ceased business within the past five years. This is a huge volume, but provides thumb tabs to assist the reader in quickly turning to listings for the U.S. states, major cities or the international banking section. For each financial organization at least some of the following data is included: branches, cable address, credit, cards issued, directors, dividend per share of stock, established date, fax, hours of operation and time zone, membership, net income, statement of condition (assets/liabilities) officers and out-of-town locations. Polk also publishes the *Polk International Banking Directory* and *Polk's World Banking Profile.*

Thomson Bank Directory. Skokie, IL: Thomson Financial Publishing. 4 Volumes.

Volumes 1 and 2 cover North America, Volume 3 is an international directory. The following information is provided for most banks in the directories: the bank's legal title, the charter type, SWIFT addresses and BIC codes for wire transfers, any banking association the institution is a member of, ownership information, some financial figures, key officers and directors, international correspondents, branches and affiliates, and foreign offices. Volume 4 provides a concise summary of principal correspondents for all banks throughout the world and performance ratios of U.S. banks for monitoring interbank liability.

Insurance.

Best's Insurance Reports. Oldwick, NJ: A.M. Best Co., 1900-present. Annual.

Best's issues hardbound series; one covering Life-Health insurance, the other covering Property-Casualty. There is also a *Best's Insurance Reports International.* These guides look at insurance companies and assign them each a "Best's Rating," (an A + + through F letter system), determined by a variety of factors. Several pages of primarily financial data is devoted to each company. There is usually comment on the history, management and operations of the company.

Manufacturers.

Directory of Foreign Manufacturers in the United States. Jeffrey S. Arpan and David A. Ricks. 5th edition. Atlanta: Georgia State University Business Press, 1993.

A directory of data on some seven thousand foreign-owned companies in the United States.

Thomas Register of American Manufacturers. New York: Thomas Publishing, 1906-present. Annual.

This bright green collection of over-sized volumes is hard to miss. The first seventeen volumes of the 1994 edition (the number of volumes is always on the rise) are labeled Products and Services. These volumes lead you to manufacturing firms by product, very much like the phone book yellow pages. A name, address and phone number are listed for each firm, with some entries also listing specific products, and, like the yellow pages, some enhanced with separate "ads" showing products and providing additional information.

Volumes 18 and 19 are the Company Profile volumes, offering more information on 145,000 of the companies listed in the first seventeen volumes: whether they export, asset ratings, company executives, locations of sales offices, distributors, plants and service/engineering offices.

The final volumes contain actual product catalogs from 11,000 of the companies, allowing the reader to find more detailed product information, including specifications, drawings, photographs and availability and performance data. (Seeing the products may be especially handy if you are describing a scene in a factory.) (On *DI-ALOG*, CD-ROM.)

Industry Information

Are you writing about the decline in going to the movies and the boom in video

rentals? This section recommends sources that assist you in determining the health and future of different industries.

Encyclopedia of American Industries. Kevin Hillstrom, editor. 2 Volumes. Detroit: Gale, 1994.

Volume 1 of this set examines Manufacturing Industries and Volume 2 surveys Service and Non-Manufacturing Industries. Over a thousand industries are explored. Each industry description supplies background, trends, current conditions, and the names of the larger companies of the sector. Bibliographic references are always supplied. The service industry descriptions are particularly useful since it can be more time-consuming for a researcher to find "quick" information on smaller industries (i.e., florists, medical equipment rental and leasing, religious organizations.) This set is a new addition to reference collections. If it lives on beyond its first year, it will probably be a standard.

Investext. Foster City, CA: Information Access Co.

Libraries that provide public access to the *Investext* electronic database have business clientele; usually academic libraries that serve schools with substantial business programs. *Investext* is comprised of foreign and U.S. full-text analysts' reports on companies and industries. The "analysts" are firms such as Lehman Brothers, The First Boston Corporation and Dean Witter Reynolds.

A securities analyst analyzes a company for its investment potential. Again, the intent of these reports is to assist investors in making decisions, but they can also help writers fruitfully fill a page by discovering more about a company or industry. More than 11,000 companies in 53 industries are featured. (On CD-ROM, *CompuServe, Data-Star, DIALOG, DJNR, LEXIS/NEXIS, NewsNet* and *STN.*)

NTDB: National Trade Data Bank. U.S. Dept. of Commerce. Monthly.

Issued by the U.S. government, this database, stored on CD-ROM, contains approximately 100,000 documents pertaining to export and foreign trade policy. *NTDB* contains lengthy market research reports, compiled by the International Trade Association, describing products and industries for many countries. Some examples of report names: "Bolivia—Average Family Spending Statistics," "Africa—Used Clothing Market Profile," and "Netherlands—Shipbuilding Overview." All libraries that are government depositories should have the *NTDB*; many others have purchased it because of the relatively low cost for the abundance of information. It is also available over the Internet.

Panorama of EU Industry. [Formerly titled *Panorama of EC Industry.*] Luxembourg: Office for Official Publications of the European Communities. Annual.

This volume describes the current situation and outlook for manufacturing and service industries in the European Union.

Standard and Poor's Industry Surveys. New York: Standard and Poor's, 1973-present.

Released quarterly, this publication surveys major industries such as bank-

ing, electronics and telecommunications. Each of the surveys includes industry background, figures, trends and outlook, as well as statistics for the leading companies in that industry. The section titled the "Earnings Supplement" ranks companies by relative profitability.

U.S. Industrial Outlook. Washington, DC: U.S. Dept. of Commerce, International Trade Administration, 1980-Present. Annual.

Each yearly volume examines approximately 350 U.S. industries with comments on the international business perspective for each industry. The focus is on industries; companies are rarely named.

Value Line Investment Survey. New York: Arnold Bernard, 1970-present.

Value Line is often consulted by those who invest in stocks, but it's also of interest to those who just want to see how particular industries and companies are faring. Each section, arranged by industry, is updated every thirteen weeks.

Market Research Reports. Market Research Reports may be another source of industry information. These reports are produced by a number of commercial publishers and are intended to describe some details of a product/service and its industry: who buys/uses it, the size and structure of the industry and other factors that affect that market. Though they can be purchased, they are often quite pricey; even in the thousands of dollars. They are priced to sell to companies or potential investors who stand to earn a good deal of money by investing in the reports.

The source *Findex: The Worldwide Directory of Market Research Reports, Studies and Surveys* (Cambridge Information Group. Annual with Supplements) lists thousands of reports available for purchase. Prices range from several hundred dollars to over $10,000.

Some market research reports are available online. These will definitely not be available for free at any library. Below are some of the databases that offer the reports, what countries they cover and what vendor systems they are available through.

- *Datamonitor*—U.S., Europe and U.K. On *Data-Star*, *DIALOG*, *FT-Profile*, and *MAID*.
- *Euromonitor*—U.S., France, Italy, Germany, Spain and U.K. On *Data-Star*, *DIALOG* and *MAID*.
- *Freedonia Industry and Business*—Mostly U.S. On *Data-Star* and *DIA-LOG*.
- *Frost and Sullivan*—Europe and U.S. On *Data-Star* and *MAID*.

The *DIALOG* database called *MARKETFULL* provides access to *Datamoniter*, *Euromonitor* and *Freedonia* in one shot.

Country Overviews

When looking into non-U.S. industries, companies or products, it's a good idea to back yourself up with some information about the specific country in which business is being conducted.

(Name of Country): A Country Study. Area Handbook Series. Washington, DC: The American University. Issued irregularly.

Each book in the *Country Study* se-ries deals with a particular foreign country, describing and analyzing its economic, military, political and social systems. Unfortunately, recent volumes are not available for every country.

Background Notes. U.S. Dept. of State, Bureau of Public Affairs, Washington, DC.

Background Notes are pamphlets, ranging from about five to nine pages, on selected countries. They (succinctly) go over the history, geography, culture, government, politics, economics, climate and transportation of each country. These notes are also reproduced in the reference resource titled *Countries of the World and Their Leaders*, described in more detail in chapter 8, "Overviews on Any Subject: Encyclopedias and Handbooks."

Doing Business in (name of country). New York: Price, Waterhouse. Issued irregularly.

Produced by the accounting, tax and management consulting firm Price Waterhouse, the *Doing Business in . . .* series is a collection of guides, each devoted to a nation, covering the country's investment climate, procedures for doing business, accounting practices and tax systems.

European Business Directory: A Comprehensive Resource Guide for Doing Business Throughout Europe and the Former Soviet States. New York: Faulkner and Gray. Annual.

This directory contains country profiles, briefly covering market/economic conditions and investment opportunities. (Also lists tons of business contacts.)

Foreign Economic Trends and Their Implications for the United States (FETs). Washington, DC: U.S. Department of Commerce, Bureau of International Commerce.

A regularly updated series of bulletins prepared by U.S. Foreign Service Officers pinpointing the economic and financial conditions of a country and marketing prospects for U.S. products.

Overseas Business Reports (OBR). Washington, DC: U.S. Dept of Commerce, International Trade Administration.

These reports, one for each country, provide information on overseas trade and investment conditions and opportunities for selected countries. Though your library will probably retain the older paper copies for some time, from 1993 forward, the OBRs will be issued in electronic format only as part of the NTDB database.

Exporters Encyclopedia. New York: Dun and Bradstreet. Annual.

The *Exporters Encyclopedia* is arranged alphabetically by country name. Each section includes marketing data, trade regulations, key contacts, description of communication and transportation services and tips on business travel. A nice feature: it is kept up-to-date with supplements found in a companion notebook called the *Fact File*.

World Economic and Business Review. Cambridge: Basil Blackwell. Annual.

The *Review* provides country profiles running from approximately one to eight pages and lists items such as entry requirements, major hotels and major public holidays.

Market Share/Rankings

What share of the high-tech market is held by the computer company you are investigating? What brands of diet soda sell the most? What are the top companies in the plastics business? Check out the following sources to find out.

Business Rankings Annual: Lists of Companies, Products, Services and Activities Compiled from a Variety of Published Sources. Compiled by the Brooklyn Public Library Business Library Staff. Detroit: Gale. Annual.

This is basically a top ten of anything related to business. The Brooklyn Library staff ransacks rankings from magazines, journals, financial services, directories, statistical compilations and other sources to come up with this volume. The book is arranged by subject, with such diverse headings as Largest Banks in Papua New Guinea (Papua New Guinea Banking Corp. was the largest in 1991), Counties with the Highest Estimated Disposable Income (Los Angeles County was ranked number one), and North America's Top Ski Resorts (with Vail, Colorado, coming out on top). The original source of information is always named so it can be referred to if needed.

Forbes 500 Annual Directory. New York: Forbes Publishing, 1917-present.

Released annually in April or May, the directory ranks companies based on sales, profits, market value and assets.

The Fortune Directory of U.S. Corporations. New York: Time/Warner, 1955-present.

A directory that combines two special annual issues of *Fortune* magazine: the five hundred largest U.S. industrial corporations (published in the April issue) and the Service 500, ranking businesses in the service sector, such as banking, insurance and retailing.

Fortune Guide to the Global 500. Time/Warner. Annual.

Ranks the five hundred largest industrial companies in the world by sales and performance within twenty-six industries, within countries.

Investext. This source, described in more detail above, often provides market share data within its reports.

The Market Share Reporter: An Annual Compilation of Reported Market Share Data on Companies, Products and Services. Arsen J. Darnay and Marlita A. Reddy, editors. Detroit: Gale. Annual.

A compilation of market share data culled from periodicals and brokerage reports. In some cases, pie charts or bar graphs are added to help the reader visualize the market share of various companies or the sales of different products or services. Don't think your product is too obscure. It might be in here. Examples of products covered include berries, bleach, greeting cards and smokeless tobacco. Some unexpected headings sneak in here, such as Sport/Compact Auto Market Shares by Color. (The favorite in 1992 was the color white, with 19.29 percent, followed by bright red at 12.39 percent and medium red at 10.60 percent.) The *Reporter* is arranged by two-digit SIC code. Also available on *NEXIS*.

NTPA: National Trade and Professional Associations of the United States. Washington, DC: Columbia Books. Annual.

Call the appropriate industry association listed and described in this single-volume directory and see if they have the ranking information you need. Associations will often keep figures and statistics regarding their industry. (Refer also to the *Encyclopedia of Associations*, described in chapter 7, "Identifying Experts.")

Standard and Poor's Industry Survey. Described above under the heading "Industry Information."

The Times 1,000: The Indispensable Annual Review of the World's Leading Industrial and Financial Companies. New York: HarperCollins. Annual.

A guide to the one thousand leading companies in the U.K. and Europe, and other leading companies in the U.S., Canada, Australia, South Africa, Hong Kong, Ireland and Japan.

Ward's Business Directory of U.S. Private and Public Companies. 5 Volumes. Belmont, CA: Information Access. Annual.

Volume 5 of *Ward's* ranks companies, by sales, within industry groupings. (Haul out the *SIC Manual*; they're arranged by SIC codes.)

U.S. Economic Censuses

A method of determining the number of businesses in an area is by looking at the *Economic Censuses*, published by the U.S. Bureau of the Census. Though they won't list the names of the individual establishments, you will be able to see if an area is *inundated* with a certain type of business. When you are using the economic censuses, be aware that minimums may be set for their data collection. Places with populations lower than 2,500 are not counted.

The *Economic Censuses* collect data about U.S. industries. They issue reports that list, for a particular region, the number of establishments and firms, employment and payroll figures, sales receipts, operating expenses, capital expenditures, assets and inventories.

Economic censuses are taken every five years. For example, the last two compilations were for 1987 and 1992. The next one is due 1997. These publications identify establishments by Standard Industrial Classification codes (SIC codes). There are census reports for the following areas:

Agriculture
Construction Industries
Governments
Manufactures
Mineral Industries
Retail Trade
Service
Transportation
Wholesale Trade

A number of libraries, especially those that are full government depositories, will also own the economic censuses on CD-ROM. Some figures are also online in the *Cendata* database, accessible through *CompuServe* and *DIALOG*.

Now, waiting five years for every update is too long to wait! So, there are a number of publications that supplement and update some of the data appearing in the Economic Censuses. Be aware that the updates to the quinquennial

census will be less detailed than the five-year reports.

Census of Manufacturers. Updated by the *Annual Survey of Manufacturers* and the *Current Industrial Reports* (*CIR*). (CIR is a series of booklets focusing on particular industries.)

Census of Service Industries and the *Census of Transportation.* Updated annually only, by the *Service Annual Survey Report* and the *Motor Freight Transportation* and *Warehousing Survey*, respectively.

The Bureau of the Census produces the *Current Business Reports* (*CBR*) series. The data included in the CBR updates a portion of the information found in some of the economic censuses. The *Census of Retail Trade* is updated by the part of CBR called *Monthly Retail Trade: Sales and Inventories*, which is cumulated in the publication *Annual Retail Trade*; the *Census of Wholesale Trade* is in part brought up to date by the report *Monthly Wholesale Trade: Sales and Inventory and Annual Wholesale Trade*.

Information from Articles

Much of the material you will be looking for will be contained in articles. Be sure to consult Appendix A under the heading "Business" for a look at the types of business indexes that are available. Newspaper indexes will also be of interest. Remember, when using an index to find articles:

• You can look under the name of a particular industry, like Fast Food.
• You can look under the name of a company or store, such as The Body

Shop. (Look under the letter B.)
- You can look under a person's name, like Donald Trump.
- You can look under a product type, for example, ice cream. (In an online or CD-ROM index you would be able to enter the specific name of the product to conduct a search, e.g., Dove Bars.)

Trade Journals

Many of the business indexes in Appendix A will lead you to trade journals, magazines devoted exclusively to one industry. You'll find these are quite useful in business research. They are both written and read by those interested in specialized industries. Examples of titles are *Footwear News*, *Nation's Restaurant News*, *Pulp and Paper* and *Supermarket News*. Trade journals also produce many special issues. Be aware that libraries will generally only own the trade journals that cater to either the interests of the people in the community or the curriculum of students on campus. You can always borrow the article through interlibrary loan or simply find the address of the publisher using one of the periodical directories listed on page 28 and buy a copy.

Newspaper Articles

Newspaper articles are of special interest to business researchers because of their timeliness—papers like the *Wall Street Journal* and the *New York Times*. There are also trade-specific newspapers, including *The Financial Times*, *Women's Wear Daily* and *Advertising Age*. Since the information you want might be recent, a newspaper will have reported on it before a weekly magazine.

Newsletters

Trade-specific publications also show up in the form of newsletters. Unfortunately, many excellent newsletters are only indexed in a limited number of areas. Two ways of locating newsletters online are:

PTS Newsletter Database. Foster City, CA: Information Access Co., 1988-present. (On *Data-Star* or *DIALOG*.) PTS lets you search the complete contents of more than five hundred business and trade newsletters.

NewsNet. Bryn Mawr, PA: NewsNet. An online system devoted to full-text coverage newsletters (as well as worldwide wire service and other business information.) Some of the full-text newsletters on this system include *Aerospace Daily*, *Central America Update*, *Drug Detection Report*, *News from France*, *South African Focus* and *Telephone News*. In all, *NewsNet* contains about five hundred newsletters on a variety of topics.

Some print options for finding newsletters include *Newsletters in Print*, *Hudson's Subscription Newsletter Directory*, and the *Oxbridge Directory of Newsletters*. Use the *Encyclopedia of Associations* to locate an association for the business you are interested in and then see if they produce a specialized newsletter.

Wire Services

Wire services are news services, such as the Associated Press or United Press International, that transmit information primarily by wire. The four majors are AP, UPI, Reuters and Agence France

Presse (AFP). Television and radio stations subscribe to wire services, hoping to pick up on breaking stories that they may follow up on. Wire services may cover new products, legal actions, and personnel changes and supply company announcements of general interest. Be aware that some of the information supplied by the wire services will be rather short and cryptic! I have had some disappointed students who paid for a wire-search article based on the title and then found it was only a few lines long. Some of the newswires available on the commercial online services:

Agence France Presse English Wire. Washington, DC: Agence France Presse. The world's oldest news agency, dating back to 1835. It covers everything from "coups to catastrophes," with 950 journalists on their payroll and an additional 2,000 "stringers" reporting from 130 countries. (On *Data Times, DIALOG, LEXIS/NEXIS* and *NewsNet.*)

AP News. New York: Associated Press. The largest supplier of general-interest news to the media worldwide, with over 15,000 newspaper and broadcast clients in 115 countries. (On *CompuServe, DIALOG, Prodigy* and others.)

Business Wire. San Francisco: Business Wire. The complete text of a quarter of a million press releases from 11,000 companies, as well as organizations such as hospitals and universities. (On *America Online, CompuServe, DELPHI, DJNR, DIALOG, NewsNet, NEXIS.*)

Japan Economic Newswire Plus (JEN).

New York: Kyodo News International. Produced by the Kyodo News Service, Japan's largest news agency, this newswire supplies all the English-language newswires from Kyodo, based in Tokyo. (On *DIALOG, DJNR, LEXIS, NEXIS.*)

PR Newswire. New York: PR Newswire Association. This service supplies the full text of news releases supplied by companies, public relations agencies, trade associations and other organizations. (On *CompuServe, Delphi, DIALOG, DJNR, NewsNet, NEXIS.*)

Reuters. New York: Reuters U.S. This file provides access to information updated around-the-clock on business and international news. This database supplies news "flashes" containing timely headlines before the complete story is written. (On *DIALOG, NewsNet, LEXIS/NEXIS.*)

UPI News. Washington, DC: United Press International. This database has news from the United Press International Wire, covering domestic and international general news, features, financial news and commentaries. (On *DIALOG, NewsNet,* and *NEXIS.*)

PR, Reuters, and UPI are also part of the database *Reuter TEXTLINE*, available through *Data-Star* and *DIALOG.*

Business Biography

For a more expanded explanation of how to track down information about people, read chapter 12, "Biographical Information." Here, I'll supply the names of some sources that look exclusively at businessmen and businesswomen.

The ABC-CLIO Companion to Women in the Workplace. Dorothy and Carl F. Schneider. Santa Barbara, CA: ABC-CLIO, 1993.

Many of the entries in this volume are biographical, touching on quite a variety of working women, including union organizers and those who were first in their field. This work also covers, in A-to-Z fashion, major events, organizations and court cases that changed working conditions for women.

Corporate Eponymy: A Biographical Dictionary of the Persons Behind the Names of Major American, British, European and Asian Businesses. Adrian Room. Jefferson, NC: McFarland and Co., 1992.

You'll find brief but interesting background narratives concerning those businesspeople whose names grace the company logos of familiar firms and the labels of well-loved products— people like Jack Daniel, of whiskey fame, and Harland Sanders, also known as the Colonel at KFC.

The Directory of Directors: Key Data on the 60,000 Directors Who Control Britain's Major Companies. 2 Volumes. Reed Information Services. Annual.

The biographical entries, which appear in Volume 1, list such information as honors, awards, education and main business interests. Volume 2 is arranged by company name.

Financial Post Directory of Directors. 2

Volumes. Toronto: Financial Post, 1947-Present. Annual.

The first volume of this set contains brief information about directors and executives of Canadian corporations; the second is in alphabetical order by the name of the company.

Reference Book of Corporate Managements. 4 Volumes. Parsipanny, NJ: Dun's Marketing Services. Annual.

This set will not tell you that old so-and-so was a helluva guy, but it will list, by years, former business positions that the person held and what school(s) they graduated from. The first three volumes are in order by company name; the major officers for those companies are profiled. The last volume, the Cross-Reference volume, enables the reader to find biographies by industry, name, college or university attended (why not track one down and write about them in the college-town paper?) and by military affiliation.

Standard and Poor's Register of Corporations, Directors and Executives. 3 Volumes. New York: Standard and Poor's. Annual.

The second volume of this collection covers about 70,000 directors and executives, providing year and place of birth, college graduation dates, principal business affiliations, business address and residence address, and fraternal (other than college) memberships.

Who's Who in Finance and Industry. New Providence, NJ: Marquis Who's Who. Biennial.

A typical Who's Who publication,

cramming a great deal of useful information into tiny, abbreviation-filled entries. Those profiled in this volume are from all over the world and in many areas of business, including accounting, advertising, banking and finance, communications, construction, engineering, manufacturing, retail trade, technological development, transportation and utilities.

Who's Who in European Business. 1st edition. New York: Bowker-Saur, 1993.

You can track down biographies of European business bigwigs by looking under company, country or the individual's name.

Who's Who of Women Executives. Jeffrey Franz, editor. Owings Mills, MD: National Reference Press, 1990.

A one-volume source listing women in all types of businesses.

Regional Biographical Directories

Very often, there will be a locally produced guide of prominent business persons in the area you're interested in. For example, here in Colorado, the Denver Business Journal produces *Who's Who in Denver Business*, a listing of area leaders in business and industry, real estate, education, finance, health care, high tech, hospitality, law and telecommunications. In Tennessee, two local directories are *Who's Who: The Business Book* (listing businesspeople in Nashville and Middle Tennessee) and *Who's Who in Memphis and Mid-South Business*. These local directory biographies tend to be more intimate than those found in national sources.

What Should Your Character Earn?

What kind of salary should the doctor in your manuscript earn? Well, that depends on where he works—India? Rhode Island? Being sure that your character's earnings match his buying habits can be important. The references in this section list both salaries that different workers can expect and descriptions of the variety of professions that exist.

American Almanac of Jobs and Salaries. New York: Avon, 1982-present. Updated irregularly.

The *Almanac* surveys hundreds of occupations, expected salary ranges and trends in the job market.

American Salaries and Wages Survey: Statistical Data Derived From More Than 300 Government, Business and News Sources. Marlita A. Reddy, editor. 2d edition. Detroit: Gale, 1993.

This survey is comprised of tables listing low, mid and high salaries for various occupations in different cities, counties, and general areas.

Career Information Center (CIC). 5th edition. 13 Volumes. New York: Macmillan Publishing Co., 1993.

In this multibook set, each volume concentrates on careers in a particular field, for example, Volume 3 covers Communication and the Arts, Volume 6 Engineering, Science and Technology careers, and Volume 11 Public and Community Services. Over a page is devoted to each career with each of the following elements explored: Definition and Nature of Work, Education and Training Requirements, Getting the Job, Advancement Possibilities and Employment Outlook, Working Conditions, Earnings and Benefits, and Where to Go for More Information. By the way, there are many options listed under "writer," including Computer Software Documentation Writer, Literary or Theatrical Agent and Fiction Writer; there is also a heading for "journalist."

Dictionary of Occupational Titles (DOT). Washington, DC: U.S. Dept. of Labor, Training and Employment Administration, 1991.

DOT lists brief job descriptions for approximately 20,000 different occupations. Most of the jobs listed are quite specialized, such as Bank Note Designer, Notch Grinder and Artificial Flower Maker. All government depository libraries (and many, many others) will own this volume.

Encyclopedia of Careers and Vocational Guidance. William E. Hopke, editor-in-chief. 4 Volumes. Chicago: J.G. Ferguson Publishing Co., 1993.

Volume 1 is comprised of seventy-four industry overviews, looking at the industry's structure and unique job paths. The next three volumes look at 540 specific jobs within those industries, supplying a description, history of the profession, requirements, opportunities for experience and exploration, methods for entering the field, advancement opportunities, employment outlook, earnings and the work environment.

Jobs Rated Almanac. Les Krantz. New York: World Almanac, 1992.

Two hundred fifty jobs are briefly evaluated under six criteria: work environment, security, stress, income, outlook and physical demands. All jobs are examined separately and then ranked for each category. Some of the "worst" jobs, as far as environment, which basically looks at hours worked weekly, include firefighters, the President of the U.S., Indy-class race car drivers and NFL football players. So if your character is a football player and he has a bad temper, this book might provide a few of the reasons why!

Municipal Year Book: The Authoritative Source Book of Urban Data and Developments. The International City/County Management Association. Washington, DC: ICMA. Annual.

The *Municipal Year Book* supplies a yearly peek at salaries for municipal workers around the U.S., including city managers, police and fire chiefs, public works directors, refuse collectors, police officers, fire fighters, mayors and heads of parks and recreation. The Municipal Year Book will also help you find the names of municipal officials (see chapter 7, "Identifying Experts").

Occupational Compensation Survey: Pay Only. (Formerly called *Area Wage Surveys.*) Washington, DC: U.S. Bureau of Labor Statistics. Annual and Biennial.

Each survey represents a specific U.S. metropolitan area. Since each report looks at wages for the same occupations, it is easy to do comparisons city-to-city. (Only the largest cities are done annually; the rest are produced biennially.)

Occupational Outlook Handbook. Washington, DC: U.S. Department of Labor, Bureau of Labor Statistics. Annual.

The *Handbook* covers about 250 occupations in almost precisely the same manner as the CIC described above. Note who's been around longer to see who's copying who! Of course, CIC does cover more jobs: 648 occupational profiles in which over 3,000 jobs are discussed.

Salaries of Scientists, Engineers and Technicians: A Summary of Salary Surveys. Washington, DC: Commission on Professionals in Science and Technology.

In order to facilitate comparison of information, this resource presents results of salary surveys for science-related positions conducted by the federal government, trade organizations, magazine publishers and educational institutions. It provides, based on factors like number of years out of college and what type of agency worked for, salary figures for those working in mathematics, chemistry, physics, geology, toxicology, pharmacology, psychology, chemical and industrial engineering and even data processing.

Vocational Careers Sourcebook: Where to Find Help Planning Careers in Skilled, Trade and Nontechnical Vocations. Kathleen M. Savage and Karen Hill, editors. 1st edition. Detroit: Gale. 1992.

One hundred thirty-five vocational jobs are described, with recommendations of where to go for contacting related associations, finding standards/ certification agencies, and locating career guides and other sources of pertinent information. A job is usually considered vocational when employment in that occupation does not rely on a college or university degree. So the spectrum of occupations covered in the VCS is quite broad, covering such varied jobs as real estate agents, correction officers, janitors, aircraft mechanics, jewelers and tool and die makers. Also put out by Gale and arranged in the same fashion is the *Professional Careers Sourcebook: Where to Find Help Planning Careers That Require College or Technical Degrees.*

To find even more detailed descriptions of jobs, it may be necessary to look at more specialized guides. To find such guides using your library's online catalog, perform a subject search, matching the word that describes the field you're interested in along with the phrase VOCATIONAL GUIDANCE. Some examples:

MUSIC VOCATIONAL GUIDANCE
BUSINESS VOCATIONAL GUIDANCE
EDUCATION VOCATIONAL GUIDANCE

You can also try matching your field word with the word CAREERS. Avoid using words that are too specific, for example, KINDERGARTEN TEACHER VOCATIONAL GUIDANCE. TEACHERS or EDUCATION would be better choices. Of course, sometimes I'm surprised to see career books on very specialized careers, such as: *Becoming an Electronics Technician* (New York: Maxwell MacMillan International.) So go ahead and try putting in a specific job . . . it only takes a moment to check.

Some examples of the type of varied job guides that are out there:

Adventure Careers: Your Guide to Exciting Jobs, Uncommon Occupations and Extraordinary Experiences. Alex Hiam and Susan Angle. Hawthorne, NJ: Career Press, 1992.

A number of "personal accounts" describe those who have found unusual occupations, including back country tours, a crafts importing business and the Peace Corps. Be aware, however, that the book is primarily a listing of organizations, etc., that can help link people with out-of-the ordinary careers.

Career Opportunities for Writers: A Comprehensive Guide to the Exciting Careers Open to You as a Writer. Rosemary Ellen Guiley. 2d edition. New York: Facts on File, 1991.

Just a few of the writing careers described include Community-Affairs Director for a TV station, a Public Information Officer of a company or organization, an Author of Fiction and a Senior Editor in publishing. Each position entry supplies a job description, income potential, work prospects, education, skills and experience needed, and the affiliated unions and associations.

Careers for Night Owls and Other Insomniacs. Lincolnwood, IL: NTC Publishing Group, 1994.

Using this book you might find a career for that rather strange young man in your story who has trouble sleeping. Other titles of books in this series include *Careers for* . . .

- *Animal Lovers and Other Zoological Types*
- *Bookworms and Other Literary Types*
- *Computer Buffs and Other Technological Types*
- *Crafty People and Other Dexterous Types*
- *Culture Lovers and Other Artsy Types*
- *Environmental Types and Others Who Respect the Earth*
- *Film Buffs and Other Hollywood Types*
- *Foreign Language Aficionados and Other Multilingual Types*
- *Good Samaritans and Other Humanitarian Types*
- *Gourmets & Others Who Relish Food*
- *History Buffs and Others Who Learn From the Past*
- *Kids at Heart and Others Who Adore Children*
- *Nature Lovers and Other Outdoor Types*
- *Number Crunchers and Other Quantitative Types*
- *Shutterbugs and Other Candid Types*
- *Sports Nuts and Other Athletic Types*
- *Travel Buffs and Other Restless Types*

Choosing an Airline Career. Carol March. Denver: Capri Publishing, 1992.

A guide to obtaining entry-level positions in the airline industry, such as reservations sales agent, flight attendant and cargo agent. Do you have a character that does not make much money but wants to travel? Give them an airline job. This book goes over what travel benefits are associated with an airline career.

Guide to Careers in World Affairs. Editors of the Foreign Policy Association. 3d edition. Manassas Park, VA: Impact Publications, 1993.

Each chapter begins by describing international careers in such areas as International Finance and Banking and International Law. Each chapter then lists specific companies that the interested job seeker might contact, describing what qualifications the company is interested in. So you could actually pick the company your character works for (or a close facsimile thereof).

Marketing and Sales Career Directory: A Practical, One-Stop Guide to Getting a Job in Marketing and Sales. 4th edition. Bradley J. Morgan, editor. Detroit: Gale, 1993.

Covering all segments of marketing, including direct mail, business-to-business marketing and services marketing, each essay describes what to expect in various job positions.

Opportunities in Sports and Athletics Careers. Lincolnwood, IL: VGM Career Horizons, 1993.

Part of the VGM *Opportunities In . . .* series. Other titles in the collection include *Opportunities in . . .*

Child Care Careers
Horticultural Careers
International Business
Occupational Therapy
Plumbing and Pipefitting Careers
Public Health Careers

Outdoor Careers: Exploring Occupations in Outdoor Fields. Ellen Shenk. Harrisburg, PA: Stackpole Books, 1992.

Outdoor Careers looks at occupations in such fields as farming, geotechnical engineering, oceanography and skydiving instruction. Profiles of some people who work in outdoor occupations are included.

If you want to bone up more on purely business research, try one or more of the following guides.

Business Information: How to Find It, How to Use It. 2d edition. Phoenix: Oryx Press, 1992.

Business Information Sources. Lorna M. Daniells. 3d edition. Berkeley: University of California Press, 1993.

Encyclopedia of Business Information Sources. Detroit: Gale. Irregular.

Handbook of Business Information: A Guide for Librarians, Students and Researchers. Diane Wheeler Strauss. Englewood, CO: Libraries Unlimited, 1988.

International Business Information: How to Find It, How to Use It. Ruth A. Pagell and Michael Halpern. Phoenix: Oryx Press, 1994.

Sourceguide to European Company Information. Detroit: Gale, 1993.

Chapter Seven

Identifying Experts

Don't be surprised if you go into a library for information and the librarian sends you home with a phone number, fax number, address, or log-on information for a computer bulletin board. As a librarian, I sometimes get the fish eye when I let a patron know that they'll need to contact someone to get the answer they need. Why doesn't a library have everything? Some reasons:

- Information is so new that it hasn't been formally published anywhere yet.
- You are seeking material on a rather obscure topic that resides in the heads of a few enthusiastic experts.
- Anecdotal feedback is something you might need that you just cannot get from a book.
- Because no one library or bookstore has everything!

A journalist friend of mine says: "I find out what I need by calling the right people." Well, this chapter leads you to the books that provide the contacts for the right people: the experts in different fields whose thoughts you can mine and quotes you can integrate into your writing. Books like the annual *Research Centers Directory* will lead you to authorities on everything from back pain to altruism.

Phone Books

The familiar phone book is a great place for hunting down experts. If you are truly lucky, you'll have a local library that maintains a paper collection of phone books from around the world. Such a collection takes up a great deal of space and is difficult to maintain, so you may need to search a bit to find a library kind enough to carry such a collection. Most larger libraries buy collections of phone books accessible through microfiche or CD-ROM.

Why use a phone book when you can call information? Because the operator may not be willing (or allowed, to be more accurate) to read the name of every person under the heading of Bakery in Berkeley. You can do that by peeking in the phone book. Don't be put off if your library does carry the phone books on microfiche. It takes half a second to learn it and only a little extra eye strain.

There are a number of advantages to using electronic phone/address/fax listings on CD-ROM or online, as opposed to paper or microfiche:

- You can quickly compile a list from a number of areas based on certain criteria, e.g., type of business, zip code and so on.
- You can search for a number of geographic areas in one shot, unlike traditional phone books.
- If you only know part of the name of a company and a general location, you still might be able to track it down through an electronic phone directory.

Some phone directories available on CD-ROM and online that cover both business and residential phone numbers:

MetroSearch Library. Lombard, IL: Metromail Corp. (On CD-ROM.)

Phone Disc. Digital Directory Assistance. (On CD-ROM.)

Phone*File. Lombard, IL: Metromail Corp. (Online on *CompuServe.*)

ProPhone National Telephone Directory. Marblehead, MA: ProCD, Inc. (On CD-ROM.)

Membership Directories

Associations and organizations of all sizes will usually publish, either formally or informally, a directory of names and addresses (and sometimes phone numbers) of its members. Your library will probably collect those that represent an interest in the community (for example, a town that makes its money the silicon way will probably have directories of computer specialists) or a curriculum specialty for the institution an academic library serves. For example, some of the specialized directories purchased at the library I work for include:

AAA [American Anthropological Association] Guide: A Guide to Departments— A Directory of Members. Arlington, VA: AAA. Annual.

ALA Handbook of Organization and Membership Directory. Chicago: American Library Association. Annual.

Directory—Transportation Research Board. Washington, DC: National Research Council. Annual.

Before I plunge into a lengthy listing of the many expert directories available, I will begin with the Mother of All Expert Directories, the one that librarians usually refer to at least once a day. If your library does not own this directory, complain bitterly.

The Encyclopedia of Associations. 4 Volumes. Detroit: Gale. Annual.

Whether looking for an association that you know the name of or looking for one to match your topic, this is the place, my friend. (Almost) every type of association I have been able to imagine is in here. To show the breadth of this directory, here are some examples of the associations listed:

Scholarly Associations:
- American Mathematical Society
- Society for Linguistic Anthropology

Fun Associations:
- Antique Phonograph Collectors Club
- *Gilligan's Island* Fan Club

Business Associations:
- Disabled Business Persons Association
- Optical Industry Association

Naughty Associations:
- National Leather Association (No, they don't make shoes.)
- North American Swing Club Association

Professional Associations:
- American Association of Physics Teachers

- American Society of Mechanical Engineers

Religious Associations:
- Global Congress of the World's Religions
- International Christian Studies Association

For each organization named, the *Encyclopedia of Associations* provides name, address, phone, fax, year founded, number of members, membership dues, number of staff, budget, a description of the organization, whether it has a library and how many volumes it contains, publications it produces, and the dates and locations of upcoming conventions or major meetings. Use the Name and Keyword Index to locate an association either by its name or by a word that describes its function. Each association in the directory is assigned an entry number, so the number you see in the index is the entry number, not the page. Also when you see the designation *IO* in the index, it is referring you to the companion volume *International Organizations*.

Research Centers Directory. Detroit: Gale. Annual.
This one is on the same level of usefulness as the *Encyclopedia of Associations*. *RCD* identifies thousands of nonprofit research organizations. Research is always being conducted in almost any field you can imagine, and of course the person doing the research is hopefully an expert. A quick browse of the subject index shows entries for termites, teeth grinding (called Bruxism,) famine, copper and brambles. The entry for each organization lists name, address, phone, and fax, and de-

scribes its research activities and lists the kinds of publications it produces. Other research directories from this publisher: *Government Research Directory: The Comprehensive Guide to U.S. and Canadian Government Research Programs and Facilities* and *Research Services Directory: A One-Stop Guide to Commercial Research Activity.*

While the *Encyclopedia of Associations* will often supply the contacts you need, there will be times when you want even more specialized directories. Below are dozens of examples, arranged by subject.

Architects and Designers

Directory to Industrial Design in the United States: A Comprehensive Guide to People, Capabilities and Information. Charles Burnette + Associates. New York: Van Nostrand Reinhold, 1992.
A directory of consulting firms, design departments, schools, institutions, organizations and resources associated with industrial design. For most of the firms in the directory, representative design projects are listed.

ENR Directory of Design Firms. New York: McGraw-Hill/ENR. Annual.
Produced by the periodical *Engineering News-Record (ENR)*, this directory is aimed at prospective buyers of architectural, engineering and environmental services related to construction. So some of the groups in this directory include engineering consultants, design firms (domestic and international) and those who will conduct energy studies.

ProFile: The Directory of U.S. Architec-

tural Design Firms. Washington, DC: AIA Press. Annual.

ProFile is subdivided by state, with a separate roster of professional interest areas, identifying architectural firms with specialties in areas such as the environment, judicial buildings and healthcare facilities.

Business

Check chapter 6, "Company, Product and Industry Information" for directories full of experts in the field of business. One general directory not mentioned in that chapter:

National Directory of Addresses and Telephone Numbers: The Business to Business Book That Covers the Entire U.S.A. New York: Nicholas Publishing Co. Annual.

This thick volume contains what the publishers have identified as the "most frequently called" businesses, associations, government agencies and media in the United States. In this directory you can find the phone and fax numbers for such disparate offerings as *National Lampoon Magazine*, the University of Alaska at Anchorage and the Butler Paper Company (the latter at seven locations). The first half of the book, the white pages, provides listings in alphabetical order; the second half is the Yellow Pages Classified Section, arranged by type of business.

Columnists

Is the person who writes the software column for a computer magazine a journalist who is very good at interpreting the words of others or an expert himself? Columnists may be subject experts who write columns as a sideline. They can

usually be reached through the magazine or newspaper they write for, or simply be listed in the phone book. (Hint: Always check the local phone book, no matter how "famous" you think someone is. Many years ago I looked up the phone number of a radio personality I admired. I was soliciting a testimonial for a local library association. I called the number, sure that it couldn't be the person I sought. They answered! "I'm surprised you don't have an unlisted number," I said, "You're famous!" He laughed and assured me that his "better half wouldn't agree.")

Some writers work with syndicators and can be reached through those organizations. One directory that will help connect you with columnists is the *Editor and Publisher Syndicate Directory.* (New York: The Editor and Publisher Co.). This is an annual special issue of the magazine *Editor and Publisher*, released every July. Other directories worth checking for finding columnists are the *Gale Directory of Publications and Broadcast Media, The Working Press of the Nation* and the *Media Yellow Pages* (see below under the heading "Media").

Criminal Justice and Law

The Best Lawyers in America. Steven Naifeh and Gregory White Smith. 5th edition. Aiken, SC: Woodward/ White, 1993.

A geographic listing of some of the lawyers in America judged to be outstanding; a mix, as the authors say, of "successful power-brokers and lawyers' lawyers." (Be aware that such lists are victim to some subjectivity. Many lawyers as capable as those in this book will not be listed.)

BNA's *Directory of State and Federal Courts, Judges and Clerks: A State-by-State Listing*. 4th edition. Washington, DC: Bureau of National Affairs, 1992. Each section opens with a family tree representation of the court system for that state. Phone numbers and addresses are provided for the many state court judges and clerks within each jurisdiction.

Judicial Staff Directory. Ann L. Brownson, editor. Mount Vernon, VA: Staff Directories, Ltd. Annual.

A directory to the federal courts and the people who work in them; includes tax, bankruptcy, circuit and district courts as well as the Supreme Court. There is also a biography section, covering almost two thousand judges and staff members.

Law Firms Yellow Book: Who's Who in the Management of the Leading U.S. Law Firms. New York: Monitor Publishing Co. Semiannual.

The largest and (in the editors' opinions) the most influential national law firms are in this directory, along with names of the members of management, the departments and department heads, administrative staff and foreign and U.S. offices. Direct numbers are often supplied for the persons named. There are indexes by department (type of law/cases handled), by law schools attended, by personnel, by geographical location and by name of the law firm.

Martindale-Hubbell Buyer's Guide: Services, Suppliers and Consultants to the Legal Profession. 1st edition. New Providence, NJ: Martindale-Hubbell, 1994.

Lawyers require the services of those in some fairly fascinating professions. Some of the names and numbers in this directory are for such people as Expert Witnesses (in over 100 categories, including Aquatic Injuries and Drownings, Dental, and Unlawful Restraint,) Bodyguards and those specializing in Repossession Services.

Martindale-Hubbell Law Directory. 17 Volumes. New Providence, NJ: Martindale-Hubbell. Annual.

One of the oldest and best-known directories of lawyers and law firms. The first fifteen volumes, arranged by city and state for the U.S. and province for Canada, are subdivided into sections that list profiles of law practices and lawyers. Volumes 16 and 17 are the index volumes. Also available: the two-volume *Martindale-Hubbell International Law Directory*, published separately (though often on the shelf with the U.S. set), and the *United States Law Digest* volumes, also published separately and described in chapter 11.

National Directory of Law Enforcement Administrators, Correctional Institutions and Related Agencies. Stevens Point, WI: National Police Chiefs and Sheriffs. Annual.

A guide to chiefs of police, city sheriffs, county sheriffs and police, county and district prosecutors, campus law enforcement, Bureau of Indian Affairs and tribal law enforcement, airport and harbor police, and state police and highway patrols. Agencies for each state are also supplied, including state criminal investigation units and conservation law enforcement agencies.

There is a fairly detailed section on Canadian law enforcement. International agencies for eighty-one countries are also listed.

National Jail and Adult Detention Directory. Laurel, MD: American Correctional Association. Biennial.

A state-by-state listing of correctional facilities. The name of the chief administrator is provided for each facility. The ACA also publishes *Directory: Juvenile and Adult Correctional Departments, Institutions, Agencies and Paroling Agencies.*

Education

How often have you heard or read "expert commentary" from a professor at a university or college? Quite often, I'd bet. Professors are normally glad to share their expertise in their particular area of study; especially if it's an opportunity to enhance his or her reputation or to promote the institution they work for.

You basically have two avenues to go in contacting subject authorities who work in higher education:

1. Call any college or university and ask if they have a program and therefore an expert in the field you are interested in. Use the phone book or your telephone company's Information service. Often, being connected with the institution's public relations department will be your best route.

2. Call a university or college that you are *sure* has the experts you need. To find these numbers, use both general and specialized higher education directories, such as:

General North American Higher Education Directories, Sample Titles:

The College Blue Book. New York: Macmillan Information. Annual.

A five-volume directory to colleges and universities in the United States and Canada. Volume 1, titled *Narrative Descriptions,* supplies phone numbers and addresses along with a description of the institution, its entrance requirements, costs per year, and college and campus environment. Use Volume 3, *Degrees Offered by College,* and Subject to look under particular majors to find the schools that offer them. Volume 4 lists institutions that offer training in *Occupational Education,* such as law enforcement, hotel and motel management and medical transcription. The remaining volumes supply *Tabular Information* (Volume 2) and *Information on Scholarships, Fellowships, Grants, and Loans* (Volume 5).

HEP Higher Education Directory. Mary Pat Rodenhouse, editor. Falls Church, VA: Higher Education Publications.

Also known as the HEP directory. Universities and two- and four-year colleges are listed in geographic order. This directory is especially useful because of the many names of administrators that it lists, including the President, various Vice Presidents and Deans, Registrar, Library Head, Directors of departments, such as athletics, handicapped services and so on.

Lovejoy's College Guide. New York: Prentice-Hall. Biennial.

Lovejoy's is a one-volume guide to

U.S. colleges that supplies data and description for each institution of interest to the potential student.

Peterson's Guide to Graduate Programs. Princeton, NJ: Peterson's Guides. Annual.
A series of six books, organized by field of study, providing descriptive information and contact information for institutions that supply accredited graduate study in the United States and U.S.-accredited programs in Canada, Mexico, Europe and Africa.
Book 1—Overview
Book 2—The Humanities
Book 3—Biological and Agricultural Sciences
Book 4—Physical Sciences and Mathematics
Book 5—Engineering and Applied Sciences
Book 6—Business

You can also try looking in some specialized higher education directories for North America, such as:

Annual Directory of Graduate Law Programs in the United States. West Hartford, CT: The Graduate Group. Annual.

Association of American Medical Colleges Directory of Medical Education. Washington, DC: AAMC. Annual.

Dance Magazine College Guide: A Directory of Dance in North American Colleges and Universities. New York: Dance Magazine. Annual.

Guide to College Programs in Hospitality and Tourism: A Directory of CHRIE

(Council of Hotel, Restaurant and Institutional Education) Member Colleges and Universities. New York: Wiley. Annual.

Guide to Programs of Geography in the United States and Canada. Washington, DC: Association of American Geographers. Annual.

Guide to Photography Workshops and Schools. Coral Gables, FL: Shaw Associates. Annual.

Handel's National Directory for the Performing Arts. Dallas: NDPA. Annual.

To find other specialized catalogs in your library's online catalog, try a subject search using the following phrases:
EDUCATION DIRECTORIES
STUDY DIRECTORIES (*If you are using a card catalog, try the heading* STUDY AND TEACHING.)

and match those phrases with a word or words that describe the field of study you are looking for, for example:
PSYCHOLOGY STUDY DIRECTORIES
BUSINESS EDUCATION DIRECTORIES

If you do hear the name of a particular instructor in higher education and want to find their campus address, try the three-volume *National Faculty Directory* (Detroit: Gale. Annual), which is an alphabetic listing of more than 600,000 faculty members around the country.

There are a number of directories that contain contact information for colleges and universities beyond North America, such as:

Some International Higher Education Directories:

International Handbook of Universities. International Association of Universities. Paris: M. Stockton Press. Biennial.

Arranged in order by country, this handbook supplies narrative concerning institutions of higher education throughout the world that grant degrees at the university level. (Other institutions of higher education are included in the biennial volume also produced by this organization, the *World List of Universities*.) Each institutional entry lists the major departments, the number of staff in each department, the name of the department head, a short history and description of the school, admission requirements, degrees granted, volumes in the library and a breakdown of the number of faculty members at different academic ranks (i.e., instructor, assistant professor, etc.).

The World of Learning. London: Europa Publications, Ltd. Annual.

There are more than 26,000 listings for institutes of higher learning in *The World of Learning*. Arranged geographically by nation, there are entries for Academies, Learned Societies, Research Institutes, Libraries, Museums and Universities. Each university listing contains address, phone, fax, telex, the number of teachers, students and volumes in the library, beginning and ending months of the academic year and the names of each of the department heads. This is a standard source at most midsized to large public and academic libraries.

To Contact Elementary and Secondary Schools, consult:

The Handbook of Private Schools: An Annual Descriptive Survey of Independent Education. Boston: Porter Sargent Publishers. Annual.

A standard guide to the many independent schools of the United States and a smattering of those abroad. The major portion of the book consists of descriptions of leading private schools, presented by geographic region, listing such data as tuition costs, student enrollment, number of faculty, entrance tests required, work program availability and a basic description of the curriculum offered (i.e., college preparatory, pre-preparatory, general academic, specialized or vocational). There is an index to schools with special features, such as all boys, all girls or boarding schools with enrollments of one hundred or less. Comparable to this volume is the *Bunting and Lyon Blue Book: Private Independent Schools* (Wallingford, CT: Bunting and Lyon. Annual).

The ISS Directory of Overseas Schools. Princeton, NJ: International Schools Services, 1994.

The ISS Directory is an international guide to K-12 learning, arranged in alphabetical order by country. These are schools that cater to English-speaking students, not the general public schools of each area. Information for each school includes foreign address, phone, fax, e-mail address, the name of the principal and other administrators, the number of full- and part-time staff, the nationalities of the staff, grade levels handled, student-to-teacher ratio, number of students enrolled, tuition and fees and the range of the school year. A narrative description is also supplied, usually highlighting aspects of the curriculum, extracurricular activities, facilities, the number of graduates who went on to college and the names of any prestigious U.S. institutions that they went on to.

Patterson's American Education. Mount Prospect, IL: Educational Directories. Annual.

Found in most libraries, *Patterson's* contains contacts for educational associations and societies and high schools, including public, Catholic, Lutheran and Seventh-Day Adventists. Also from this publisher: *Patterson's Elementary Education.*

Environment

Access EPA. 3d edition. Washington, DC: U.S. Environmental Protection Agency, 1993.

A guide to environmental products and services available from the Environmental Protection Agency and other related agencies. A contact name is generally provided. This guide is distributed to all full depository libraries (and others may have purchased it).

Conservation Directory: A List of Organizations, Agencies and Officials Concerned With Natural Resource Use and Management. Rue E. Gordon, editor. Washington, DC: National Wildlife Federation. Annual.

The National Wildlife Federation, with over 5.3 million members, sup-

porters and affiliate organizations, is also the publisher of the periodicals *National Wildlife, International Wildlife* and *Ranger Rick,* the nature magazine for children. You might guess that they have some pretty good connections in the field of conservation! You would be right, and they're listed in this directory. There are name, subject and publication indexes (the latter listing alphabetically all publications listed throughout the directory).

Environmental Telephone Directory. Editorial Staff. Government Institutes. Biennial.

Contact information is supplied for environmental contacts in federal and state government, including: the aides to U.S. Senators and Representatives that work with environmental issues, Senate and House Committees and Subcommittees, and staff at the Environmental Protection Agency and state environmental agencies.

People of Color Environmental Groups. Robert D. Bullard. Atlanta: Environmental Justice Resource Center, Clark Atlanta University, 1994-95.

A listing of more than three hundred groups from forty states, Washington DC, Puerto Rico, Canada and Mexico who are working on environmental and economic justice issues. The mission, issues and activities of each group are stated.

World Directory of Environmental Organizations. 4th edition. Claremont, CA: California Institute of Public Affairs. Updated Irregularly.

A listing of green organizations in the United States and around the world.

Gay and Lesbian

The Alyson Almanac 1994-1995: The Fact Book of the Gay and Lesbian Community. Boston: Alyson Publications, 1993.

The *Alyson Almanac* lists events in the history of homosexuality, reports on current events and provides biographies. Essays are featured that discuss health issues and romance. And like most almanacs, there's lots more, like a dictionary of slang and a judging of the best and worst literary and dramatic portrayals of gays and lesbians. And finally (since this is the chapter on experts, isn't it?)—*Alyson's* lists directory information for organizations such as the Gay and Lesbian Press Association and the National Coalition for Black Lesbians and Gays.

The 100 Best Companies for Gay Men and Lesbians. Ed Mickens. New York: Pocket Books, 1994.

This directory pinpoints firms with such practices as: inclusion of gay and lesbian issues in their training programs, rules forbidding discrimination based on sexual orientation and the provision of healthcare benefits for same-sex partners.

Spartacus International Gay Guide. Amsterdam: Spartacus International. Annual.

You should *see* the guy on the cover of this guide . . . Fabio stand aside. *Spartacus International* is a travel guide for "men who like men." For each

travel destination the directory includes names, locations and some descriptions of local attractions and organizations of particular interest to the gay community. Listings include restaurants, hotels, groups such as the Gay Amateur Surfers in Australia and the Gay and Lesbian Youth of Buffalo, cruising areas (and they don't mean using a sailboat), gay radio and television, shops, sex clubs, escort services and health spas. The text is in English, German, French, Italian and Spanish.

General—Listings of Experts in All Areas

Directory of British Associations and Associations in Ireland. G.P. Henderson and S.P.A. Henderson. Kent, England: CBD Research, Ltd. Annual.

Though there are directories in this section that are international in coverage, you will probably find more information when looking at a guide that focuses on one or two countries, like this one does. Unfortunately, such directories will be less plentiful on library shelves. The reason: they are fairly expensive and it can be a big pain to order non-U.S. items that are not distributed in the United States. Also from this publisher: *Directory of European Industrial and Trade Associations* (1971-present) and the *Directory of European Professional and Learned Societies* (1975-present).

Lesko's Info-Power II. Matthew Lesko. 2d edition. Detroit: Visible Ink Press, 1994.

A veritable library of phone numbers and addresses of experts and contacts for almost any information need. Organizations and agencies are listed that represent needs of consumers, job-seekers, artists, employers, travelers and, of course, writers. (Also available on disc and through *CompuServe*.)

The National Fax Directory. Karin E. Koek, editor. Detroit: Gale. Annual.

Both geographic and subject access are provided in this compilation of more than ten thousand fax and phone numbers at corporations, financial institutions, government agencies, media and publishing organizations, nonprofit groups, libraries and educational institutions.

The Yearbook of Experts, Authorities and Spokespersons: An Encyclopedia of Sources. Washington, DC: Broadcast Interview Source. Annual.

The *Yearbook* opens with over 150 pages of possible topic ideas, including Cat Allergies, Corn, Electric Toothbrushes, Hunger, Living Wills, Sex and Yugoslavia. The listings of experts follows, an assortment of Universities, Foundations, Companies and Organizations. There is a geographic index, arranged by ZIP code, which can be used to quickly see if there is an expert available in a specific location.

Yearbook of International Organizations. K.G. Sauer. 3 Volumes. Annual.

Organizations of all types are included, both nongovernment-related (i.e., the International Weightlifting Federation) and governmental (i.e., the United Nations). Volume 1 describes the organizations and gives contact information, listing the associations alphabetically by name, Volume 2 is the Geographic Volume, with organizations arranged and identified by country, and Volume 3 is the Subject Directory and Index.

Labor Organizations

American Directory of Organized Labor: Unions, Locals, Agreements and Employers. Cynthia Russell Spommer, editor. Detroit: Gale, 1992.

Address, phone, affiliation and contact name are supplied for regional, state and local labor unions. More data is provided for "parent" unions, including the year founded, number of members, election date, convention date, the names of key officials and their salaries, union financial data, a general description, present activities, summary of agreements and any special services offered. Selected bargaining agreements are highlighted in two separate sections; one arranged by union, the other in order by the name of the employer. There are indexes by Industry, Geography, AFL-CIO Affiliated Union and Master Name/Keyword.

Directory of U.S. Labor Organizations. Courtney D. Gifford, Washington, DC: Bureau of National Affairs. Biennial.

Address, phone, fax and administrator information is provided for AFL-CIO Trade and Industrial Departments and Staff Departments in Washington, DC, and state federations and central labor councils throughout the United States. Part III, the List of Labor Organizations, lists contact information, date of convention, number of members, year founded, any publications produced, and the names of individuals responsible for areas such as research, organizing, accounting and education. There are indexes arranged by abbreviation (of organization), organization and name. Contact information for local chapters is not provided, as it is in the *American Directory of Organized Labor*, described above.

Libraries

The most highly used directories to libraries are fully described in chapter 1, "Navigating the Library."

Media

Broadcasting and Cable Yearbook. [Formerly called *Broadcasting and Cable Market Place* and *Broadcasting Yearbook*.] 2 Volumes. New Providence, NJ: R.R. Bowker. Annual.

A standard source in most midsize to large academic and public libraries. In addition to major broadcast stations, the *Yearbook* lists low-power, Spanish-language and experimental stations along with those that are college, university or school-owned. There are listings for Multiple System (Cable) Operators, satellite owners and operators, advertising and marketing specialists, and suppliers of programming, technical and professional services. There are also quite a few varied statistics scattered throughout these volumes, including sales of radios, TV usage per home per week at different times of the day and week, and cable "penetration" broken down by "Designated Market Areas" (geographic areas determined by the A.C. Nielsen Company).

News Media Yellow Book: Who's Who Among Reporters, Writers, Editors and Producers in the Leading National News Media. New York: Monitor Leadership Directories. Semiannual.

The *Yellow Book* provides names and professional titles for those in news services (such as feature syndicates or news bureaus), newspapers, cable-radio-television stations, programs, networks and some periodical publishers. A highlight: Some direct numbers are listed for individuals.

Radio Amateur Callbook. New York: Watson-Guptill Publications. Annual.

A listing of calls, names and addresses for hundreds of thousands of licensed radio amateurs. One volume covers North America, another contains international listings.

WRTH: World Radio TV Handbook. Andrew G. Sennitt, editor. Amsterdam, The Netherlands: Billboard Books, 1994.

WRTH lists, country-by-country, long, medium and shortwave broadcasters, with such extras as an hour-by-hour guide to broadcasts in English directed to particular areas, and listings of stations in frequency order to help facilitate finding them quickly.

Medical Professionals/Health Support Organizations

The AIDS Directory: An Essential Guide to the 1500 Leaders in Research, Services, Policy, Advocacy and Funding. 1st edition. Washington, DC: Buraff Publications, 1993.

A compilation of names and numbers of those working on AIDS from all angles: looking for a cure, helping those that are already ill, and working to prevent others from becoming infected.

Alternative Health Care Resources: A Directory and Guide. Brett Jason Sinclair. West Nyack, NY: Parker Publishing Co., 1992.

Organized by health condition or health-related topic (such as Childbirth, Longevity and Aging, and Mind-Body Connection), each chapter recommends alternative organizations, self-help groups and publications that offer healing techniques or education. There are two sections for each entry, The Background (of the organization, and sometimes the health topic) and What's Offered (a description of what can be expected from the organization or publication).

Alternative Medicine Yellow Pages: The Comprehensive Guide to the New World of Health. Puyallup, WA: Future Medicine Publishing, 1994.

A phone-book-like guide to alternative-therapies practitioners and groups, including those who work with Biofeedback Training, Enzyme Therapy, Meditation, Sound Therapy and Yoga.

American Dental Directory. Chicago, IL: American Dental Association. Annual.

A directory to names and addresses of all U.S. dentists, including those living abroad and affiliate, associate and honorary ADA members. Check the codes in the front of the book; they will help you find the additional

information provided in each entry, which includes each doctor's specialty, dental school attended and year of graduation. There is a separate index by specialty. The main directory is in geographic order.

The Best Doctors in America, 1994-1995. Steven Naifeh and Gregory White Smith. Aiken, SC: Woodward/White, 1994.

The men and women listed in this directory are the physicians that other physicians and professionals in the medical field would choose to send their loved ones to. (Now this book must be, of course, selective. So if your physician is not listed, don't worry!) Still, these may be the people to give a call to when you need some expert input for your writing. The doctors are listed in chapters divided by specialties, such as Pain, Hand Surgery, Thyroid and Herpes.

The Complete Directory for People with Chronic Illness. Leslie MacKenzie, editor. Lakeville, CT: Grey House Publishing, 1994.

If you are trying to find information about some of the persistent illnesses plaguing humankind, use this directory to find experts. It lists associations, research groups and support groups (as well as informative publications) for such disorders as Chronic Fatigue Syndrome, Cystic Fibrosis and Charcot-Marie-Tooth disease (the latter characterized by weakness and wasting away of the muscles in the legs).

Drug, Alcohol and Other Addictions: A Directory of Treatment Centers and Pre-

vention Programs Nationwide. 2d edition. Phoenix, AZ: Oryx Press, 1993.

Over twelve thousand U.S. programs and facilities are identified that work with the prevention and treatment of alcohol, drug and behavioral addictions. Each listing specifies the type of addiction the program or institution works with, and what treatment programs they use.

Hospital Blue Book. Atlanta: Billian Publishing. Annual.

A nationwide directory of hospitals, diagnosis-related groups (DRGs), Healthcare Systems Listings, Health Maintenance Organizations (HMOs and PPOs). Other hospital and health facility directories that may be in your local academic, public or hospital library:

   The Directory of Nursing Homes. Baltimore: HCIA. 1994.
   The Directory of U.S. Hospitals. Baltimore: HCIA. Annual.
   Guide to the Nation's Hospices. Arlington, VA: National Hospice Organization. Annual.
   Register of North American Hospitals. South River, NJ: American Preeminent Registry. Annual.

International Directory of Bioethics Organizations. Anita L. Nolen and Mary Carrington Coutts. Washington, DC: Kennedy Institute of Ethics, Georgetown University, 1993.

There are many controversies when it comes to ethics in medical research and treatment. Should there be physician-assisted suicides? Should fetal tissue be used for research? Talk to some of the experts at these organizations and get their opinion.

The Medical Directory. Harlow, Essex: Longman Group, Ltd. Annual.

A multivolume set listing physicians of the United Kingdom. A work address is usually provided. Medical organizations are also listed in the last volume, including hospitals and medical schools.

National Healthlines Directory (Toll-Free Numbers). Louanne Marinos, compiler. Arlington, VA: Information Resources Press, 1992.

This directory supplies "800" numbers for over two hundred organizations that provide telephone responses to health topic queries. The list is alphabetical by name of organization and there is a subject index. Of interest to writers: two organizations can help with "headache" problems and there is one for smoking cessation (but none for writer's cramp or writer's block).

The Official ABMS Directory of Board Certified Medical Specialists. New Providence, NJ: Marquis Who's Who. Annual.

You can find names of physicians in this multivolume directory two ways: by Specialty (such as Dermatology or Family Practice) and alphabetically. The Specialty Sections, which comprise most of this directory, are broken down geographically by states and cities (and some foreign countries), with the doctors listed alphabetically within each geographic region. Biographical information is provided for each physician, with a typical sketch including such elements as type of practice, place where residency was fulfilled, staff positions and professional memberships. Take a moment to look at the pointers, located in the front of the first volume, on how to read each entry.

Minorities

Black Americans Information Directory. Wendy S. de Sande, editor. 3d edition. Detroit: Gale, 1993.

More than 53,000 names of organizations, agencies, institutions, programs and publications concerned with black American life and culture are listed in this information guide. Other publications in this series:

Asian Americans Information Directory

Hispanic Americans Information Directory

Native American Information Directory

Older Americans Information Directory

Hispanic Resource Directory: A Comprehensive Guide to Over 6,000 National, Regional and Local Organizations, Associations, Agencies, Programs and Media Pertaining to Hispanic Americans. Alan Edward Schorr. Juneau, Alaska: The Denali Press, 1992.

The names and addresses of the contacts are listed in sixteen chapters. Headings include State and Local Hispanic Commissions, Hispanic Chambers of Commerce, Research Centers, Libraries and Museums, and Media. Also from this publisher: *The Refugee and Immigrant Resource Directory*, produced every three years.

Reference Encyclopedia of the American Indian. Barry T. Klein. 6th edition.

West Nyack, NY: Todd Publications, 1993.

A compendium of Native American facts and contacts. Some of the facts: Federally Recognized Tribes, Biographies of prominent Native Americans and a lengthy bibliography of resources; some of the contacts: Reservations, Tribal Councils, National Associations, Museums, Monuments, Parks and Arts and Crafts Shops. This volume covers both the United States and Canada.

The Occult

Encyclopedia of Occultism & Parapsychology: A Compendium of Information on the Occult Sciences, Magic, Demonology, Superstitions, Spiritism, Mysticism, Metaphysics, Psychical Science, and Parapsychology, with Biographical and Bibliographical Notes and Comprehensive Indexes. Leslie Shepard, editor. 3d edition. Detroit: Gale, 1991.

An eclectic compendium of otherworldly (or perhaps just beyond our understanding?) information. Notable is this work's inclusion of prominent modern-day and historic figures in the occult sciences, including academics, scientists and psychologists. The Societies and Organizations heading in the Topical Index lists a number of associations, groups and academies for those with an interest in wraiths and unexplained phenomena, including the Ghost Club, the Ghost Research Society, the Society for Research on Rapport and Telekinesis (SORRAT), and the Spiritualist Mediums' Alliance.

Guide to the American Occult: Directory and Bibliography. Wilcox, Laird.

Olathe, KS: Editorial Research Service, 1990.

The organizations listed in this directory have some connection to things occult, paranormal, metaphysical, mystical, parapsychological or psychic, which actually makes for quite a variety. Just a few of the organizations identified include the American Celtic Order of Wicca in St. Paul, the Institute of Metaphysics in L.A., and the New York School of Astrology in Manhattan. Organizations are listed in both alphabetic and geographic order. (Remember—those geographically arranged listings in any directory may always be useful to a writer in pinpointing groups of interest in his or her town.) This guide also lists occult publications and associations that oppose the occult, and it contains a glossary of terms (such as Animatism—the attraction of consciousness to inanimate objects, and Zener Cards—cards used in experimental tests for ESP).

Performing, Visual and Fine Arts

Art Marketing Sourcebook for the Fine Artist: Where to Sell Your Artwork. Constance Franklin-Smith. Renaissance, CA: Directors Guild Publishers, 1992.

This is a guide to more than two thousand art world professionals: dealers, galleries, art organizations and publishers. Each dealer listing describes the type of art work the dealer is interested in, what the review process entails, rate of commission and how many artists he or she represents. For each U.S. and foreign art gallery, exhibit space and museum listed the

entries state some of the following information: founding year, days and hours of operation, number of shows annually, number of artists represented, some financial information, what type of artistic medium is preferred, who the art is offered for sale to and whether or not gallery/museum is looking for new artists.

The Artist's Resource Handbook. Daniel Grant. New York: Allworth Press and the American Council for the Arts, 1994.

The names and addresses in this guide cover organizations that assist with career-finding in the field of art, professional services for artists, art associations, financial assistance outlets, artist-in-residence programs, art colonies and public art programs.

Celebrity Access: The Directory. Mill Valley, CA: Celebrity Access Publications. Annual.

Celebrity Access furnishes names and mailing addresses (these are not home addresses) of actors, actresses and selected people in politics, science and the arts. (Just as a test I looked up one of my favorites, Tom Hanks. There were three possible listings.)

Christianson's Movie, T.V., Rock 'n' Roll, and Sports Address Directory. 4th revised edition. San Diego: Cardiff-By-The-Sea, 1992.

Over forty thousand addresses of actors, rock musicians and sports players are listed.

Film Producers, Studios, Agents and Casting Directors Guide. David M. Kipen and Jack Lechner. 3d edition. Los

Angeles: Lone Eagle Publishing Co., 1992.

There is a business address, phone and fax listed for most of the filmmakers in this directory. In addition to contact information, the film producer section lists U.S. film credits of the past few decades for each producer. The film title index makes it simple to find the producer of a particular film you have admired. There are also credits listed for some of the casting directors. Other directories from this publisher include *Film Director: A Complete Guide* (Michael Singer, 1992) and *Film Actors Guide* (Steven LuKanic, 1991).

Motion Picture, TV and Theatre Directory for Services and Products. Tarrytown, NY: Motion Picture Enterprises Publications. Semiannual.

A mini-yellow pages to those who are the backbone of the broadcast, film and theatre industries: camera crews, scenic designers, editing services, lighting consultants, producers, public relations people and, of course, caterers.

Musical America: International Directory of the Performing Arts. New York: Musical America Publishing. Annual.

In this international directory you will be able to locate names and addresses of managers, orchestras, opera and dance companies, choral groups, record companies, state arts agencies, those directing performing arts series and festivals, and schools for arts administration study and music study. There are also entries for contests, foundations, awards and music publications.

National Directory of Record Labels and Music Publishing. 4th edition. Atlanta: Rising Star Publishing, 1994.

Each listing indicates the style of music that the publisher or label specializes in. Just calling one of these interesting-sounding labels, such as Hula Records in Honolulu, might generate an article. Or perhaps Jungle Boy Music, publishers in Santa Monica.

Stern's Performing Arts Directory. Allen E. McCormack, editor-in-chief. New York: Robert D. Stern. Annual.

A directory for dance and music information, with entries for dance companies, instructors, choreographers and educators, and music ensembles, orchestras, composers and conductors. Others who supply services or resources for dance and music ensembles are also named.

TCG Theatre Directory. New York: Theatre Communications Group. Annual.

A guide to nonprofit professional theaters in the United States. There is also a section devoted to arts organizations that serve nonprofit theaters and performing artists, such as Volunteer Lawyers for the Arts, who provide free legal assistance to eligible performers and nonprofit theaters whose problems are arts-related, and the Non-Traditional Casting Project, an advocacy group that works to increase the use of women, disabled people and a variety of ethnic groups in theater, film and television.

Want's Theatre Directory. Washington, DC: WANT Publishing Co. Annual.

Want's has names and numbers of about seven hundred U.S. and Canadian theaters for the performing arts, as well as some major theaters in London and Western Europe. Also provided are seating charts for selected Broadway theaters and a nationwide tour schedule for major Broadway shows.

Political and Judicial Figures and Government Agencies—U.S. and Foreign

Remember that you are a voting constituent and the staff members in both federal and state legislators' offices are often available to help you (the constituent) out with answers to your research questions. There are plenty of directories that will get you to the right people.

County Executive Directory. Washington, DC: Carroll Publishing Co. Annual.

A directory to key contacts in county governments. Also from this publisher:
Federal Executive Directory
Federal Regional Executive Directory
Municipal Executive Directory
State Executive Directory

Congressional Yellow Book: Who's Who in Congress Including Committees and Key Staff. Washington, DC: Monitor Leadership Directories, 1976-present.

Updated quarterly, this volume is packed with useful information. A page of information is provided for each senator and representative that includes a photo of the legislator, phone, fax, address, the names and responsibilities of his or her staff aides, a listing of the lawmaker's committee assignments and brief biographical data that includes date of birth, area

of residence, educational degree(s) and religion. In separate sections committees and organizations are described, listing current membership address and phone number. E-mail addresses are also included when available. This publisher also produces:
Federal Yellow Book
Municipal Yellow Book
State Yellow Book

Encyclopedia of Governmental Advisory Organizations: A Reference Guide to Over 6,500 Permanent, Continuing and Ad Hoc U.S. Presidential Advisory Committees, Congressional Advisory Committees, Public Advisory Committees, Interagency Committees and Other Government-Related Boards, Panels, Task Forces, Commissions, Conferences and Other Similar Bodies Serving in a Consultative, Coordinating, Advisory, Research or Investigative Capacity. Donna Batten, editor. 9th edition. Detroit: Gale Research, 1994-95.

This directory is just as wide-ranging a source for experts in all fields as the *Encyclopedia of Associations* and the *Research Centers Directory.* Just think of the thousands of laws and regulations our country is run by, and the many people the government consults with to uphold, institute or regulate those laws, and you get a good idea of how many experts this directory can put you in touch with. Examples of the varied Committees listed include: The Indian Arts and Crafts Board, The Technical Pipeline Safety Standards Committee and The Women's Health Initiate Advisory Committee.

Each entry explains the History and Authority of the Committee (i.e., if it was established by a particular Public

Law, by Executive Order or at the request of an agency), describes the Program (function) of the Committee, the number of members (though only the name of the chair is provided), and what publications, if any, they produce.

Congressional Quarterly's Federal Regulatory Directory. Washington, DC: Congressional Quarterly. Updated Irregularly.

This book contains in-depth profiles of major U.S. regulatory agencies, including their history, powers, methods, name, phone, addresses of key officials and listings of branch offices. Examples of the types of agencies listed include the Securities and Exchange Commission, the Social Security Administration, the Interstate Commerce Commission, the Federal Railroad Administration and the Federal Reserve System.

Offical Congressional Directory. Washington, DC: U.S. Congress, Joint Committee on Printing. Annual.

A list of who is in Congress and how to contact them. The emphasis is on the legislative branch, but there are listings for the judicial and executive branches as well.

Municipal Year Book: The Authoritative Source Book of Urban Data and Developments. The International City/County Management Association. Washington, DC: ICMA. Annual.

Commonly found in midsize to large public and academic libraries, the *Municipal Year Book* is a combination of articles concerning the cutting edge of county/city administration, statistics that cover salaries of municipal employees, and a directory of names, addresses and phone numbers for state municipal leagues, state, provincial, and international municipal management associations, directors of councils of government, and appointed and elected municipal officials. I use this yearly volume fairly often in my work as a reference librarian, usually to find the name of a fire chief, police chief, mayor or city clerk. This book does not usually provide the direct phone number you need for a particular official, just the general information number for the municipality or county.

Staff Directory on CD-ROM. Mount Vernon, VA: Staff Directories. Semiannual.

A detailed list of the staff who work for each member of Congress, more than 20,000 employees of the executive branch of government, and over 1,000 federal judges and their staffs. This information is also available in three print directories produced by the same publisher:
Congressional Staff Directory (also available on floppy disk)
Federal Staff Directory
Judicial Staff Directory

Washington Information Directory. Jerry A. Orvedahl, editor. Washington, DC: Congressional Quarterly. Annual.

Each of the eighteen chapters in this guide covers a broad subject area, such as Education and Culture, Health and Transportation. Within each of these chapters you will find contacts for federal governmental agencies and committees associated with the topic, as well as relevant private and nonprofit associations. All of the agencies, organizations and groups listed are in Washington, DC. Take advantage of the detailed table of contents preceding each chapter.

Washington Representatives: Who Does What for Whom in the Nation's Capital. Arthur C. Close, J. Valerie Steele and Michael E. Buckner, editors. New York: Columbia Books. Annual.

This directory will help get you in touch with lobbyists, consultants, legal advisors and public affairs and government relations representatives.

Political Figures and Government Agencies—Foreign

Diplomatic List. Washington, DC: U.S. Dept. of State. Quarterly.

The addresses for foreign U.S. embassies are listed along with the names and titles of all of the diplomatic staffs and their spouses. You will find this publication in all government depository libraries and some other libraries.

EC Information Handbook. Brussels: EC Committee of the American Chamber of Commerce in Belgium. Annual.

There are many institutions that comprise the European Community, such as the Commission of the European Community, the European Parliament and the EC Courts. This guide supplies descriptions of these bodies and the names and addresses of administrators and others. Also listed are some related nongovernmental agencies, like The Association of the Monetary Union of Europe, and world

organizations, including the Organization for Economic Cooperation and Development (OECD).

Foreign Consular Offices in the United States. U.S. Dept. of State. Quarterly.

A "complete and official" listing of the foreign consular offices in the U.S. These offices and their consular officers, located throughout the United States, act as representatives to foreign governments for a variety of purposes. They can supply business information, such as license requirements, trade quotas and even ideas on the needs and preferences of consumers of the country the office represents.

Key Officers of Foreign Service Posts: Guide for Business Representatives. Department of State, Office of Information Services, Publishing Services Division. Washington, DC: Updated twice a year.

A listing of officials at foreign service posts whom American business representatives would most likely want to contact, including representatives at embassies, missions and consulates. The first few pages of the book explain the duties of various officials, to help you decide who would be the best person to contact. For example, Scientific Attachés follow the technological and scientific developments in a country; Political Officers analyze and report on political developments and their potential impact on U.S. interests. Abbreviations are listed in the back.

Russian Government Today. New York: Carroll Publishing Co. Biannual.

A listing of almost nine thousand

Russian government contacts. A description of Russian government organizations and their functions is also given.

Worldwide Governments Directory: With International Organizations. Ken Gause, editor-in-chief. Bethesda, MD: Worldwide Government Directories. Annual.

This directory outlines, country by country, the structure of government for almost two hundred nations. Name, phone, fax and address are supplied for thousands of officials of world government, including heads of state, ministries and departments, and officials of legislative and judicial entities, the central bank, the country's United Nations mission and foreign embassies located in that country. In addition, more than one hundred major international and regional organizations are named, along with names of their executive officers and contact information. Examples of organizations listed include The European Committee for Standardization (CEN-CENELEC), the United Nations Children's Fund (UNICEF) and the Association of Southeast Asian Nations (ASEAN).

Social Services and Public Interest Organizations

Your library will own many specialized social services directories that are unique to your city or town. Some national directories:

Public Interest Profiles. Foundation for Public Affairs. Washington, DC: Congressional Quarterly. Biennial.

The public interest groups described

in this volume fall under twelve major headings. The headings, with an example of a representative organization for each, are: Business/Economic (Citizens for Tax Justice), Civil/Constitutional Rights (National Council of La Raza), Community/Grassroots (Nuclear Free America), Consumer/Health (Center for Science in the Public Interest), Corporate Accountability/Responsibility (United Shareholders Association), Environmental (Sierra Club), International Affairs (Human Rights Watch), Media (Accuracy in Media), Political/ Governmental Process (Council for Excellence in Government), Public Interest Law (Trial Lawyers for Public Justice), Religious (National Council of the Churches of Christ in the U.S.A.) and Think Tanks (Cato Institute).

The Self-Help Directory: A Sourcebook for Self-Help in the United States and Canada. Joseph K. Donovan. New York: Facts on File, 1994.

Support groups, self-help and mutual-aid groups are listed for physical ailments, addictions and everyday problems that have become overwhelming. Some of the varied topics covered by these groups include people who have had one or more limbs amputated, manic-depression, formerly employed mothers, cancer and ex-offender rehabilitation.

Sports

Directory of European Sports Organizations. Martyn P. Glanville. Beckenham, Kent, England: CBD Research, Ltd., 1992.

This directory lists and describes

governing bodies of sports organizations throughout the nations of Europe, such as the Israeli Athletic Association and the German Racquetball Federation.

The National Directory of College Athletics: The Official Directory of the National Association of Collegiate Directors of Athletics (Men's Edition). Cleveland, OH: Collegiate Directories. Annual.

A listing of sports conferences (as in the American Midwest Conference or the Middle Atlantic Conference) and related associations (i.e., The Track and Field Writers of America, College Athletic Business Management Association). Senior and Junior Colleges are listed along with information on what sports they offer and the person responsible for each one. A Women's Edition is also available.

The Sports Address Bible: The Comprehensive Directory of Sports Addresses. Edward T. Kobak, Jr. 7th edition. Santa Monica, CA: Global Sports Productions, Ltd., 1994.

A name and address guide to U.S. and international teams, leagues, publications and organizations associated with baseball, basketball, bowling, boxing, cricket, cycling, football, golf, hockey, motor sports, polo, road running, rugby, soccer, softball, tennis, volleyball, water and winter sports. There are additional listings for sports museums and halls of fame, sports for the disabled, state high school athletic federations and the media.

Sports Fan's Connection: An All-Sports-in-One Directory to Professional, Collegiate and Olympic Organizations, Events

and Information Sources. Bradley J. Morgan, editor. Detroit: Gale, 1992.

This directory will help you connect with leagues, teams, athletic programs, organizers of sporting events, associations, fan clubs, halls of fame, fantasy camps, and radio and TV stations. Some of the sports included are Auto Racing, Boxing, Equestrian Sports, LaCrosse, Racquet Sports, Rodeo, Soccer and Wrestling, plus all the sports that would immediately come to mind, like Baseball.

Sports Halls of Fame: A Directory of Over 100 Sports Museums in the United States. Doug Gelbert. Jefferson, NC: McFarland and Co. Publishers, 1992.

With this guide you will be able to contact the curators of such museums as the United States Bicycling Hall of Fame (in Somerville, NJ), Big Daddy Don Garlits' Museum of Drag Racing (Ocala, Florida) and the Trapshooting Hall of Fame and Museum (Vandalia, Ohio).

Travel Information

Worldwide Travel Information Contact Book: A Country by Country Listing of Approximately 45,000 Sources of Information for Individual and Business Travelers, the Tourist Industry, the Travel Trade Press, Researchers and Students. Herbote Burkhard, editor. 2d edition. Detroit: Gale, 1993.

Whether you need to locate tour operators in Micronesia or the tourism authority in Azerbaijan, you will be able to find their name, number, address and fax in this hefty one-volume source.

The Writer's Ultimate Research Guide

Women

Encyclopedia of Women's Associations Worldwide: A Guide to Over 3,400 National and Multinational NonProfit Women's and Women-Related Organizations. Jaqueline K. Barrett, editor. Detroit: Gale, 1993.

The format is the same as that of the *Encyclopedia of Associations* and covers a wide spectrum of organizations: business, political, women's studies and social issues.

Resourceful Woman. Shawn Brennan and Julie Winklepleck. Detroit: Visible Ink, 1994.

Fifteen subject-oriented chapters, covering such topics as Aging, Global Issues, History, Spirituality and Violence Against Women, with listings for organizations, publications, videos, government agencies, programs, libraries and museums related to the chapter's theme. Sidebar information, pieces from writings, and poetry are also tucked in among the resources.

Women's Information Directory: A Guide to Organizations, Agencies, Institutions, Programs, Publications, Services and Other Resources Concerned with Women in the United States. Shawn Brennan, editor. 1st edition. Detroit: Gale, 1993.

If the number you are looking for has something to do with women, then it's probably in here. Some of the categories covered: Awards and Scholarships, Electronic Resources, Research Centers, Videos and Women's Centers.

And finally, if you need a great big number of experts in one field (perhaps for a mailing list), use the guide *Directories in Print.* DIP is a list of directories on all topics, with information about each guide that includes cost and ordering information. Some of the varied directories I found described in the 1994 edition of *DIP*:

Directory of Law Teachers. Washington, DC: Association of American Law Schools. Annual. Phone: (202) 296-8851.

Fossil Collections of the World: An International Guide. Lawrence, KS: University of Kansas, International Paleontological Association. Updated irregularly. Phone: (913) 864-3338.

Human Rights: A Directory of Resources. Oakland, CA: Third World Resources. Published in November 1989 and updated in the quarterly magazine *Third World Resources.*

International Directory of Primatology. (Primate Research). Madison, WI: Wisconsin Regional Primate Research Center Library. Biennial.

North American Guide to Nude Recreation. Kissimmee, FL: American Sunbathing Association. Phone: (407) 933-2064.

Parachuting: The Skydiver's Handbook. Santa Barbara, CA: Para Publishing. Phone: (805) 968-7277.

Experts in Cyberspace

One of the greatest uses of the information highway is the ability to quickly connect with experts (or those who profess to be). First, a quick refresher from chapter 1 on ways of chatting online, that is, using electronic bulletin board systems, abbreviated as BBSs. At the time of this writing, there were almost 50,000 (known) BBSs in the United States; about 100,000 publicly accessible boards worldwide. Some are run by companies or organizations, others by enthusiastic individuals.

Most of the home-oriented online services offer BBS-type services as part of their package (along with access to information databases, services and gateways to other systems): *America Online* and *CompuServe* call them "forums"—*GEnie* has "RoundTables." The *WELL*—*The Whole Earth 'Lectronic Link*—has public and private "conferences." All offer special times when members can participate in "real time" chatting ("Chat Lines"), that is, sending and receiving typed messages instantaneously—having a typed conversation. (For additional information on *America Online, CompuServe, GEnie* and the *WELL*, see Appendix B.)

In addition to the services mentioned above, there are dozens of other companies that can tie you to the Internet. Check with your local computer store or library for some names of local systems you might join to connect with the Internet. Some of these companies or nonprofit systems may offer competitive pricing to the larger, better known online systems. For example, in my home state Colorado, the Colorado Supernet, a government-subsidized service, offers competitive pricing to users in the state—(303) 273-3471. To be fair, many of the well-known systems do have pretty moderate pricing, and they

offer a lot of assistance.

One way to access BBSs is by dialing in to them with computer, modem and communications software. Many are free (run by hobbyists, enthusiasts and experts); others have an annual rate ranging about $15 to $75.

If you join, or just want to browse a BBS-type service that is part of a commercial online vendor, there will usually be online and hotline help available to you. Here are some tips for calling dial-up BBSs: Once you have your computer, modem and communications software, you can dial in to the BBSs. (You will find the numbers you need to dial in some of the directories I've listed below.) Once the connection is made, you may need to hit the <Return> or <Enter> key a few times. You will be prompted to set up communication parameters, and usually asked a number of questions in order to register. BBSs will often let you browse once or twice for free, even if they charge a fee.

It is a much cheaper option to use BBSs in your local dialing area or for dialing boards with 800 numbers. Once you dial outside that area, you are paying long distance charges! Those can add up when you are reading the latest exciting news on your very favorite BBS. If you do intend to call long distance often, you may want to subscribe to a packet-switching network; sort of a long distance phone company for computer communication. They will lower your long distance bills. Two are PC Pursuit (SprintNet), (800) 336-0437, and Star*Link, (505) 881-6980. Another simple way of saving on phone costs is by downloading information (copying it to disc or the computer's hard drive) and then reading off line, thereby saving the online charges.

Many of the BBS/Internet/Online Information books you browse through will not provide you with phone numbers; they give you e-mail addresses. (That's what those weird numbers and letters are in those directories!) Some of the groups these addresses are attached to are known as Listservs. A listserv is basically a BBS. With a listserv you register via e-mail with a standard subscription message. After you're registered, all of the messages of the group automatically pop into your e-mail. So you must have an e-mail account and Internet access to get to most listservs. Fortunately, most of the companies that connect you to the Internet provide you with an e-mail account.

Usually there are two e-mail messages provided for listservs. One address is used for registering; the other address is the one you will use to send messages to the list. A common beginner mistake is to send subscription request messages to the entire list. If you are lucky (like I was once), a kind member of the list will e-mail you and give you the proper "address" to subscribe. (And they won't make you feel too bad when they do it.)

One format for subscribing to a listserv is to send an e-mail message to the SYSOP (systems operator), (that's the address used for subscribing); leave the subject header blank and put only the following words in the body of the message:

subscribe[space]nameoflistserv[space] yourname

For example, when I joined a business librarian listserv, this is what I entered in the message field:

subscribe buslib-l ellen metter

Some books, like the *New Rider's Official Internet Yellow Pages* spell out very clearly the method for signing up for listservs and other conferences or bulletin boards. For example, for the listserv known as *Journet*, which conducts discussion on topics of interest to journalists and journalism instructors, the entry spells out the steps for joining.

> *To subscribe to the list, send an e-mail message to the URL(Uniform Resource Locator) address (listserv@qucdn. queensu.ca) consisting of a single line reading: SUB journet YourFirstName YourLastName.*
>
> *To send a message to the entire list address it to: journet@qucdn. queensu.ca.*

So, when I joined *Journet*, I typed in to my e-mail

> *Subscribe journet ellen metter*

Later, I received a message over my e-mail saying that my request to join had been acknowledged and accepted. I am now reading about some interesting censorship issues on *Journet*.

There are variations in this subscription format. Other formats might be:

> *subscribe firstname lastname*
> *subscribe lastname firstname*

To ascertain the format you should follow when you want to subscribe to a listserv, send a message to the administrative address that simply says: help.

Example of Using a Listserv: As a librarian in an academic setting, I have access to the Internet through the munificence of my employer. I connect to my account using "Kermit" communications software on my personal computer. My account allows me to access e-mail and to telnet to a variety of databases (among many other functions).

The listserv I use most often is the Business Librarians listserv known as buslib-l. A co-worker told me about this listserv and gave me the e-mail address I needed to subscribe. On my system, the questions, answers and thoughts of the group members now simply show up in my e-mail. I can choose to respond to queries by sending an e-mail reply that the whole group will see, I can just ignore the messages or I can just delete them without reading them. (I do the latter quite a bit.)

I especially appreciate buslib-l when I have a difficult question I need an answer to in the field of business. Occasionally, someone will survey the members of the group on a topic of interest to all of us and then summarize the answers for the group. See? A group of my peers who are experts in a field of interest to me are there at the touch of a keyboard or mouse. And I try to reciprocate when I can by answering questions or surveys. (For tips on etiquette on the Internet, see the book titled *Netiquette* by Virginia Shea [San Francisco: Albion Books. 1994].)

Depending on your Internet connection, you may find groups that you have read about but cannot reach. These groups may be associated with FidoNet, Bitnet or Usenet, for example. Talk to your technical support person for the service you are part of to see if there may be a way you could connect.

Yet another conglomeration of BBS-type entities you may have heard about are the Usenet Newsgroups. They are particularly infamous for their so-called "ALT" groups, which are the really-out-there or just super-specialized forums that aren't part of the Usenet mainstream topics. They have titles like alt.alien.visitors and alt.animals.dolphins. To access Usenet newsgroups, you need to be a part of service that will let you link up to UUNET. Inquire when you select your service. (Of course, almost any service you select will get you to at least a few unusual, weird BBSs/Conferences/Listservs!) (And of the more than nine thousand Usenet groups, there are many mainstream/academic/informative ones available through Usenet. They are designated by a different letter-combination code at the beginning of their address than ALT, such as SCI, for science and COMP, for computer information-related newsgroups.)

How do you find out what up-to-date BBSs are out there? BBSs have unpredictable survival rates. When checking for BBSs using print directories at the library, be sure you look at a very up-to-date one. You may also inquire at your local computer store, or check a regionally produced computer magazine. A national magazine to check is the *Boardwatch Magazine: Guide to Online Information Services and Electronic Bulletin Boards*.

Other sources to use to find current BBSs:

Modem USA: Low Cost and Free Online Sources for Information, Databases and Electronic Bulletin Boards via Computer and Modem in 50 States. Lynne Motley. 2d edition. Washington, DC: Allium Press, 1993.

One thousand bulletin boards are listed and briefly described.

National Directory of Bulletin Board Services. Patrick Dewey. Westport, CT: Meckler Publishing. Annual.
Lists about ten thousand BBSs.

New Rider's Official Internet Yellow Pages. 2d edition. Indianapolis, IN: New Riders Publishing, 1994.
More than ten thousand listings.

What topics do BBS's cover? Well, with the number that exist you'd be right to guess Almost Anything. Here are some wide-ranging examples to show you the variety out there:

- alt.alien.visitors—A Usenet newsgroup that features dialogue on space aliens on earth and other stories.
- Backstreets—Discussion of Bruce Springsteen's music.
- fwake-l—A formum for discussion of James Joyce's *Finnegan's Wake.*
- sci.astro.hubble—Information about NASA's Hubble Space Telescope.

Going online into BBSs can be a fabulous way to find experts. But be wary! Anyone can set themselves up as an expert online. As the online universe starts creating self-policing devices, it will probably be simpler to identify those groups that have some sort of seal of approval, akin to the referee process in journals. (Of course, it can't hurt to grab some info on Internet and then confirm it elsewhere!) See Appendix B for a description of online services and what they offer.

There are many online groups where writers get together to learn about the art and craft of writing—and schmooze. Some are:

America Online: Members can join the "Writer's Club," where there are bulletin boards for fiction, nonfiction and poetry. "Real-time" workshops are offered online, where writers can upload drafts of their materials to a reading library. Others may then download it, read it and return comments and critique.

CompuServe: The "Journalism Forum" has information on all aspects of professional journalism, with access to job listings and freelance opportunities. The "Literary Forum" is a BBS for the discussion of literary topics, including books, poetry, writing, stage, screen, journalism and comic books. Also of interest, the "Sci-Fi and Fantasy Forum," which offers discussion for science fiction lovers and provides conferences with well-known authors, producers and publishers.

GEnie: There is a bulletin board on GEnie known as "Writers Ink," comprised of novelists, journalists, technical writers, dramatists, poets, humorists and screenwriters. The "Science Fiction and Fantasy RoundTable" covers discussion of science fiction, fantasy and horror. GEnie is also home to the "Romance Writers Exchange."

Prodigy: Subscribers can become part of the "Arts Club," which features three bulletin boards: Writing/Poetry, Writing/Prose and Writing/Technique.

The WELL: "The Writers Conference" is used for sharing information on writing and getting answers on submissions, query letters, grants, awards and writers' colonies. *"WELL Writers"* is an online workshop where members post their writings and others post constructive criticism. Related conferences of interest to the writer discuss Computers, Freedom and Privacy, Computer Journalism, the First Amendment and Media. The conference "Firearms, Military, Police and True Crime," discusses topics like police, true crime books, military technology, arms and self-defense. "Science Fiction and Fantasy" may be of interest to science fiction/fantasy writers or aficiondos.

Biographical Sources

Many of the sources that are recommended in chapter 12, "Biographical Information," will include addresses and phone numbers, so take a look there for some additional expert sources.

TV and Radio Transcripts

For a fee, you can often obtain the transcripts of television and radio programs. Having a chance to slowly pore over the written words of a political debate, for example, can be quite fascinating, offering a closer look, different perspective and opportunity for pulling interesting

quotations. A major transcript service:

Journal Graphics, 1535 Grant Street, Denver, CO 80203, (303) 831-6400.
Journal Graphics supplies transcripts to broadcasts that appeared on CNN, ABC, CBS, PBS and National Public Radio.

Some libraries maintain collections of transcripts. Below are some you might find in larger libraries:

CBS *News Television Broadcasts.* Microfilming Corp. of America. 1963-present.

Face the Nation. Microfilming Corp. of America. 1954-present.

MacNeil Lehrer Report. Microfilming Corp. of America. 1976-present.

Summary of World Broadcasts by the British Broadcasting Corp. University Microfilms International. 1939-present.

Additionally, larger libraries may own videos of famous speeches or video copies of documentary or news programs that originally aired on television.

Chapter Eight

Overviews on Any Subject: Encyclopedias and Handbooks

There will be plenty of times when you just need to get a grip on a subject: in preparation for an interview, to learn the background of an event you mention in your writing or simply to gear up for more in-depth research you will do later. Using handbooks, encyclopedias, textbooks and short articles is a great method of painlessly familiarizing yourself with varied subjects.

Have you referred to an encyclopedia lately? They are amazing. I find, even as a librarian, that I forget just how much information is contained in a good, general encyclopedia set. In this chapter I want to alert you to the hundreds of subject-specific encyclopedias available, but also to remind you to use the ones that are as familiar to you as phone books.

General Encyclopedias

Sometimes a "general," multisubject encyclopedia will have as much, or more, information as a specialized one. In fact, a subject-specific encyclopedia that is not updated for years will eventually lag behind an updated section of a general encyclopedia.

The elements that are available in most encyclopedias:

- Biographies of well-known people.
- Statistics of a wide variety.
- Historical surveys and contemporary information on almost any topic, major organization or event.

- Basic explanations of complex concepts in terms understandable to the layman.
- Photographs, drawings, diagrams, maps and other illustrations that complement the text and further the reader's understanding of a topic.

Some major encyclopedias commonly found in libraries:

Academic American Encyclopedia. 21 Volumes. Danbury, CT: Grolier.

Collier's Encyclopedia with Bibliography and Index. 24 Volumes. New York: P.F. Collier.

Encyclopedia Americana: International Edition. 30 Volumes. Danbury, CT: Grolier.

New Encyclopedia Britannica. 32 Volumes. Chicago: Encyclopaedia Britannica.

The World Book Encyclopedia. 22 Volumes. Chicago: World Book.

Most encyclopedia sets are reprinted annually with revisions. Since larger libraries own several sets of encyclopedias, few can afford to replace all of them each year. That is why your library may have the most recent edition of, say, the *Lexicon Universal Encyclopedia*, but an edition from two years back of

Funk & Wagnalls New Encyclopedia.

When using encyclopedias, remember the back-of-the-book-index tip from chapter 1, "Navigating the Library": Don't just look alphabetically where you think your subject is. A more foolproof method: Look in the index, which is almost always in the last volume of the series (or actually is the last volume).

In addition to multivolume, multisubject encyclopedias, there are also "concise" multisubject encyclopedias; an entire encyclopedia set jammed into a volume that you would not want dropped on your head. Ranging in price from about $50 to $140, you might even consider purchasing one of these for your very own home writer's library. Some sample titles:

The Cambridge Encyclopedia. David Crystal, editor. New York: Cambridge University Press. 1st Reprint with revisions, 1992.

The Random House Encyclopedia: The World's Knowledge Presented in 11,325 Full-Color Illustrations and 3 Million Words of Text. James Mitchell, editor-in-chief. 3d edition. New York: Random House, 1990.

Webster's New World Encyclopedia. New York: Prentice-Hall, 1992.

Electronic Encyclopedias

Dozens of encyclopedias are now available online and on disc. Electronic access to encyclopedias improves your searching capabilities, enabling you to do a word search of the complete text of the encyclopedia. Though such a universal search will result in some terribly "false hits," it will also enable you to quickly find every occurrence of your topic throughout the encyclopedia.

You will find encyclopedias showing up as part of your library's online information system, on disc and on the home dial-in services listed in Appendix B. All of the general multivolume encyclopedias listed above are available electronically. Ask your library what they have available.

Many encyclopedias are fairly affordable on CD-ROM, so you might consider them for home use if you have a personal computer with a CD-ROM drive. Some sources to consult to find the latest encyclopedias on CD-ROM and their prices:

CD-ROMS in Print: An International Guide to CD-ROM, Multimedia and Electronic Book Products. Westport, CT: Mecklermedia. Annual.

A straightforward guide to resources available on CD-ROM, supplying such data as what type and how fast a computer is needed to run the disc, a description of the product, its intended level (i.e., child, adult), price and any multimedia features.

Kister's Best Encyclopedias: A Comparative Guide to General and Specialized Encyclopedias. Kenneth Kister. 2d edition. Phoenix: Oryx Press, 1994.

Kister's supplies in-depth reviews of both print and electronic encyclopedias for all subject areas. A thorough volume, written by a librarian, offering qualitative reviews of each resource.

Specialized Encyclopedias

I think one of the best ways to illustrate the incredible variety of encyclopedias available is to list major and minor topics and provide an example or two of an encyclopedia devoted to it. You will notice that many of these encyclopedic sources bear the label "dictionary" in their title. Believe me, these so-called dictionaries provide far more than a sentence or two of description on the subjects they cover. Another misnomer is the word "handbook." There are quite a few reference sources, arranged A to Z, that look for all the world like an encyclopedia, but are called handbooks.

Animals and Insects

Atlas of Cats of the World: Domesticated and Wild. Dennis Kelsey-Wood. Neptune City, NJ: T.F.H. Publications, 1989.

The *Atlas of Cats* supplies information on the psychological and physiological needs of cats, detailing their general, health and nutritional needs. The author also explains feline anatomy and discusses what is known about cat behavior. There are also tips on purchasing, exhibiting, breeding and exporting cats. There are hundreds of colorful kitty photos. Also by this publisher is the *Atlas of Dog Breeds of the World* (1991).

Audubon Society Encyclopedia of North American Birds. John K. Terres. New York: Alfred A. Knopf, 1980

A hefty one-volume survey of the birds of North America penned by former *Audubon* magazine editor John Terres. Written in non-technical form, data covered includes facts about the lives of different types of birds, including flight, nesting, egg laying, migration, size, life span, speed of flight, and altitude achievable. There are also entries detailing some behaviors and psychological occurrences associated with birds, including molting, swimming and singing. High-quality color photographs are included.

The Complete Dog Book. Official Publication of the American Kennel Club. 18th edition. New York: Howell Book House, 1992.

Don't look for your poor loveable mutt in here. This guide lists breeds, such as the Giant Schnauzer and the Welsh Terrier, and supplies the "official standard" that each dog must meet to be allowed registration with the American Kennel Club (AKC). The breeds are arranged in seven groups: Sporting Dogs, Hounds, Working Dogs, Terriers, Toys, Non-Sporting Dogs and Herding Dogs. A sample photograph of each breed begins each section, along with two or more pages describing the history of the breed and the usual temperament of that particular type of dog. This guide also contains chapters that instruct in selecting, training, breeding and caring for purebred dogs. Many a rich character owns a dog or two like the kind featured in this book. (By the way—note the name of the publisher of this collection!)

Encyclopedia of Endangered Species. Mary Emanoil in association with IUCN—The World Conservation Union. Detroit: Gale, 1994.

Descriptions of more than seven hundred animals and plants worldwide that are threatened with extinction. Each animal or plant is described, including its physical dimensions and reproductive and social behavior; its preferred habitat is listed along with recent population estimates, if available; and a look at the factors currently threatening the species, any conservation efforts thus far taken and the survival outlook for the species. Unfortunately, photographs were not available for each plant and animal.

Encyclopedia of Insects. Christopher O'Toole. New York: Facts on File, 1986.

Particularly notable for showing full-color, in-focus insects blown up to the size of your head. It is easy to see every detail. Besides being a learning tool for your entomologist character, this book might serve as a real idea-stimulator for horror writers. Those with just a slight aversion to tiny insects blown up to be rainforest-sized might prefer looking through the *Illustrated Book of Insects: A Comprehensive Color Guide to the Lives and Habitats of the Insects of the World* (Chartwell Books, 1991), which features friendly pastel drawings of the little buggers. The *Encyclopedia of Insects* is part of the Facts on File Animal Series, which includes:
The Encyclopedia of Reptiles and Amphibians
The Encyclopedia of Mammals
The Encyclopedia of Birds
The Encyclopedia of Aquatic Life

Grzimek's Animal Life Encyclopedia. 13 Volumes. Bernhard Grzimek, editor. New York: Van Nostrand, 1972-75.

Grzimek's is a well-respected standard, supplying information on the physiology and habits of animals. Several volumes are dedicated to different parts of the animal kingdom; four volumes cover mammals, three are devoted to birds, two to fish and amphibians, and one each to reptiles, insects, mollusks, and echinoderms and lower forms. *Grzimek's* is well illustrated with color drawings and photographs. The mammals volumes have been updated in *Grzimek's Encyclopedia of Mammals* (5 Volumes, 1990).

Art and Architecture

The Art Business Encyclopedia: For Artists, Collectors, Dealers, Galleries, Museums and Their Attorneys. Leonard DuBoff. New York: Allworth Press/ The American Council for the Arts, 1994.

How many times have you seen gallery owners and art dealers portrayed in fiction? Often, I would suspect. This tiny encyclopedia defines some of the activities of those on the business side of the art world.

Encyclopedia of Architecture: Design, Engineering and Construction. 5 Volumes. Joseph A. Wilkes and Robert T. Packard, editors. New York: Wiley, 1988-90.

The essays in this set examine architectural design, the regulations it is bound by, methods and materials of construction and engineering, and the educational field of architecture. Many photographs, line drawings and graphs accent lengthy entries. The lives and work of well-known architects are also included.

The Encyclopedia of Photography. International Center of Photography. New York: Crown Publishers, 1984.

The Encylopedia of Photography will help demystify the processes, materials and equipment associated with photography. This encyclopedia also looks at such fields of photography as Advertising Photography and such types of photography as Documentary Photography. The lives and works of influential photographers are also examined. As might be expected, this volume is filled with fabulous examples of well-executed and artistic photography; many of the images should be quite familiar.

Encyclopedia of World Art. 17 Volumes. New York: McGraw-Hill, 1959-68 [Vol. 1-15], 1983 [1st Supplement], 1987 [Second Supplement].

Known as one of the finest reference sources on international art, the *Encyclopedia of World Art*, as it says in the Preface, tries to "encompass our present knowledge of the arts within a single work." Surveyed at length are the artistic movements around the world and throughout history and the great and/or influential artists. Each volume contains dozens of beautifully reproduced color and black-and-white plates; each an example of the work of a particular artist or artistic movement. You would find this set in almost all larger public and academic libraries.

Aviation

See chapter 5, "Modes of Travel."

Business

Encyclopedia of Accounting Systems. Tom

M. and Lois R. Plank. 2d edition. 2 Volumes. New York: Prentice-Hall, 1993.

This set supplies information about the accounting systems of specific enterprises, for example, Churches, Commercial Banks and Travel Agencies. Even Scuba Diving Stores and Cement Producers are covered.

The Encyclopedia of Banking and Finance. Charles J. Woelfel. 10th edition. Chicago: Probus Publishing Company, 1994.

This resource, commonly found in larger libraries, contains definitions of thousands of banking, business and financial terms, explanations of relevant laws and regulations, historical tidbits, descriptions of financial organizations (such as the Financial Analysts Federation) and analysis of past and recent financial trends.

The Encyclopedia of Career Change and Work Issues. Lawrence K. Jones. Phoenix: Oryx Press, 1992.

This volume supplies advice and information on topics of interest to those looking for work, involved in day-to-day work or running a business. Substantial essays are devoted to such topics as Career Changes at Midlife, Networking and Office Romance.

The Prentice-Hall Real Estate Investor's Encyclopedia. Frank J. Blankenship. Englewood Cliffs, NJ: Prentice-Hall, 1989.

An A to Z listing of terms and concepts commonly encountered in the field of real estate investing. The author also supplies tips and advice for maximizing investments.

Computer Science

Encyclopedia of Artificial Intelligence. Stuart C. Shapiro, editor-in-chief. 2d edition. 2 Volumes. New York: John Wiley and Sons, 1992.

Those in Artificial Intelligence (AI) research attempt to program computers to perform advanced tasks that would normally require human intelligence and reasoning. In this research, scientists must first understand the human cognitive process so that it can be duplicated in computer form. The essays in this encyclopedia look at the many functions that computers are "learning," such as speech and image cognition. The essays cover major work and findings in the field and social issues related to AI.

Encyclopedia of Computer Science. 3d edition. Anthony Ralston and Edwin D. Reilly, editors. New York: Van Nostrand Reinhold, 1993.

All the information your computer nerd character already knows: over seven hundred substantive entries classified under nine major headings: Hardware, Software, Computer Systems, Information and Data, Mathematics and Computing, Theory of Computing, Methodologies, Applications and Computing Milieux. (I knew I would get that word in this book somehow!) Some helpful information in the appendices includes abbreviations and acronyms, mathematical notation, units of measure, and a glossary of major computer science terms in five languages.

Crime

The Encyclopedia of Crime and Justice.
Sanford H. Kadish, editor-in-chief. 4 Volumes. New York: The Free Press, 1983.

The essays in this set examine types of criminal conduct, methods of crime prevention and control, careers in criminal justice, and treatment, punishment and rehabilitation of criminals.

The Encyclopedia of Drug Abuse. Robert O'Brien, Sidney Cohen, Glen Evans and James Fine. 2d edition. New York: Facts on File, 1992.

All aspects of drug abuse are examined and explained in this volume: types of drugs, their biological effects, legality, the social and economic impact of drug abuse, the occurrence of abuse around the world and descriptions of intervention and prevention programs. Appendix A of this volume lists street drug language.

The Encyclopedia of Police Science. William G. Bailey. New York: Garland Publishing, 1989.

The Encyclopedia of Police Science explains what U.S. law enforcers do on the job, describes notable police officers and departments, and details some of the stress and pitfalls of working in such a dangerous profession.

Encyclopedia of Violence: Origins, Attitudes, Consequences. Margaret Di-Canio. New York: Facts on File, 1993.

A look at what the author terms "the world's most serious health problem"—violence. The focus is primarily on the United States and to a lesser extent on Canada. This encyclopedia attempts to find the origins of violent behavior, the attitudes that sustain it in modern-day society, and the consequences it has on our bodies, our minds and our institutions. Sample headings include Arson, Hate Crimes, and Relapse Prevention: Treatment for Sex Offenders.

Encyclopedia of World Crime: Criminal Justice, Criminology and Law Enforcement. Jay Robert Nash. Wilmette, IL: CrimeBooks, 1990.

A six-volume compendium detailing the vicious antics of murderers and other ne'er-do-wells around the world. The good guys are also represented: Law enforcement officials and many victims who suffered crimes that are yet unsolved are also featured. Volume 5 of this set is a dictionary of more than twenty thousand terms used in America, the United Kingdom and elsewhere by criminals and those in law enforcement, from ancient time through the present.

Communication

The Encyclopedia of Language and Linguistics (ELL). 10 Volumes. R.E. Asher, editor-in-chief. New York: Pergamon Press, 1994.

ELL offers essays about and allied with the field of linguistics. The editors have tried to make "even the most technical articles . . . intelligible to those who are not experts in the subject under discussion," though to be honest, I do not think they always succeed, since there are many heady and complex subjects discussed. Some of those subjects are: Apes and Language, Marathi ("a major outer language of the Indo-Aryan group"), and Sociophonetics (the study of speech in

its social context). Volume 10, in addition to a name and subject index, contains an inventory of the languages of the world, major language and linguistics journals, abbreviations, and the logical symbols used in the text.

Economics

Encyclopedia of American Economic History: Studies of the Principle Movements and Ideas. Glenn Porter, editor. 3 Volumes. New York: Charles Scribner's Sons, 1980.

The essays in this set examine classic economic theories and views, written for the "intelligent layperson."

The New Palgrave Dictionary of Economics. John Eatwell, Murray Mulgate and Peter Newman. 4 Volumes. New York: Stockton Press, 1987.

A standard economics reference resource, defining such concepts as Bioeconomics, Intertemporal Equilibrium and Efficiency and Taylorism. Noted economists are featured throughout.

Espionage

The Encyclopedia of American Intelligence and Espionage: From the Revolutionary War to the Present. G.J.A. O'Toole. New York: Facts on File, 1988.

This volume is dedicated to the field of "espionology," which is, according to the author, studied in more than forty U.S. colleges and universities. The subject matter includes coverage of the missions and activities of U.S. intelligence agencies like the CIA and the OSS, the role of intelligence in major wars that the U.S. was involved in, specific events of note, such as the

Bay of Pigs Invasion, and biographies of major figures in espionage, including the author William Somerset Maugham.

Encyclopedia of Espionage. Ronald Seth. London: New English Library, 1975.

Essentially a who's who of spies throughout the ages, including several pages of information on such figures as Fleming B. Muus, a Danish Resistance leader in World War II, and Caron de Beaumarchais, French dramatist and secret agent in the eighteenth century. The entries are filled with enjoyable hyperbole. In addition to biographical information, the author also describes the mission of intelligence agencies and groups such as the FBI and KGB. Descriptions of devices of the trade such as Secret Inks and Letter Boxes are also supplied.

Performing Arts and Media

Encyclopedia of Folk, Country & Western Music. Irwin Stambler and Grelun Landon. 2d edition. New York: St. Martin's Press, 1983.

A compilation of descriptions of those who were (or are) part of, influenced by, or had an impact on the country music genre.

Encyclopedia of Music in Canada. Helmut Kallmann and Gilles Potvin, editors. 2d edition. Toronto: University of Toronto Press, 1992.

A sourcebook concentrating on music and creators of music in Canada. This also examines Canada's musical relations with the world.

Encyclopedia of the Blues. Gérard Herz-

haft. Fayetteville, AR: The University of Arkansas Press, 1992.

A one-volume examination of a genre of music that was born in America. The author looks at blues instruments, trends, recordings and producers, with an emphasis on the musical biographies of performers. Some black-and-white photographs are included. There is a select discography of blues recordings to help new blues aficionados begin their collections.

Encyclopedia of the Musical Theatre. 2 Volumes. Kurt Gänzl. New York: Schirmer Books, 1994.

An international survey of the plays of musical theater and the people who brought them to life.

The Encyclopedia of Vaudeville. Anthony Slide. Westport, CT: Greenwood Press, 1994.

A look at the vaudevillians themselves, those behind the scenes, types of vaudeville and descriptions of particular vaudeville houses.

The Film Encylopedia. Ephraim Katz. 2d edition. New York: HarperCollins. 1994.

The author's aim in writing *The Film Encyclopedia* was to create the "most comprehensive one-volume encyclopedia of world cinema ever published in the English language." *The Film Encyclopedia* contains biographical entries on filmmakers and performers, the history of major film industries around the world, descriptions of important film organizations, and definitions and explanations of filmmaking inventions, techniques, processes, equipment and jargon. To hold the volume to a manageable length (it is almost 1500 pages long), the author elected to forego any review or critical analyses of specific films. The lack of an index is a drawback to this volume.

Les Brown's Encyclopedia of Television. Les Brown. 3d edition. Detroit: Gale, 1992.

Covering television from its inception to present day in the U.S. and in major international markets, *Les Brown's Encyclopedia of Television* supplies short entries covering television personalities, programs and companies, along with legal, regulatory and technological issues associated with the medium. Many references in this genre concentrate only on programs or only on stars, so this is a useful all-in-one television reference source. Very sparsely illustrated.

Magill's Survey of Cinema. 21 Volumes. Frank N. Magill, editor. Englewood Cliffs, NJ: Salem Press, 1980-85. [Kept up-to-date with the title *Magill's Cinema Annual.*]

If your heroine is a film buff, she will certainly know how to critique a film. *Magill's* critiques over 3,000 of them in its original set. The twenty-one volumes are actually comprised of three parts which may be shelved in slightly different areas of the library. Ten volumes are devoted to *English Language Films*, eight to *Foreign Language Films*, and three look at *Silent Films*.

McGraw-Hill Encyclopedia of World Drama. 5 Volumes. Stanley Hochman, editor-in-chief. 2d edition. New York: McGraw-Hill, 1984.

The standard international theater reference encyclopedia, which presents surveys of the drama of different nations and of many genres and critical biographies of dramatists and seminal directors. This collection is brimming with incredible photographs, including some of actors and actresses that we now associate with screen acting, performing in runs of classic plays that we now associate with the movies (such as Katherine Hepburn in *The Philadelphia Story*). Volume 5 contains a glossary of terms, forms, movements and styles of drama. The index assists in matching play titles to playwrights.

The New Grove Dictionary of Jazz. 2 Volumes. Barry Kernfeld. New York: Macmillan Press, Ltd., 1988.

This set surveys all periods and styles of jazz worldwide. Six categories of articles are presented: individual biographies, background on groups and bands, definitions of terms, playing technique and use of musical instruments of jazz, information on record companies and labels, and details on institutions that are devoted to furthering jazz scholarship and performance. Small portions of this work were first published in the *New Grove Dictionary of Music and Musicians* and *The New Grove Dictionary of Musical Instruments.*

The New Grove Dictionary of Music and Musicians. Stanley Sadie, editor. 20 Volumes. London: MacMillan Publishers, Ltd., 1980.

Begun in the 1870s by Sir George Grove, *Grove's* is the first place to look for scholarly biographical and informational essays in music. Over 50 percent of the entries discuss composers, from ancient to contemporary times. The only contemporary performers included are those who have earned worldwide repute or are known for "specially important national achievement." In other words, The Archies are not listed, but Felix Mendelssohn earned over twenty-four pages. Essays cover international musical concepts, influences, theories, styles, instruments and terminology. This is a standard in most mid-size to large libraries.

The Rolling Stone Illustrated History of Rock & Roll: The Definitive History of the Most Important Artists and Their Music. Anthony DeCurtis, James Henke and Holly George-Warren. 3d edition. Original Editor Jim Miller. New York: Random House, 1992.

Each chapter in this historical survey covers either a particularly influential artist or group (Presley, Dylan, The Byrds, U2) or a passing fad or lasting genre (teen idols, folk music, MTV). Each essay has a personal ring, with many of the essay authors recounting a personal experience at a concert or a feeling for a specific type of music. Many black-and-white photographs are included. This one has become a standard rock music reference.

Tune In Yesterday:The Ultimate Encyclopedia of Old-Time Radio, 1925-1976. John Dunning. Englewood Cliffs, NJ: Prentice-Hall, 1976.

Tune In Yesterday is a listing of the dramatic, entertainment radio programs stilled by the advent of television. For each program the author lists dates, networks, sponsors, time changes and personnel. The premise

of each show is described and biographical data is supplied for many of the shows' stars. Listed alphabetically by program title, you can find stars and staff using the index. Some of the shows described include *Ethel and Albert*, a fifteen-minute program built around the daily goings-on of the couple's life, *Our Daily Food*, a quarter-hour discussion of recipes and meal menus, and *The Witch's Tale*, the first "significant horror show of the air," which began in 1931.

Fashion

Encyclopedia of American Indian Costume. Josephine Paterek. Denver: ABC-CLIO, 1994.

A compilation of descriptions and cultural contexts of the traditional dress and ornamentation of the American Indians of ten cultural regions (Southeast, Northeast, Plains, Southwest, Great Basin, Plateau, California, Northwest Coast, Subarctic and Arctic), covering men's and women's basic dress, footwear, outerwear, hairstyles, headgear, accessories, jewelry, armor, special costumes, face and body embellishment, and transitional dress after European contact.

Esquire's Encyclopedia of 20th Century Men's Fashions. O.E. Schoeffler and William Gale. New York: McGraw-Hill, 1973.

This volume describes the clothing and grooming styles of U.S. and European men from 1900 to about 1970. Illustrations and photographs are provided running the gamut from Ivy League Fashions to the Mr. T Look. The entries are varied and lengthy, including one section for Socks and another for Toiletries (allotted a respectable ten pages apiece). The glossary helps to define such tricky terms as Impregnated Fabric (material made water-repellent by filling the openings between the threads with a chemical compound). Biographical backgrounds on fashion designers are also included.

The Encyclopedia of World Costume. Doreen Yarwood. New York: Charles Scribner's Sons, 1978.

An A-to-Z volume with simple, black-and-white line drawings. Terms defined include material types (such as cotton and sackcloth), fashion accessories (including furs and collars), types of clothing (coats, sandals, ponchos) and costume of particular countries (for example, Afghan dress and Japanese dress).

The Historical Encyclopedia of Costumes [The Classic Work of the 19th Century Re-edited and Re-designed with Over 2,000 illustrations]. Albert Racinet. New York: Facts on File, 1988.

Based on *Le Costume Historique of 1888,* the detailed color plates featured throughout this volume, published a century later, make it both useful and beautiful. Details of clothing accessories and hairstyles are also easily seen in these illustrations.

One illustration that evokes a particularly dark mood is part of the ecclesiastical dress in seventeenth-century Italy: The Penitent. With dark hood and gown, wielding a whip ("an instrument symbolic of penitence and self-punishment"), this fellow looks like a cross between Darth Vader, an executioner and a monk. With hood fully covering his face, he would be the perfect undercover character!

This resource covers clothing in the ancient world through the 1880s. Do read the introduction to this book by scholar Aileen Ribeiro, who offers insights and a few "buyer beware" warnings concerning this collection. This is one of the few general costume encyclopedias I looked through that features some detailed drawings of non-caucasian/non-European apparel.

The Pictorial Encyclopedia of Fashion. Ludmila Kybalová, Olga Herbenová and Milena Lamarová. New York: Crown Publishers, 1968.

A profusely illustrated volume with paintings, statues, photographs and drawings depicting styles of dress and ornamentation from Early Egypt through the 1960s. A volume of similar coverage is *Fashion: From Ancient Egypt to the Present Day* (Mila Contini. New York: The Odyssey Press, 1965). The larger size of the latter book and use of more color (instead of black-and-white) photographs and drawings make the details of the illustrations more pronounced.

Food and Nutrition

Encyclopedia of Food Science, Food Technology and Nutrition. Robert Macrae, editor. 8 Volumes. San Diego: Academic Press, 1993.

Experts in the fields of food science and nutrition from around the world wrote the five hundred essays that comprise this set. Though this encyclopedic set has received rave reviews in the library press, it may not be at all larger libraries because of its hefty price tag (over two thousand dollars). The topics in this scholarly set encompass food processing, the origin, chemical composition, and nutritive value of many foodstuffs, food additives, and the effects of nutrition on disease.

Foods and Nutrition Encyclopedia. Audrey Ensminger, M.E. Ensminger, James E. Konlande and John R.K. Robson, 2d edition. 2 Volumes. Boca Raton, FL: CRC Press, 1993.

The authors care about food on its own merits along with its effects on the health of humans. The entries in this set range from two-sentence descriptions of particular foods (i.e., "The Abernathy Biscuit—a hard biscuit containing caraway seeds, named after an English surgeon who, in the early 1800s, treated maladies with diet") to several pages on topics like Fats and Other Lipids and the Soybean (which examines the origin, history, uses and processing of the soybean). Volume 1 contains almost two hundred pages under the heading "Food Compositions" and lists the composition of generic foods (including such compositional elements as Calories, Fats, Fiber, Calcium, Minerals and Water-Soluble Vitamins).

The Wellness Encyclopedia of Food and Nutrition: How to Buy, Store and Prepare Every Variety of Fresh Food. The Editors of the *University of California, Berkeley Wellness Letter.* Boston: Houghton Mifflin, 1991.

This one-volume encyclopedia deals with choosing, storing and preparing fruits, vegetables, grains, legumes, nuts, seeds, fish, dairy products, meat

and poultry. This book taught me that peppers are not pepper! That is, the grey/black stuff we shake on our food is not related to those yellow, green and red vegetables we cook with and put in salads. It also taught me that red peppers have three times as much vitamin C as oranges.

Health—Western and Eastern Traditions

See chapter 16, "Diseases and Mental Illnesses."

History (U.S./World) and Archaeology

(Other historic overview collections are listed in chapter 9, "Chronologies and Calenders," under the headings "General World Chronologies" and "U.S. History and Events.")

Dictionary of American History. Revised edition. 8 Volumes. New York: Charles Scribner's Sons, 1976.

An A-to-Z compilation of an impressive array of the achievements and events that comprise the history of the United States. If it happened in the United States, it is probably noted in here: Beekeeping, Black Cavalry in the West, Elevators and Washington's Farewell Address are all included.

Dictionary of Historic Documents. George C. Kohn. New York: Facts on File, 1990.

Influential documents from the world over, ranging from B.C. times to the present day, are described in short paragraphs. A wide variety of texts are described, including proclamations, treaties, encyclicals, petitions, decrees and manifestos. Some sample documents described include: a synopsis of William Faulkner's Nobel Prize acceptance speech, a description of the 1620 Mayflower Compact, signed by Pilgrims in Provincetown Harbor, and a summary of the intent of the British Riot Act of 1715.

Dictionary of the Middle Ages. Joseph Strayer, editor-in-chief. 13 Volumes. New York: Charles Scribner's Sons, 1982.

The creators of this set have attempted to record ideas, names and terminology associated with art, law, literature, music, numismatics, economics, politics, philosophy, theology, technology and everyday life in the Middle Ages, roughly A.D. 500 to 1500.

Encyclopedia of American Social History. 3 Volumes. Mary Kupiec Cayton, Elliott J. Gorn and Peter W. Williams, editors. New York: Scribner, 1992.

The Encyclopedia of American Social History is comprised of 180 essays that examine U.S. history in terms of the processes and the people of the American social structure. The writings are arranged under fourteen thematic sections, which include Ethnic and Racial Subcultures, Patterns of Everyday Life, Family History, and Education and Literacy. This set is part of the Scribner American Civilization Series. Other volumes in the series include:

Encyclopedia of American Economic History (1980)
Encyclopedia of American Foreign Policy (1978)
Encyclopedia of the American Judicial System (1987)

Encyclopedia of the North American Colonies (1993)
Encyclopedia of American Political History (1984)

Encyclopedia of Historic Places. Courtlandt Canby. New York: Facts on File, 1984.

More detailed than most gazetteers, the *Encyclopedia of Historic Places* supplies information on places of historic importance throughout the world. Each entry is designed to pinpoint the importance of each place in history. Thus, the entry for Death Valley lists the area's length (about 140 miles), number of feet below sea level (approximately 280), and mentions that in the mid-1800s many people died trying to cross the desolate region in search of gold. Areas covered in this set include towns, cities, countries, provinces, regions, empires, deserts, forts, battle sites, lakes, mountains, rivers, shrines and archaeological sites.

Encyclopedia of the Renaissance. Thomas Bergin, consulting editor. New York: Facts on File, 1987.

This volume examines the events and personalities that filled the three centuries in European history known as the Renaissance. The entries tend to be quite brief, only a paragraph or so. Beyond the thirty-two color plates of Renaissance art, there are few illustrations.

Larousse Encyclopedia of Archaeology. [Translation of *Larousse L'Archaeologie Découvertedes Civilisations Disparues,* 1969.] Gilbert Charles-Picard. New York: G.P. Putnam's Sons, 1972.

A one-volume work devoted to the work and findings of the "detectives of the past," archaeologists. The first portion of the encyclopedia is devoted to explaining some of the work of archaeologists. The remainder of the encyclopedia examines findings from many ages, peoples and locations, including Prehistoric Archaeology, Europe in the Bronze and Iron Ages, and the Etruscans. The majority of photographs are black-and-white.

Magill's History of Europe. Frank N. Magill, 6 Volumes. Danbury, CT: Grolier Educational Corporation, 1993.

These six volumes describe, in chronological order, 288 events selected as major events that shaped the Western world. Some of the events described include the Battle of Zama (a military engagement between Roman and Carthaginian armies in 202 B.C.), the proclamation of Italy as a constitutional monarchy (on March 17, 1861), and the recovery of Great Britain from its military intervention on the Falkland Islands.

The Reader's Companion to American History. The Society of American Historians. Eric Foner and John A. Garraty, editors. Boston: Houghton Mifflin Co., 1991.

Need a quick refresher on some elements of the Civil Rights Movement? A review of the history of the Panama Canal? This sourcebook contains concise overviews of U.S. historical happenings and the people involved in making them happen.

World Guide to Antiquities. Seymour Kurtz. New York: Vineyard Books, 1975.

A reference guide to ancient, Oriental and primitive art and artifacts, liberally illustrated with color photographs. With the world to choose from, it is to be expected that the variety discussed is phenomenal and that some of the art and artifacts pictured are stunning. For example, there is a full-page photograph of an Aztec Skull, a human skull that has been inlaid with an elaborate turquoise and obsidian mosaic. This book is purely a launching point for more in-depth research.

Government, Politics, and Social Movements

Encyclopedia of the American Left. Mari Jo Buhle, Paul Buhle and Dan Georgakas, editors. New York: Garland Publishing, 1990.

Essentially, this is a history of Left-leaning movement in the United States, supplying articles on people like Emma Goldman, recounting the activities of such groups as the Congress of American Women, surveying movements like the Catholic Worker Movement, and looking at the "left-wing" activities of people of many descents and beliefs, including Irish Americans, Chinese Americans and Portuguese Americans.

Encyclopedia of Third Parties in the United States. Earl R. Kruschke. Santa Barbara, CA: ABC-CLIO, 1991.

This resource offers descriptions, ranging from about one to five pages, of the political third parties that have emerged throughout the history of the United States. Among those described are The Free Soil Party (established in 1848, comprised of people who opposed slavery and wanted cheap land), the Peace and Freedom Party (founded in 1967, they nominated Eldridge Cleaver as their Presidential candidate), and the Progressive Party (founded in 1912 as a result of a split in the Republican Party; the Progressives favored Roosevelt's ideas over Taft's).

The Middle East: A Political Dictionary. Lawrence Zirig. Santa Barbara, CA: ABC-CLIO, 1992.

This book identifies the terms, events, characteristics, movements and institutions that describe latter twentieth-century Middle East politics. Some major areas examined in this book include Political Geography and Geopolitics, Islam, Ethnicity and Political Culture, Political Parties and Movements, and Israelis and Palestinians. Also by this publisher, *Latin America: A Political Dictionary*, 1992.

World Encyclopedia of Peace. Ervin Laszlo and Jong Youl Yoo, executive editors. 4 Volumes. New York: Pergamon Press, 1986.

Published in 1986, the "International Year of Peace," the editors labored over this set in the hope that "the *Encyclopedia* will contribute greatly to the promotion of peaceloving ideas among the peoples of the world [providing] a fertile source of material both for governments and policy makers as well as peace researchers." Focusing on peace research and peace activism, some headings in the first two volumes include Arms

Conversion, Spirit of Geneva, Deterrence and Quakerism. Volume 3 lists treaties, a chronology of the peace movement, and information about Nobel Prize laureates; Volume 4 lists peace institutes, organizations and journals.

Political Handbook of the World. Arthur S. Banks, editor. Binghamton, NY: CSA Publications. Annual.

This *Handbook* goes over the political background and current politics and parties for all countries of the world. Want to send your character to a politically tumultuous clime? Look for a country in uproar.

The United States Government Manual. Washington, DC: Government Printing Office. Annual.

This is the "official handbook of the federal government," with overview information on the agencies of the legislative, judicial and executive branches, as well as "quasi-official" agencies, boards, commissions, committees and international organizations the government is involved with. The main numbers and addresses for the federal and regional offices of the organizations covered are provided. This manual is usually kept within grabbing distance of the librarian. I would say I use this manual most when a library user wants to find out a little about what a certain regulatory agency, like the FDA, is actually supposed to do.

Literature

Benét's Reader's Encyclopedia. New York: Harper and Row, 1987.

An excellent standard quick-guide to contemporary and classic world literature. Items listed, with descriptions ranging from a few sentences to several paragraphs, include plot summaries of important literary works, myths, legend and folklore often encountered in literature, biographies of writers and historians, and literary terminology, movements, schools and awards.

Dictionary of Concepts in Literary Criticism and Theory. Wendell V. Harris. Westport, CT: Greenwood Press, 1992.

Treatments of seventy concepts of literary theory and commentary are presented. Sample headings include Deconstruction, Humanism, Narrative and Semiotics.

Encyclopedia Mysteriosa: A Comprehensive Guide to the Art of Detection in Print, Film, Radio and Television. William L. DeAndrea. New York: Prentice Hall General Reference, 1994.

Dedicated to the art of the mystery as presented in all media, this encyclopedia supplies portraits of mystery writers and many of their characters, along with commentary on themes, styles and specific mystery works. Some of the entries on characters are far longer than those for actual authors! Sections in the back of *Encyclopedia Mysteriosa* list mystery bookstores, organizations, awards, magazines and journals. Of related interest, from the same publisher, would be the *Encyclopedia Sherlockiana: The Complete A-to-Z Guide to the World of the Great Detective* (1994).

Encyclopedia of World Literature in the

20th Century. 5 Volumes. New York: Frederick Ungar Publishing. Volumes 1-4, 1981. Volume 5 (Supplement and Index), 1993.

This encylopedia is well known among literary researchers for its national literature surveys, biographical pieces on the writers of the world, and explanations of concepts in literary scholarship. Volume 5, the supplement volume, updates some of the information in the base volume along with completely new entries on contemporary literary topics (such as feminist criticism and poststructuralism). This is a standard at larger libraries.

The New Princeton Encyclopedia of Poetry and Poetics. Alex Preminger and T.V.F. Brogan, co-editors. Princeton, NJ: Princeton University Press, 1993.

The standard dictionary in this field, the *Princeton Encyclopedia* surveys the national poetries of 106 countries, contains essays on poetic forms, major and minor genres, principal schools and movements in poetry, issues in criticism and literary theory, and the relation of poetry to other fields, such as history, politics, religion and science.

Nations

Europa Yearbook. London: Europa Publications. Annual.

Despite its name, the *Europa Yearbook* covers all countries and continents. It provides detailed country overviews and statistics for such elements as area and population, births and deaths per thousand, agriculture data, denominations of currency, central bank reserves, trade figures, number of tourist arrivals, principal trading partners, and number of radios, televisions and automobiles in use. There are seven regional *Europa* editions that supply even more information on the geography, history and economy of nations: *The Middle East and North Africa, Africa South of the Sahara, Eastern Europe and the Commonwealth of Independent States, The Far East and Australia, South America, Central America and the Caribbean, Western Europe* and *The USA and Canada.* Most larger libraries will at least own the general *Europa* set.

Countries of the World and Their Leaders Yearbook. Detroit: Gale Research. Annual.

A wealth of concise information for over 170 nations. The book opens with listings of the chiefs of state and their cabinets, so if you need to know the name of the Minister of Public Health and Social Affairs in the Republic of Guinea, start with this section. The factual data supplied for each nation includes descriptions of the country's geography, peoples, government, economy, political conditions, foreign relations and defense capabilities. The second volume contains health information for the international traveler, e.g., the need for vaccinations and hints on how to stay healthy while abroad.

See chapter 3, "Geography, Climate and Local Customs," for more examples of reference resources that provide national overviews.

Nature

Earth's Natural Forces. Kenneth J.

Gregory, editor. New York: Oxford University Press, 1990.

An illustrated, around-the-world look at climate, rivers, oceans, glaciers, earthquakes and volcanoes.

The Encyclopedia of Earthquakes and Volcanoes. David Ritchie. New York: Facts on File, 1994.

An alphabetically arranged listing of some of the better-known volcanoes and earthquakes, along with some that serve as good examples of these phenomena. Illustrated only with some scattered black-and-white photographs.

Encyclopedia of the Environment. The René Dubos Center for Human Environments, Ruth A. Eblen and William R. Eblen, editors. Boston: Houghton Mifflin Co., 1994.

Regional, national and international environmental concerns and issues are discussed.

Handbook of Unusual Natural Phenomena. William R. Corliss. Glen Arm, MD: The Sourcebook Project, 1988.

A sourcebook of strange natural phenomena as reported by witnesses. The editor's criteria for inclusion: "1) Beyond the reach of present scientific explanation, and 2) curious (to the author) personally." Some of the phenomena described include a slow meteor reportedly seen over the mid-Oregon coastline in 1934, so slow that it was dubbed the "Lazy Meteor" by the local media and the sighting of a pillar of fire "resembl[ing] an ordinary gate-post in size and shape" floating in the sky for about ten miles before it exploded (1869). Earlier titles in this series: *Strange Planet: A Sourcebook of Unusual Geological Facts*, 1975, and *Strange Phenomenon: A Sourcebook of Unusual Natural Phenomena*, 1974.

Hugh Johnson's Encyclopedia of Trees: With 1,000 Full-Color Illustrations. 2d edition. [First edition was called *The International Book of Trees*.] New York: Portland House, 1990.

Written by Hugh Johnson, connoisseur of both trees and wine (!), this volume explains the structure, history and life cycle of trees, with advice on their placement, planting and care.

The Illustrated Encyclopedia of Fossils. Giovanni Pinna. New York: Facts on File, 1990.

More than a thousand color photographs of fossil specimens found worldwide are in this one-volume compendium of the work of paleontologists. Some remarkable creatures are shown imbedded in or imprinted on substances such as rocks and shells. One photo shows a gecko preserved in amber, a la *Jurassic Park*.

The New York Botanical Garden Illustrated Encyclopedia of Horticulture. Thomas H. Everett. 10 Volumes. New York: Garland Publishing, 1981.

The author defines horticulture as gardening—not to be confused with botany or other field practices associated with agriculture and forestry. These ten large volumes are filled with descriptions and both color and black-and-white photos of the majority of plant genera in the U.S. and Canada (though the author ruefully admits that not all the plants of such large expanses are included).

The Way Nature Works. Robin Rees, senior executive editor. New York: Macmillan Publishing Co., 1992.

Cross-sectional diagrams, colorful illustration and photographs are used along with simply comprehended descriptions answering questions about nature. Some of the questions answered include "What Causes Ice Ages," "How Islands Form," "How the Greenhouse Effect Warms the Globe," "How Birds are Adapted to Flight," and "How Color is Created in Nature."

Oxford Companions

Oxford Companions, published by Oxford University Press, exist for virtually all subjects. They are essentially encyclopedic sets, usually one or two volumes, which supply concise and authoritative information on the subject at hand. Some sample titles include:

The Oxford Companion to Canadian Theatre (1989)

The Oxford Companion to French Literature (1959)

The Oxford Companion to Law (1980)

The Oxford Companion to Medicine (1986)

The Oxford Companion to Politics of the World (1993)

Philosophy, Psychology, Social Work and Sociology

Encyclopedia of Adoption. Christine Adamec and William L. Pierce. New York: Facts on File, 1991.

Over five million people in the United States were adopted, certainly a large readership if you are considering penning a story on adoption.

Encyclopedia of Adoption will supply you with explanations of the social, legal, economic, psychological and political issues surrounding the system of U.S. adoption.

Encyclopedia of Marriage, Divorce and the Family. Margaret DiCaniio. New York: Facts on File, 1989.

This resource is devoted to issues surrounding the formation and dissolution of married couples and nuclear families. Topics are varied, encompassing such topics as Childbirth Anxieties, Nonsupport of Children, Credit Ratings and Elderly Alcoholics.

Encyclopedia of Philosophy. 8 Volumes. Paul Edwards, editor-in-chief. New York: The Macmillan Co. and The Free Press, 1967.

This is where you head to learn the basics of major philosophical movements and the ideas of the giants in the field. It's hard to keep this physically ragged collection (from almost thirty years of continuous use) on the shelf.

Encyclopedia of Memory and Memory Disorders. Richard Noll and Carol Turkington. New York: Facts on File, 1994.

How do people remember things? What portions of the brain play a part in the ability to remember? What might cause amnesia? These and other questions relating to the human memory are answered in this encyclopedia.

Encyclopedia of Psychology. Raymond J. Corsini, editor. 4 Volumes. New York: John Wiley and Sons, 1994.

A standard series found in all midsize

and large libraries, the *Encyclopedia of Psychology* looks at the theorists and theories of psychology. Some of the theorists mentioned include Sigmund Freud, Karl and William Menninger and Edward Tolman; among the psychological schools and ideas described are Gestalt Psychology, Operant Conditioning and Scapegoating.

Encyclopedia of Sociology. Edgar F. Borgatta and Marie L. Borgatta, editors. 4 Volumes. New York: Macmillan Publishing Co., 1992.

The lengthy articles in this set (generally none are shorter than four pages) cover topics of particular research interest to sociologists, such as Death and Dying and Quality of Life, and sociological concepts like Replication, Anomie and Alienation, and sociology as practiced in such countries as Scandinavia and Japan.

Encyclopedia of Sleep and Dreaming. Mary A. Carskadon, editor-in-chief. New York: Macmillan Publishing Co., 1993.

A look at the biological, medical and psychological research on sleep and dreams. Some of the entries: All-Nighters, Deafness and Dreaming, Individual Differences, Tea, Telepathy and Dreaming, and Teddy Bears!

Human Sexuality: An Encyclopedia. Vern L. Bullough and Bonnie Bullough. New York: Garland Publishing, 1994.

Over two hundred articles related to human sexuality fill this volume. Some discuss attitudes toward sex, such as Catholic Attitudes Toward Sexuality; some describe types of sexual behavior and specific practices, including Petting and Greeks: Sexual Customs of the Ancient Greeks. The physiology and psychology of sex, diseases, homosexuality and many aspects of reproduction are also examined. No illustrations.

International Encyclopedia of the Social Sciences. David L. Sills, editor. 17 Volumes. New York: The MacMillan Co. and The Free Press, 1968.

Lengthy essays discuss concepts, theories and methods in the social sciences, that is, politics, economics, law, anthropology, sociology, penology and social work. Also touched upon are the "semi-social sciences," ethics, education, philosophy and psychology, and the "sciences with social implications," biology, geography, medicine, linguistics and art. There are also lengthy biographies for six hundred individuals whose research and writings have had an impact on the social sciences. Just a few sample headings in this exceedingly varied set: The State: The Concept, Chinese Political Thought, and Interaction: Social Exchange. Despite its age, this set is still a standard, found in the reference collections of most larger libraries.

The Oxford Companion to the Mind. Richard L. Gregory, editor. New York: Oxford University Press, 1987.

One volume of 1001 entries that looks at the physiology of the brain, and psychological and philosophical concepts related to brain function. Concepts from major thinkers like Carl Jung and Sir Isaac Newton are also presented.

World Philosophy: Essay-Reviews of 225 Major Works. Frank Magill, editor. 5 Volumes. Englewood Cliffs, NJ: Salem Press, 1982.

A compilation of essays distilling and critiquing philosophical concepts from the Sixth Century B.C. to 1971. Among the philosophers covered— Roy Wood Sellars (the philosophy of Physical Realism), William James (on Pragmatism) and Niccolo Machiavelli (*The Prince*).

Science

Encyclopedia of Human Biology. 8 Volumes. Renato Dulbecco, editor-in-chief. San Diego: Academic Press, 1991.

A highly accessible guide to human physiology and the forces that shape it and effect it. Each lengthy article supplies a glossary of terminology employed in that particular section. Just a few of the topics covered include Depth Perception, Life Expectancy, the Retina, and Viral Infections.

McGraw-Hill Encyclopedia of Science & Technology. 20 Volumes. Sybil P. Parker. 7th edition. New York: McGraw-Hill, 1992.

Updated about every half-decade, this set is commonly found in good-sized public and academic libraries. Providing information in every field of contemporary science and technology, the entries are generally lengthy, running several pages or more. Drawings, tables and graphs are included in (with few exceptions) subdued colors (blue, grey, black, white.) Some subjects are updated annually in the *McGraw-Hill Yearbook of Science and Technology.*

Sports

Be aware that there are many sports reference books that use the term "Encyclopedia" in their title, but are really books of sports records and statistics. For those type of books see chapter 10, "Facts and Statistics Books." Below are examples of books that follow what we think of as more traditional encyclopedias, books that provide history, descriptions and biography.

The Complete Encyclopedia of Hockey. Zander Hollander, editor. 4th edition. Detroit: Gale, 1993.

The history of NHL hockey, covering every NHL season, including the Stanley Cup playoffs. Outstanding players are profiled, and the All-Time Player Register lists the record of every player who has ever appeared in a National Hockey League game.

Barnaby Conrad's Encyclopedia of Bullfighting: Illustrated. Boston: Houghton Mifflin Co., 1961.

If you haven't seen photographs of bulls with implements in their bodies or bullfighters scarred and torn, then you haven't yet opened up the *Encyclopedia of Bullfighting.* Since bullfighting is a tad more violent than butterfly catching, such illustrations are to be expected. Many photos also capture the movements common to bullfighting. This volume defines words of the sport and supplies short biographies of well-known matadors and novilleras (apprentice bullfighters). There are also biographies of such people as painters, announcers and horn-wound specialists!

Encyclopedia of North American Sports

History. Ralph Hickok. New York: Facts on File, 1992.

Coverage of both contemporary and obsolete sporting events of Canada and the United States. In addition to historical coverage of dozens of sports, this single-volume work surveys major records, places, organizations and people of sports.

Encyclopedia of Track and Field. New York: Prentice-Hall Press, 1986.

Each entry in this guide looks at a particular "run" or event (for example, the 100 Meter or High Jump) and looks at the training, technique, and people who have excelled in that event.

Golf Magazine's Encyclopedia of Golf: The Complete Reference. The editors of *Golf Magazine.* 2d edition. New York: HarperCollins Publishers, 1993.

A look at the history of golf, major championships and tournaments, who's who in golfdom, golf course architecture, and equipment, principles and rules of the game.

The World Encyclopedia of Soccer. Michael L. LaBlanc and Richard Henshaw. Detroit: Gale Research, 1994.

This encyclopedia goes over the history of soccer, its rules and tactics, biographies of players, major soccer associations in countries worldwide, disasters and tragedies, women's soccer, Olympic soccer and FIFA (the international governing body of soccer).

Wars

The Cold War: 1945-1991. Benjamin Frankel, editor. 3 Volumes. Detroit: Gale, 1992.

The first two volumes are comprised of biographical essays looking at leaders and other "participants" during the so-called Cold War period. Some figures featured include past presidents and prime ministers of the United States, Western and Eastern Europe, the Soviet Union, China and other Communist (at that time) nations. The third volume contains a chronology of the Cold War and coverage of the history, concepts, events and organizations of the era.

Encyclopedia of the Confederacy. Richard N. Current, editor-in-chief. 4 Volumes. New York: Simon and Schuster, 1993.

A sourcebook to the Confederate States of America, which was in existence for the four years of the Civil War, 1861-1865. In addition to an abundance of war-related information and biography, some social and cultural topics are also addressed.

Encyclopedia of the Holocaust. Israel Gutman, editor-in-chief. 4 Volumes. New York: Macmillan, 1990.

This set covers individuals, major events, countries involved, concentration and extermination camps, ghettos, and political movements and trends from pre-World War II times to the postwar consequences of the attempt by the Third Reich to expel and destroy European Jews.

International Military and Defense Encyclopedia (IMADE). Trevor N. Dupuy, editor-in-chief. 6 Volumes. New York: Brassey's (US), 1993.

IMADE was developed with seventeen major subject areas in mind, in-cluding Combat Theory and Operations, Logistics, Armed Forces and Society, Leadership, Command and Management, Defense and International Security Policy, Material and Weapons, and History and Biography. Some of the weapons systems examined include Armored Ground Vehicles and Guided Missiles. Types of skirmishes covered include Mountain Warfare and Naval Warfare. Some miscellaneous topics addressed include Legal Aspects of Terrorism and Night Vision Technology Applications. Essays are also devoted to most countries of the world, examining such elements as strategic problems or advantages associated with its geography and other factors, military alliances and total armed forces.

The Simon and Schuster Encyclopedia of World War II. Thomas Parrish, editor. New York: Simon and Schuster, 1978.

A one-volume, A-to-Z overview of the people, places, forces and invasions of WWII.

The Vietnam War. 12 Volumes. New York: Marshall Cavendish, 1989.

A simply written, highly illustrated account of the Vietnam War, with each short volume of fifty to sixty pages looking at specific aspects, fighting units and events. Some volume titles include The Grunts, Tet'6 and After the War.

Bibliographies

When you are beginning your research on a topic, why not find out if someone has already compiled a nice neat list of resources for you to peruse? Bibliographies, not to be confused with biographies, are lists that recommend research resources on a particular subject. Sometimes, bibliographies are the result of an author's research on a particular aspect of a topic. After writing his book, article or encyclopedia entry, he will collect all of the titles of the resources he used and list them at the end of his writing. Sometimes this list is referred to as "Suggested Further Readings" or "Other Sources."

At other times, those interested in a particular subject will simply compile bibliographies that are book-length. They hope that other researchers will use pieces of the information they recommend to continue burrowing into the subject. Actually, this book, that you are reading at this very moment, is in large measure an annotated bibliography . . . with lots of side comment. Sample titles of full book-length bibliographies are:

> *Runaway Children and Youth: A Bibliography*
>
> *Black Holes: An Annotated Bibliography*
>
> *Employment Discrimination in the Public Sector: An Annotated Bibliography.*

Bibliographies may list books, articles, films, sound recordings, special library collections, special newsletters, associations, and anything else that might assist enthusiastic researchers identify what information exists on their topic. (Hint: When browsing a bibliography, look for the kind of information on the subject that is not there. That's what you might want to write about.)

An excellent way to locate bibliographies is by using the *Bibliographic Index* (H.W. Wilson Company. 1937/42-present). Arranged by subject heading, the *Bibliographic Index* cites bibliographies with at least 50 references that show up in books, pamphlets, magazines and journals or that are published separately. The 50-reference-limit rule is broken only when the topic is unique enough to warrant mention. Some examples from the index include, under the heading "Soyfoods," the *Soy Yogurt: Bibliography and Sourcebook, 1934-1993*, which includes original interviews and unpublished archival documents, published by the Soyfoods Center in 1994; and under "Mentally Handicapped Children," pages 411-418 of the book *Children with Mental Retardation: A Parent's Guide* (Woodbine House, 1993).

Chapter Nine

Chronologies and Calendars

It's A.D. 500. Your character is sipping a cup of coffee. But in that year he was probably sipping it for its medicinal value. Coffee wasn't recorded as a beverage until around A.D. 1000. That's the kind of detail you want to be aware of and be able to find to add historic authenticity . . . or at least to find a factual point from which you can then jump off into a flight of fancy.

The time is now. You want to trace the roots of a contemporary story from its first appearance a few years earlier. No problem—many resources commonly found in libraries and described in this chapter will help you track major news happenings and events quickly.

Anniversaries, Commemorations, Holidays, Holy Days and Festivals

If you know about certain anniversaries well in advance, you might be able to write something about them before others do. Just remember, if you are thinking of writing about National Magic Day, which happens in October, don't submit it a week before. Submit it in April. The following directories will help alert you well in advance:

Chase's Annual Events: The Day-by-Day Directory to (Year). Chicago: Contemporary Books. Annual.

Chase's lists, by day, anniversaries, holidays, birthdays, festivals and

events—unofficial, official, legal and silly. Some events listed in *Chase's*: January 10-16: Man Watchers Week; June: Dairy Month; September 16: Stay Away From Seattle Day; and December 2-5: The Festival of Trees in Topeka, Kansas. *Chase's* also acts as a mini-almanac, supplying such facts as major annual awards, astronomical phenomena of the year recorded and years ahead, a list of the names of U.S. Supreme Court justices, and a world map of time zones.

The Folklore of American Holidays: A Compilation of More Than 400 Beliefs, Legends, Superstitions, Proverbs, Riddles, Poems, Songs, Dances, Games, Plays, Pageants, Fairs, Foods and Processions Associated with Over 100 American Calendar Customs and Festivals. Hennig Cohen and Tristam Potter Coffin, editors. 2d edition. Detroit: Gale, 1991.

Roughly in chronological order (though there are many date overlaps). This volume looks at the lore and legend associated with American holidays. The descriptions are informative and interesting. Some of the holidays discussed are well known (like St. Valentines Day), other celebrations listed are more obscure (such as Buzzard Day). Now, can't you imagine a local periodical being interested in your article coverage of Buzzard Day? (It happens the first Sunday after

March 15 near Hinckley, Ohio, where a flock of red-headed turkey buzzards returns annually to Hinckley Ridge. The celebration includes a pancake breakfast, souvenir buying and selling and a walk to Hinckley Ridge).

The Folklore of World Holidays (1992), is set up in the same manner as the U.S. holiday compendium. This international volume describes holidays unique to different countries, and also recounts how widely observed holidays, such as Christmas, are celebrated in various nations. Even a few yummy-looking recipes are included, like the "*Kringle Coffee Cake*" from Estonia and the "*Anoush Abar*," a sweet soup traditionally made at Yuletide in Armenia.

Frew's Daily Archive: A Calendar of Commemorations. Andrew W. Frew. Jefferson, NC: McFarland, 1984.

A month-by-month listing of commemorations worldwide for each day of the year. Some are major religious and sectarian holidays; some remember events of national or international importance. Some examples, using the 12th of September: In 1910, Ms. A.S. Wells became the first policewoman in the United States, it is the Mid-Autumn Festival in Macao, and Ethiopian Popular Revolution Commemoration Day is celebrated.

Holidays, Festivals and Celebrations of the World Dictionary: Detailing More Than 1,400 Observances from All 50 States and More Than 100 Nations. Sue Ellen Thompson and Barbara W. Carlson, compilers. Detroit: Omnigraphics, 1994.

The volume opens by briefly listing holidays chronologically, by state and then by nation. Each holiday is then listed alphabetically, with its history and associated activities described. For example, in Geisenheim, Germany, a six hundred-year-old Linden tree is the center of attention for the annual Lindenfest. Visitors come to taste the wine from the local, renowned vineyards and to visit a local Franciscan shrine. It is held the second weekend in July.

Chronologies

Chronologies list events in date order. Chronologies are often used by teachers or librarians who want to be able to plan exhibits for special days and by broadcasters and news writers who want to throw out some it-happened-on-this-day-200-years-ago trivia. Be aware that many chronologies do not supply a great deal of information for each event; for example, the *Timetables of American History* reports that in 1790 "John Greenwood invents foot-powered dental drill." Although the words are few, you do know for sure that you can have a character in the late 1700s being operated on by a dentist who is using a foot-powered dental drill. Multisubject chronologies, like the *Timetables of American History*, which look at happenings and important events in a variety of areas (such as science, the arts and so on), help paint a quick picture of what the world (or a particular region) was like in a particular year or for a specific time period. As James Trager says in the preface of his work *The People's Chronology* (described below), chronologies "help to show interrelationships (often obscured in conventional history) between political, economic, scientific, social and artistic facets of life."

Aeronautics

Chronicle of Aviation. Mark S. Pyle. London: Chronicle Communications, Ltd., 1992.

Unlike most chronologies, this one is chock full of drawings and photographs of aircraft and aviators. Each year begins with just one page chronologically summarizing major aviation events of that year. That page is followed by a series of short articles, some from writings of the time, touching on the year's most important happenings. There are a number of *Chronicle* books set up in a like manner, including:
Chronicle of Britain
Chronicle of Canada
Chronicle of the Royal Family (U.K.)
Chronicle of the Second World War
Chronicle of the 20th Century, Australia
Chronicle of the 20th Century, United States
Chronicle of the 20th Century, United Kingdom
Chronicle of the World

Flight and Flying: A Chronology. David Baker. New York: Facts On File, 1994.

This chronology is a listing of those events that the author feels contributed "in some measurable way" to the development of flight and flying. It lists record-breaking civil and military flights and dates for development and first flights of prototypes and other aircraft. (I was interested in a more mundane date: May 15, 1930, the day Ellen Church, registered nurse, became the world's first in-flight stewardess. The requirements of the job called for

a height of not more than 5'4", and a weight of no more than 115 lbs.)

The Arts, Literature and Media

American Musical Theatre: A Chronicle. Gerald Bordman. 2d edition. New York: Oxford University Press, 1992.

Arranged year by year (show by show and season by season), this chronicle is written in narrative format with the author discussing musical plays, players, composers and playwrights of each time period, interweaving reviews, descriptions and biographies along the way. Many of the descriptions are quite entertaining as well as enlightening.

Calendar of Literary Facts: A Daily and Yearly Guide to Noteworthy Events in World Literature from 1450 to the Present. Samuel J. Rogal, editor. Detroit: Gale, 1991.

The *Calendar of Literary Facts* was primarily designed to answer "who wrote what when?" Other facts it supplies: authors' births and deaths, their nationalities, publication dates of titles and the literary forms and plots of many writings. Did you see the Kenneth Branagh film version of *Much Ado About Nothing*? This volume reminds us of the sobering fact that Shakespeare wrote that piece in 1598. Will your writing be as long-lasting?

A Chronological Outline of World Theatre. Walter J. Meserve and Mollie Ann Meserve. New York: Feedback Theatrebooks and Prospero Press, 1992.

Beginning with 3,000 B.C., this small volume touches on the origins of theater, theater movements and births and deaths of influential persons of world drama. The authors alternate sections that briefly outline events, with pages of text that go into more detail for each country. Also provided are simple line diagrams depicting the shape and elements (i.e., stage area, audience section, etc.) of the Greek, Roman, Sanskrit, *Noh*, Chinese, *Kabuki*, Elizabethan and modern-day proscenium theaters.

The Ghost Walks: A Chronological History of Blacks in Show Business: 1865-1910. Henry T. Sampson. Metuchen, NJ: Scarecrow Press, 1988.

A look at black performances and performers starting just after the Civil War. The book has many rare photographs of dramatic players, sheet music, playbills and advertising. In many cases the author has included critiques or article excerpts concerning a particular show. (Note: The title came from a reference to the manager or owner of a show who would go to each performer, once a week, dressed in a white outfit—thus the ghost comparison. If the "ghost was walking" that meant people were getting regularly paid.)

Mass Media: A Chronological Encyclopedia of Television, Radio, Motion Pictures, Magazines, Newspapers and Books in the United States. Robert V. Hudson. New York: Garland Publishing, 1987.

The author has divided this book into sixteen eras, consisting of between five and thirty-plus years. For example, 1638-1764 is labeled the Founding Period for various mass me-

dia, and 1954-1963, the Era of Fear and Hope. This volume traces the origin and development of each of the mediums discussed, including the birth of great (or significant) movies, monographs, periodicals, broadcasts, newspapers, key technology, publishing houses and networks.

A few pages of major media "firsts" are listed at the beginning of the volume, including: "1774—The first magazine of distinction" (*The Royal American*, which during its publication included some of the copper engravings of Paul Revere), and "1868—The first woman reporter on a major (New York) daily newspaper" (Mrs. Emily Verder Bettey was hired by the *Sun*).

Timelines of the Arts and Literature: A Chronology of Culture in Human History—From the Magdalenian Cave Paintings to Madonna. David Brownstone and Irene Franck. New York: HarperCollins, 1994.

The scope of this book encompasses film, broadcasting, theater, music and dance of all varieties, literature, photography, vaudeville, circuses and architecture. Early entries are grouped in longer time periods; as material increases, the groupings go from decades to year-by-year accounting. This is a highly useful chronology for finding any entertainment/media-related event, including births, deaths, completion/publication/production of great works, openings and the founding of art forms. Very briefly, in each time period, the authors outline other world events outside of cultural events for added historical context.

Business

American Dreams: One Hundred Years of Business Ideas and Innovation from the Wall Street Journal. Kenneth Morris, Marc Robinson and Richard Kroll. New York: Lightbulb Press, 1990.

A compilation of memorable events in American business from 1889 to 1989. Moving year by year, the text is fascinating and the photographs of people, new technology, advertising and events are varied—touching, humorous or just plain interesting. Some of the highlights touched upon include the formation of U.S. Steel (a merger of eight companies) in 1901, the death of garters and birth of pantyhose in 1959, and the Three Mile Island nuclear plant disaster in 1979.

Business History of the World: A Chronology. Richard Robinson. Westport, CT: Greenwood Press, 1993.

A basic timeline of representative worldwide business events that represent the evolution of business from 10,000 B.C. through the 1980s. Beginning with the entries for 1600, the author lists some General Events for each year along with Business Events. This book is meant to complement the title *United States Business History: 1602-1988*, also by this author.

General World Chronologies

Asimov's Chronology of the World. Isaac Asimov. New York: HarperCollins Publishers, 1991.

Asimov divides each time period into twenty- to fifty-year chunks (earlier eras have longer spans) and provides overviews, generally divided geographically, worldwide. For example, for the period 1300-1350, each of the following areas is allotted between a few sentences to over a page each: England, Scotland, Ireland, France, Castile, Venice, Milan, Florence, Naples, the Holy Roman Empire, Denmark, Poland, Switzerland, Lithuania, Hungary, Russia, Serbia, the Byzantine Empire, Africa, Persia, China, the Ottoman Empire and North America. Another chronology by Isaac Asimov: *Asimov's Chronology of Science and Discovery* (1989).

Book of Ages. Desmond Morris. New York: Viking Press, 1983.

A very clever book—wish I'd thought of it first! The author numbers the book from zero to one hundred-plus, each number representing a person's age. For each age, a significant achievement or happening is listed for a person of that age. Some examples: Age 8—Franz Liszt had actually been playing piano for years, but at age 8 he *finally* began to compose; Age 22—Rudolph Nureyev defected from Russia to the West during a visit to Paris in 1961; and Age 88—Mae West died at that age, but not before appearing in the film *Myra Breckinridge* at age 78 and *Sextette* at the age of 85.

Chronological History of the United States: Foreign Relations. 3 Volumes. New York: Garland Publishing.

Each entry has a title in capital letters that looks like a headline, which is followed by a few sentences or paragraphs of description. For example: "June 29th, 1984—THE SOVIET UNION SEEKS NEGOTIATIONS

TO BAN SPACE WEAPONS, BUT COUNTER-PROPOSALS BY THE UNITED STATES ARE REJECTED." The description goes on to say that at this time, the Soviet Union is not interested in folding the discussion of space weapons into broader arms control talks, as the White House is. However, a few weeks later both sides do agree to modernize the "Hot-Line" communications between their two capitals. Volumes 1 and 2 (published 1985) cover the time period 1776-1981; Volume 3 (published 1991) looks at January 21, 1981, to January 20, 1989.

Chronology of the Modern World: 1763 to the Present Time [1965]. Neville Williams. New York: David McKay Company, 1967.

Arranged year by year, twenty-four event elements, labeled A-Z, are presented. The first dozen are simply events of note for each of the twelve months, and then there are categories for Music, Philosophy, Scholarship and so on. Item Z lists births and deaths of notable international figures in that year. The events are described in just a few words. For example, in 1882, under Sport, it says: "American Baseball Association founded." The thorough back-of-the-book index makes it simple to look up a person or event of interest, which then refers you to the proper year.

The New York Public Library Book of Chronologies. Bruce Wetterau. New York: Stonesong Press Book, 1990.

An excellent, multisubject first-place-to-look chronicle of international events. This volume briefly notes events of consequence worldwide, under fourteen broad subject categories. Some of the subcategories include (under the heading "Politics and Law"): The U.S. Criminal Justice System, Historic Assassinations, and Uprisings and Revolts; (under the heading "War and Military History"): the English Civil War, the Chinese Civil War, and the Korean War. This volume has a little bit on *a lot* of subjects.

The People's Chronology: A Year-by-Year Record of Human Events from Prehistory to the Present. Revised and updated edition. James Trager. New York: Henry Holt and Co., 1994.

A chronology of everything. In addition to the major categories covered in other chronologies, the *People's Chronology* has created specific headings for matters of everyday interest such as Nutrition, Consumer Protection, Energy and Food Availability. Ordered by year, each section denotes the topic of different paragraphs with icons, e.g., a small clenched fist represents Human Rights and Social Justice, and a little fish is used for Marine Resources. The symbols make is easy to quickly spot the section you need.

Timelines on File. The Diagram Group. New York: Facts on File, 1988.

The publisher Facts on File has put out a number of books physically constructed as this one is: in a large loose-leaf notebook with straightforward charts or illustrations on heavy paper intended for reproduction (intended to accompany, for example, a speech). The publishers explicitly state on the front inside cover of the book that all are welcome to copy at will . . . for nonprofit, private or educational use). The timelines are divided into seven sections: American, Canadian, European and World History, Religion/ Ideas, Science/Technology and The Arts.

Events are listed only by year, with just a few-word description for each. For example: "1941—Penicillin introduced," and "1555—Coach introduced in England." Though the wording is brief, the amount of information is immense. However, since the Index only lists names and not areas, subjects or events, there is no simple way to check for most of it. Other Facts on File publications set up like this one: *Environment on File*. (1983. Environmental Analysis.) *Human Body on File*. (1983.) *Maps on File*. (1981-present. Updated Annually.)

Timelines. Paul Dickson. Reading, MA: Addison-Wesley Publishing Co., 1990.

The unique aspect of this chronology is its listing of key phrases and slogans, fads, movers and shakers, and major statistics representing each year from 1945 to 1989. For example, in 1958, the list titled "People Most Likely to Be on the Cover" includes Charles de Gaulle, Eleanor Roosevelt and Jack Paar; in 1982, the popular buttons and bumper stickers included: "Warning! I Stop for No Apparent Reason" and "Happiness is Coming."

Timetables of History: A Horizontal Linkage of People and Events. Bernard Grun. New York: Simon and Schuster, 1979.

Based on the original German work *Kulturfahrplan* of 1946 (by Werner Stein). I have found this volume to be exceedingly useful in my reference work, since it covers the world and a number of topics: History/Politics, Literature/Theater, Religion/Learning Philosophy, the Visual Arts, Music, Science/Technology/Growth and Daily Life. The layout of the book, in grid fashion, makes it simple to easily see the events in all of the topic areas for one year.

The Timetables of History begins in 4,241 B.C. (or as the author refers to it: -4,241) and winds up in 1978. There is much minutiae of interest, such as: 1269—The first toll roads in Europe; 1578—Catacombs of Rome discovered; and 1918—Daylight saving time introduced in America.

Music

I've given a separate heading to Music, in addition to the Arts category mentioned previously (note that some of the books in that category do include music), to point out the wealth of material available on the chronology of modern-day music. By browsing the reference music area (the 780s) of a midsize public library, you shouldn't have any problem identifying "top 40 hits" type chronologies. Below are examples of some unique compilations:

Calendar of Music and Musicians. Adele P. Manson. Metuchen, NJ: Scarecrow Press, 1981.

This guide was designed to assist those who want to be able to look at a day of the year and see what musical event occurred on that day, anywhere from the sixteenth to twentieth centuries. This listing focuses on the achievements of musical performers, composers, conductors and scholars. Each entry begins with a person's name and records one of the following: birth, death, famous performance, debut or premiere.

Country Music: 70 Years of America's Favorite Music. Bob Millard. New York: HarperPerennial, 1993.

For each year the author lists the most important records and milestones of country music. In later years, awards and debut artists for the year are also cited. For example, just a few of the facts from 1990: Garth Brook's "Friends in Low Places" was named one of the most important recordings of the year, the debut artist was Mary Chapin-Carpenter, the Kentucky Headhunters received the Grammy award for Best Country Performance by a Group or Duo with a Vocal, the album *Reba McEntire Live* was a huge success, and Naomi Judd announced that she was retiring, after revealing that she has a potentially fatal liver disease.

An Eighteenth-Century Musical Chronicle: Events 1750-1799. Charles J. Hall. New York: Greenwood Press, 1990.

This book is compiled from program notes for a radio program in which the announcer provided political, social or cultural commentary to go along with musical selections of a given year. The music featured is primarily what the author calls "art" music; that is, there is less emphasis on "popular" music. Some points covered for each year include New Positions (for example, new conductors being appointed),

Prizes and Honors, and the publishing or performance of musical compositions. The author has also put together two other chronologies: *A Twentieth-Century Musical Chronicle: Events 1900-1988* and *A Nineteenth-Century Musical Chronicle: Events 1800-1899* (both published 1989).

Music Since 1900. Nicolas Slonimsky. 5th edition. New York: Schirmer Books, 1994.

A descriptive chronology of ninety-one years of primarily classical music and opera events. The language is not directed to the layman. For example, one of the few nonclassical/opera references, hopefully tongue in cheek, reads: "11 September 1962. John Lennon, Paul McCartney, George Harrison and Richard Starkey ("Ringo Starr"), four young, brash and pert Liverpudlians destined to ascend the empyrean heights of fame, fortune and ubiquitous adulation under the inspired sobriquet The Beatles phonemically related to the rhythmic beat and the order of coleoptera, make their first recording together in a hallucinogenic rendering of two vocal quartets, "*Love Me Do!*" and "*P.S. I Love You.*"

Rock On Almanac—The First Four Decades of Rock 'N' Roll: A Chronology. Norm N. Nite. New York: Harper and Row Publishers, 1989.

A year-by-year review of mainstream rock music from 1945 through 1989. For each year, categories include names of debut artists, top albums, top singles, Grammy winners, Rock and Roll Hall of Fame inductees, movies featuring pop music artists, deaths and music news stories of the year (i.e., in 1987 George Michael's hit song "I Want Your Sex" was banned by many U.S. stations).

This Day in African American Music. Ted Holland. San Francisco: Pomegranate Artbooks, 1993.

Arranged day by day, this chronicle looks at events for different years on that particular day. It includes the days that African-American singers, musicians and composers of all musical genres were born and notes important showings on the musical charts.

This Day in Rock: Day by Day Record of Rock's Biggest News Stories. John Tobler. New York: Carroll and Graf, 1993.

The layout of this book looks like a slick scrapbook of news stories, with headlines, short "articles," and many black-and-white photos. The author documents the highs and lows that made rock headlines, with some good humor thrown in. For example, a picture of Sid Vicious wearing his typical sneer is captioned as "Sid looks lovable." Still, this does have the facts and is actually an enjoyable read.

News Events: United States and Worldwide

The Annual Register: A Record of World Events. Harlow, Essex: Longman Group UK Limited, 1758-present.

Arranged alphabetically by nation, this yearly compilation contains articles covering events of world interest. (For each country, some quick, key data is also included, such as the main language(s), capital and main export

earners.) Some of the major occurrences noted in the 1993 edition were: IRA bombings in Britain, the death of King Baudouin, the Israel-PLO agreement and the creation of the Czech and Slovak republics.

Facts on File: Weekly World News Digest. New York: Facts on File.

Very similar to *Keesing's*, described below, this loose-leaf source supplies synopses, on a weekly basis, of worldwide news events. *Facts on File* gives more space to U.S. events than *Keesing's*. Under its heading for miscellaneous news happenings each week, *Facts on File* includes highlights of major sporting events, award listings, obituaries and outlines of the generally more "popular" news stories of the week e.g., Michael Jackson revealing his skin-lightening disease on *Oprah* (*Facts on File,* 2/18/93, p. 108).

Keesing's Record of World Events (Formerly titled *Keesing's Contemporary Archives: Weekly Diary of World Events.*) Harlow, Essex: Longman. Monthly. 1931-present.

Each monthly issue of *Keesings's* (collected in annual binders) gives an overview of world events under six geographic headings: Africa, The Americas, Asia-Pacific, Europe, Middle-East/Arab World and International. Items covered are those of political or economic importance to the world or a region.

Politics

Almanac of Modern Terrorism. Jay M. Shafritz, E.F. Gibbons, Jr., and Gregory E.J. Scott. New York: Facts on File, 1991.

Part I of the *Almanac of Modern Terrorism* supplies a timeline of violent political incidents since World War II. Part II is a minidictionary of terms of terrorism, including slang like Necklace (the term for the abominable practice of putting a gasoline-soaked tire, which is then set aflame, around a victim's neck) and names of organizations both those involved in terroristic activities and those formed to propel their downfall, such as Amnesty International.

Assassinations and Executions: An Encyclopedia of Political Violence: 1865-1986. Harris M. Lentz, III. Jefferson, NC: McFarland and Co., 1988.

A listing of world leaders, from the mid-nineteenth century to the third quarter of the twentieth century, who were killed during or after their term, assignment or reign. The first leader recorded is Abraham Lincoln.

Kings, Rulers and Statesmen. Edward W. Egan, compiler and editor. New York: Sterling Publishing, 1976.

A chronology of the rulers of the world from earliest recorded history through the mid-1960s, arranged alphabetically by country. For each "ruler," the birthdate, death date, family relationships and years of reign or term are listed.

The Presidential Chronology Series. Dobbs Ferry, New York: Oceana Publications.

For all of the Presidents from George Washington through Ronald Reagan, each volume in this series represents a brief chronology of major events in the man's life, significant documents

and speeches during his Presidency and titles of additional research materials on that particular President.

Rulers and Governments of the World. 3 Volumes. Martha Ross, Volume 1; Bertold Spuler, Volume 2; and Bertold Spuler, C.J. Allen and Neil Sauners, Volume 3. New York: Bowker, 1978.

Each volume, covering a different time period, is listed in alphabetic order by nation or territory. Rulers and statesmen are named along with dates of their accession, nomination, election or usurpation. When available, the compilers have also supplied the birth and death dates of the leaders. The periods covered: Volume 1—Earliest Times to 1491, Volume 2—1492 to 1929, Volume 3—1930 to 1975.

Religion

Chronological and Background Charts of Church History. Robert C. Walton. Grand Rapids, MI: Academic Books, 1986.

Moving in calendar order, this book pinpoints the leaders, scholars and reformers of Christian religions, shows contrasting theology between the different sects, and draws the "family trees" of different religions.

This Day in Religion. Ernie Gross. New York: Neal Schuman, 1990.

With an emphasis on Christianity and a leaner look at Judaism and Eastern religions, *This Day in Religion* provides synopses for those events and individuals responsible for shaping modern-day religious beliefs.

Timetables of Jewish History: A Chronol-

ogy of the Most Important People and Events in Jewish History. Judah Gribetz. New York: Simon and Schuster, 1993.

There are five headings for each year: General History, Jews in North and South America, Jews in Europe, Jews in the Middle East and Elsewhere, and Jewish Culture. Following the heading "Jews in Europe" provides a chronicle of events before and during the Holocaust.

Science and Technology

A Chronology of Noteworthy Events in American Psychology. Warren R. Street. Washington, DC: American Psychological Association, 1994.

Some of the daily events recorded in this volume, with the majority ranging from 1892 to the present, include dates of publication of important writings (such as Harry Harlow's article, "*The Nature of Love*"), dates of birth of influential psychological thinkers and practitioners, passage of significant legislation (such as the passing of psychology licensure laws in Maryland and New Hampshire, both in 1957), events in the history of the American Psychological Association and listings of awards.

A Chronology of the History of Science: 1450-1900. Robert Mortimer Gascoigne. New York: Garland Publishing, 1987.

Part I is divided into nineteen areas of science, with events occurring within each area listed chronologically by decade. Some of the more specialized divisions not seen in similar compendiums are Mineralogy and Crystallography, Evolution and He-

redity, Human Anatomy, and Embryology.

Part II is arranged by twelve countries and regions, allowing the reader to pinpoint the discoveries of one of those geographical areas.

Landmarks in Science. Robert Bingham Downs. Littleton, CO: Libraries Unlimited, 1982.

In seventy-four biographical sections, listed chronologically, the author describes individuals who have made breakthrough discoveries or had history-changing ideas. Each two- to four-page section discusses the achievements of the person within the context of the goings-on of their time period, and touches on past ideas that inspired each thinker. Some of the scientists: Pliny the Elder (Natural History, 23A.D.-79A.D.,) Tycho Brahe (Astronomy, 1546-1601), and William Beaumont (Digestion, 1785-1853).

On the Move: A Chronology of Advances in Transportation. Leonard C. Bruno. Detroit: Gale, 1993.

On the Move focuses on civilian (nonmilitary) modes and means of transportation from 30,000 B.C., when some seagoing crafts were believed to have existed, through the 1990s and the "Smart Card" electronic toll collection system. In addition to specific vehicles, this chronology notes the building of roads, bridges, railways and airports, and comments on milestones such as major transportation companies going out of business, solo flights, and ever-increasing speed records.

Timetables of Science: A Chronology of

the Most Important People and Events in the History of Science. Alexander Hellemans and Bryan Bunch. New York: Simon and Schuster, 1988.

An excellent year-by-year breakdown of achievements and discoveries in six categories: General Science, Astronomy, Life Science, Mathematics, Physical Science and Technology. In addition to the fairly short descriptions common to chronologies, the author provides several-page overviews of the scientific scene for nine major periods. Also by these authors: *The Timetables of Technology* (1993). In the *Technology* volume, you can easily scan the yearly accomplishments in the fields of Architecture and Construction, Communications/ Transportation, Food and Agriculture, Materials/Medical Technology and Tools and Devices.

Sports

American Women in Sport: 1887-1987: A 100-Year Chronology. Ruth M. Sparhawk, Mary E. Leslie, Phyllis Y. Turbow and Zina R. Rose. Metuchen, NJ: Scarecrow Press, 1989.

A chronological listing of the female competitors, winners, record-breakers and role-breakers in U.S. sports.

The Baseball Chronology: The Complete History of the Most Important Events in the Game of Baseball. James Charlton, editor. New York: Macmillan Publishing Co., 1991.

A linear account of noteworthy baseball moments: record breakers, pennant races, player and franchise shifts, many "firsts" (such as the first steal of first base) and "lasts" (like the

last park to install lights), and individual highlights from the majors and the minors, Negro leagues, Japanese leagues, Latin American baseball and college ball.

Facts and Dates of American Sports: From Colonial Days to the Present. Gorton Carruth and Eugene Ehrlich. New York: Perennial Library, 1988.

The firsts, bests and notables are listed for almost every athletic activity under the sun, including handball, field hockey, horse racing, dog racing, car racing, air racing, boxing, tennis, walking, wrestling, skiing . . . well, you get the idea. Some biographies of sports notables are also sprinkled throughout the volume.

Timetables of Sports History: Baseball. William S. Jarrett. New York: Facts on File, 1989.

Beginning with 1903, a year-by-year look at major events under three categories: Regular Season: American and National League, World Series (and beginning 1933, All-Star Games and World Series games), and Awards and Honors. Also by this author: *Timetables of Sports History: Football* (1993), *Timetables of Sports History: The Olympic Games* (1990), and the *Timetables of Sports History: Basketball* (1990).

U.S. History and Events

American Decades: 1950-1959. Richard Layman, editor. Detroit: Gale, 1994.

This is a collection in progress, with this volume, covering the 1950s, the first volume of the series. There will be eight more, each chronicling a twentieth-century decade. Each of the thirteen chapters, which include the Arts, Business, Education, Fashion, Law, Lifestyles, Media, Medicine, Politics, Religion, Science and Technology and Sports, contains the following elements: a chronology of significant events in the field, topics in the news, short biographies and deaths of important people of that time, and awards of note.

Chronology of the Old West. William P. Hardy, New York: Vantage Press, 1988.

The author puts the events and developments in the western United States between 1860 and 1900 (from the point of view of the non-Native Americans) in time order. Some events: "October 29, 1861—California Chief Justice Stephen Field transmits the first coast-to-coast telegraph to President Lincoln. This California-to-Washington, DC, message was one that expressed hope and unity for the nation," and "April 6, 1882—Jesse James is buried at his family homestead near Kearney. His gravestone notes that he was 'murdered by a traitor and coward whose name is not worthy to appear here.' " The book also contains photos of lifeless bandits, transport of the time, upstanding citizens and main streets of the era.

Chronology of African-American History: Significant Events and People from 1619 to the Present [1990]. Alton Hornsby, Jr. Detroit: Gale, 1991.

The chapter titles reflect the overall situation of African-Americans in the United States, including Chapter 1—Involuntary Servitude, 1619-1860,

Chapter 4—The Age of Booker T. Washington, 1901-1917, and Chapter 11—The Attack Against Segregation, 1946-1954. A chronicling of victories, breakthroughs and setbacks throughout the centuries.

Chronology of the American Indian. Newport Beach, CA: American Indian Publishers, 1985.

A listing of major events of the pre-Columbian and post-Columbian periods. There are black-and-white photos and drawings on almost every page showing people, craft, art, dwellings and paintings depicting everyday life, ceremony and battle.

Day by Day: The Sixties. Thomas Parker and Douglas Nelson. New York: Facts on File, 1983.

This is part of an ongoing series, with currently available editions covering the fifties, sixties and seventies. Major world and U.S. events are presented in a sentence or two for each day of each decade. Headings for U.S. events are Politics and Social Issues, Foreign Policy and Defense, Economy and Environment, Science, Technology and Nature, and Culture, Leisure and Life Style, with an emphasis on happenings covered by the mainstream news media. Much of the material comes from the *Facts on File* reports listed above.

The Day in American History. Ernie Gross. New York: Neal-Schuman Publishers, 1990.

Look up any day of the year and see what significant U.S. historical events occurred on that day, beginning with the 1400s (though the majority of listings are from the eighteenth, nineteenth twentieth centuries). Many of the important dates noted are the birthdates of those who were influential in the shaping of America. The entries are no more than a sentence or two, and record such great moments of U.S. history as September 4, 1882, when the first Labor Day parade was held in New York City, and July 27, 1922, the birth of TV producer and director Norman Lear, creator of the shows *All in the Family, Maude, The Jeffersons* and *Sanford and Son*.

The Encyclopedia of American Facts and Dates. Gorton Carruth. 9th edition. New York: HarperCollins, 1993.

This is a very readable chronology; the author consistently writes complete sentences instead of the sentence fragments so common in chronologies. The big landmarks are included, as are some other small but interesting facts, such as the June 24, 1882, fact: "The only major league baseball umpire expelled for dishonesty, Richard Higham, left the National League." The subject index is quite detailed.

For each year, the author places the events in four groupings containing related topics: I—Exploration and Settlement, Wars, Government, Civil Rights, Statistics; II—Publishing, Arts and Music, Popular Entertainment, Architecture, Theater; III—Business and Industry, Science, Education, Philosophy and Religion; and IV—Sports, Social Issues and Crime, Folkways, Fashion and Holidays. This book begins its reporting with the first Norse explorers of 986 and ends with a 1992 statement by the nation's Catholic bishops: "Women need not submit to abusive husbands."

Ethnic Chronology Series. Dobbs Ferry, New York: Oceana Publications.

Each volume in this series focuses on immigrant groups now living in America. At least a portion of each of these books presents important events for each group. Some titles in this series include:

Estonians in America—1627-1975: A Chronology and Fact Book. Jaan Pennar, editor. 1975.

The Filipinos in America—1898-1974: A Chronology and Fact Book. Hyungchan Kim and Cynthia C. Mejia. 1976.

The Greeks in America—1528-1977. Heike Fenton and Melvin Hecker. 1978.

Great Events from History. Frank N. Magill, editor. Englewood Cliffs, NJ: Salem. A series of multivolume sets.

Ancient and Medieval Series. 3V. 4000 B.C.-A.D. 1500. (1972)

American Series. 3V. [?]-1963.

Arts and Culture Series. 5V. 1897-1992. (1993)

Human Rights Series. 5V. 1900-1991. (1992)

Modern European Series. 3V. 1469-1969. (1973)

Science and Technology. 5V. 1888-1991. (1991)

Worldwide Twentieth Century Series. 3V. 1900-1979. (1980)

Great events such as the discovery of the wheel, development of gothic architecture, the Supreme Court of the U.S. ruling that states cannot compel flag salutes, and *The Honeymooners* (TV show) enchant(ing) audiences of all ages, are examined in essays of a few pages each that contain four elements: quick reference material (which supplies time, locale and major players of the event); a summary (which explains what took place, with cause-and-effect commentary); pertinent literature (which is described in essay/review format); and a listing of additional recommended readings.

Historic Documents of [year]. Washington, DC: Congressional Quarterly. Annual.

Begun in 1972, this annual compiles documents deemed of "basic importance in the broad range of public affairs." The documents include political speeches (including the annual presidential "State of the Union" address), interviews, court decisions and excerpts from studies and reports. For example, Historic Documents of 1975 includes excerpts from the report "*Fluorocarbons and the Environment,*" in which a federal task force recommends that fluorocarbons 11 and 12 be banned by January 1978; the 1992 edition includes the text of Saudi Arabia's first constitution as well as a letter from Earvin "Magic" Johnson to President George Bush, in which Johnson resigns from the National Commission on AIDS. Each document is put into perspective, with a background summary provided.

Racial and Religious Violence in America: A Chronology. Michael Newton and Judy Ann Newton. New York: Garland Publishing, 1991.

A timeline of acts of violence spawned from intolerance in the United States, beginning with a Portuguese explorer kidnapping fifty Indians in 1501 (he intends to sell them as slaves; the ship he has them on disappears—it is assumed to have been due to a mutiny of the Indians). The last incidents in the book are from 1988, including the murder of civil rights sympathizer Judge Robert Vance, who is killed when opening a parcel bomb.

The Timetables of American History. Laurence Urdang, editor. New York: Touchstone Books, 1981.

Described well on the cover as "What happened and who did what in America at the same time in history—plus major concurrent events elsewhere." The categories for each year are History and Politics, The Arts, Science and Technology, and Miscellaneous; each grouping lists incidents that occurred in America and "Elsewhere." For example, under the Miscellaneous/America category in 1776, a major event was "fire destroys most of the old parts of New York City;" elsewhere it was "famine strikes Bengal, India; one third of the population dies."

Wars and Battles

At War in the Gulf: A Chronology. Arthur H. Blair. College Station, Texas: A&M University Press, 1992.

A recounting of the U.S. operations known as Desert Shield and Desert Storm, from mid-1990 to its after-war implications, following February 1991. The war was a U.S. retaliation against Iraq and its leader Sadam Hussein after the Iraqi invasion of Kuwait.

Battle Chronicles of the Civil War. 6 Volumes. James McPherson. New York: Macmillan Publishing Co., 1989.

Each volume is devoted to one year of the Civil War (1861-1865), primarily comprised of long chapters on each battle, but which also include essays on topics such as *"Life in Civil War America."* (This is actually not, in the strictest sense, a chronology, but like a chronology, you would be able to quickly pinpoint certain activities of a particular year.)

The Civil War Day by Day: An Almanac, 1861-1865. E.B. Long. Garden City, New York: Doubleday and Co., 1971.

The text is divided into years, months and days. The author writes of each and every day of the Civil War, following the belief of the historian that "history is all events, all time, all people everywhere," meaning that this compendium contains more than a record of only the "principle" happenings. This book can be read and enjoyed from beginning to end or used to find the activities of select days. The entries for each day are generally several paragraphs long.

Chronicle of the First World War. Randal Gray. 2 Volumes. New York: Facts on File, 1990.

For each day of World War I, from 1914 to 1921, you can look across nine columns of information under the headings: Western Front, Eastern Front, Southern Fronts, Turkish Fronts, African Operations, Sea War, Air War, International Events and Home Fronts. These volumes also contain a who's who of World War I figures, and maps depicting sites of

significant wartime activities.

Cold War Chronology: Soviet-American Relations, 1945-1991. Kenneth L. Hill. Washington, DC: Congressional Quarterly, 1993.

A record of the many proclamations, defections, misunderstandings, negotiations and policies during the "Cold War" period. Events recorded include violations of treaties, comments on summit meetings and very brief synopses of the opinions of Soviet and American leaders relating to elements effecting the relationship of the two "superpowers."

The Harper Encyclopedia of Military History from 3500 B.C. to the Present. 4th edition. R. Ernest Dupuy and Trevor N. Dupuy. New York: HarperCollins Publishers, 1993.

This volume chronicles the military history of the world, looking at specific wars and battles along with the changes over time in military tactics, strategy and weaponry. Though most entries are comprised of no more than a short paragraph, the authors supply essays for each section that provide history and context for the events that they list. Some representative chapter headings include: War Becomes An Art: 600-400 B.C., The Dark Ages— Battle Ax and Mace: 800-1000, The Era of Napoleon: 1800-1850, and The Dominance of Technology: 1975-1990.

Vietnam Battle Chronology: U.S. Army and Marine Corps Combat Operations, 1965-1973. David Burns Sigler. Jefferson, NC: McFarland and Co., 1992.

The author chronicles the time period in which the vast majority of combat occurred involving the Army and the Marines. For each combat operation, the author lists, in a succinct fashion, the name that was given to the particular operation, its general location, objectives, which units participated (U.S., allied and Vietnamese), the events and casualties.

The Vietnam War: An Almanac. John S. Bowman, general editor. New York: World Almanac Publications, 1985.

The greater portion of this book is made up of a chronological accounting of the occurrences of centuries earlier that culminated in the Vietnam War, and a day-by-day listing of events during the war itself (from a U.S. perspective). The *Almanac* also contains essays that discuss the land, air, naval and irregular forces, and short biographies or selected government, political and military figures involved in the conflict.

World War II: America at War, 1941-1945. Norman Polmar and Thomas B. Allen. New York: Random House, 1991.

This volume opens with a brief daily chronology for the years America was involved in World War II. The majority of the volume is more of a encyclopedic dictionary, with over two thousand entries on battles, weapons, notable figures, places and events.

A Chronological Atlas of World War Two. Charles Messenger. New York: Macmillan Publishing Co., 1989.

This chronology looks at events preceding, during and after what the author calls the "largest and most inten-

sive conflict that the world has ever known." This volume is filled with annotated maps that assist in both explaining events and pinpointing the locations in which they occurred.

Women

Almanac of American Women in the 20th Century. Judith Freeman Clark. New York: Prentice Hall Press, 1987.

A decade-by-decade listing of women's actions and involvement in all walks of life. The *Almanac* includes many (small, but striking) photographic portraits of women. Biographies of notable women, about a page or so in length, are interspersed in appropriate time periods of the chronology.

Chronology of Women's History. Kirstin Olsen. Westport, CT: Greenwood Press, 1994.

A chronicle of major occurrences that have impacted or involved the women of the world; the actions of almost five thousand women are recorded. Arranged by year, some of the topic areas include Athletics and Exploration, Education and Scholarship, Government/ Military and the Law, and General Status/Daily Life.

Feminist Chronicles: 1953-1993. Toni Carabillo, Judith Meuli and June Bundy Csida. Los Angeles: Women's Graphics, 1993.

This work documents the work of the feminist movement, crediting the National Organization of Women (NOW) as a main instigator in its progression, through the years covered: the early 1950s through the early

1990s. The year-by-year grid presentation is divided into three major areas: Events, such as the appointment of the House of Representative's first female page on May 31, 1973; Issues (including Lifestyles and Economic, Religious, Legal and Political Issues), and examples of "Backlash," such as the 1955 urging of Adlai Stevenson for women to participate in politics "through the role of wife and mother."

This work is actually excerpted from a larger work still in progress called the *Feminist Chronicles of the Twentieth Century*. This volume also reproduces, in full text, some major NOW documents, including the original Statement of Purpose, written in Autumn 1966, and various position papers, including *"NOW's Position on the Current Proposal to Institute a Compulsory Registration of Young People"* (1980).

Chapter Ten

Facts and Statistics Books

No writer would impress a reader by saying that "lots" of people supported an issue. Saying that a scientifically conducted study showed that 73 percent of all people were supporters would of course be more convincing.

Along with statistics, fascinating facts, sometimes elusive, also serve to spice up writing. How often have you been in need of just one tiny bit of information that you knew could be easily found . . . somewhere!

The resources in this chapter will help you track the facts—the biggest and smallest, the most popular and the population of anywhere.

Let me first mention the two compilations I always check first when looking for almost any statistic: *The Statistical Abstract of the United States* and the *World Almanac.* (More detailed descriptions of both will be provided later.) If you can't find what you want in one of those books, start using the hints and resources outlined in this chapter!

Browsing the Reference Collection to Find Statistics

Statistical compilations will usually be shelved in a library's Reference Collection. There are two basic types of statistical books:

Subject-Specific Statistical Compilations.

One way of finding specialized statistical directories is by simply browsing in the area of a Reference Collection that represents your subject area. For example, compilations of health statistics will be in the R section of the Reference stacks in a Library of Congress arranged library, and in the 610-619 area of a Dewey library, where the medical/health books are.

General Statistical Compilations.

General statistical compilations, which often cover a wide variety of topics, are shelved in the HA reference section of LC collections, and 310-319 in Dewey. On page 174 is a further breakdown of the kinds of statistical books found in different call number areas.

Using an Online Library Catalog to Find Statistics

There are several approaches for finding statistical books in an online library catalog:

By Subject

Try a subject search in the catalog to find statistics. Use a word describing the kind of statistics you want (or an area you'd like statistics for) combined with the word STATISTICS. Some examples:

CALIFORNIA STATISTICS
ST. PAUL STATISTICS
POPULATION STATISTICS

Other possibilities:
OPINION POLLS

Library Of Congress:

HA154—4737	Statistical Data
HA154—155	Universal Statistics
HA175—4737	By Region or Country
HA195—730	United States
HA221—724	Individual States
HA730.A1—739	U.S. Cities, A-Z

Dewey Decimal:

310—	General Statistics
312—	Demographic Statistics
314-319—	Statistics of Specific Regional Areas

PUBLIC OPINION (combined with a subject word, such as CRIME)

Combining a subject word with the heading MISCELLANEA also brings up some interesting books, resources with a variety of facts and statistics. The result of an online search using SCIENCE and MISCELLANEA on my local public library catalog came up with the titles *365 Surprising Scientific Facts, Breakthroughs and Discoveries* (Wiley, 1994) and *Great UnSolved Mysteries of Science: From the End of the Dinosaurs to Interstellar Travel and Life on Other Planets* (Betterway Books, 1993).

By Name

If you know the name of a particular organization or issuing agency, doing an author search with the name of the organization is another way of locating statistics. When searching for a U.S. agency, spell out "United States." (Online catalogs usually have you drop words such as "the" and "of." Check the

instructions for your online system.) Examples of name searches:

BUREAU CENSUS UNITED STATES
BUREAU LABOR STATISTICS UNITED STATES
DEPARTMENT DEFENSE

By Title

If you already know the exact title of the source you need, your catalog will allow you to search by that title to see if your library owns the book and to give you the location.

Statistics Tip: Keep in mind that many useful books containing statistics are not found in statistical compilations; they're just in general, run-of-the-mill books. For example, a general book that discusses capital punishment will most likely quote statistics dealing with the death penalty, and a book about divorce will likely list figures for marriage breakups.

Almanacs and Everything Books

Many books are published that one might call "everything" books. They are crammed with facts, sometimes related to each other, sometimes not.

Perhaps because it has assisted me innumerable times in answering questions, I think of the World Almanac as the quintessential "everything" book. Some questions I have answered using the World Almanac include:

> What is the height of the taller of the twin Trade Center towers in Manhattan? 1,368 feet.
> What is the Roman numeral for 90? XC.
> How much does the governor of Colorado earn annually? Only $70,000! Far below most other governors. Hasn't anyone heard that our cost of living has risen?

Other annually published almanacs covering the same type of information as that found in the World Almanac:

Canadian Almanac & Directory. Toronto: Canadian Almanac and Directory Publishing Company Limited, 1847-present.

Information Please Almanac. Boston: Houghton Mifflin, 1947-present.

Universal Almanac. Kansas City, MO: Andrews and McMeel, 1989-present.

Whittaker's Almanack. (Great Britain.) London: J. Whitaker and Sons, Ltd., 1868-present.

Another excellent source of answers to quick look-up questions is the New York

Public Library Desk Reference, really a miniencyclopedia of commonly asked questions (2d edition. New York: Prentice Hall General Reference, 1993). There are items in here that you won't find in an almanac, including Pseudonyms of Famous Authors, Spelling Guidelines, Anatomical Drawings with Parts of the Body Labeled and Real Estate Terminology. But it does also include many of the most popular features of the general almanacs, including weights and measures, major holidays and population statistics. This is the type of reference book that might be good as a home reference for your writing.

Opinions

Do you want to know the number of people that favor a certain issue you'd like to address in a feature? Or do you want to include what percentage of a given population feels strongly (in one way or another) about a current trend that you are writing about? Try these compendiums of public sentiment:

American Public Opinion Index. Louisville, KY: Opinion Research Service, 1981-present. Annual.

An index to the public opinion surveys conducted by a variety of market research organizations, universities, associations and media companies. The index leads you to the accompanying microfiche set, called American Public Opinion Data, which provides summary results of the surveys. If you can not get the microfiche set, the Index provides the information needed to contact the pollster.

Gallup Poll Monthly. [Formerly called

The Gallup Report.] Princeton, NJ: The Gallup Poll, 1964-present.

The *Gallup Poll* presents results of monthly surveys that the organization conducts. About one hundred surveys are conducted annually. Some of the same topics repeated each year, for comparison, include Religion in America, Alcohol Consumption, and the most admired men and women in America. A survey of the President's performance is conducted bimonthly.

Index to International Public Opinion. Westport, CT: Greenwood Press. Annual.

This annually updated volume shows results of surveys conducted in single countries as well as those given to groups of nations. The polling data includes items of general international interest, for example, "In your opinion, how much of an effect can individual citizens and citizens' groups have on solving our environmental problems?" as well as questions about values and everyday habits, such as use of media and eating habits.

Public Opinion Online (POLL). Storrs, CT: Roper Center for Public Opinion Research, 1960-present. (Some questions pre-1960.) Monthly.

Each record in this online database represents a survey question, with answers usually shown as percentages. POLL covers a wide spectrum of public-interest topics, including politics, international affairs, social issues and attitudes, business, and consumer issues and preferences. (Available online through *DIALOG* and *GEnie.*)

Statistical Indexes

Just as periodical indexes lead you to the articles found in magazines, statistical indexes help you find particular statistics buried in statistical compilations. Some are:

American Statistics Index (ASI). Washington, DC: Congressional Information Service, 1973-.

A detailed subject index to statistics published in U.S. Government publications. Since the U.S. government publishes material on virtually all subjects, the variety of statistics is impressive.

How to use *ASI*:

ASI is published monthly and cumulated annually. It is published in two volumes: an Index volume and an Abstract volume. Start with the Index volume and either search for statistics by name or subject (e.g., homicide) or by category (e.g., by age). The Index entries provide an abstract number that you can look up in the accompanying Abstract volume. In the Abstract volume you will find a summary description of the resource along with a citation (so that you can find the resource). Note of interest: All items marked with a black dot in this publication should be owned by libraries that are full government depositories. (Other libraries should have at least some of the publications.)

Two indexes that you search using the same methodology as *ASI* are:

Index to International Statistics (IIS). Washington, DC: 1983-.

An index to the statistical international government publications from such organizations as the United Nations (UN), the World Health Organization (WHO) and the International Monetary Fund (IMF).

Statistical Reference Index (SRI). Washington, DC: Congressional Information Service, 1980-.

A subject index to a variety of publications produced by sources other than the U.S. government. Sources include: state agencies, associations, magazines and journals, business organizations and universities.

More statistical indexes include:

Datamap 1990: Index of Published Tables of Statistical Data. Phoenix, AZ: Oryx Press, 1990.

Datamap is an index to several dozen common statistical sources (many of them are listed in this chapter). Though *Datamap* may point you to volumes that contain statistics older than you need, it is still useful. Since many compilations print similar statistics each year, knowing that your statistic appeared in a 1988 source indicates that it will probably appear in that source for the current year as well.

Statistics Sources. Paul Wasserman. 17th edition. Detroit, Michigan: Gale Research, 1994.

A subject guide to statistical data on industrial, business, social, educational, financial and other topics for the United States and internationally. This index recommends a wide variety of publications as well the names of agencies and organizations who may supply statistics.

Fact and Statistics Compilations

Statistics are not always fast and easy to come by, but you may find just the ones you are after in one of these compilations, listed by subject category.

Awards

Performing arts.

The Academy Awards Index: The Complete Categorical and Chronological Record. Richard Shale. Westport, CT: Greenwood Press, 1993.

This index lists both the winners and the nominees for all Oscars from 1927 to 1992. The award winners for the "extra" awards, including Special Achievement and the Irving G. Thalberg Memorial Award, are also named.

Award Winning Films: A Viewer's Reference to 2700 Acclaimed Motion Pictures. Peter C. Mowrey. Jefferson, NC: McFarland and Co., Publishers, 1994.

A compilation of award-winning films from the silent era through 1990. Not all films listed were judged best picture; some won for categories such as Best Song. Each film won at least one award from the thirty-one award organizations surveyed (including the Academy Awards, the Berlin Film Festival Awards, the New York Film Critics Circle Awards and Film Comments "Best Ever" Poll). Entries for each film include the country of origin, year made, color or black and white, length, production credit, director, screenwriter, actors, brief description, notable features, what awards it won, sequels or remakes and rating. The guide is very well indexed, providing cross-reference by Studios and Countries of Production, Actors, Writers, Directors and Subject. The Appendix lists the top award-winning movies of all time; *A Man for All Seasons* (the original) was number one, having won thirty-one awards.

The Golden Turkeys Awards: Nominees and Winners—The Worst Achievements in Hollywood History. Harry Medved and Michael Medved. New York: Perigee Books, 1980.

A sequel to the authors' 1978 effort, *The Fifty Worst Films of All Times.* This book awards the Golden Turkey for such categories as The Worst Performance By an Actor as Jesus Christ, and The Worst Rodent Movie of All Time. The awards are completely subjective (based on the authors' opinions) and quite fun.

International Film Prizes: An Encyclopedia. Tad Bentley Hammer. New York: Garland Publishing, 1991.

Arranged in order by the forty-three countries featured, this "encyclopedia" is actually a chronological listing, within prize category, of the award winners for a variety of national film prizes through 1990 (though most end in 1989). For example, in Bulgaria, they award the Zlatnata Roza (The Gold Rose) during the annual Festival of Bulgarian Films at Varna. China awards the Golden Rooster. Several U.S. awards are included as well.

Tony, Grammy, Emmy, Country: A Broadway, Television and Records Awards Reference. Don Franks, compiler. Jefferson, NC: McFarland and Co., 1986.

A listing of winners in all categories from the time each award began through 1984. (Except Emmys, which are listed through 1983.)

Variety's Directory of Major U.S. Show Business Awards. New York: R.R. Bowker, 1989.

The winners and nominees in a total of over four thousand categories are named for Pulitzer Prize plays, Oscars, Tonys, Emmys and Grammys through 1988.

General award compendium.

World of Winners: A Current and Historical Perspective on Awards and Their Winners. Gita Siegman, editor. 2d edition. 1992.

World of Winners claims to identify winners of awards in "all areas of human endeavor." Some of those areas include Education, Librarianship, Public Affairs and Technology. Some specific awards (out of the 2,500 included!) are the Beyond War Award, the National Inventor's Hall of Fame, the Scientific Medal and the American Bar Association Medal.

Nobel Prizes.

The Nobel Prize Winners. Frank N. Magill, editor. Pasadena, CA: Salem Press, 1987-91.

This series of multi-volume sets looks at all the Nobel Laureates in all six categories of the Nobel Prize: Literature, Physics, Chemistry, Peace, Economic Sciences and Physiology or Medicine. Each multivolume set is devoted to a category and comprised of articles that look at the Laureate's life and career and describe the speeches and commentary that accompanied the awarding of the prize. The articles are presented in chronological order by year of award.

Nobel Prize Winners. Tyler Wasson, editor. New York: H.W. Wilson, 1987. *Supplement: 1987-91.* Paula McGuire, editor.

Fairly lengthy biographies and small photographs are provided for Nobel Prize winners in all categories since 1901.

Science and invention.

Spirit of Enterprise: The Rolex Awards. Bern, Switzerland: Buri.

Awarded every three years, Rolex Awards recognize excellence in Applied Sciences and Invention, Exploration and Discovery, and the Environment. This book devotes several pages of description and photographs to projects submitted by 267 of the candidates. Some of the projects featured in the 1990 edition included work on a solar-wind power system, and deep-ocean camera, video and lighting systems (which were used to explore the Titanic wreckage).

Writing.

Foreign Literary Prizes: Romance and Germanic Languages. E.C. Bufkin, editor. New York: R.R. Bowker Co., 1980.

A representative listing of literary awards of twenty-five countries that includes "the famous and the obscure, the old and recent, the discontinued and continuing." The criteria for each prize is described only briefly; winners are listed from the beginning of each award to as recently as 1980. U.S. awards are not listed.

Index to American Short Story Award Collections: 1970-1990. Thomas E. Kennedy. New York: G.K. Hall and Co.

A slim volume that will identify the titles and authors of award-winning short fiction for the past two decades. Titles of winning stories for the following prizes are listed: Pushcart Prize, American Fiction Series, AWP Short Fiction Award, Drue Heinz Literature Prize, Flannery O'Connor Award, University of Illinois Short Fiction Series and Iowa School of Letters Award. The awards themselves are very briefly described, though details for entering are not provided.

Literary and Library Prizes. [Originally titled *Famous Literary Prizes and Their Winners.*] 10th edition. New York: R.R. Bowker, 1980.

Divided into four sections—International Prizes, American Prizes, British Prizes and Canadian Prizes—this guide describes each award and lists past winners along with the title of their winning work (though some prizes are awarded on lifetime or general achievements, and not just one piece of writing).

Newbery and Caldecott Medalists and Honor Book Winners: 1922-1992. Muriel W. Brown. New York: Neal-Schuman Publishers, 1992.

Arranged alphabetically by author's name, this directory identifies that book or books by the author that won an award, and then lists the other materials written by the author. Newbery recognizes the children's book of the year; Caldecott honors the children's picture book of the year, with the emphasis on illustration.

Reginald's Science Fiction and Fantasy Awards: A Complete Guide to the Awards and Their Winners. Daryl F. Mallett and Robert Reginald. San Bernardino, CA: Borgo Press, 1993.

Brief descriptions of 228 awards and listings of the winners and the piece of writing they were recognized for.

Athletics

Almost all reference sources involving sports include statistics! Either player stats or records. So here I'll list just a few examples. For assistance in actually interpreting these figures, try Jeremy Feinberg's *Reading the Sports Page: Guide to Understanding Sports Statistics* (New Discovery Books, 1992).

The Complete Book of the Olympics. David Wallechinsky. Boston: Little, Brown and Co., 1992.

This handbook contains the complete statistics for the final results of every Olympic event from 1896 through 1988.

The Guinness Book of Sports Records. New York: Facts on File. Annual.

A listing of both "serious" sports, such as the winners of hockey's Stanley Cup beginning from 1893 to the present, and some that are a tad more trivial, like the completion of 46,001 push-ups in twenty-four hours performed by Charles Servizio in April 1993.

The Information Please Sports Almanac. Mike Meserole, editor. Boston: Houghton Mifflin Co. Annual.

This almanac contains information on sports happenings for the current year, historical and contemporary stats for most major college and professional sporting events, and brief who's who entries for sports figures. There are many statistics tucked away in this volume, such as the capacity of major arenas and ballparks, athletic awards bestowed by journalists, and a listing of the top twenty-five horses in horse racing and the money they earned for others.

The Sports Encyclopedia: Baseball. David S. Neft and Richard Cohen. New York: St. Martin's Press. Updated irregularly.

Arranged in chronological order by year, *The Sports Encyclopedia* provides thousands of baseball statistics and facts including every player's vital statistics and lifetime totals, hall of fame inductees and yearly batting and pitching leaders. A similar source is *The Baseball Encyclopedia* (Macmillan Publishing Company). Other encyclopedias from St. Martin's Press:
The Sports Encyclopedia: Football
The Sports Encyclopedia: Pro Football-The Modern Era
The Sports Encyclopedia: Pro Basketball

Many of the official sports organizations regularly produce yearbooks and statistics and rule books. For example, the National Collegiate Athletic Association (NCAA) annually publishes rule books that detail dimensions of playing space, standards for equipment, a description of events and procedures and the duties of officials. (You can make your character realistically cheat if you know what the real rules are.) Some of the athletic and sporting events covered by the NCAA booklets include:

Baseball and Softball
Football
Men's and Women's Basketball
Men's and Women's Rifle
Men's and Women's Soccer
Men's and Women's Skiing
Swimming and Diving

Best, First and Worst

A word of caution about books that proclaim that something is the "best" or "worst." Look at their methodology; how they came to the conclusion. For example, in *The Best and Worst of Everything* the authors in the category "All Time Greatest Writers" were determined by the number of scholarly articles written about each author from 1981 to 1990. While this seems somewhat "scientific," since concrete numbers were used to determine the "winners," many literary experts would dispute the choices.

African-American Firsts: Famous, Little-Known and Unsung Triumphs in America. Joan Potter and Constance Claytor. Elizabethtown, NY: Pinto Press, 1994.

Many "firsts" books list only a line or phrase about an accomplishment. *African-American Firsts* has entries that average about a half page. Some examples of firsts: The First African-American-Owned Company to Produce Serious Films—The Lincoln Motion Picture Company, founded in L.A. in 1915 by Noble Johnson, Clarence Brooks, James T. Smith and

Harry Gant; the First African-American Wounded in the Civil War—Nicholas Biddle, an escaped slave, in April 1861, and The First African-American Anchor of a TV Morning News Show—Bryant Gumble on NBC's *Today* show; he debuted on January 4, 1982.

The Best and Worst of Everything. Les Krantz, editor-in-chief. New York: Prentice Hall General Reference, 1991.

Ratings fall into three categories: *People*, *Places* and *Things*. People categories include such headings as highest salaries in a variety of professions, most valuable autographs and many lists of "greatest" writers in a number of genres. The Places and Things sections cover a weird hodgepodge of items like states with the highest beer consumption and the incidence of leprosy. The lack of indexing limits this book's usefulness.

The Book of Lists: The 90's Edition. David Wallechinsky and Amy Wallace. New York: Little, Brown and Co., 1993.

Oh, this is a truly fun one. Lists include: "10 Celebrities Who Have Seen U.F.O.'s" (Muhammad Ali and Mel Tormé are among the alien spotters) and "Writers Watched by the FBI" (Sinclair Lewis and Pearl S. Buck were two). Some "Odd Jobs of Celebrities"? Gregory Hines was a karate instructor, Lawrence Welk was a farmer, and Sinead O'Connor was a singing kiss-o-gram French maid in Dublin.

The Book of Women's Firsts: Break-

through Achievements of Almost 1,000 American Women. Phyllis J. Read and Bernard L. Witlieb. New York: Random House, 1992.

This book is arranged in alphabetic order by each woman's last name, but the back-of-the-book index assists you in linking the achievement with the name. More than one-line blurbs are provided about each woman; each entry contains some solid biographical data. Some of the firsts: Laura Blears Ching was the first woman to compete against men in an international surfing competition, and in 1869, Amy Bradley was the first woman to supervise a public school system.

Everyman's Dictionary of Dates. Audrey Butler. 7th edition, revised. London: Dent, 1987.

A list of discovery/founding/starting dates of concepts, people, institutions and areas, birth and death dates of well-known figures, and construction dates of famous works of architecture. The dates of closures/endings are also noted. Everything is in alphabetic order, so, for example, in the As you'll find Algebra and the Aztecs, and in the Ms Mexico City and Monasteries.

Famous First Facts: A Record of First Happenings, Discoveries and Inventions in American History. Joseph N. Kane, 4th edition. New York: H.W. Wilson, 1981.

A fabulous quick look-up source to find the very first time U.S. events occurred, or when products or concepts were introduced. The first national park? Yellowstone National Park, established in 1871. The first electric blanket to warm our soles? Manufac-

tured October 9, 1946. Particularly useful are the "Index by Years," allowing an easy glance at "firsts" for a particular year, and the "Index by Days," for an overview of "firsts" that happened on a particular day as far back as the year 1007.

The Geographical Index lets you pinpoint "firsts" in particular U.S. towns and cities. Some towns have more auspicious "firsts" than others. Mount Vernon, Ohio, was home to the inventor of chewing gum (1869), while it was in Ripon, Wisconsin, that a local group suggested the moniker "Republicans" for the new political party they wished to create (1854). (I leave it to you to determine the importance of each event.)

The Gay Book of Lists. Leigh W. Rutledge. Boston: Alyson Publications, 1987.

Lists involving the lives, loves, thoughts and accomplishments of lesbians and gays (and related topics). Some sample lists include 6 Famous People Who Disliked the Word Gay (including Truman Capote, who thought the word spelled backwards was better—Yags), 43 Notable Actors Who Have Appeared in Drag in the Movies (that includes Anthony Perkins in *Psycho*, Dustin Hoffman in *Tootsie*, and Jack Lemmon and Tony Curtis in *Some Like it Hot*), and 7 Famous Gay Men Who Also Had a Gay Brother (3 on the list are Sir Francis Bacon, Francois Duquesnoy and A.E. Housman).

The Guinness Book of Records. New York: Facts on File. Annual.

You probably hear about this book

all the time, but have you ever picked it up? It does indeed cover the antics and feats that show up on local news programs, such as the accomplishment of building the biggest snowman (1992—76′2″) or making a bed awfully quickly (1990—17.3 seconds). It also lists "biggests," "smallests," "bests," "longests," "fastests," and so on for natural phenomena, sports, science and human events. *Guinness* has both a subject and name index, and unlike most quick fact books, features colorful photographs and an attractive layout.

The 100 Best Companies to Work For in America. Robert Levering and Milton Moskowitz. New York: Doubleday, 1993.

Did you know that the employees of John Deere feel truly connected to their work? Or that the Hallmark Card staff enjoy each other's company and get paid well to boot? Firms in this volume were ranked on Pay/Benefits, Opportunities, Job Security, Openness/Fairness, Camaraderie/Friendliness and Pride in Work/Company. Each item is discussed for each business.

Children and Youth

Statistical Record of Children. Linda Schmittroth, editor. Detroit: Gale, 1994. Biennial.

How many children are awaiting adoption? (In 1988, 2,600 were waiting in Illinois alone.) What percentage of children live in poverty? (In 1991 it was 21.8 percent.) What is the percentage of children that are read to? (In 1991, 47 percent of nursery

school kids were read to every day!) If you are looking for a statistic dealing with youth, give this volume a try. The statistics are gathered from many other sources. This does deal exclusively with children in the United States.

Youth Indicators: Trends in the Well-Being of American Youth. National Center for Education Statistics. Washington, DC: U.S. Dept. of Education, Office of Educational Research and Improvement. Annual.

Are modern-day kids in good physical shape? Are they proficient in science? *Youth Indicators* is a statistical compilation of data on the world of young people: family structure, economic factors, extracurricular activities, education, substance use and abuse, health and values.

Crime

Correctional Populations in the United States. Office of Justice Programs, Bureau of Justice Statistics. Washington, DC: U.S. Department of Justice. Annual.

This report looks at the number of inmates in local, state and federal jails, including those who were executed and those who are awaiting the death sentence. Breakdowns are generally provided by gender, age, race and type of crime. The publication of these figures tends to lag about two years (for example, the figures for 1991 were released in 1993.)

The Corrections Yearbook: Instant Answers to Key Questions in Corrections. South Salem, NY: Criminal Justice Institute. Annual.

The *Corrections Yearbook* is actually comprised of four pamphlet-like books, each concentrating on an area of criminal justice: Adult Corrections, Probation and Parole, Jail Systems and Juvenile Corrections. Small, but statistic-packed.

Crime in the United States: Uniform Crime Reports for the U.S. Washington, DC: U.S. Department of Justice, Federal Bureau of Investigation, 1930-present. Annual.
    Published by the F.B.I., this report presents annual statistics on U.S. crime rates, trends and arrests.

Criminal Victimization in the United States. Washington, DC: U.S. Department of Justice. Bureau of Justice Statistics, 1973-.
    A compilation of the characteristics of victims, offenders and crimes, and data on the reporting of crimes to police.

Sourcebook of Criminal Justice Statistics. Washington, DC: U.S. Department of Justice, Bureau of Justice Statistics, 1973-present. Annual.
    A yearly publication, supplying statistics on criminal offenses, arrests, prosecutions, courts, correctional facilities, releases and paroles.

Countries (Foreign)

Statesman's Year-book: Statistical and Historical Annual of the States of the World for the Year. New York: St. Martin's Press. Annual.
    This resource has been around for over one hundred years and is commonly found in larger libraries. For ev-

ery country in the world, facts and brief overviews are furnished concerning each country's history, area and population, climate, constitution and government, defense capabilities, economy, communications, religions, educational offerings and health systems.

World Factbook. Washington, DC: Central Intelligence Agency. Annual.
    Issued by the CIA, dozens of brief "facts" are listed for all of the countries of the world. Some facts listed include voting age, birth and death rate, life expectancy, literacy, general climate, environmental problems, natural hazards and religions.

Many other books listing facts and statistics about non-U.S. nations are listed in chapter 3, "Geography, Climate and Local Customs."

Economic Statistics (U.S.)

Budget of the U.S. Government. Washington, DC: Executive Office of the President. Annual.
    This lengthy document includes actual and projected government spending for a range of fiscal years. As of FY 1992, the budget includes "Historical Tables"; they were previously published separately. Highlights of the budget are published in the significantly more compact *U.S. Budget in Brief.*

Economic Indicators. Washington, DC: Government Printing Office, 1948-present.
    A monthly report of dozens of economic indicators, including those re-

lated to income, spending, employment, prices, money, credit, security markets and production and business activities. Generally, each table presents a ten-year series, with the most recent year broken down quarterly or monthly. This is actually an update to the statistical portion of the *Economic Report of the President* listed below.

Economic Report of the President Transmitted to the Congress. U.S. President. Washington, DC: U.S. Government Printing Office, 1947-present.

An annual publication that offers a review of the nation's economic condition, documented by statistics.

Federal Reserve Bulletin. Washington, DC: 1915-present.

A monthly periodical that provides current information, including statistics, on financial conditions in the United States. It also reports on financial developments in foreign countries.

Education

CIC's School Directory. Westport, CT: Market Data Retrieval, 1983/84-present.

Updated yearly, this directory provides data on public school districts and schools, Catholic and other independent schools, and regional and county centers for all fifty states and the District of Columbia. It supplies such information as address, name of principal and librarian, level of expenditure per student and the percentage of students falling below the poverty line.

The Condition of Education. Washington, DC: U.S. Department of Education, Office of Educational Research and Improvement. Vocational Center for Educational Statistics. 1975-present.

An annual statistical report covering enrollment, curricula, finance, student and faculty/staff characteristics and other indicators relevant in assessing the condition of U.S. education for the elementary, secondary and post-secondary levels.

Digest of Education Statistics. Washington, DC: Department of Health, Education and Welfare, Education Division. National Center for Education Statistics. 1975-present.

An annual compilation of a large variety of American educational statistics covering students, faculty and staff for kindergarten through graduate school. Figures are provided for enrollments, finance and expenditures, population characteristics and salaries. Examples of tables include: "Profile of Scholastic Aptitude Test Takers" and "Selected Characteristics of Participants in Adult Education."

Fact Book on Women in Higher Education. Judith G. Touchton and Lynne Davis, compilers. New York: Council on Education, 1991.

A compendium of data on women faculty, students, administrators, staff and trustees.

Projections of Education Statistics to 2003. National Center for Education Statistics. Washington, DC: U.S. Dept. of Education. Annual.

Projected statistics for elementary,

secondary and higher education. Some projections included cover enrollment, graduates and expenditures.

World Education Report. Paris: UNESCO Publishing, 1993.

In addition to a narrative look at such issues as Overcoming the Knowledge Gap, Expanding Educational Choice and Searching for Standards, this report provides worldwide statistics that include access to schooling, illiteracy rates and pupil-teacher ratio.

Energy

Annual Energy Outlook: With Projections to 2010. Washington, DC: Energy Information Administration, Department of Energy. Annual.

The *Outlook* looks at energy consumption and production of oil for gas, electricity and coal. Information is also provided on nuclear energy and renewable energies.

Annual Bulletin of Electric Energy Statistics for Europe and North America. Economic Commission for Europe. Geneva: United Nations. Annual.

This is a compendium of electricity and heat statistics for the nations of Europe, Canada and the United States. Some statistics presented cover electricity consumption and capacity of conventional thermal power plants. Presented in three languages: English, French and Russian.

Gas Facts. Arlington, Virginia: The American Gas Association. Annual.

Some section headings are: Natural Gas Supply, Prices, Energy Consumption, Appliance and Housing Data, and Energy Reserves.

ICAO Statistical Yearbook: Civil Aviation Statistics of the World. Montreal: International Civil Aviation Organization. Annual.

Some statistics presented in this international compilation include Number of Aircraft and Hours Flown by Type of Operation, Traffic of Commercial Air Carriers, Aircraft Accidents Involving Passenger Fatalities, and Airports with Highest International Traffic.

State Energy Data Book: Consumption Estimates 1960-1990. Washington, DC: Energy Information Administration, 1992.

A thirty-year look at energy consumption by various means and of a variety of types at both state and national levels.

Transportation Energy Data Book. Stacy Davis. Oak Ridge, TN: Oak Ridge National Laboratory, Prepared for the Office of Transportation Technologies, U.S. Department of Energy. Annual.

How much gas are we Americans guzzling? What are typical commute times for U.S. workers? This data book presents information on the type, age and use of public and commercial vehicles, detailing the amount of fuel or power needed to run them and the type of emissions that result.

Environment

The European Environmental Yearbook. London: DocTer International. Annual.

Much more than a book of statistics, this reference uses essays, accompanied by figures, in examining the efforts in nature conservation and planning in European nations. The Yearbook also looks at the extent of various types of pollution in these areas and at what efforts are being made to stem the tide.

The Information Please Environmental Almanac. Compiled by The World Resources Institute. Boston: Houghton Mifflin Co., 1992.

A plethora of data for the environmentally concerned. Environmental problems in different areas of the world are surveyed, the "greenness" of U.S. cities is investigated, and statistics are provided for such areas as waste production, recycling and water use.

Statistical Record of the Environment. Detroit: Gale, 1991.

Imagine a U.S. environmental question that requires a statistical answer. Look up the answer in this resource. Chances are, you'll find it. Some topics covered: Mine Ore and Waste Production, Air Pollution Control Costs, and Soil Conservation Methods. (There is a smattering of international information in here as well.)

Food

The Corinne T. Netzer Encyclopedia of Food Values. New York: Dell, 1992.

Nutritional data is provided for both brand-name and generic foods. Aspects covered include calories, carbohydrates, cholesterol, protein, fiber, sodium, total and saturated fat and vitamin content. I looked up "Twinkie" to see how it fared. The regular type

was 150 calories per Twinkie with 5 total grams of fat; the light was 110 calories and contained 2 total fat grams.

Nutritive Value of Foods. Washington, DC: United States Department of Agriculture, 1991.

Tables in this guide list nutritive value and nutrients in generic foods. The values examined are Water, Calories, Protein and Fat (Saturated, Monounsaturated and Polyunsaturated). Some of the nutrients mentioned include calcium, iron and potassium.

General Statistics—All Topics—U.S.

Gale Book of Averages. Kathleen Droste, editor. Detroit: Gale, 1994.

The *Book of Averages* looks at averages of all kinds, for activities, consumption, manufacturing, costs, weights, life cycles, temperatures and speeds. Some examples from this volume include: the average prison sentence for burglary in 1989—41.7 months; average calories burned per hour during housework—180; and driest city in the U.S.—Reno, Nevada, with average yearly rainfall of 7.53 inches.

A Matter of Fact: Statements Containing Statistics on Current Social, Economic and Political Issues. Ann Arbor, MI: Pieran Press. Semi-annual.

Arranged by subject, *A Matter of Fact* pulls out statistical statements from newspapers, magazines and congressional hearings. The statements from politicians may be of particular interest if you are looking for some broad, statistics-filled quotes on a topic of current political interest. (Also available on CD-ROM and *FirstSearch*.)

Statistical Abstract of the United States. Washington, DC: U.S. Department of Commerce, Bureau of the Census, 1878-. Annual.

Known as *Stat Abstracts*, this source is called the "bible" of statistics by some librarians. As mentioned in the beginning of this chapter, *Stat Abstracts* is a great "first place" to look for any statistic. This is an annual compilation of statistics gathered by government organizations and trade and industry groups. It includes data on subjects covered by U.S. government agencies—almost everything.

General Statistics— All Topics—International

European Historical Statistics, 1750-1975. New York: Facts on File, 1980.

A wide range of economic, demographic and education statistics for over a twenty-year period. (Although statistics for every year, for every country, are not always listed.)

Main Economic Indicators. Organization for Economic Cooperation and Development. Monthly.

Main Economic Indicators supplies economic data for the OECD member countries: Austria, Australia, Canada, Belgium, Denmark, Finland, France, Germany, Greece, Iceland, Ireland, Italy, Japan, Luxembourg, Mexico, Netherlands, New Zealand, Norway, Portugal, Spain, Sweden, Switzerland, Turkey, the United Kingdom and the

United States. Some of the figures provided cover Permits Issued for Construction, Rate of Unemployment, Average Labor Costs in Engineering Industries, and Producer and Consumer Price Indexes. As a monthly publication, this resource will often be found in the periodicals collections of libraries.

Monthly Bulletin of Statistics. Lake Sucess, NY: Statistical Office of the United Nations, 1947-present. Monthly.

This bulletin has figures for industrial production, population, employment and finance. Not all countries are included on every table.

Statistical Abstract of Latin America. Los Angeles: UCLA Latin American Center Publications. Annual.

This *Stat Abstracts* supplies a great variety of statistics (like the *U.S. Stat Abstracts*) for the twenty nations of Latin America.

Statistical Abstract of the World. Detroit: Gale, 1994.

Each chapter is arranged by country with headings covering Human Factors, Education, Science and Technology, Government and Law, Labor Force, Production and Manufacturing Sectors, and Finance and Economics.

Statistical Handbook of the Former USSR. Washington, DC: The World Bank, 1992.

Part of the *Studies in Economies in Transition* series from the World Bank. The countries of the former USSR are still in transition, as are their methods of maintaining statistics. They are now working to collect many of the statistics that are useful in a market economy. The first section of the book presents comparative data for the countries; the second section presents main statistical indicators by country.

Statistical Yearbook. Paris: U.N. Educational, Scientific and Cultural Organization. Annual.

A compilation of international cultural, educational, research and media data. It includes figures for educational attainment, research expenditures and viewing and production of film, radio and television.

Statistical Yearbook for Asia and the Pacific. Bangkok, Thailand: Economic and Social Commission for Asia and the Pacific, United Nations. Annual.

A wide spectrum of data is presented: population figures, employment and unemployment data, trade, industry, transport, communication, wages and prices. There are also some social statistics, such as education, housing and causes of death.

World Factbook. Washington, DC: Central Intelligence Agency. Annual.

Issued by the CIA, dozens of brief "facts" are listed for each country in this thin volume, including population, voting age, birth and death rate, life expectancy and literacy.

Health/Medical

AHA Hospital Statistics. Chicago, IL: American Hospital Association, 1972-present.

An annual compilation of statistical tables gathered by the American Hospital Association. The tables present a profile of services, use, personnel and finances of hospitals in the United States and associated areas.

Health Care State Rankings: Health Care in the 50 United States. Kathleen O'Leary Morgan, et al., editor. Lawrence, KS: Morgan Quitno Corporation, 1993-present. Annual.

This guide supplies basic health-related information, derived from federal and state government agencies and private organizations, listed state-by-state and ranked high-to-low. There are a variety of statistical rankings under seven major headings: Births and Reproductive Health, Deaths, Facilities, Finance, Incidence of Disease, Personnel and Physical Fitness.

Health, United States. Rockville, Maryland: U.S. Department of Health and Human Services, National Center for Health Services Research, 1975-present.

Published yearly, this report is divided into two sections. The first is a "chartbook" with tables and graphs on minority health. The second contains detailed tables organized around four major subject areas: health status and determinants, utilization of health resources, and healthcare resources and expenditures. The 1991 edition was the last edition issued in paper. It is now available on CD-ROM and should be at all government depository libraries.

Mental Health, United States. Rockville, MD: U.S. Department of Health and Human Services, 1992.

Some of the mental health statistics covered include Specialty Mental Health System Characteristics, the Training of Mental Health Providers, Mental Health Services in State Adult Correctional Facilities, and Serious Mental Illness and Disability in the Adult Household Population.

World Health Statistics Annual. Geneva, Switzerland: World Health Organization.

This is a statistic-packed volume containing both French- and English-language text. Worldwide vital statistics and causes of death are included.

Labor/Employment

Employment and Earnings. Washington, DC: U.S. Department of Labor, Bureau of Labor Statistics, 1954-present.

This periodical provides a monthly update of employment statistics, including characteristics of the employed, unemployed and persons not in the labor force. Data is usually given by age, gender, industry and occupation.

Employment, Hours and Earnings, 1909-1990. Washington, DC: U.S. Department of Labor, Bureau of Labor Statistics, 1991.

This two-volume set presents historical monthly and annual average data on employment, hours and earnings for U.S. industries. This book is arranged by SIC code. Most of the data in this bulletin is updated by *Employment and Earnings,* described above.

Handbook of Labor Statistics Washington, DC: U.S. Bureau of Labor Statistics, 1924-present.

An annual collection of statistics on labor force and employment status with figures on family relationships and earnings, work experience, job schedules, absences, turnover, earnings by state, unions and occupational injuries.

Monthly Labor Review. Washington, DC: U.S. Department of Labor, Bureau of Labor Statistics, 1918-present.

This journal supplies a wide variety of current labor statistics, updated monthly.

Year Book of Labour Statistics. Geneva: International Labour Office. Annual.

Employment, unemployment, hours of work, wages and industrial disputes are among the topics covered for more than 180 countries, areas and territories.

Minorities/Women

European Women's Almanac. Paula Snyder. New York: Columbia University Press, 1992.

This almanac presents statistics and information dealing with immigration and residence rights, equal rights, birth, life, death, lesbian rights, health care, parental pay, leave, benefits, child care provision, education, politics, detention and employment for all the countries of Europe. This book claims that of all European women, Romanian females have the shortest average life expectancy: seventy-three years.

Hispanic Databook of U.S. Cities and Counties. Research Staff. Milpitas, CA: Toucan Valley Publications, 1994.

This databook documents Hispanic population figures at state, county, city and ZIP code levels for the United States. Some of the following are included for different levels: the percentage of people who speak Spanish; the percentage of people who speak *only* Spanish, region of origin or ancestry (including Mexico, Cuba, Dominican Republic, Central America or South America), per capita income and percentage of high school graduates.

Statistical Handbook of Women in America. Phoenix, AZ: Oryx Press, 1991.

Statistical figures culled from a variety of federal agencies covering women's demographic and social characteristics, health issues and employment and economic status are presented. This book is most useful for looking at a statistic over a period of time. Despite its name, this handbook also touches on women worldwide, not just America. Helpful phone numbers for the Bureau of the Census and Department of Labor Statistics are provided in the Guide to Relevant Information Sources section.

Statistical Record of Older Americans. Arsen J. Darnay, editor. Detroit: Gale, 1994.

This resource supplies a wide variety of data concerning aging Americans. Some examples: Population Distribution by Age, Educational Attainment for People Aged Twenty-Five Plus and Sixty-Five Plus, and Median Income of Elderly Men and Women by Marital Status.

Statistical Record of Black America. Car-

rell Peterson-Horton and Jessie Carney Smith, editors. Detroit, MI: Gale Research, 1990.

This volume touches on a wide assortment of statistics, including social, political, economic and vital.

Statistical Record of Native North Americans. Marlita A. Reddy, editor. Detroit: Gale, 1993.

There are many sections of statistics available in this massive volume, including: Historical, with population statistics from pre-1492; Demographic, recording current populations of Native Americans in the U.S. and Canada; The Family, looking at selected characteristics of Native American families; Education, which records educational attainment, enrollment, academic progress and costs; and Culture and Tradition, focusing on languages spoken and occupations held.

Statistical Handbook on U.S. Hispanics. Frank L. Schick and Renee Schick. Phoenix, AZ: Oryx Press, 1991.

The statistical tables and charts in this book cover demographics, immigration and naturalization, social characteristics, education, health, politics, labor force and economic conditions.

Statistical Record of Women Worldwide. Linda Schmittroth, editor. Detroit: Gale, 1991.

This book contains a wide range of figures culled from articles, reports, studies, reference books and newspapers. They range from opinions (i.e., How important would you say religion is in your life?) to diverse statistics (e.g., the percentage of women who

hold roles on prime time television—
43 percent in 1990).

Misleading Statistics

You may want to educate yourself in the
ways statistics can be misused. You
probably don't want to be quoting faulty
statistics in your writing; they'll come
back to haunt you. It's easy to misrepre-
sent and mislead with numbers, graphs
and maps. Even simple phrasing can
sway the reader. Notice the difference
in tone in these phrases: "a minority of
48 percent have suppressed their doubts
and taken the plunge in deciding to
back the candidate," compared with
"fully 48 percent in this small region
dedicated their full support to the candidate." Two books that discuss such
maneuvers:

How to Lie With Maps. Mark Monmo-
nier. Chicago: The University of Chicago Press, 1991.

Written by a professor of geography,
How to Lie With Maps first concedes
that it is almost essential for maps to
lie when trying to portray certain relationships. That is, portions of the map
will be terribly out of scale, or show
only a selective view. However, the
author's main intent is to alert map
users to the fact that "maps, like
speeches and paintings, are authored
collections of information and also are
subject to distortions arising from ig-
norance, greed, ideological blindness
or malice." Many samples of misleading maps are provided.

*Misused Statistics: Straight Talk for Twis-
ted Numbers.* A.J. Jaffe and Herbert F.
Spirer. New York: Marcel Dekker,
1987.

The authors hope to make the readers "critical observer(s) of the statistics scene." They use examples of
common statistical errors, misrepre-
sentations and biases to help you look
at statistics and determine whether or
not they should be reasonably accurate based on how they were derived.

Political/Government

*America Votes: A Handbook of Contem-
porary American Election Statistics.*
Elections Research Center. Washington, DC: Congressional Quarterly.
Annual.

America Votes is arranged by state,
showing the precise number of votes
cast, and the percentage of votes, for
major candidates in the races for governor, congress and the presidency. A
map of each state's voting districts is
also provided.

*American National Election Studies Data
Sourcebook: 1952-1986.* Warren E.
Miller and Santa A. Traugott. Cambridge, MA: Harvard University Press,
1989.

This sourcebook supplies data, between 1952 and 1986, on a number
of election elements, including Social
Characteristics of the Electorate,
Party Identification, Trust in/Confi-
dence in Government, and Involvement and Turnout.

*Congressional Quarterly's Congressional
Districts in the 1990s: A Portrait of
America.* Washington, DC: Congres-
sional Quarterly, 1993.

A compilation of narrative, description and facts on each of the congressional districts in all of the states of

America. Some facts presented for each district include the percentage of different races and ancestry in the area, names/enrollment of local colleges and universities, the total population of the district along with the population of each county represented, and a breakdown of the percentage of those who voted Republican or Democrat for President, Congressman or Governor over the last several elections. There are six indexes: by city, county, university, military base, cable company and major business employer. The indexes assist in quickly pinpointing the district that any of those entities is a part of.

Vital Statistics on Congress. American Enterprise Institute. Washington, DC: Congressional Quarterly. Biennial.

The "vital" in this title is meant to mean "important," not "vital" statistics, as in birth and death statistics. Okay. Examples of the important statistics about Congress listed in this volume include Political Action Committee Contributions to Senate Candidates, Amount Raised by Candidate, Blacks in Congress and Women in Congress. The Appendix lists information about the members of the current Congress, providing their name, party, years of service, percentage of vote received and how they were rated (numerically) by several organizations and based on support from the White House and their party.

Population census publications.
(Note: Many of the books in this chapter note some population statistics.)

Every ten years the U.S. Bureau of the Census conducts major surveys that theoretically involve the entire population of the United States. After they complete this admittedly large-scale endeavor and add up the millions of answers, the census results are available in many libraries (and especially in government depository libraries). Many libraries now own the latest census results in CD-ROM format.

The Census asks individuals various questions; all participants are asked to answer some questions, but a smaller population answers additional questions. The STF 1 series asks 100 percent of the population questions; the STF 3 asks a sample of the population. However, the STF 3 folks get asked more questions.

The major census publications include:

Census of Population—Social and Economic Characteristics.

Contains median income figures, number of people living below the poverty line, race and ancestry, income type, levels of income and family characteristics.

Census of Population and Housing, Summary Tape File 3A (Referred to as STF 3A).

Lists place of birth, education, ancestry, migration, language spoken at home, disability, journey to work, occupation, industry, class of worker, 1989 income, year moved into residence, number of bedrooms, plumbing and kitchen facilities, telephone, heating fuel, year structure built, condominium status and shelter costs. Figures are supplied for states and their subareas in hierarchical sequence down to the block group level. Also summaries for the State portion of American Indian and Alaska Native areas, whole places, whole tracts and whole block groups.

Census of Population and Housing, Summary Tape File 3C (STF 3C).

Provides the same information as 3A for the following geographic segments: the United States, regions, divisions, states, counties, places of 10,000 or more inhabitants, county subdivisions of 10,000 or more inhabitants in selected states, American Indian and Alaska Native areas, metropolitan areas, and urban areas.

Population and Housing Characteristics for Census Tracts and Block Numbering Areas.

Looks at income levels, including mean, median, and per capita, family type and percent below the poverty level for specialized areas.

Regional (U.S.)

County and City Data Book. Washington, DC: U.S. Department of Commerce, Bureau of the Census, 1947-present.

A good source of county statistics. The data coverage includes population, health, crime, income, labor force, agriculture, wholesale and retail trade and poverty status for U.S. counties and cities.

CQ's State Fact Finder: Rankings Across America. Victoria Van Son. Washington, DC: Congressional Quarterly, 1993.

Which state spent the most on highways? (In 1991 it was Alaska.) The

most reported cases of rabies? (In 1992, Delaware.) Dozens of statistics on business, agriculture, crime, defense, education, energy, environment, health, population, recreation, government and transportation are reported and ranked within the states of the United States. Be aware that some tables report figures a number of years out of date.

Historical Statistics of the United States: Colonial Times to 1970. Washington, DC: U.S. Department of Commerce, Bureau of the Census, 1975.

A two-volume compilation containing U.S. historical statistical data on subjects ranging from rape statistics to figures for men's shoe production. This set is commonly found in midsize to large public and academic libraries.

Sourcebook of County Demographics. 7th edition. Arlington, VA: CACI Marketing Systems, 1986-present.

Every county in the United States is profiled with over seventy demographic variables, including median household income, age distribution in each county, race breakdown and "Purchase Potential Profiles," which measure potential demand for a product or service in a county.

State and Metropolitan Data Book. Washington, DC: U.S. Department of Commerce, Bureau of the Census, 1979-. Biennial.

The *Data Book* provides statistics on such items as population, housing, education, employment, industry and crime for Metropolitan Statistical Areas (MSAs) and their component counties and central cities. Published biennially, this book and the *County and City Data Book* described above, are great sources to consult between the major ten-year census periods. (By the end of each decade the major census figures are pretty stale.) Both sources are frequently found in larger public and academic libraries.

State Names, Seals, Flags and Symbols: A Historical Guide. Benjamin F. Shearer and Barbara S. Shearer. Westport, CT: Greenwood Press, 1994.

In addition to the items mentioned in the title, this book names state mottoes, capitals, flowers, trees, birds and songs. The flags, flowers, trees and birds are also illustrated in color. By the way, New Jersey, New York and Pennsylvania have no official state songs, but Tennessee has five.

Rand McNally Commercial Atlas and Marketing Guide. Chicago, IL: Rand McNally and Co. Annual.

This atlas offers a yearly update of U.S. economic and geographic information through maps, tables and charts. Population, income and sales figures are supplied for major and basic trading areas, Metropolitan Statistical Areas (MSAs) and counties. Some sample headings include "Largest Corporations in American Business" and "Railroads of the U.S." This is an oversized volume, making the state maps included especially easy to examine. Most larger libraries will carry this atlas.

Note: Some states compile their own statistical directories, like Colorado's *Statistical Abstract*. These are generally found in the libraries of that state or of nearby states.

Science and Engineering

Basic Science and Technology Statistics. Paris: Organization for Economic Cooperation and Development, 1991.

An international data book, covering OECD countries, which looks at each country's expenditures on research and development and the number of patent applications generated.

Science and Engineering Indicators. Washington, DC: National Science Board. Biennial.

Produced biennially, this series provides quantitative information about the structure and function of U.S. Science and Technology. Some areas covered include the Science and Engineering Workforce and Financial Resources for Research and Development.

Times and Dates

The International Time Tables. Gary L. Fitzpatrick. Metuchen, NJ: Scarecrow Press, 1990.

What time is it in Afghanistan when it's 10 P.M. in Albania on June 15? This book answers that question. Its tables allow you to determine time around the world.

The Book of Calendars. Frank Parise, editor. New York: Facts on File, 1982.

This reference work allows you to transfer dates from over sixty calendars of modern and ancient times to the appropriate Julian or Gregorian date. Thus, for example, you would know that the Babylonian New Year fell on April 18 in 573 B.C.

Transportation

AAMA *World Motor Vehicle Data*. Economic and International Affairs Department, AAMA. Washington, DC: American Automobile Manufacturers Association. Annual.

Statistics on production, sales, registrations, exports and imports of passenger and commercial vehicles worldwide. This data guide will be available in many larger libraries.

Automotive News: Market Data Book. Detroit: Crain Communications. Annual.

The trade publication *Automotive News* publishes this *Market Data Book* yearly. It gives numbers for production and sales of cars and trucks, by country, worldwide, with individual types of vehicles named for the United States, Canada and Mexico; it compares retail prices of U.S.-built and imported cars and light trucks, and lists the top U.S retail dealers and suppliers of vehicle accessories (the suppliers listed are primarily North American).

The Aviation and Aerospace Almanac. Compiled by the editors of *Aerospace Daily* and *Aviation Daily*. New York: TAB Books. Annual.

An almanac of information and statistics concerning international and U.S. airlines, airports, the U.S. Department of Transportation, the Federal Aviation Administration, the National Transportation Safety Board,

the Department of Defense, the U.S. Air Force, Army and Navy, NASA and the Aerospace Industry. Just some of the facts available in this almanac include Average Speed of U.S. Air Carriers, the Market Share of U.S. Airports (by carrier), and the total flight hours for different types of airplanes. Names and addresses are also included for the many departments of the agencies covered.

Highway Statistics. Federal Highway Administration. Washington, DC: U.S. Department of Transportation, 1945-present. Annual.

Statistics of general interest are listed for motor fuel, motor vehicles, driver licensing, highway-user taxation, federal and state highway finance and highway mileage.

Ward's Automotive Yearbook. Southfield, MI: Ward's Communications. Annual.

Ward's looks at the automotive industry worldwide over a year's time and discusses it in text, statistics and photographs of new vehicles. The volume begins with a Year in Review section, and goes on to examine the use of various materials and components in the manufacture of vehicles. Each world market gets a section of the book: Asia/Pacific, South America and North America, with reports for sales, wages, exports, imports, production and registrations. New and existing car models are discussed for the different automobile companies, accompanied by photographs of the cars and trucks.

Vital Statistics

Accident Facts. Chicago, IL: National Safety Council. Annual.

A booklet of tables, graphs and text concerning injuries and deaths. Examples of headings include: Motor-Vehicle Deaths on Major Holidays and School Bus Accidents.

Vital Statistics of the United States. Washington, DC: U.S. Department of Health and Human Services. Public Health Service. Office of Health Research, Statistics and Technology. National Center for Health Statistics. 1937-.

The National Center of Health Statistics produces this three-volume set covering data concerning Natality (fertility, live births, birth rates), Mortality (infant and fetal mortality, death by accidents, life tables), and Marriage and Divorce.

Wages and Salaries

See chapter 6, "Company, Product and Industry Information."

Finding Statistics in Articles

Many newly gathered statistics will appear first in newspaper, magazine or journal articles. When I can't find a statistic in one of the sources I've listed in this chapter, I start digging through the periodicals. Even if I do find statistics in reference compilations, I often look for them within articles because I know they may be more up-to-date and may offer additional commentary. Use some of the indexes/abstracts listed in Appendix A to find articles with statistics.

Chapter Eleven

Legal Details: Laws, Court Cases and Law Enforcement

State and federal laws and cases are simple to find . . . once you master a few jargon terms and learn how the resources are presented. This chapter will help you access the publications of the U.S. legal and judicial systems. Also included are books and journals that will assist you in understanding the everyday duties of those in law enforcement.

Where Can You Find Law Books?

An obvious answer to "where can you find law books" would be "law libraries." But a law library may not be your most convenient choice. Luckily, there are more options available.

Academic libraries and large public libraries. These libraries will generally offer a good solid collection of basic law books. At the very least, they should provide access to federal laws and laws of that particular state. Finding federal and state supreme court cases (for the state the library is in) would also be common in these libraries. Academic libraries that offer degrees in Criminal Justice, Paralegal Studies or other law-related programs will usually have more than the minimum, since the students of their programs will need to look into case law and statutory law (these types of law are defined below).

Court libraries. Check in your town—

there may be a state- or county-sponsored library associated with the courts that is open to the public and carries primarily law material for the use of lawyers and judges.

Government depository libraries. All full-depository libraries will have the basic collection of laws and cases that must, by law, be published and distributed by the U.S. government. For a refresher on the Depository concept, check chapter 1, "Navigating the Library."

Law Libraries. Academic libraries that cater to law students will have the widest spectrum of law materials. Alas! Most law libraries are not keen on swinging their doors open wide to the public. Generally there will be a fee, sometimes token, sometimes large, for those who are not students or faculty to gain entry to academic law libraries. But it can be worth it. Law libraries will generally own cases and laws for all the states of America, as well as some non-U.S. law materials. (Law libraries will also subscribe to sophisticated search systems such as *LEXIS/NEXIS* and *WESTLAW*. Though I feel you should be aware of those systems, you should also know: because law libraries have a strict agreement with these online vendors, only law students and faculty of the particular school each library serves have access to those databases.

Law Updates: Pocket Parts

There are thousands of laws, rules and cases. And they are in constant evolution! Law-book sets usually consist of dozens or hundreds of volumes, with each volume representing a specific legal topic or agency (or a part of the alphabet, like encyclopedias). Instead of publishing a new set of all laws each time a change occurs, many legal volumes are updated with *pocket parts*.

Pocket parts are just pages with updated information on them that get stuck into a little pocket in the back of the book. Always check your law or case in the main volume, and then flip to the pocket part to be certain that no changes have occurred. Always remember to check the pocket part! (Sometimes a law will be brand new and won't even show up in the main volume yet—it will just be in the pocket part.)

Legal Citations

When being referred to law materials, the citation might look a bit foreign. Some examples:

107 Stat 1909

122 LE2d 525

Law citations appear far more cryptic than they are; they're actually quite simple. Most citations to legal materials follow a standard format consisting of three elements:

1. The name of the court case, law or law review article.

2. The location, consisting of the volume number, an abbreviation of the name of the series or volume and the page number.

3. The date (not always included; sometimes the date will appear right after the name of the case, law or review).

Example: Roe v. Wade, 410 U.S. 113 (1973)

Read as: The case Roe versus Wade, which can be found in volume 410 of the *United States Reports* on page 113. The case was decided in 1973.

Easy, easy.

Other Legal Citation Elements You May Run Across

Sections and subsections. This symbol, §, refers to the section you should turn to in a law book if no page is indicated. When the symbol is doubled, it stands for a subsection (i.e., §§).

"And the following." The words *et seq* stand for a Latin phrase translated as "and the following." For example, here is how it would look in a citation:

Okla.Stat. 1991, Title 62, 910 et seq.

Interpretation: You will find the particular state law that this citation represents in the *Oklahoma Statutes*, the main volume of which was published in 1991, in the Title 62 volume, in section 910 and subsequent sections. Easy.

Sections denoted by two or three numbers. A section of a law may be denoted by a series of two or three numbers separated by hyphens. For example, here's a sample citation:

N.M. Stat. Anno. 1978, 32-6-1 et seq

A.	*Atlantic Reporter*
A.2d	*Atlantic Reporter, 2d Series*
A.L.R.	*American Law Reports*
Am.Jur.2d	*American Jurisprudence, 2d Series*
C.F.R.	*Code of Federal Regulations*
F.	*Federal Reporter*
F.2d	*Federal Reporter, 2d Series*
F. Supp.	*Federal Supplement*
L.Ed.	*Lawyer's Edition, Supreme Court Reports*
L.Ed.2d	*Lawyer's Edition, Supreme Court Reports, 2d Series*
N.E.	*North Eastern Reporter*
N.E.2d	*North Eastern Reporter, 2d Series*
N.W.	*North Western Reporter*
N.W.2d	*North Western Reporter, 2d Series*
P.	*Pacific Reporter*
P.2d	*Pacific Reporter, 2d Series*
P.L.	*Public law*
S.Ct	*Supreme Court Reporter*
S.E.	*South Eastern Reporter*
S.E.2d	*South Eastern Reporter, 2d Series*
So.	*Southern Reporter*
So.2d	*Southern Reporter 2d Series*
Stat.	*Statutes at Large*
U.S.	*United States Reports*
U.S.C.	*United States Code*
U.S.C.A.	*United States Code Annotated*
U.S.C.S.	*United States Code Service*

Interpretation: You will find this New Mexico state law in the *New Mexico Statutes Annotated*, originally published in 1978, in section 32-6-1, and in the pages following.

Abbreviations

Law books are chock full of abbreviations. A quick reference list of some that are commonly seen appears above (most of these books will be discussed later in the chapter).

Be aware that law publications are sometimes a bit wild and free about slightly altering these citations. For example, some listings may drop the periods after the letter; others may drop a whole letter. Also, there are times when one abbreviation may mean several things. For example O. may stand for Law Opinions, Oregon or Ohio (among other possibilities!).

One very handy collection of legal abbreviations is the *Dictionary of Legal Abbreviations Used in American Law*

Books (Doris M. Bieber. Buffalo, NY: William S. Hein and Co., 1985). For a more complete explanation of legal terms and abbreviations, see *The Bluebook: A Uniform System of Citation* (15th edition, Cambridge, MA: The Harvard Law Review Association, 1991). A volume that calls itself "a companion to the *Bluebook*" is *Bieber's Dictionary of Legal Citations: A Reference Guide for Attorneys, Legal Secretaries, Paralegals, Law Students* (4th edition. Buffalo, NY: William S. Hein and Co., 1992); it provides sample citations and abbreviations based on the *Bluebook's* rules and guidelines.

Before plunging into the ways you can find court cases and laws, be aware that several publishers produce these materials. There are "official" versions and "unofficial" versions.

The official versions:
These are the cases or statutes that are required, by law, to be published so that the general public will have access to them. These are published by the U.S. government.

The unofficial versions:
These versions, published by private publishing companies such as The Lawyers Cooperative and West Publishing Company contain the exact same text (laws, cases) as the official versions, but generally have two advantages:

1. They are annotated with additional information, which makes them more useful to researchers.

2. They are published a heck of a lot faster than the official versions.

Unofficial versions are just as authoritative as official versions.

Dictionaries and Thesauri

When looking into law issues or putting some legalese in the mouth of the lawyer in your novel, I can almost guarantee that there will be times when you need a law dictionary! Law is filled with jargon and abbreviations. The best-known law dictionary:

Black's Law Dictionary. Centennial Edition. Henry C. Black. St.Paul, MN: West Publishing Co., 1990.

Both American and English contemporary and ancient legal terminology are covered. Definitions often cite authoritative cases. I occasionally have difficulty, as a layperson, interpreting *Black's* definitions, but am usually satisfied.

Others are:

Ballantine's Law Dictionary. Rochester, NY: Lawyer's Cooperative Publishing Co., 1969.

The definitions of most words and phrases commonly used in law. Like *Black's*, the definitions will often cite the cases that help to define the word or term.

Ballantine's Thesaurus for Legal Research and Writing. Jonathan Lynton, Albany, NY: Delmar Publishers and Lawyers Cooperative Publishing, 1994.

An alphabetic list of words commonly used in legal writings with pronunciations, part of speech and synonyms. Many entries also supply a sentence or phrase that illustrates the meaning of the word (though no formal definitions are provided).

Latin Words and Phrases for Lawyers. Datinder S. Sodhi, publisher, and R.S. Vasan, editor-in-chief. Don Mills, Ontario: Law and Business Publications, 1980.

This is a great dictionary to consult if you run across a legal phrase in Latin that you need translated.

Law Dictionary for NonLawyers. Daniel Oran. St. Paul, MN: West Publishing Co., 1991.

In his introduction the author says "this is a guide to a foreign language." How true. So many legal words simply don't mean what the layman might think. The definitions here are simple and written in English (and I referred to it several times while writing this chapter).

Legal Thesaurus. William C. Burton. 2d edition. New York: Macmillan Publishing Co., 1992.

A book born from the author's dismay over the repetitive use of words in legal documents. Provided for each entry: definition, part of speech, synonyms, associated legal concepts, foreign phrases and translations and any multiple meanings. Words included are those that are strictly legal, some that are not absolutely legal (but popular with those in the law profession), and sophisticated words that attorneys may want at hand.

Mellinkoff's Dictionary of American Legal Usage. St.Paul, MN: West Publishing Co., 1992.

The definitions in this volume are fairly lengthy and easy to understand. In addition to the definition, the author also often adds a sentence in which the use of the term is illustrated. Many cross-references between terms are provided.

Encyclopedias

When I want to look up a famous case or a legal concept and need more than a quick definition, I will turn first to a law encyclopedia geared to the layperson:

The Guide to American Law: Everyone's Legal Encyclopedia. 11 Volumes, Plus Annual Supplements. St. Paul, MN: West Publishing Co., 1985-present.

The premiere layperson's law encyclopedia, commonly found in all main branch public and academic libraries. It contains readable articles on most aspects of U.S. law, including overviews of major cases. Additional sources and cases are often cited.

There are two "standard" law encyclopedias. Some collections with law materials (other than law libraries) will at least own one or the other, sometimes both. These two collections are geared to those in the legal profession, but with a good law dictionary at hand, they are certainly accessible.

American Jurisprudence, 2d: A Modern Comprehensive Text Statement of American Law—State and Federal. 82 Volumes. San Francisco: Bancroft-Whitney Co., 1962-present. (Updated with pocket parts.) [Cited as AmJur2d.]

Corpus Juris Secundum: A Contemporary Statement of American Law as Derived from Reported Cases and Legislation.

102 Volumes. St. Paul, MN: West Publishing Co. 1936-present. (Updated with pocket parts.) [Cited as C.J.S.]

Other encyclopedias that will be handy:

Encyclopedia of the American Constitution. Leonard Levy, editor. 5 Volumes. New York: Macmillan. Vol. 1-4, 1986. Supplement 1, 1992.

An encyclopedic analysis of the United States Constitution's doctrines, the people who created it and shaped it and judicial decisions, laws, treaties and executive orders based on it. Examples of some of the elements covered: the concept of Civil Liberties is discussed at length; the career of Supreme Court Justice Hugo L. Black is surveyed; and the case *One Book Entitled Ulysses* v. United States is included as a "harbinger of modern decisions on obscenity."

Encyclopedia of the American Presidency. Leonard Levy and Louis Fisher, editors. 4 Volumes. New York: Simon and Schuster, 1994.

This set looks at the powers and prerogatives of the U.S. president. It provides biographical sketches of all past and present vice-presidents, presidents, first-ladies, presidential candidates, judges and other notable officials through the beginning of the Clinton administration. If you can't figure out why the president has authority in some areas, check this set.

Two Types of Law

There are two different kinds of law:

Statutory law—Laws enacted by bodies (groups) legally authorized to pass laws: The U.S. Congress, State Legislatures, Counties and Municipalities. The precepts in the U.S. Constitution are also statutory law. The quasi-statutory by-product of Statutes are Rules or Regulations. Once a law is passed, federal, state and municipal agencies (such as the FCC or FDA) are authorized to create the rules needed to support the law. These rules and regulations have the force of law.

Case law—When cases are appealed (in appellate courts), they may present an opinion and decision that differ from previous decisions on the same point of law (or be a totally new point). This is then a precedent-setting case, one which the lower courts in the same jurisdiction will have to follow. It is law.

Just as agencies create rules and regulations, many, including the Internal Revenue Service, may decide cases. These administrative law hearings can spawn changes or additions to the rules and regulations.

Law Nomenclature

A law may be referred to in a variety of ways, so here's a list to make you wise to the variety:

Act—Law passed by one or both houses of a legislature (the law-making branches of government).

Ordinance—Law passed by a city, town or other municipality.

Statute—Same as Act.

Finding Court Cases

As long as you change the names and a few details to protect the innocent and guilty, feel free to get some ideas for invented court battles from actual cases.

You may be interested in finding court cases for a number of reasons when writing nonfiction. For example, since court cases are won or lost based on different points of law, you may use a particular court case to make a point that supports a general rule of our society. You may be writing about a specific court case and need to find out about that particular case as well as other similar cases.

Federal or State?

Remember that there are two distinct court systems in the United States: the federal courts and the state courts.

The methods of finding state or federal cases does not vary drastically, but it will certainly be a factor in the law reference books you need to consult!

Federal courts.

These courts have jurisdiction in all cases that involve the U.S. Constitution, federal laws and treaties. The federal courts are comprised of:

The U.S. district courts. It is in district court that most cases dealing with *national law* both begin and end.

The U.S. Court of Appeals. When a case in a district court is appealed, it comes to the U.S. Court of Appeals. This Court also hears cases from the U.S. Tax Court and from the rulings of some regulatory agencies, such as the FCC and the National Labor Relations Board.

The United States Supreme Court. The "highest court in the land," may hear appeals of cases from the Court of Appeals, or the U.S. District Courts, but only a very few cases submitted are ever heard; the U.S. Supreme Court has discretionary power over which cases it will accept.

State Courts

These courts deal with infractions of, and challenges to, state law. Names of courts may vary slightly from state to state.

The minor courts. The bottom rung of the state court hierarchy consists of the minor courts, such as the municipal courts, traffic courts and juvenile courts. (This is the court many of us have had occasion to visit for our driving "mistakes."

The trial courts. The bulk of major cases dealing with state law are brought to these courts, known as District, Superior or Circuit Courts.

The intermediate appellate courts. Corresponds to the U.S. Court of Appeals, only at the state level.

The State Court of Last Resort. Usually called the State Supreme Court. A case that has been rejected at this level may be presented to the U.S. Supreme Court for appeal if the question involves either a federal law or a constitutional question.

Please realize: NOT all court decisions are published! Here's what is:

At the federal level:
All Supreme Court Opinions

Selected Decisions of the U.S. Court of Appeals

Selected Decisions of the U.S. District Courts

At the state level:

(with very few exceptions) Only Cases Appealed to a Higher Court (Courts of Appeals, state Supreme Court).

Sets Containing Supreme Court Cases:

United States Reports. 1790-present. [Cited as *U.S.*]

The official publication set, containing all opinions handed down from the U.S Supreme Court. Before the cases are bound into full volumes, they are released in pamphlet format and called *Slip Opinions*.

United States Supreme Court Reports, Lawyers Edition. Rochester, NY: Lawyer's Cooperative Publishing. 1754-present. [The first 100 volumes are cited as *L.Ed.*, the second series began in 1956 and is cited as *L.Ed.2d.*]

An unofficial version of the Supreme Court opinions. This version has annotations and headnotes concerning the main points of law covered in each case, and summaries of the briefs of counsel prepared by the publisher's editorial staff.

Supreme Court Reporter. St. Paul, MN: West Publishing Co. [Cited as *S.Ct.*]

Another unofficial version of Supreme Court opinions.

Note: When you see a citation to a case or statutory law, you will often see *paral-*

lel citations, that is, citations to the same law or case appearing in different publications. For example, a case called the *Employee Drug Testing Case* is cited in *Shepard's Acts and Cases by Popular Name* as being available in three sources:

489 U.S. 656—Volume 489 of the *United States Reports*, page 656.

103 L.Ed.2d 685—Volume 103 of the *Lawyer's Edition 2d*, page 685.

109 S.Ct. 1384—Volume 109 of the *Supreme Court Reporter*, page 1384.

You will find precisely the same case in each of those volumes. (But the "unofficial" versions will also be annotated, providing additional notes of interest.)

United States Law Week. Washington, DC: Washington Bureau of National Affairs. 1966-present. [Cited as *U.S.L.W.*]

Several weeks after Supreme Court decisions are handed down, they are reproduced in this loose-leaf format (allowing for easy updates) resource. *U.S. Law Week* is comprised of two sections:

• The Supreme Court section containing opinions and summaries of new cases.

• The General Law section, consisting of selected statutes and summaries of recent federal laws and federal and state court decisions.

Landmark Briefs and Arguments of the Supreme Court of the United States. Arlington, VA: University Publications of America. 1975-present.

Lengthy presentations of the legal debates, for and against, of cases brought before the U.S. Supreme

Court. This is a source to look into if you want to analyze a specific case. Keep that legal dictionary close at hand.

Sets Containing U.S. Court of Appeals and District Court Cases

The Federal Reporter. St. Paul: West Publishing Co., 1880-1924 [*1st Series*, cited as *F.*] 1924-present [*2d Series*, cited as *F2d.*]

The Federal Reporter contains all decisions from the U.S. Court of Appeals (and for volumes from 1880-1932, decisions from the U.S. Court of Claims and the U.S. District Courts).

Federal Supplement. St. Paul: West Publishing Co., 1932-present. [Cited as *F.Supp.*]

The *Supplement* contains the decisions of the U.S. Customs Court and select decisions of the U.S. District Courts.

Federal Rules Decisions. St. Paul: West Publishing Co., 1941-present. [Cited as *FRD.*]

The decisions in these volumes meet two criteria:
- They are not included in the *Federal Supplement*.
- The opinions selected are those that involve the federal rules of criminal procedure.

Sets Containing State Court Cases

The State Reporters.

There are reporters for each segment of the United States that contain cases from each state's highest court and Court of Appeals. They are all

"unofficial" and all published by West Publishing Company.

Atlantic Reporter. [Cited as *A.*]

Includes Connecticut, Delaware, Maine, Maryland, New Hampshire, New Jersey, Pennsylvania, Rhode Island and Vermont.

North Eastern Reporter. [Cited as *NE.*]

Includes Illinois, Indiana, Massachusetts, New York and Ohio.

North Western Reporter. [Cited as *NW.*]

Includes Iowa, Michigan, Minnesota, Nebraska, North Dakota, South Dakota and Wisconsin.

Pacific Reporter. [Cited as *P.* and *P2d.*]

Includes Alaska, Arizona, California, Colorado, Hawaii, Idaho, Kansas, Montana, Nevada, New Mexico, Oklahoma, Oregon, Utah, Washington and Wyoming.

South Eastern Reporter. [Cited as *SE.*]

Includes Georgia, North Carolina, South Carolina, Virginia and West Virginia.

Southern Reporter. [Cited as *SO.*]

Includes Alabama, Florida, Louisiana and Mississippi.

South Western Reporter. [Cited as *SW.*]

Includes Arkansas, Kentucky, Missouri, Tennessee and Texas.

Each state also has its own series, which only reports cases for that state. For example, in Ohio, the set that includes their Supreme Court cases is called *Ohio State Reports*; the volumes that include their Court of Appeals is called *Ohio*

Appellate Reports. The cases in those volumes are the same cases for Ohio that you would find in the *North Eastern Reporter.* Documentation of cases from lower courts will vary from state to state.

Finding Cases by Subject

One method of finding cases by subject (for example, cases dealing with property rights) is by using digests. Digests are multivolume collections containing summaries of court cases, arranged by subject. The subject is the point (or points) of law discussed in court cases. Digests are also often used to find the correct citation for a case you already know of.

Since there are two major purposes of digests (finding citations for cases and finding cases on particular subjects), there are two types of indexes included with the collection: Descriptive-Word Indexes and the Table of Cases (arranged by the "name" of the case, i.e., the plaintiff vs. the defendant. Example: Smith v. United States). There are digests for both state and federal cases.

United States Supreme Court Digest. 1754-present.
 Supreme Court cases.

The Federal Digest. 1754-1939.
 Decisions of all the Federal Courts. Continued by:
 Modern Federal Practice Digest
 West's Federal Practice Digest 2d.
 West's Federal Practice Digest
 West's Federal Practice Digest 4th.

Series that get you to state appellate court cases by subject:
 Atlantic Digest
 North Western Digest

Pacific Digest
South Eastern Digest
Southern Digest

There are also digests for 45 states, e.g., *West's California Digest.* There are no digests for Delaware, Nevada and Utah. West Virginia and Virginia are combined in one digest as are North Dakota and South Dakota.

Sources that can help you find well-known cases (and laws, too):

Shepard's Acts and Cases by Popular Names—Federal and State. Colorado Springs: Shepard's. 1968-present; six supplements per year.

A great quick look-up source for laws and cases that are fairly well known and, in some cases, have come to be known by a "popular" name. This set of books will provide you with the citation you need to find the act or case you are interested in.

American Law Reports. [Cited as *A.L.R.*] Rochester, NY: Lawyers Cooperative Publishing Co.

ALR is great for finding in-depth analysis and critique on precedent-setting cases. Each case that is chosen is summarized and discussed as it relates to other cases. If you have a law topic in mind and want to see how it's been handled in state and federal cases, this is an excellent source to turn to.

The Quick Indexes are separate volumes that lead you to the cases in the ALR set by topic. There are now four series of ALRs:

State Cases:
 ALR (1st Series)—1919-1948

ALR 2d—1948-1965
ALR 3d—1965-1980
ALR 4th—1980-1992
ALR 5th—1992-present.

Federal Cases:
ALR Fed—1969-present.

Finding Statutory Law

Final laws at both the state and federal level are found in two different forms:

- In *chronological* order, appearing in full text and printed in the order they are passed.
- In *subject* order, with each volume dedicated to a major topic, and each law or piece of law that pertains to that subject included in that volume.

Again, there are both official and unofficial versions. (Stay with me!)

Sets Listing Federal Laws in Chronological Order

United States Statutes at Large. [Cited as *Stat.*]

These volumes contain U.S. laws listed in chronological order (that is, as they were passed.) This one's "official."

United States Code Congressional and Administrative News [Cited as USCCAN or *U.S.Code Cong. & Admin. News*] St. Paul, MN: West Publishing. 1952-present.

The "unofficial" source of U.S. laws in chronological order that comes out aeons before the *Statutes at Large*. Another unofficial source is the *USCS* (*United States Code Service*) *Advance*, a monthly advance sheet service listing new public laws.

Sets Listing Federal Laws in Subject Order

United States Code. [Cited as *U.S.C.*] 1926-present.

The *U.S.C.* is a listing of all the laws of the U.S. arranged by subject. The *Code* is divided into fifty broad subject categories called "titles" (e.g., Title 18 covers Crime and Criminal Procedure; Title 21 is Food and Drugs). There is a very detailed subject index to the collection. This is the official version. Two unofficial (but very widely used and preferred) versions are:

The United States Code Annotated. [Cited as *U.S.C.A.*] St. Paul, MN: West Publishing.

The United States Code Service. [Cited as *U.S.C.S.*] Rochester, NY: Lawyer's Co-operative.

By the way, a *Code* is any systematic collection of laws, rules or regulations. So the *United States Code* is a collection of the U.S. laws that has been codified, that is, arranged by subject.

Sets Listing State Laws in Subject Order

State codes.
Again, as with session laws, all states have collections of their laws in subject order, similar to the *U.S. Code*. Some put out their own collections, but all have at least one, and sometimes two, unofficial versions. Some sample titles:

Colorado Revised Statutes
Montana Code Annotated

Probably the quickest way to find the set that leads you, by subject, to the laws of the state you are interested in: Check with the librarian. You'll be in front of the correct volumes in a flash.

Surveys of Laws

How do laws compare from state to state? Seeing some of the vast differences between regions can be quite thought-provoking. There are a number of reference sources that provide a quick overview and comparison of laws of many states:

Digest of Motor Laws. Traffic Safety and Engineering Department, American Automobile Association. Heathrow, Florida: AAA. Annual.

Do you want the imaginary adolescent in your story stopped by the police in Michigan? One way to do it would be to put him on a moped and be sure he's under age 15. This digest lists, by region, the laws and regulations related to the operation of automobiles, motorcycles, mopeds and vehicle towing devices in the United States, its territories, and the provinces of Canada.

Highlights of State Unemployment Compensation Laws. Washington, DC: The National Foundation for Unemployment Compensation and Workers' Compensation.

A presentation of selected features of compensation laws, state by state, such as Qualifying Requirements, Duration of Benefits and Seasonality Provisions.

Martindale-Hubbell Law Digest: United States Law Digests and International Law Digests. New Providence, NJ: Martindale-Hubbell. Annual.

These volumes summarize laws for each of the United States, the District of Columbia, Puerto Rico the Virgin Islands, Canada and its provinces and sixty other nations. The topic index preceding each region makes it simple to find the summary you need. Examples of law topics: Banks and Banking, Consumer Protection, Taxation, Foreclosure and Wills.

National Survey of State Laws. Richard A. Leiter, 1st edition. Detroit: Gale, 1993. (Biennial updates are anticipated.)

A look at common legal requirements for each state in the United States for selected topics, such as marriage age, leases and rental agreements, gun control, lemon laws and child custody.

Two sources that act as indexes to compilations of laws:

Subject Compilations of State Laws. Cheryl Rae Nyberg. [1st edition by Lynn Foster and Carol Boast.] Twin Falls, ID: Carol Boast and Cheryl Nyberg, 1979-present.

If there is a document in existence that lists or discusses a law or laws compared among different states, then it should be referred to in this collection. Each volume in this series is in subject order and indexes law reviews, U.S. and state government documents, loose-leaf services and U.S. Supreme Court opinions that contain variations of a law in several states.

Another source with the same aim:

Statutes Compared: A U.S., Canadian, Multinational Research Guide to Statutes by Subject. Jon S. Schultz. Buffalo, NY: William S. Hein & Co., 1992.

Law Enforcement

Is your hero (or villain) a police officer? Detective? Do you know the rules of those professions? There aren't too many reference books that will go into detail, but there are plenty of textbooks and handbooks that will give you insight into the work of law enforcers.

You will do particularly well using an academic collection at a library that caters to criminal justice majors. Large public libraries should also contain some information, since citizens are often looking into the field of policing and security. Libraries may also have study guides for the examinations that police personnel are required to take, such as *Norman Hall's Police Exam Preparation Book* (Holbrook, MA: Bob Adams, 1994).

Law Enforcement Handbooks and Textbooks—Sample Titles

Fundamentals of Criminal Investigation. Charles E. O'Hara and Gregory L. O'Hara. 6th edition. Springfield, IL: Charles C. Thomas, publisher, 1994.

This thick handbook will help move you quickly along the investigative road. The O'Haras (father and son authors; the father is now deceased) cover the details, like Care of Evidence, Interviews and Interrogations, and Photographing the Crime Scene, and also give guidance for specific types of crimes, including Burglary, Larceny, Arson and Homicide. Up-to-date techniques for such activities as fingerprinting and studying documentary evidence are described.

K9 Officer's Manual. Robert S. Eden. Calgary, Alberta: Detselig Enterprises, 1993.

This manual explores the many techniques for handling canine law enforcement companions and examines the many ways they can contribute. There are many illustrations and photographs of such situations as the proper positioning of a dog in a building search and confronting a suspect with a dog. Also by this author: *Dog Training for Law Enforcement.*

The Law Enforcement Handbook. Desmond Rowland. New York: Barnes and Noble Books, 1994.

A small book that you could slip into a pocket for quick referral. It describes the "methods and techniques of the art of policemanship." The author gives tips on such subjects as Developing Your Powers of Observation, Approaching Crime Scenes, and Stopping and Searching Vehicles.

Management and Supervision in Law Enforcement. Wayne W. Bennett and Karen M. Hess, St. Paul, MN: West Publishing Co., 1992.

This is just one example of the type of police administration textbooks available by the dozen. They generally cover topics like management skills, problem-solving, dealing with unions, morale-boosting, discipline, training and performance appraisals.

Practical Gambling Investigation Techniques. Kevin B. Kinnee. New York: Elsevier, 1992.

The author looks at crooked gambling from many angles, including how a police raid should be planned, methods of infiltrating sports bookmaking operations and common poker machine cheating.

Requirements to Become P.I. in the 50 States and Elsewhere: A Reference Manual. Joseph J. Culligan. Hallmark Press, 1992.

Listed by the states of the United States and provinces of Canada, this book supplies examples of the legal forms required in different areas for those who wish to become private investigators.

The Howdunit Series. Writer's Digest Books has published a series of books that deal with the various "howzit-done?" questions, such as "How is a crime scene investigation handled?" and "What precisely do Private Eyes do?" These books are part of the Howdunit Writing Series. Titles in the series include:

Malicious Intent: A Writer's Guide to How Murderers, Robbers, Rapists and Other Criminals Think. Sean Mactire. 1995.

Modus Operandi: A Writer's Guide to How Criminals Work. Mauro Corvasce and Joseph Paglino. 1995.

Police Procedural: A Writer's Guide to the Police and How They Work. Russell Bintliff. 1993.

Private Eyes: A Writer's Guide to Private Investigators. Hal Blythe, Chalie Sweet and Johan Landreth. 1993.

Scene of the Crime: A Writer's Guide to Crime Scene Investigation. Anne Wingate. 1992.

Other titles in the *Howdunit Writing Series* are listed in chapter 5, "How to Kill Your Character."

Articles and reviews

Often, I find that students in my library are not actually looking for the law itself; instead they want articles that discuss the law, the debates surrounding it or its ramifications. There are hundreds of U.S. and foreign periodicals in the field of criminal justice and law. Just to show you the variety, here are some sample titles:

> *American Criminal Law Review*
> *Journal of Forensic Sciences*
> *Journal of Offender Counseling, Services and Rehabilitation*
> *Juvenile and Family Court Journal*
> *Narcotics Control Digest*
> *Police Chief*

Check Appendix A for a list of law indexes. And remember, a huge number of articles discussing laws will not only be in law journals, but in magazines and journals that are simply interested in that law. For example, laws affecting freedom of speech will certainly show up in library science journals, and laws affecting corporations will be included in business journals. And of course newspapers and general news magazines like *Time* and *Newsweek* will be interested in almost anything that is considered news. So be sure to consider more than legal indexes when searching for articles by checking general and subject-specific indexes.

Some common law questions dealing with the rights of the citizens of a state may be answered by the office of the State Attorney General for the area you are interested in. The number is available in the phone book government pages as well as a number of government sources listed in chapter 7, "Identifying Experts."

"Loony" Laws

After searching through dry law books you may need a break from legalese.

Grab a copy of *Loony Laws: That You Never Knew You Were Breaking.* [Robert Wayne Pelton. New York: Walker and Co., 1990.] The author discusses what he calls Laughable Laws. Some examples: Women in Minnesota may *not* dress up as Santa Claus on any city street; doing so will risk a $25 fine or a 30-day sentence in the local jail. In Orlando, Florida, don't think that using an elephant for transportation will save you parking fees: If your pachyderm is left tied to a parking meter, you must pay the parking fee. Also by this author: *Loony Sex Laws.*

Chapter Twelve

Biographical Information

People are endlessly fascinating to other people. There are quite a few reasons why a writer might delve into research on a person. The author could be writing a full-blown biography or screenplay based on a little-known but intriguing individual. Or they may be about to interview someone and know that it's logical to know something of the interviewee's ideas and background before meeting him or her. At times writers just need some quick facts like place or year of birth.

No one can better tell you about a person than that person, along with those that were closest to him or her. Of course that is not always possible. The person and their loved ones may be unwilling to be interviewed or they may simply be deceased. After an interview, writers sometimes find that there are gaps they want to fill in but don't feel it's appropriate to ask the person for a follow-up interview. The books, indexes, bibliographies, directories, anthologies and general tips in this chapter will help you find out things that you need to know about people.

Finding Book-Length Biographies and Autobiographies

There are full-length books written by and about thousands of people, so it can never hurt to look and see if one or more exist about an individual you are inter-

ested in. Remember, when you are looking for information about a person, the person is the subject. That means you would look in the *Subject Guide to Books in Print* under the person's name to see if any books were written about him or her. You might also do a subject search under the person's name on your library's online catalog. (Some online catalogs offer a combined search option that will look for sources both by or about a person when you type in a name and put in a special command. As mentioned before, familiarize yourself with the particulars of your library's system.)

Of course there will be times when the person you're interested in has written a book about themselves, an autobiography. In that case, you would try an author search in your library's catalog or look in the Author edition of *Books in Print*.

There might be a great deal of information about a person within a book that covers a broader topic. For example, let's say that a library only owns one full book about Buddy Holly called *Buddy Holly: A Biography in Words, Photographs and Music*. (Elizabeth and Ralph Peer. New York: Peer International Corp., 1972). Well, let's also say it's checked out. So think about it: what kinds of books would Buddy Holly likely show up in? Books about the history of rock music. So, go to your online library catalog and type in ROCK MUSIC HISTORY. You will most likely come up with a few books, such as *The Rolling Stone Illustrated History of Rock and Roll* (Anthony DeCurtis, editor. New York: Random House, 1992) and *The Ultimate Encyclopedia of Rock* (Michael Heatley, editor. New York: HarperPerennial, 1993). Though the catalog record usually won't list the names of all the artists included in these books, you could safely assume that a rock legend like Buddy Holly would show up in these sources. I find that books containing hefty chapters on people will still be on the shelves when full biographies are checked out.

One of the print sources that will lead you to book-length biographies is the series *International Bibliography of Biography* (12 Volumes. New York: K.G. Saur, 1988), arranged in both subject sequence and author/title order. It lists approximately one hundred thousand biographical and autobiographical titles.

General and Specialized Encyclopedias

Marvelous biographical articles appear in all sorts of encyclopedias. For example, the *International Encyclopedia of the Social Sciences* (New York: Macmillan and Co. and The Free Press, 1968) devotes ten substantial pages to the life of Sigmund Freud, plus over a page of bibliographic references. For listings of specific titles and tips on finding specialized encyclopedias, see chapter 8, "Overviews on Any Subject—Encyclopedias and Handbooks."

Book Reviews

A lengthy book review will sometimes devote a certain amount of space to a description of the author. Unfortunately, the mention is often brief at best, saying, for example, that the author is a "much admired business professor at the University of Colorado in Denver." But it's a lead. You could then call the University of Colorado to find out more. So remember—if you need information about someone who has published a book or books, check past book reviews for information. For that matter, check the book flaps and cover of the book, which usually supply basic data.

There are a number of indexes that lead you to book reviews, and most are released monthly and cumulated yearly. (See the list below.) To use one, first check the copyright date of the book you want a review for. Grab the book review index volume for that year and look under the author's name. The index will supply you with citations of book reviews in a variety of sources. Also check the book review index for the year after the book you want a review for was published. If a book was released late in one year its reviews may show up in indexes for both that year and the next. For example, the 1974 edition of *The Book Review Digest* lists eleven book reviews for *Zen and the Art of Motorcycle Maintenance*, which was published that year. The 1975 edition has five additional reviews.

As mentioned, book review indexes provide the citation of the review, telling you which periodical or book contains the review you need. Some book review indexes, such as *The Book Review Digest*, also reprint a few sentences from the review. Just keep in mind that indexes that provide summaries tend to have fewer citations overall because of space limitations. Some book review indexes:

The Book Review Digest. New York: H.W. Wilson, 1905-present.

The Book Review Index. Detroit: Gale, 1965-present.

Combined Retrospective Index to Book Reviews in . . . Arlington, VA: Carrollton Press.
Political Science. 1886-1974
Scholarly Journals. 1896-1974
History. 1838-1974
Sociology. 1895-1974
The Humanities. 1802-1974

SFBRI—Science Fiction Book Review Index (Still referred to as SFBRI though the new name is Science Fiction and Fantasy Book Review Index). San Bernadino, CA: Borgo Press, 1970-.

Many reviews from scholarly journals and magazines are indexed in a section in the back of periodical indexes. Some indexes that do this, all published by H.W. Wilson (known by librarians as The Wilson Indexes) include The Reader's Guide to Periodical Literature, The Social Science Index, The Business Periodicals Index, The Humanities Index, The General Science Index, The Applied Science and Technology Index, The Art Index and the Biological and Agricultural Index.

Newspapers are also an excellent source of book reviews. Some, like the New York Times and TLS: The Times Literary Supplement, have separate weekly sections devoted to nothing but reviews. Some newspaper reviews will be included in such sources as The Book Review Index and The Book Review Di-

gest. You can also check the unique index that indexes each newspaper. The New York Times Index puts book reviews under the heading Book Reviews and lists the books by title. Both the Washington Post Index and the Wall Street Journal Index have two headings for reviews; one under Books-Authors, the other under Books-Titles.

Articles

Just as you can find articles about artichokes in magazines and journals, you can also find articles about people. In fact, many of the journals with tiny circulation figures and a tight subject focus will write about people who are eminent in that tiny field (but will not show up in US magazine). These folks may be fascinating! For example, you might try the Philosopher's Index to find articles on great thinkers, or the Humanities Index or the Art Index to dig up pieces on an illustrator. See Appendix A for a list of possible indexes. Use the tips in chapter 2, "Exploring Articles," to find biographical articles. Remember that the person is your subject, so you will look under that person's name in the indexes.

A particularly helpful biographical newspaper index is the Personal Name Index to the New York Times Index: 1851-1974. 22 Volumes. Byron A. Falk, Jr. and Valerie R. Falk, editors. Succasunna, NJ: Roxbury Data Interface, 1976. Supplements: 1975-79 (3 Volumes), 1975-84 (4 Volumes), and 1975-89 (5 Volumes). More are forthcoming. This is an "index to an index." And it's wonderful! So many people of note or of 15-minute fame have been included in The Times. If you have ever tried to find information on a person using the regular *New York Times Index*, you'll find that names are, of course, scattered among indexes for different time periods. The *Personal Name Index* quickly leads you to the specific index volumes where a person's name appears, providing the year of the Index and the page number. For example, I looked under the name Clark Gable and found references to thirty-one articles between 1932 and 1974. Those citations will in turn bring you to articles in the *New York Times*.

Tip—even if you are looking up a person who was written about in the late 1800s, also do a quick look-up in the supplements to the main collection since some names were missed in the earlier volumes and stuck into the supplements.

As for finding articles in smaller newspapers, be sure to check with the publishers of local newspapers of the region where your biographee lives, vacations or used to live. Again, as mentioned in chapter 2, there may be no index to small newspapers. Give the newspaper office a polite call or send a concise letter. Many people are willing to help.

Interviews

Of course, a prime way of learning about a person is by talking to them or those who know them. Contact the high school they went to. Does their high school yearbook show them in a picture for the Young Scientists Club with the nickname "Gummy" under their photo? Call organizations that they were involved in. You may get a listing of the individual's great contributions or a story of them dancing on a table! There are a number of books that will guide you through the interview process and help you understand the nuances required to actually obtain an interview. A few:

How to Locate Anyone Anywhere Without Leaving Home. Ted Gunderson. New York: E.P. Dutton, 1989.

Though this book is not an interview book per se, it does direct you to do a lot of contacting people via phone and letter (and I just had to fit this source in somewhere). This book proves that the Salvation Army and Bankruptcy Court may be founts of information. Author Gunderson was a former FBI agent who went on to head a private investigative firm in Los Angeles. He shares his secrets on finding information about people by listing sleuthing opportunities at a variety of organizations and agencies. (Including, yes, the Salvation Army.)

How to Talk to Practically Anybody About Practically Anything. Barbara Walters. New York: Doubleday, 1983.

Advice from the interview diva herself. Ms. Walters's book is friendly, entertaining, and, of course, full of rock-solid tips on speaking with all kinds of people, including tycoons, celebrities, royalty, the young, old, bereaved, handicapped, boring, drunk or belligerent. The postscript shares Twenty-Five Sure-Fire Conversation Starters along with anecdotes illustrating their successful use.

The Writer's Complete Guide to Conducting Interviews. Michael Schumacher. Cincinnati: Writer's Digest Books, 1990.

"Complete" is perhaps an understatement of what this book contains. If covers pre-interview research, many approaches for contacting sources, the specifics of interviewing techniques and even ethical and legal points.

Diaries, Letters, and Collected Papers

If the person you are interested in is no longer living or simply not willing to speak with you, you may try tracking documents they have written. See chapter 1: "Navigating the Library," and the description of Special Libraries and Special Collections. You may think that the papers in a special collection will already have been thoroughly mined by others. Not so. Many collections are filled with folders of correspondence and other writings that have been barely touched (if at all). Of course it could require some dedication and expense if you live in Alabama and the papers of the person you are researching are in a collection in Oregon; such manuscripts will usually not be loaned. If you can't travel, check with the library to see if they have a photocopying service.

There are a number of bibliographies that will point you to the location of diaries and letters. Some are:

American Diaries: An Annotated Bibliography of Published American Diaries and Journals. Volume 1: Diaries Written from 1492 to 1844; Volume 2: Diaries Written from 1845 to 1980. Laura Arksey. 1st edition. Detroit: Gale, 1987.

A guide to the whereabouts of reprints of almost ten thousand diaries. There is a Name Index, Geographic Index and Subject Index, the latter with such entries as Marriage, Attitude Toward, and Whaling Ships.

American Diaries in Manuscript, 1580-1954: A Descriptive Bibliography. William Matthews. Athens, GA: University of Georgia Press, 1974.

Over five thousand diaries are described with generally short statements (i.e., "Trip across the plains from Wis. to Cal." or "Mexican War Diary"). The historical society or library that houses each manuscript is identified.

And So to Bed: A Bibliography of Diaries Published in English. Patricia Pate Havlice. Metuchen, NJ: Scarecrow Press, 1987.

The majority of diaries in this bibliography were published as books, book chapters, journal articles or dissertations. Though many nationalities are represented, all the diaries were either written in or translated to English. *And So to Bed* is arranged in chronological order beginning with 838 A.D. The first and last entry dates of each diary are included, along with a very brief description (such as John Edward Hamilton's diary: "Military diary; Presbyterian Minister; with the Army of the Potomac; service in Virginia").

National Union Catalog of Manuscript Collections. Washington, DC: Library of Congress, 1959-present. Annual.

A regularly updated guide to the location of personal papers of people and the business files for organizations and businesses. The holdings of U.S. special collections, historical societies and archives are detailed, including such items as letters, diaries, photographs, account books and genealogies. The people whose papers are included are representative of quite a few careers and lifestyles, including legislators, teachers and pioneers. Some examples of the extremely varied holdings: Papers of Nancy Hamilton (at Smith College), in part known for her production of the documentary film *Helen Keller—Her Story*, and the records of the Fargo Rotary Club (at the North Dakota Institute for Regional Studies).

Through a Woman's I: An Annotated Bibliography of American Women's Autobiographical Writings, 1946-1976. Patricia K. Addis. Metuchen, NJ: Scarecrow Press, 1983.

This bibliography identifies books, of at least twenty-five pages in length, that include in their pages letters, diaries, journals, memoirs, reminiscences and travel accounts of American women from all areas of society.

Women's Diaries, Journals and Letters: an Annotated Bibliography. Cheryl Cline. New York: Garland Publishing, 1989.

The author has tried to allude to only those diaries and letters deemed "personal, private writing." This collection identifies such writings that have appeared in articles and books and refers to some that are not in English. There is an index of the writers by profession and a subject index that covers such topics as Quakers, Child Prodigies, Plantation Owners and Temperance Workers.

To find personal letters and writings using an online catalog try using the words PERSONAL NARRATIVES, CORRESPONDENCE or DIARIES. For example, I tried a search in my local library's online catalog using the words PIONEERS and CORRESPONDENCE and came up with the book *Letters From Honeyhill: A Woman's View of Homesteading, 1914-1931* (Cecilia Henna Hendricks. Boulder, CO: Pruett Publishers, 1986).

Biographical Indexes

Just as periodical indexes lead you to articles in magazines, newspapers and journals, biographical indexes identify articles and books that contain biographical information. Some include:

An Analytical Bibliography of Universal Collected Biography. Phyllis M. Riches. London: The Library Association, 1934.

All of the over fifty thousand biographical sources listed in this bibliography were published before 1933.

Biography Almanac: A Comprehensive Reference Guide to More than 23,000 Famous and Infamous Newsmakers from Biblical Times to the Present as Found in Over 300 Readily Available Biographical Sources. Susan L. Stet., 3d edition. Detroit: Gale, 1987.

For each person listed, the *Almanac* lists birthdate and place, and death date. The reader is then directed to one or more of the three hundred resources indexed by this guide to find further information. The *Biography Almanac* is continued by the *Almanac of Famous People* (Detroit: Gale, 1988-present. Biennial).

Biography and Genealogy Master Index: A

Consolidated Index to More Than 450,000 Biographical Sketches in Over 95 Current and Retrospective Biographical Dictionaries. Detroit: Gale, 1981-present. Annual with Supplements.

This directory, with little, tiny print, helps you quickly determine which biographical compilation you need to go to for information on an individual. Sample titles of biographies indexed in this ongoing set are Hollywood Baby Boomers, Polish Biographical Dictionary and Contemporary Gay American Novelists. This Index is part of the ten-part Gale Biographical Index Series, which includes:

Author Biographies Master Index. 4th edition. 1993.

Children's Authors and Illustrators: An Index to Biographical Dictionaries. Joyce Nakamura. 1986.

The Performing Arts Biography Master Index: A Consolidated Guide to Over 270,000 Biographical Sketches of Persons Living and Dead, As They Appear in Over 100 of the Principal Biographical Dictionaries Devoted to the Performing Arts. Barbara McNeil and Miranda C. Herbert. 2d edition. 1982.

Historical Biographical Dictionaries Master Index. Barbara McNeil and Miranda C. Herbert. 1980.

Journalists Biographies Master Index. 1979.

Writers for Young Adults: Biographies Master Index. 3d edition. 1988.

Biography Index: A Cumulative Index to Biographical Material in Books and Magazines. New York: H.W. Wilson Co., 1946-present.

The Biography Index points you to biographical sources that include full books, book sections, periodical articles, obituaries, letters, diaries, memoirs and bibliographies. The word biography may bring to mind contemporary figures, but this index includes both historical and modern persons.

The first half of the Biography Index is arranged by person's name, the second is an Index to Professions and Occupations. Some pretty obscure (outside of their professions) folks get in here, since many of the specialized magazines included in this index are apt to write specialized articles. Thus, the 1986 edition lists six calligraphers, nineteen cooks and ten mystics.

In Black and White: A Guide to Magazine Articles, Newspaper Articles and Books Concerning More Than 15,000 Black Individuals and Groups. Mary Mace Spradling, editor. 3d edition. 2 volumes. Detroit: Gale, 1980.

The editor chose the entrants by scanning newspapers, magazines, books, pamphlets, calendars and the dictionary catalogs for libraries with extensive black history holdings, including New York's Schomberg collection, and Washington DC's Moorland.

Index to Collective Biographies for Young Readers. Karen Breen. 4th edition. New York: Bowker, 1988.

An index to biographies of almost 10,000 people covered in 1,129 books of biography for youth. Every work referred to in this collection is one that could be easily understood by a sixth grade student. So, if you want to be pointed to some easy reads, here's a good place to look. Of course, the biographies recommended might not be a great place to find certain "adult"

Who's Who in . . .

America	Finance and Industry
American Art	International Banking
American Education	Religion
American Law	Science and Engineering
American Nursing	South African Politics
American Politics	The East
Asian and Australasian Politics	The Midwest
Entertainment	The South and Southwest
European Business	The West
European Research and Development	The World

and *Who's Who of . . .*

American Women	Australian Writers
Emerging Leaders in America	Women in World Politics

---

information, like the small details of an infamous person's peculiar sexual wonts. No, the titles cited here include such volumes as *Picture Book of Famous Immigrants* (Sterling, 1962), *Baseball's Hottest Hitters* (Lerner, 1975), and *Valiant Women* (Vantage, 1972).

Biographical Directories

Biographical compilations come in three stripes:

- By region (such as *Who's Who in the West*).
- By occupation (such as *Who's Who in Venture Capital*).
- Encompassing many occupations and regions, with a broad scope (such as *Who's Who in the World*).

Marquis Who's Who is the publisher of many well-known *Who's Who* collections. Most of these collections are for-matted in a similar fashion, providing name, profession, vital statistics, family data, education, listings of writings and creative works, community and political activities, military service, awards, association memberships, political affiliation, religion, hobbies, home address and office address. There are no photographs.

Some *Who's Who* volumes are updated regularly; others were a one-shot deal. There is an index to the collection called *Marquis Who's Who Publications: Index to All Books* (1974-present). Some current Marquis *Who's Who* titles are listed above.

There are also a number of compilations that begin with the words *Who Was Who*, including *Who Was Who in America* (12 Volumes, 1607-present), also published by Marquis.

Quite a few biographies put out by any number of publishers begin with the words *Who's Who*. One of particular interest is *Who's Who in Writers, Editors and Poets: United States and Canada* (Highland Park, IL: December Press. Biennial). Check the Titles edition of *Books in Print*, or type in the words WHO'S WHO in your library's online catalog and you will get an eyeful! The 1994 *BIP* lists over 200 volumes beginning with the words *Who's Who*, and the online catalog for the medium-sized academic library I work for lists 174 titles, including *Who's Who in Health Care*, *Who's Who in Boxing*, and *Who's Who in Dickens: A Complete Dickens Repertory in Dicken's Own Words.*

Note: *Who's Who in America* is also available through *DIALOG* and *CompuServe.*

Specialized Biographies

Though it may seem lengthy, the titles listed below, presented by subject area, are just a sampling of the many biographical collections available. Let these pique your interest.

Activists and Social Movement Leaders

American Reformers. Alden Whitman. New York: H.W. Wilson, 1985.

From the seventeenth century to the present, *American Reformers* offers an alphabetic list of 504 men and women involved in the evolution of American society. The essays examine the societal influences that helped form the reformer and excite them to action, and then offers an assessment of the activist's significance to the general reform movement in the United States.

American Social Leaders: From Colonial Times to the Present. William McGuire and Leslie Wheeler. Santa Barbara, CA: ABC-CLIO, 1993.

Similar to *American Reformers*, described above, *American Social Leaders* profiles pioneers of U.S. social and intellectual movements, such as labor leader John Llewellyn Lewis and civil rights activist (and well-known athlete and actor) Paul Robeson.

American Women Civil Rights Activists: Biobibliographies of 68 Leaders, 1825-1992. Gayle J. Hardy. Jefferson, NC: McFarland, 1993.

Some activities these women helped spearhead include Hispanic American Rights, Antilynching, Adoptee/Adoption Rights and Consumer Rights.

Biographical Dictionary of Modern Peace Leaders. Harold Josephson, editor-in-chief. Westport, CT: Greenwood Press, 1984.

Highlights western world individuals from 1815 through the early 1980s who, in a wide variety of ways, worked for a world with less war.

Biographical Dictionary of Social Welfare in America. Walter I. Trattner, editor. Westport, CT: Greenwood Press, 1986.

Features those individuals associated with such events as the 1843 creation of the New York Association for Improving the Condition of the Poor, the 1899 establishment of America's first juvenile court (in Chicago), and the 1964 passage of the Food Stamp Act. Appendix One lists reformers by birthdate and Appendix Two lists their place of birth. Have there been recent writings on some of your state's notable reformers? Perhaps their anniversary is coming up and an article would be welcome.

Aeronautics

Men and Women of Space. Douglas B. Hawthorne. San Diego: Univelt, Publishers, 1992.

Biographical information is provided for every (yes, every) person who has received spaceflight training since the beginning of the space age. That covers NASA astronauts and candidates, Soviet cosmonauts and candidates, X-15 military and civilian research pilots and many others.

Space People—From A-Z. Ray Spangenburg. New York: Facts on File, 1990.

This is the fourth volume in the Facts on File *Space Exploration* series. The biographees are those who were actually space travelers or those who helped make space flight a reality. Some of the "others" include aeronautical engineer and physicist Theodore von Karman, who was one of the pioneer theorists of supersonic flight, and the "space artist" Chesley Bonestall, who specialized in works depicting "the facts and wonders of space."

African Americans, Blacks of Non-U.S. Nationality, Hispanics and Native Americans

Black Women in America: An Historical Encyclopedia. Darlene Clark Hine, editor. 2 Volumes. Brooklyn, NY: Carlson Publishing, 1993.

This set is labeled as an encyclopedia and does include nonbiographical top-

ics, such as Feminism in the Twentieth Century and Aunt Jemima, but the bulk of entries are biographical. Photos are provided for most of the women and further reading sources are recommended.

Black Women in United States History. Darlene Clark Hine, editor. 16 Volumes. Brooklyn, NY: Carlson Publishing, 1990.

The editor comments that this multivolume work assists in pulling black women out of "historical oblivion." Though some names are familiar, like Harriet Tubman and Sojourner Truth, most will be new. The women in these volumes represent all aspects of American life. Some of the articles are purely biographical; others are thematic, such as "Marital and Sexual Norms Among Slave Women" by Herbert G. Gutman. All pieces are lengthy and scholarly.

Contemporary Black Biography: Profiles from the International Black Community. Barbara Carlisle Bigelow, editor. 5 Volumes. Detroit: Gale, 1994.

The introduction to this set proclaims that it is designed for "quick research *and* interesting reading." Influential black people from a variety of countries and fields are featured. Along with several pages of biographical coverage, a photo, mailing address and further reading suggestions are usually included. The set is indexed by Nationality (including American, Nigerian and Ugandan), Occupation (including Law, Music and Writing), and a Cumulative Subject Index (with such headings as Grammy Awards, Pediatrics and Tennis).

Hispanic American Almanac: A Reference Work on Hispanics in the United States. Nicolas Kanellos. Detroit: Gale Research, 1993.

Facts, dates, biographies and essays cover the facets of Hispanic life in the United States. Some areas covered include historic landmarks, education, literature, film and religion. Other, similar works from Gale Research:

The African American Almanac.
1994.
The Native North American Almanac.
1994

Mexican American Biographies: A Historical Dictionary, 1836-1987. Matt S. Meier. New York: Greenwood, 1988.

The author identifies "*prominentes* in the Mexican American experience" from the 1830s to the late 1980s. There is an index to the collection by field, including Finance, Engineering and the Military, and a geographic index by state.

Native American Women: A Biographical Dictionary. Gretchen M. Bataille, editor. New York: Garland, 1993.

This work describes individual American Indian women representing a diversity of rôles within their culture, both contemporary and historic.

Notable Hispanic American Women. Diane Telgen and Jim Kamp, editors. 1st edition. Detroit: Gale, 1993.

Many of the women in this compilation were actually interviewed, with some entries being wholly comprised of information from an interview. Consequently, a good deal of the biographical material is unique to this collection. Most figures, like singer/composer Joan Baez and tennis player

Gigi Fernández, are contemporary. The Ethnicity Index cross-references the women under their birth countries, such as Cuba, Spain and Puerto Rico. The Ethnicity Index also serves as a reminder that the word "Hispanic" refers to people from many geographic areas.

The Ancients

A Dictionary of Greek and Roman Biography and Mythology. William Smith, editor. 3 Volumes. London: John Murray, 1876.

Do be sure to bring a magnifying glass with you when you look at this one. (Did people once have much better eyesight than we do now?) These volumes cover the lives of the "ancients" of myriad fields and professions—jurists, artists, mathematicians and philosophers being among those included. The writers are careful to distinguish between what is true historical biography and what is myth.

Who Was Who in the Greek World: 776 B.C.-30 B.C. Diana Bowder, editor. Ithaca, NY: Phaidon. 1982.

This volume begins in the year of the first Olympiad, the first Olympic Games ever presented. Many of the short biographies are accompanied by photographs of images on sculptures, coins and architecture. Also compiled by the same editor: *Who Was Who in the Roman World: 753 B.C.-A.D. 476.*

Anthropologists

International Dictionary of Anthropologists. Christopher Winters, general editor. New York: Garland, 1991.

This worldwide volume interprets

"anthropologists" broadly, and includes social, cultural, physical and biological anthropologists, as well as some archaeologists, folklorists and linguists. Travelers, missionaries and others are listed along with the scholars and academics. For example, fur trader George Nelson never had his writings of Northern Algonquian life, myth and religion recognized in his lifetime, though this anthropological work is now seen as valuable.

Women Anthropologists: A Biographical Dictionary. Ute Gacs, editor. Westport, CT: Greenwood Press, 1988.

Fifty-eight female anthropologists, encompassing a one-hundred-year span, are represented in this dictionary. Several pages are devoted to each scholar.

Architects, Artists and Designers

A Biographical Dictionary of Science Fiction and Fantasy Artists. Robert Weinberg. Westport, CT: Greenwood Press, 1988.

What? No illustrations? Unfortunately that is true of this volume. Still, this source provides a neat package of biographic sketches on this unique genre of illustration. Whenever possible, the author has used information provided by the artist.

A Biographical Dictionary of Women Artists in Europe and America Since 1850. Penny Dunford. Philadelphia: University of Pennsylvania Press, 1989.

A quick source to many artists who you would have had to dig for previously. Includes women who are still creating art as well as those long gone.

There are full-color photographs of twenty-six art pieces.

Contemporary Designers. Colin Naylor, editor. 2d edition. Chicago: St. James Press, 1990.

Over six hundred contemporary designers are represented from the fields of architecture, interior display, graphic, textile, fashion, product, industrial, stage and film design. Each entry consists of a biography, a selected list of design works, a bibliography of works by and about the designer and an illustration of one of their works. The next scheduled release of this work is 1996. Also by this publisher:

Contemporary Artists. Colin Naylor. 3d edition. 1989. 4th edition due 1995.

Contemporary Architects. Muriel Emanuel. 3d edition. 1994.

Contemporary Fashion. Richard Martin. 1st edition. Chicago: St. James Press, 1994.

There had not been a good, all-in-one fashion reference source for some time until this was published. Included are the many people who are part of the fashion industry, including milliners and footwear designers. Also described are the design companies and textile houses. And as the publishers say, it's "lavishly illustrated."

Designers International Index. Janette Jagger and Roger Towe, compilers. 3 Volumes. New York: Bowker-Saur, 1991.

An index to books and periodicals about designers of all types: animation, computer-aided design, glass, metalwork, even wallpaper. The first two volumes are arranged alphabetically by designer's name; Volume 3 is arranged by design category.

Dictionary of American Sculptors: 18th Century to the Present. Glenn B. Opitz, editor. Poughkeepsie, NY: Apollo, 1984.

A compendium of basic information on over five thousand U.S. sculptors (though many were born elsewhere). Each brief listing supplies the artist's birthdate and place, institution(s) of study, museums, galleries and so forth that have exhibited the sculptor's pieces, and the area where the artist lived or lives. There are full addresses provided (as of the early 1980s) for some of the contemporary sculptors.

International Dictionary of Art and Artists: Artists. James Vinson, editor. Chicago: St. James Press, 1990.

Artists is Volume 1 of this series; the second volume, titled *Art*, discusses individual works of art. *Artists* names the most important artists from the thirteenth through the twentieth centuries and presents essential facts of their lives, the most important public and private collections of their work, a bibliography and a critical essay that discusses historical and critical aspects of each artist's work. Black-and-white photographs of the artist's work, usually a full page in size, printed on good paper stock, accompany each biography.

Macmillan Encyclopedia of Architects. Adolf K. Placzek. 4 Volumes. New York: Free Press, 1982.

Most of these biographies encompass more than life history by discussing how the era of each architect, with its particular influences, contributed to the designer's ideas and approach to design. A good number of black-and-white photographs are shown.

Museum of American Folk Art Encyclopedia of Twentieth-Century American Folk Art and Artists. Chuck Rosenak and Jan Rosenak. New York: Abbeville Press, 1990.

This volume is filled with beautifully reproduced photographs of the work of painters, sculptors and potters recognized as the foremost twentieth-century folk artists of the United States. A lengthy biography is supplied for each of the 257 artists included, supplying personal biographical data, general and artistic background, description of the artist's subjects, sources, materials and techniques, and what formal recognition the artist has received.

Twentieth-Century American Folk Art and Artists. Herbert W. Hemphill, Jr. and Julia Weissman. New York: E.P. Dutton, 1974.

Arranged, as the authors say, "more or less" chronologically, this volume looks at over one hundred fifty artists, from 1900 through the early 1970s, known as folk artists. A generous portion of this book includes color and black-and-white examples of the artwork discussed.

Athletes

Biographical Dictionary of American Sports. David L. Porter. Westport, CT: Greenwood Press, 1987-92.

The *Biographical Dictionary of American Sports* is a series, with each volume highlighting a different sport: *Football* (published 1987), *Baseball* (1987), *Outdoor Sports* (1988), *Basketball and Other Indoor Sports* (1989). There is also a *1989-1992 Supplement* updating all the volumes.

The Biographical Encyclopedia of the Negro Baseball Leagues. James A. Riley. New York: Carroll and Graf, 1994.

This book represents the author's goal of "preserving a complete and accurate history of the Negro leagues." He accomplished this task in part by traveling nationwide and interviewing those players still living, and by scouring the microfilmed collections of black newspapers. (See, researchers *do* use these collections!) Members of such teams as the Harlem Stars, the New York Cubans and New York Black Yankees are included.

Great Athletes. Editors of Salem Press. 20 Volumes. Pasadena, CA: Salem Press, 1992.

Huge photos accompany each biography. All the essays have the same elements: Early Life, The Road to Excellence, The Emerging Champion, Continuing the Story and Summary. The honors, awards and statistics for each athlete are tacked on the end. This collection is great for basic facts, but the writing is simple, geared to younger readers. But it's not bereft of drama. Boxer Bob Foster, for example, has this Early Life story: "In a playground fight, Bob shattered a classmate's jaw with a punch of ferocious power. Despite getting into trouble with the school authorities, for the first time Bob was made aware of the frightening power he possessed within his wiry frame. From that moment on, Bob realized he had a talent for boxing."

Greek and Roman Sport: A Dictionary of Athletes and Events from the Eight Century B.C. to the Third Century A.D. David Matz. Jefferson, NC: McFarland and Co., 1991.

The earliest known athlete listed in this book is the "stade racer" Coroebus, from the eighth century B.C. In case you didn't know (I certainly didn't), a stade race is a "straight Greek foot race covering approximately 200 yards."

Outstanding Women Athletes: Who They Are and How They Influenced Sports in America. Janet Woolum. Phoenix, AZ: Oryx Press, 1992.

The first section of *Outstanding Women Athletes* briefly covers the history of women's involvement in sports in America. The biographical section of this book covers sixty athletes in nineteen sports from the end of the nineteenth century through 1991. Appendix A lists female Olympic medal winners, arranged by sport.

Autobiographies

American Autobiography, 1945-1980: A Bibliography. Mary Louise Briscoe, editor. Madison, WI: University of Wisconsin Press, 1982.

A listing of thousands of books, diaries, journals and collected papers that U.S. citizens wrote about themselves. It doesn't say who owns them; just identifies the existence of the manuscript. Remember, just identifying a source *is* helpful, because you can often borrow it through Interlibrary Loan. This serves as a companion volume to *A Bibliography of American Autobiographies* (described below).

A Bibliography of American Autobiographies. Louis Kaplan. Madison, WI: University of Wisconsin Press, 1961.

Louis Kaplan provides a worthwhile reminder in his introduction: Keep in mind that some autobiographies are ghost written (and perhaps don't precisely reflect the narrative style of the person). All works in this collection were published before 1946.

Three books by Anne Ellis listed in this collection are noteworthy. Her first book, *The Life of an Ordinary Woman* (New York: Houghton Mifflin, 1929), discusses the pioneer living of Coloradan Anne Ellis, a dressmaker and cook for a sheep camp. Her next book, *Plain Anne Ellis: More About the Life of an Ordinary Woman* (1931), talks about the author's forays into local politics. Her third book, by which time I guess she isn't so ordinary anymore, is called *Sunshine Preferred* (1934) and discusses her life as an asthmatic in the Southwest!

Contemporary Authors Autobiographies Series. Detroit: Gale, 1984-. Irregular.

Reading an entire book that someone has written about themselves might occasionally be more than you need. Here you can look through a few pages. Writers in this series were invited to write about ten thousand to fifteen thousand words about themselves. They were also asked to supply family photographs that represented a

range of years and a number of people who were important in their lives.

Business

See chapter 6, "Company, Product and Industry Information."

Crime

Bloodletters and Badmen: A Narrative Encyclopedia of American Criminals from the Pilgrims to the Present. Jay Robert Nash. New York: M. Evans and Co., 1973.

Describes only those criminals with "known and proven records . . . whose convictions and crimes were never in doubt." So don't look for Lizzie Borden, who was never actually convicted. The hard data section for each criminal is a litany of sequentially arranged crimes and arrests. The data is followed by a general narrative of the criminal's life and crimes.

Dictionary of Culprits and Criminals. George C. Kohn. Metuchen, NJ: Scarecrow Press, 1986.

Brief, straightforward descriptions of criminals of notoriety over the past six centuries from several countries. No illustrations.

FBI Most Wanted: An Encyclopedia. Michael Newton and Judy Ann Newton. New York: Garland, 1989.

A chronologically arranged, case-by-case description of those named on the FBI's "Most Wanted" lists from the lists' inception in 1950 through mid-1988. Just a few of these criminals have never been located; the Profiles section of the book lists these men as "still at large." Perhaps an enterprising writer would like to guess what the continuing life story of these fugitives may be.

Hunting Humans: An Encyclopedia of Modern Serial Killers. Michael Newton. Port Townsend, WA: Loompanics Unlimited, 1990.

You may be interested to know that the United States boasts 74 percent of serial killers worldwide! Of course the author points out that the communist nations, which supposedly only contribute 1.8 percent of the total, do have a tendency to "lose" bad news. Reading just a few of these case histories should be fodder for innumerable horror stories (not to mention nightmares).

Look for the Woman: A Narrative Encyclopedia of Female Poisoners, Kidnappers, Thieves, Extortionists, Terrorists, Swindlers and Spies from Elizabethan Times to the Present. Jay Robert Nash. New York: M. Evans and Co., 1981.

Rather sensationalist accounts of law-breaking women with some pretty nasty photos.

Encyclopedia of Western Lawmen and Outlaws. Jay Robert Nash. New York: Paragon House, 1992.

Did you know that John Wesley Hardin was once the "most feared gunman in Texas, killer of at least twenty-one men?" I didn't know that. There are six pages on John Wesley Hardin and hundreds of photos and detailed stories on other desperados and those who tracked them down.

Murderers' Who's Who: Outstanding International Cases from the Literature of Murder in the Last 150 Years. J.H.H. Gaute and Robin Odell. New York: Methuen, 1979.

A story could probably be written about every murderer and victim in this chilling, but well-written, collection. The bibliography leads the reader to further reading on each killer.

Women in Espionage: A Biographical Dictionary. M.H. Mahoney. Santa Barbara, CA: ABC-CLIO, 1993.

Worldwide female spies of the past and present representing various areas of the "intelligence business." Fascinating narratives of their goings-on, including the story of Alexandra Kollanti, who was born into a wealthy (but "liberal") Russian family and who from 1910 on sent detailed reports to Lenin regarding conditions inside Russia. Another essay concerns Aphra Behn, who lived in the seventeenth century, a novelist and dramatist who is remembered as one of Britain's most famous spies.

Film and Theater Folk

Contemporary Theatre, Film and Television: A Biographical Guide Featuring Performers, Directors, Writers, Producers, Designers, Managers, Choreographers, Technicians, Composers, Executives, Dancers and Critics in the United States and Great Britain. Detroit: Gale, 1984-.

Published annually since 1984, each entry lists name, personal data, addresses, career highlights, memberships, awards, honors, credits, recordings, writings, adaptations and sources of further information. This set is a continuation of *Who's Who in the Theatre*, which began in 1912.

The Encyclopedia of Magic and Magicians. T.A. Water. New York: Facts on File, 1988.

The author, a magician himself, offers concise biographical essays on past and present creators and performers of magic. This work also provides basic descriptions of magical effects and routines. An interesting addendum was added to the author's introduction. He writes, "In the entries that follow, many books are suggested for further reading. The great majority of these books are available only through magic shops and magic publishers and booksellers, and are thus not listed in *Books in Print* or similar sources." (And this can also serve as a reminder that even a massive resource such as *BIP* has omissions, missing such items as those that are self-published.)

International Dictionary of Films and Filmmakers. Nicholas Thomas, editor. 2d edition. Chicago: St. James Press, 1990-.

Each volume covers a different aspect of movies and moviemakers: Volume 1: *Films*, Volume 2: *Directors/Filmmakers*, Volume 3: *Actors and Actresses*, Volume 4: *Writers and Production Artists*, Volume 5: *Title Index*. The biographical editions each contain *Who's Who*-type biographies, complete filmographies, a selected bibliography of works on and by the entrant and an essay by a specialist in the field. St. James Press (1994) also published the *International Dictionary of the Theatre* (3 volumes; the biographical volumes cover *Playwrights* and *Actors*, *Directors and Designers*; the latter volume is forthcoming) and the *International Dictionary of Ballet*, 2 volumes.

Notable Women in the American Theatre: A Biographical Dictionary. Alice M. Robinson, editor. Westport, CT: Greenwood Press, 1989.

The editors have attempted to go beyond simple biography of each woman by trying to evaluate the biographee's life and accomplishments. Each entrant is a woman who was born or worked in the United States as an actress, producer, director, designer, critic, agent, manager, patron, dancer, choreographer, educator, scholar or administrator. They are women who were influential in their own lifetime in the American Theatre.

Theatrical Designers: An International Biographical Dictionary. Thomas J. Mikotowicz. Westport, CT: Greenwood Press, 1992.

Think of the stories some of these people have to tell about the shows they have put on and the people they have worked with! All types of stage designers are featured in this compilation, including painters, sculptors, costumers, lighting designers, stage machinists and theatrical architects.

Variety Obituaries: 1905-1986. 11 Volumes. New York: Garland Publishing, 1988. Annually updated beginning with Volume 12.

Variety is the official newspaper of show business, including entertainment news items, reviews and casting notices. This set reproduces the obituaries published in *Variety* from 1905 on as well as articles in the newspaper that refer to deaths in show business. Some of the more unusual headlines reported include *Breaking Diet Brought Death to June Mathis* and *Freddie Welsh Died of a Broken Heart*, both stories reported on August 3, 1927.

Europe

The Dictionary of National Biography: From the Earliest Times to 1900. 22 Volumes. London: Oxford University Press. Updated with Supplements through 1985. New volumes are scheduled to appear every five years.

A standard biographical reference set to noteworthy, deceased British Isle and British Colony citizens (and Americans of the Colonial period).

European Biographical Directory. 8th edition. Waterloo-Belgique: Editions Database, 1989.

The four hundred men and women in this directory are covered at length. Each article contains A Biographical Chronology (a life synopsis), Activities of Historical Significance, Overview of Biographical Stories (examining the changing interpretation of the subject's life over the years), Evaluation of Principal Biographical Sources (annotations of the most important readings), and Overview and Evaluation of Primary Sources.

Research Guide to European Historical Biography: 1450-Present. James A. Moncure, editor. 8 Volumes. Washington, DC: Beacham Publishing, 1992.

The first four volumes cover explorers, government leaders and social reformers; the last four volumes cover scientists, philosophers, political theorists, theologians, popes, artists, writers and musicians.

Explorers

Explorers and Discoverers of the World. Daniel B. Baker, editor. Detroit: Gale, 1993.

Has there been a movie, short story, or article based on every one of these adventurers? Is there one whose life would spice up an inspirational speech? Page through this compilation of over three hundred explorers and find out!

World Explorers and Discoverers. Richard E. Bohlander. New York: MacMillan Publishing Co., 1992.

Similar to the Gale source listed above, providing, on the average, about a page of information about each explorer. Some of the adventurers covered include Sebastian Cabot, the Italian-born cartographer, who was the first explorer to search for the Northwest Passage to the Orient in 1508, and the "ruthless and aggressive" Spanish conquistador Alonso de Ojeda, who was commander of a ship on Christopher Columbus's second voyage to the New World.

General

Current Biography. New York: H.W. Wilson, 1940-present.

Since 1940, *Current Biography* has provided fact-filled background on anyone whose name has been bandied about in the media. This paperback publication comes out eleven times a year with a year-end cumulated and revised edition in hardcover called *Current Biography Yearbook.*

From Fashion Designers to Prime Ministers, *Current Biography* provides four to six pages of coverage with references to further readings. The *Yearbook* has a "Classification by Profession" Index, handy for jogging your memory about who was newsworthy for what in a given year. This series also provides updates for especially newsworthy folks (so Ronald Reagan has an entry in the 1967 yearbook, which was updated in the 1982 yearbook), and "whenever feasible" obituary notices are included for persons who were once profiled.

New York Times Biographical Service: A Compilation of Current Biographical Information of General Interest. New York: The New York Times, 1970-present.

Released monthly, with six months' worth generally stored in loose-leaf notebooks, the *New York Times* plucks stories and obituaries from its pages and reproduces them in this series. Interesting to browse through.

Health Professionals

American Psychiatric Association Biographical Directory. Washington, DC: American Psychiatric Press, 1989. Updated irregularly.

Some of the data provided for each psychiatrist includes current work status, medical education and degrees, hospital affiliations, special interest areas, languages spoken and writings.

Biographical Dictionary of Medicine. Jessica Bendiner. New York: Facts on File, 1990.

The authors fish through the history of medicine and offer glimpses of heal-ers through the ages and around the world. Ancient herbalists share the stage with modern eastern physicians and researchers. The addition of a subject index, not common in such biographical sources, is very handy, allowing the reader to see exactly who was noted for his or her involvement with the bubonic plague, midwifery and so on.

Historians

Biographical Dictionary of Latin American Historians and Historiography. Jack Ray Thomas. Westport, CT: Greenwood Press, 1984.

English-speaking-only people should be aware that many of the references to further reading about these historians are to pieces written in Spanish.

Blackwell Dictionary of Historians. John Cannon, editor. New York: Blackwell, 1988.

For each scholar covered, an essay looks at the circumstances in which they worked and to what extent their work was refuted or corroborated.

Great Historians from Antiquity to 1800: An International Dictionary. Lucian Boia, editor-in-chief. Westport, CT: Greenwood Press, 1989.

Historians from numerous nations and cultures are profiled, with the entries arranged by countries or geographic areas and alphabetized within these divisions. The companion volume is *Great Historians of the Modern Age: An International Dictionary* (1991).

Musicians, Singers and Composers

The New Grove Dictionary of Music and

Musicians. Stanley Sadie, editor. 20 Volumes. London: MacMillan Publishers, Ltd., 1980.

Begun in the 1870s by Sir George Grove, *Grove's* is the first place to look for scholarly biographical and informational essays in music. Over 50 percent of the entries discuss composers, from ancient to contemporary times. The only contemporary performers included are those who have earned worldwide repute or are known for "specially important national achievement." In other words, The Archies are not listed, but Felix Mendelssohn earned over twenty-four pages. Essays cover international musical concepts, influences, theories, styles, instruments and terminology. This is a standard in most midsize to large libraries.

American Songwriters. David Ewan. New York: H.W. Wilson, 1987.

Almost 150 life overviews of "popular" songwriters such as Henry Clay Work, who penned the classic American patriotic song "Marching Through Georgia," and Woody Guthrie, who wrote or adapted nearly one thousand songs between 1932 and 1952.

Blues Who's Who: A Biographical Dictionary of Blues Singers. Sheldon Harris. New Rochelle, NY: Arlington House, 1979.

For each of the hundreds of blues figures listed, a career chronology is provided along with nicknames, quotes about those who influenced the musical style of the performer, personal data and references for further reading.

Contemporary Composers. Brian Morton and Pamela Collins. New York: St. James Press, 1992.

Biographies, discographies and critical analysis of about five hundred twentieth-century composers worldwide.

Contemporary Musicians: Profiles of People in Music. Michael L. LaBlanc, editor. Detroit: Gale, 1989-present.

Published twice yearly, each volume of *Contemporary Musicians* covers eighty to one hundred music writers and performers in rock, pop, jazz, blues, country, new wave, New Age, folk, R&B, gospel, bluegrass and reggae. Artists range from Desi Arnaz to the Beastie Boys. Each entry features biographical/critical essays, selected discographies, photos and sources of additional information.

Headbangers: The Worldwide Megabook of Heavy Metal Bands. Mark Hale. Ann Arbor, MI: Popular Culture, Ink. (No, "Ink" is not a mistake!), 1993.

This guide actually gives little biographical information other than the names of the members of the bands and the instruments they play. There are some memorable group names like Thrashholes, Mayhem and Vatican.

Hollywood Songsters: A Biographical Dictionary. James Robert Parish, editor. New York: Garland Publishing, 1991.

This volume writes of performers who were successful as both singers and film stars. Some of those who fit the bill are Shirley Temple, Dean Martin, June Haver, Lena Horne and Maurice Chevalier. Even Madonna gets a spot.

Illustrated Guide to Composers of Opera. Peter Gammond. London: Salamander Books, Ltd., 1980.

A look at over one hundred international opera composers, with many photographs and illustrations of both the composers and scenes from performances of their works.

International Dictionary of Opera. 2 Volumes. C. Steven LaRue, editor. Detroit: St. James Press, 1993.

Biographies of influential composers, librettists, performers, conductors, designers, directors and producers are supplied. Each biographical outline contains the person's occupation, birth and death dates, marriages and names of children, training and career data, including milestones. The individual's circle of important friends is also noted. In addition to biographies, this set covers major operatic works, supplying a description and listing the composer, librettist, roles for different voices and citations to publications that have commented on the work.

Pickers, Slickers, Cheatin' Hearts and Superstars: Country—The Music and the Musicians. The Country Music Foundation. New York: Abbeville Press, 1988.

This thick volume supplies coverage of the stars and starmakers in one of America's most popular musical genres. Stage, screen, radio and recording personalities are all included, with more than seven hundred color and black-and-white photos of the stars in action.

Rock Movers and Shakers: An A to Z of the People Who Made Rock Happen. Dafydd Rees and Luke Crampton, editors. Santa Barbara, CA: ABC-CLIO, 1991.

The editors identify those they consider to be the most influential and popular figures in Rock and Roll. Each entry is written chronologically, making it simple to identify at a glance the major events in the artist's life and career.

Obituaries

Annual Obituaries. New York: St. James Press, 1980-present.

Annual Obituaries offers biographical essays on international individuals of note. The sketches range from five hundred to two thousand words in length, covering, in addition to basic birth/death data, events, achievements and influences of the person's life.

Obituaries of the Gunfighters: Dust to Dust. Jerry J. Gaddy, compiler. Fort Collins, CO: The Old Army Press, 1977.

While most books in this section highlight hundreds of people, this one looks at only twenty-two gunfighters, like Billy the Kid and Doc Holliday, as recorded in papers of the day such as *The Galveston Daily News, The Fort Smith Elevator Extra* and *The Denver Republican.*

Obituaries: A Guide to Sources. Betty M. Jarboe. 2d edition. Boston: G.K. Hall, 1989.

Arranged geographically, beginning with listings for international obituaries, then U.S.-wide, followed by a chapter for each state. In addition to listing where to find obituaries in newspapers, collected genealogical works, and cemetery and burial records for a variety of areas, the author has also included publications that list tombstone inscriptions. She points out that "tombstone inscriptions often give valuable biographical information other than birth and death dates, as many of the older tombstones give place of birth, military service and sometimes family relationships."

Obituaries From the Times. Reading, England: Newspaper Archive Developments, Ltd., 1975-79.

In three volumes, each covering a different time period: 1951-1960, 1961-1970 and 1971-1975. In each volume there are about a thousand plus full-text reproductions of obituaries that originally appeared in the *Times* (of London) along with citations to other obituaries, listing the edition of the *Times* to check for the full notice.

The New York Times Obituaries Index, 1858-1978. 2 Volumes. New York: New York Times Co., 1970.

Volume I of this index is a single alphabetic listing of all names listed under the "Death" heading in the *New York Times Index* from September 1858 to December 1968, over 363,000 names. Volume II lists an additional 36,000 names, and also includes fifty full-text reprints of *New York Times* obituaries of celebrated people, including Maria Callas, who died at age 53, Bing Crosby, who lived until 73, and Jack Benny, who was 80 when he died in 1974.

Volume II indexes names of well-known persons who were listed under the "suicide" or "murder" headings, something not done in Volume I.

See also *Variety Obituaries* under the heading Film and Theater Folk.

Politicians, Legislators, Political Theorists and Rulers

American Political Scientists: A Dictionary. Glenn H. Utter and Charles Lockhart, editors. Westport, CT: Greenwood Press, 1993.

Presents "capsule careers" of political science scholars in the United States, from early theorists on. The editors say that few who entered the field after 1970 are included.

American Presidential Families. Hugh Brogan and Charles Mosley. New York: MacMillan Publishing Co., 1993.

A fascinating compilation describing ancestors and descendants of all U.S. presidents from George Washington through Bill Clinton (although Clinton's is incomplete since he was only in office a short time at the time of this work's publication). For each president there is an essay about his career and family background. An annotated family tree is also provided.

Biographical Dictionary of Marxism. Robert A. Gorman, editor. Westport, CT: Greenwood Press, 1986.

A spectrum of Communist and Socialist philosophers and activists who espouse materialist Marxism is presented. Greenwood Press has also issued *The Biographical Dictionary of Neo-Marxism* (Gorman, 1985), which encompasses nontraditional philosophical variations of Marxian theory.

Biographical Directory of the Governors of the United States: 1983-1988. Marie Marmo Mullaney. Westport, CT: Meckler, 1989.

Past volumes put out by Meckler also covering governors include:
Biographical Directory of American Colonial and Revolutionary Governors: 1607-1789. John W. Raimo. 1980.
Biographical Directory of American Territorial Governors. Thomas A. MacMullin and David A. Walker. 1984.
Biographical Directory of the Governors of the United States: 1789-1983. John W. Raimo. 1985.

Biographical Directory of the United States Congress: 1774-1989. Joint Committee on Printing, Congress of the United States. Bicentennial edition. Washington, DC: U.S. Government Printing Office, 1989.

There are a lot of politicians in here. To find out who was in Congress for a certain time period, check the first part of the book that lists all Representatives and Senators by state from the first to the one hundredth Congress. Once you've got the name, flip to the next part, which is in order by last name, where you will find a description of each statesman.

Debrett's Kings and Queens of Europe. David Williamson. Topsfield, MA: Salem House, 1988.

You'll learn of Alphonso II the Fat, Pedro I the Severe and Ferdinand I the Handsome! This book is a companion volume to *Debrett's Kings and Queens of Europe* (1986). Birth, marriage, ancestry and descendant data is provided for each monarch, with an essay providing details of each ruler's reign.

International Year Book and Statesman's Who's Who: International and National Organizations of the World and 8,000 Biographies of Leading Personalities in Public Life. West Sussex, England: Reed Information Services. Annual.

The first half of the book is in order by country, supplying facts and figures about each nation. The second half is comprised of thousands of short biographies arranged alphabetically by name. So, in order to find out a little about the Prime Minister of Belgium, for example, look under the country Belgium under the heading "Members of Government." Once you have the name, you can look it up in the alphabetic name section.

Women in Congress: 1917-1990. Staff of the Office of the Historian, U.S. House of Representatives. Washington, DC: Government Printing Office, 1991.

This collection was produced as part of a publication program, under the direction of the Commission on the Bicentenary of the U.S. House of Representatives, meant to commemorate the two-hundred-year history of Congress. For the record, the first woman to serve in the U.S. House of Representatives was Jeannette Rankin in 1917. Arranged in order by the name of the politician with a nice black-and-white photo for each one.

Women Who Ruled. Guida M. Jackson. Santa Barbara, CA: ABC-CLIO, 1990.

Included in this work are all women heads-of-state, de-facto rulers and constitutional monarchs throughout the ages, from the world's "kingdoms, islands, empires, nations and tribes." Yes, Cleopatra is in here, as is Margaret Thatcher, but the lesser known (by the general modern populace) are more intriguing—women like Zabel, also known as Isabella, ruler of Little Armenia in the thirteenth century, and Agnes of Poitou, regent for the Holy Roman Emperor Henry IV, who was characterized as being "pious and colorless . . . she gave away the duchies of Bavaria, Swabia and Carinthia to relatives."

Scientists and Engineers

The Biographical Dictionary of Scientists. Ray Porter, editor. 2d edition. Oxford: Helicon, 1994.

The *Biographical Dictionary of Scientists* is a series of six books. The first four are: *Astronomers, Biologists, Chemists* and *Physicists* (1984), and the final two are *Mathematicians* (1986) and *Engineers and Inventors* (1986). Volumes are set up identically, containing biographies that are (almost) understandable to the layman, a glossary of terms of the field and in-depth subject indexes.

The entry on Charles Lutwidge Dodgson in the *Mathematicians* volume caught my eye. After reading the new book *Alice in Wonderland*, Queen Victoria requested the complete works of Lewis Carroll, a.k.a Charles Dodgson. She was rather surprised to receive in her shipment some scholarly papers on mathematical subjects!

Blacks in Science and Medicine. Vivian Ovelton Sammons. New York: Hemisphere Publishing Corp., 1990.

A biographical listing of about fifteen hundred men and women in such fields as bacteriology, dentistry, biology, engineering, chemistry, mathematics and opthamology.

Dictionary of Scientific Biography. Charles Coulston Gillispie, editor-in-chief. 15 Volumes. New York: Scribner's, 1970. *Supplement.* 1 Volume (Vol.16), 1978. *Index.* 1 Volume (Vol.17) , 1980.

Don't be fooled by the word *dictionary* in the title. The articles in these volumes are not short! Though some are less than a page, a good number of them range from several pages to over ten pages in length. This work, which is a standard in many libraries, covers principal mathematicians and natural scientists worldwide, from all historical periods. The bibliographical references are numerous and cover non-English-language works in addition to English-language ones.

War Figures

An Account of the Organization of the Army of the United States: With Biographies of Distinguished Officers of All Grades. Fayette Robinson. 2 Volumes. Philadelphia: E.H. Butler, 1848.

Robinson, described as "late an officer of the army," writes in the Preface, "I have written this book to fill a vacuum in the history of our country—to preserve if possible the memory of the services of many distinguished men, the achievement of whom were apt in the general annals of the United States to be overlooked." Includes thirty-six "authentic portraits." This title can be found in *LAC: The Microbook Library of American Civilization* ultrafiche collection. (For a description of *LAC* see chapter 3, "Geography, Climate and Local Customs," under the heading "Collections on Microform.")

The American Navy: Being an Authentic History of the United States Navy, and Biographical Sketches of American Naval Heroes, from the Formation of the Navy to the Close of the Mexican War. Charles J. Peterson. Ann Arbor, MI: University Microfilms International, 1979.

Illustrated with over one hundred engravings, this source is available on a microfilm reel, part of the (ACS) *American Culture Series: 1493-1875*.

Biographical Dictionary of the Confederacy. Jon L. Wakelyn. Westport, CT: Greenwood Press, 1977.

In addition to biographical sketches of Southern wartime leaders, the author adds appendices that track Geographical Mobility Before and After the War, the Principal Occupations of these notable men, Religious Affiliations, Education and Prewar and Postwar Political Party Affiliation.

Biographical Dictionary of World War I. Holger H. Herwig. Westport, CT: Greenwood Press, 1982.

Military personnel, politicians, journalists and others for all countries involved in World War I are described.

Biographical Dictionary of World War II. Christopher Tunney. New York: St. Martin's Press, 1972.

The author follows the maxim that "war is a lifetime within a lifetime," with no biography in this collection going beyond the year 1945, the ending of World War II. The men and women profiled in this collection were military officers and soldiers, politicians, spies, royalty, religious figures, agitators and advisors during the second World War.

Dictionary of American Military Biography. Robert J. Spiller, editor. 3 Volumes. Westport, CT: Greenwood Press, 1984.

A wide range of biographees who have been influential in the military field, including inventors, writers, educators, physicians and explorers, along with, as expected, soldiers and officers. A detailed narrative describing the person's career and influence is provided.

The Encyclopedia of Amazons: Women Warriors From Antiquity to the Modern Era. Jessica Amanda Salmonson. New York: Paragon House, 1991.

The *Encyclopedia's* author defines an Amazon as a woman who is a duelist or soldier. The contents are heavy on Amazons of ancient and medieval times, favoring, as the author says, "the romance of the sword, the ax and the bow over the romance of the firearms." Among the Amazons listed are Cattle Kate, who was an Indian fighter and later a cattle rustler (hanged for her transgression); Hilda, a samurai; and Itagaki, who "led a charge of three thousand warriors of the Taira clan against ten thousand of the Heike in A.D. 119."

Who Was Who in the American Revolution. L. Edward Purcell. New York: Facts on File, 1993.

The majority of the biographies are those of American soldiers. All Continental generals are covered; few private soldiers or noncommissioned officers are here since few can be tracked through historical records. Loyalists, political leaders, British foes of the Revolution, "Hessians" and French allies are also featured.

Women Patriots of the American Revolution: A Biographical Dictionary. Charles E. Claghorn. Metuchen, NJ: Scarecrow Press, 1991.

Synopses of the lives of six hundred of the heroines and female patriots of the Revolutionary War. An additional five thousand are mentioned briefly. By the way, the editor says of the story of Betsy Ross designing the American flag "[it is] traditional and has never been proved." But she did definitely make ships' flags for the Pennsylvania Navy!

World Military Leaders. Paul Martell and Grace P. Hayes, editors. New York: R.R. Bowker, 1974.

These biographies of military and civilian personnel in senior positions of worldwide military establishments are definitely not home-life oriented; they list name, rank, current assignment or position, date of assuming that position, date and place of birth, education and professional training, date of commissioning, experience in active theaters of war, professional affiliations, most important honors, decorations, awards and dates of promotion to senior grades.

Women

An Annotated Index of Medieval Women. Ann Echols and Marty Williams. New York: Markus Wiener Publishing, 1992.

Approximately fifteen hundred entries present a cross-section of women over seven centuries (beginning A.D. 800), from almost thirty countries. The women who get the most coverage are English and French upper-class women from the thirteenth and fourteenth centuries, based in part on the availability of published materials from that era and those areas. Though the main purpose of this index is to direct the reader to other sources that talk about the women in question, the biographical annotations, which run from one sentence to a few dozen sentences, give the reader a start. It is possible to look up women by date, name, profession/subject, country, city or region.

History of Women. New Haven, CT: Research Publications, 1977.

This is a collection on microfilm of works from the late eighteenth century to 1920 on women worldwide. Items filmed for this collection include books, pamphlets, journals, diaries and photographs. Many women of the early American West are included, as are a variety of social reformers.

Lesser-Known Women: A Biographical Dictionary. Beverly E. Golemba. Boulder, CO: Lynne Rienner Publishers, 1992.

The book is arranged chronologically, beginning in 1600, and covers women from all over the world. *Lesser Known Women* tells of people like Anne Dacier, a French translator of Greek and Latin works, noted for her 1699 translation of the *Iliad* and of the *Odyssey* some years later, and Donaldina Cameron, a native Scotswoman who worked in the late 1800s and early 1900s in San Francisco's Chinatown, to turn young Chinese girls away from prostitution. These are the women to whom a good writer could give a new life. Since history has not regaled them as much as others, a little fiction added to the fact of their lives might make a good story. The author hopes her work will help others to "re-evaluate history by bringing to light accomplishments of women that have largely gone unrecognized for centuries."

Notable American Women, 1607-1950: A Biographical Dictionary. Edward T. James, editor. 3 Volumes. Cambridge, MA: Belknap Press, 1971.

Most entries are at least a page in length and include such fascinating women as Belle Boyd, who lived from 1844-1900 and is described as a confederate spy, actress and lecturer. This set is supplemented by a volume covering *The Modern Period* (Barbara Sicherman, editor. Cambridge, MA: Belknap, 1980), which covers women who died between January 1, 1951, and December 31, 1975.

The World Who's Who of Women. Ernest Kay, hon. general editor. Cambridge, England: International Biographical Centre, 1973-present.

At the time of this writing, this set had reached twelve volumes. Earlier volumes are notable for having included small photographs of almost all of the women named, unusual for this type of who's who book. Recent editions contain only large black-and-white pictures of a few dozen women singled out in that edition for their achievements. All editions contain basic biographical data on prominent women in all careers.

Writers: Fiction and Nonfiction Authors, Journalists and Poets

Dictionary of Literary Biography. Detroit: Gale. 1978-present.

At last count this series, including the *Dictionary of Literary Biography Yearbook* and the *Documentary Series*, was up to over 175 volumes. Each volume focuses on specialized areas of the writing field, providing biographies that focus on the career of the writer (or editor, publisher, etc.) and look at his or her work within the historical context of the time. Some titles in this varied collection include:
American Magazine Journalists, 1900-1960. Vol. 137. 1994.
American Screenwriters. Vol. 44. 1986.
Austrian Fiction Writers After 1914. Vol. 85. 1989.
Canadian Writers, 1920-1959. Vol. 68. 1988.
Twentieth Century Spanish Poets. Vol. 108. 1991.

Biographical Dictionary of American Journalism. Joseph P. McKerns. New York: Greenwood Press, 1989.

The Appendix in the back of this work assists readers in locating those listed in the directory by the type of work they did, including War Correspondents, Radio and Television, and Washington Correspondents. The main body is an A-to-Z compilation, by name.

Contemporary Authors: A Bio-Bibliographical Guide to Current Writers in Fiction, General Nonfiction, Poetry, Journalism, Drama, Motion Pictures, Television and Other Fields. 100 Volumes. Detroit: Gale Research, 1962-.

This popular set is commonly recommended in libraries. The biographies tend to be long, including personal data, career dates and highlights, organization memberships, awards, lists of writings both by and about the author and, when available, comments from the author.

The *Contemporary Authors* series is being continually updated. It is not uncommon to find an author's life recounted in one volume, an update to that narrative in another and an obituary in a later volume. At the time of this writing, the *Contemporary Authors* series was up to Volume 143, and the *Contemporary Authors New Revision Series*, with sketches from earlier volumes requiring extensive changes, was comprised of 43 volumes.

There is also a *Contemporary Authors Autobiography* series. See above under the heading "Autobiographies."

Hint on using the *Contemporary Authors* series: look for the *Contemporary Authors Cumulative Index*, a skinny book, containing authors' names listed alphabetically, that points you to the proper volumes to look at from any of the *Contemporary Authors* series. A cumulative index can also be found in even-numbered volumes of the original

Contemporary Authors series, and odd-numbered volumes of the *New Revision* series.

Contemporary Novelists. Lesley Henderson, editor. 5th edition. Chicago: St. James Press, 1991.

Selected novelists are featured in each edition. Each listing details the author's awards, the address of the literary agent, titles of publications, and essays that critique and describe the author's body of work. Of particular interest are some comments from some of the novelists themselves, as each one was "invited to comment on their work," though not every entrant chose to do so. The next scheduled update for *Contemporary Novelists* is 1995. St. James Press also publishes:

Contemporary American Dramatists. Kate Berney and Nina Templeton, editors. 1st edition. 1994.

Contemporary British Dramatists. Kate Berney and Nina Templeton, editors. 1st edition. 1994.

Contemporary Dramatists. K.A. Berney. 5th edition. 1993.

Contemporary Literary Critics. Elmer Borklund. 2d edition. 1982. (Next scheduled update is 1998.)

Contemporary Poets. Tracy Chevalier. 6th edition. 1995.

Contemporary Women Dramatists. Kate Berney and Nina Templeton, editors. 1st edition. 1994.

Contemporary World Writers. Tracy Chevalier, editor. 2d edition. 1993. (Next scheduled update is 1998.)

Cyclopedia of World Authors II. Frank Magill. 4 Volumes. Pasadena, CA: Salem Press, 1989.

Contemporary international poets,

writers and dramatists representing dozens of genres, including science fiction, literary criticism, mystery, politics and theology are discussed. Companion volume to the *Cyclopedia of World Authors*, last revised in 1974.

Film Writer's Guide. Susan Avallone. 4th edition. Los Angeles: Lone Eagle Publishing Co., 1993.

For each screenwriter, his or her agent or contact is listed, usually with an address and phone number, along with a list of the writer's screenplays. Another guide by this publisher is the *Television Writer's Guide*.

Forbes MediaGuide 500: A Review of the Nation's Most Influential Journalists. New York: Forbes. Annual.

Forbes MediaGuide is a yearly supplement to the quarterly periodical *Forbes MediaCritic*. It lists who the editors believe are the five hundred most influential journalists in five categories: Politics and Culture, Business and Economics, Science and Technology, Foreign, and Commentary. Each entry briefly reviews the journalist's works and style and determines his or her overall influence. Some publications represented include the *New York Times*, *The New York Post*, *The Wall Street Journal*, the *Los Angeles Times*, the *Boston Globe*, *The National Journal* and, of course, *Forbes*.

Journalists of the United States: Biographical Sketches of Print and Broadcast News Shapers from the Late 17th Century to the Present. Robert B. Downs and Jane B. Downs. Jefferson, NC: McFarland and Co., 1991.

Those featured range from gossip columnists to major publishers with a few paragraphs to a page dedicated to each. Some of those featured include Duff Green, a Kentucky-born journalist whose inflammatory editorial involved Green in several duels in the early 1800s, and Anne Royall, who, in 1820, launched the weekly paper titled *Paul Pry*, with a stated mission of exposing "all and every species of political evil and religious fraud without fear or affection." (Ms. Royall's follow-up paper that she ran for fourteen years was called the *Huntress*.)

Something About the Author: Facts and Pictures About Contemporary Authors and Illustrators of Books for Young People. Anne Commire, editor. Detroit: Gale, 1971-.

Basically, this is very similar to *Contemporary Authors*, except that this series looks at the authors of books geared to children, adolescents and teenagers. Since illustration is usually an essential part of books for young people, illustrators are also included along with examples of their illustration work.

Spanish American Authors: The Twentieth Century. Angel Flores. New York: H.W. Wilson, 1992.

This is part of the *Wilson Author Series*, and extensively profiles 330 novelists and poets with roots in the Caribbean, Central America and South America.

Twentieth Century Authors, First Supplement. Stanley J. Kunitz and Vineta Colby. New York: H.W. Wilson, 1955.

Each biography contains comments

on the author's life and writings and lists his or her principal works. This "supplement" brought all of the eighteen hundred biographies of the original volume up to date and added seven hundred more. Newer volumes in this series are titled *World Authors* and include:

World Authors: 1950-1970. John Wakeman, editor. 1975.

World Authors: 1970-1975. John Wakeman, editor. 1980.

World Authors: 1975-1980. Vineta Colby. 1985.

Twentieth Century Crime and Mystery Writers. Lesley Henderson, editor. 3d edition. Chicago: St. James Press, 1991.

Basic data and critical essays are presented. There are some writers that were in the first and second edition that are not in this latest edition; their names are listed in the front of this edition. Other editions in the *Twentieth Century Writers Series*:

Twentieth-Century Western Writers. Geoff Sadler, editor. 2d edition. 1991.

Twentieth-Century Science-Fiction Writers. Noelle Watson and Paul E. Schellinger, editors. 3d edition. 1992.

Twentieth-Century Young Adult Writers. Laura Standley, editor. 1st edition. 1993.

Twentieth-Century Children's Writers. Laura Standley, editor. 4th edition. 1994.

Twentieth-Century Romance and Historical Writers. Aruna Vasudevan, editor. 3d edition. 1994.

The Writers Directory. Miranda H. Ferrara and George W. Schmidt. Detroit: St. James Press. Biennial.

More than fifteen thousand living writers from Australia, Canada, Ireland, New Zealand, South Africa, the United Kingdom and the United States are listed, with each entry consisting of name, pseudonym, nationality, birth year, genres, brief career information, publications and address. This directory opens with an Index to Writing Categories, listing the names of writers under specific genres, such as Romance/Historical, Poetry, Computers and Social Commentary.

Chapter Thirteen

Language and Speech

The way people speak says volumes about them. Likewise, the way your character speaks will influence the way your reader reacts to him. Your character might occasionally say some words that are unique to a particular profession. Or he might use words that are now obsolete but were quite common in the period in which your story is set. He may simply have an accent or manner of speech common to where he lives.

Just as there are specialized encyclopedias on just about every subject, there are also subject-specific dictionaries. There are dictionaries for different professions and specialties, each revealing the jargon of the field. There are guides to obscure, obsolete, slang or colloquial terms. Use these resources to help your character speak.

Accents

Authors use various devices for conveying an accent. They may adapt only a few words in the dialog to show there is a difference in the way certain characters speak, or they may alter all spellings and show phonetically how dialog is being pronounced. Sometimes the writer will allude to a difference in speech, but then not bother to actually show it through any word changes, italics or altered spellings. Whatever method you choose, you will need to know how a particular accent you want to depict actually sounds.

Audio recordings of accents are commonly found in libraries. Some are actual foreign language learning tapes, allowing you to hear a native language spoken by a native speaker. Others are geared to actors and provide examples of how the English language sounds when spoken by a variety of foreign speakers.

To find foreign language learning tapes, try a subject search in your library's online catalog using the name of the LANGUAGE in one of the following phrases, for example:

SPANISH LANGUAGE STUDY SOUND RECORDING
DUTCH LANGUAGE STUDY AUDIOCASSETTES
AFRIKAANS LANGUAGE SELF INSTRUCTION

To locate tapes of speakers from other countries speaking English (and books that describe the accents), try a subject search using the name of the LANGUAGE, combined with the words ENGLISH LANGUAGE FOREIGN PRONUNCIATION. For example:

FRENCH ENGLISH LANGUAGE FOREIGN PRONUNCIATION
SLOVAK ENGLISH LANGUAGE FOREIGN PRONUNCIATION

Some sample titles in this category:

English With an Accent: Examples of the Ways in Which People from Many Parts of the World Speak English. New York: Gillette-Madison Communications Co., 1974.

Examples, on an LP record, of English as spoken by natives of twenty-three countries, including New Zealand, Kenya, Poland and India. Note: Libraries now routinely make LP recordings available on cassette, since fewer people own turntables. Oy, does that make me feel old, or what?

Acting With An Accent. David Allen Stern. Los Angeles: Dialect/Accent Specialists, 1979-83.

Twenty-five audio cassettes with instruction on twenty-five accents, including Farsi, Texas, Kennedyesque and Australian.

There are also guides that spell out foreign pronunciations, such as the *Actor's Encyclopedia of Dialects* (Donald Molin. New York: Sterling Publishing Co., 1984), which uses an elaborate system of symbols and the like to help the reader "hear" the more than one hundred dialects described in this book. (There is also a tape companion to this book, though the library I visited only owned the book.)

Of course, there are many marvelous entertainment movies you could watch and enjoy while absorbing accents. Try your public library, the foreign film area in your local video store or the foreign film cinema in your neighborhood.

Special Dictionaries

Sometimes Webster's just isn't enough. Or Funk & Wagnall. There will be times when you need to find some less contemporary or common words for your character to say—perhaps some profanity from the 1800s or some local expressions from Georgia. Luckily, there are specialized dictionaries that present popular expressions, phrases and word-types that share either meaning, intent or geography.

Clichés

You may create a character who is uncreative, dogmatic or just plain ignorant enough to use some clichés. Clichés have a bad name—but why did they become clichés? Because many of them are wise sayings that were repeated again and again. So perhaps your sage characters will also use one of the phrases found in the books below.

A Dictionary of Clichés. Eric Partridge. 5th edition. New York: Routledge, 1978.

The over two thousand commonly used words and phrases in this book are listed in alphabetical order, with the key word of the phrase listed first. There is no subject index, making it difficult to locate several phrases of similar meaning. Some sample phrases:

Hundred-to-one chance. (Originated in horse racing.)

To be a little thin on top. (From barbers trying to sell hair preparations to their balding male customers.)

To read the riot act. (The Riot Act passed around 1720. This cliché is now used when insisting that someone cease objectionable action or conduct.)

Have a Nice Day—No Problem! A Dictionary of Clichés. Christine Ammer. New York: A Dutton Book, 1992.

Clichés, their meaning and sometimes their origin. Some include:

Clear as a Bell—"Describing a tone free from harshness, rasping, or hoarseness, pure as the sound of a bell ... it appeared in John Ray's proverb collection of 1670."

To Hell and Gone—"A long way off; forever ... Margaret Miller used it in her *Soft Talkers* (1957): "I can contradict myself to hell and gone if I feel like it.""

Euphemisms, Regionalisms and Just Plain Isms

British English: A to Zed. Norman W. Schur. New York: Facts on File, 1987.

A lexicon of Briticisms for Americans, such as:

Bob's Your Uncle—Used at the end of instructions, it means "There you are!" or "Voilà!"

Dutch—wife. Used as an endearment, as in "My old dutch."

O.N.O.—Or Nearest Offer. Seen in ads for such items as real estate and automobiles.

Wrap Up—Shut up!

Dictionary of Alaskan English. Russell Tabbert. Juneau, AL: Denali Press, 1991.

A compilation of what the author calls "Alaskanisms," including:

Jumper—"A salmon fisherman's term for jumping fish, which is interpreted as a sign that fishing will probably be good."

Oosik—"The penis bone from the walrus ... polished, decorated and sold as an Alaskan souvenir."

A Dictionary of Euphemisms and Other Doubletalk: Being a Compilation of Linguistic Fig Leaves and Verbal Flourishes for Artful Users of the English Language. Hugh Rawson. New York: Crown Publishers, 1981.

A book that shows phrases that *don't* say it like it is. Euphemisms are words and phrases that are used to replace other, perhaps more vulgar, personal or uncomfortable terms. Such as:

Disadvantaged—Poor.

Endowed—Large Breasts.

Golden Years—Old.

Previously Owned—Used.

Dictionary of American Regional English (DARE). Frederic G. Cassidy. Cambridge, MA: Belknap Press of Harvard University, 1983.

The results of a massive scholarly study, involving thousands of conversations and questionnaires with people in communities throughout the United States. *DARE* looks at the way those in particular areas and social groups of the United States speak. In addition to providing word origins and characteristics of those who use specific words (i.e., age, gender, educational level), *DARE* supplies maps showing exactly the regions of the United States in which a word is used. Only volumes 1 (A-C) and 2 (D-H) are completed.

A Fine Kettle of Fish: And Other Figurative Phrases. Laurence Urdang. Detroit: Visible Ink Press, 1991.

A compilation of figurative phrases, their origin and definition; for example:

Penny-Ante—"Insignificant or unimportant ... originally, pennyante

was a poker game in which the minimum wager (ante) was one penny."
Put the Screws to—"To compel action by exercise of coercion. The expression derives from an early method of torture involving the use of thumbscrews to extract confessions."

Isms: A Compendium of Concepts, Doctrines, Traits and Beliefs from Ableism to Zygodactylism. Alan von Altendorf and Theresa von Altendorf. Memphis, TN: Mustang Publishing Co., 1991.
Almost anything can be "ism'd," and if you read this book it will seem that everything indeed has (though the authors claim to have left out plenty they've seen). Some examples of those defined:
Attitudinarianism—"Striking poses for effect. Today known as Vogueing."
Lookism—"A person or group unfairly favoring someone based on his or her physical traits."

Kind Words: A Thesaurus of Euphemisms. Judith S. Neaman and Carole G. Silver. New York: Facts on File, 1983.
The Green Man—"A twentieth-century British name for a men's bathroom."
To Frag—"To kill a fellow soldier or officer by setting off a fragmentation grenade."
To Have a Hollow Leg—"To eat voraciously."
Juniper Juice—Gin (whose main ingredient comes from the berry of the juniper tree).

Mountain-ese: Basic Grammar for Appalachia. Aubrey Garber. Radford, VA:

Commonwealth Press, 1976.
A glossary of words and phrases used by those in the rural sections of America called Appalachia. The author puts these into three categories: words mispronounced, verbs used as nouns or nouns and adjectives used as verbs, and words and phrases that have been coined by the mountain people. There is a sample sentence for each word. Examples:
Agonies—sickness. "Mary hain't been doin' her work since she's been sufferin' with the agonies."
Holp—help. "Zack, bring the boys over and holp us run off a stir uv lasses."
Quituate—fail to graduate. "Johnnie couldn't pass his grades so he decided to quituate school."

NTC's American Idioms Dictionary: The Most Practical Reference to Everyday Expressions of American English. Richard A. Spears. Lincolnwood, IL: National Textbook Co., 1987.
A dictionary of American slangs, clichés, proverbs, and folksy and formal expressions, with sample sentences illustrating their usage. Some included are:
Run That By Again—Say that again. "Run that by again. I don't believe my ears."
Forever and a Day—Forever. "We have enough money to last forever and a day."

NTC's Thesaurus of Everyday American English. Anne Bertram. Lincolnwood, IL: National Textbook Co., 1995.
A thesaurus focusing on the best choices for plain old English words commonly used in daily conversation.

For example, some of the choices for the word Friendly include Affable, Amiable, Genial, Sociable and Warm. There are several sample sentences for each word, showing how it might be used in conversation. This type of book is especially useful for writers whose first language is not English.

Western Words: A Dictionary of the American West. [Revised edition of *Western Words: A Dictionary of the Range, Cow Camp and Trail.*] Ramon E. Adams. Norman, OK: University of Oklahoma Press, 1968.

The most common early West words of the cowman, rodeo performer, sheepman, freighter and packer, trapper, buffalo hunter, stagecoach driver, western-river boatman, logger, sawmill operator, miner and western gambler. Some words included:

High salty—"A name for the foreman of a ranch."

Necktie social—"A hanging."

Road stake—"A logger's term for money he had earned and saved to carry him to the next job."

What Do You Call a Person From . . .? A Dictionary of Resident Names. Paul Dickson. New York: Facts on File, 1990. Very handy! Samples of proper residential nomenclature:

Someone from Dallas, Texas—A Dallasite.

Someone from Louisville, Kentucky—A Louisvillian.

Someone from Australia—An Aussie or Ozzie.

Someone from Amsterdam, Netherlands—An Amsterdamer or Amsterdammer.

Whistlin' Dixie: A Dictionary of Southern Expressions. Robert Hendrickson. New York: Facts on File, 1992.

Thousands of words and expressions of the historic and modern South, including:

Don't get crosslegged—Don't lose your temper.

Make the riffle—make the grade, succeed.

Vanity cake—a Mississippi dessert often served at tea time.

Also in this vein is the book *Southern Stuff: Down-Home Talk and Bodacious Lore from Deep in the Heart of Dixie* (Mildred Jordan Brooks. New York: Avon Books, 1992). *Whistlin' Dixie* is Volume 1 of the Facts on File series called *Dictionary of American Regional Expressions.* Also in this series: *Happy Trails: A Dictionary of Western Expressions.* Robert Hendrickson. 1994.

Metaphors and Similes

Happy as a Clam: And 9,999 Other Similes. Larry Wright. New York: Prentice Hall, 1994.

A listing of words and the phrases used to describe them. Careful though . . . some of these could easily fit in a book of clichés! Still, browsing these phrases may spark some ideas of other similes. Some sample similes:

About as easy as nailing a glob of mercury to the wall.

About as much zip as road kill.

Happy as a dog with five tails.

Hard as a harlot's smile.

Shrieked like children after an ice cream truck.

Sports Talk: A Dictionary of Sports Metaphors. Robert A. Palmatier and Harold L. Ray. Westport, CT: Greenwood Press, 1989.

The coach in your novel will no doubt use many of these phrases:

To Deck Someone—"To knock someone to the ground." Source—Sailing, as in knocking someone to the deck of a ship.

To Muddy the Water—"To confuse the issue." Source—Fishing, as in stirring up stream water when others are fly-fishing.

Similes Dictionary. Elyse Sommer and Mike Sommer, editors. Detroit: Gale, 1988.

The *Similes Dictionary*, arranged in alphabetic order by theme, allows you to look under a concept to find the many similes that have been used to describe the idea in books, magazines, plays, oratory, film and television. Some examples:

Hand Movements—"Hands rose and floated in the air, graceful and helpless as doves."—Marge Piercy.

Pallor—"Pale as a white rose."—Nathaniel Hawthorne.

Violence—"I'll crush his ribs in like a rotten hazelnut."—Emily Brontë.

Obsolete Words

Loose Cannons and Red Herrings: A Book of Lost Metaphors. Robert Claiborne. New York: W.W. Norton and Co., 1988.

Metaphors and other terms whose origins may be somewhat obscure nowadays, such as:

Despicable, Despise—"From Latin *de-spicere*, look down. A despicable person is one you look down on—or should."

Straddle—"When you straddle a horse, you've got one leg on either side of the animal. When a politician straddles an issue, he's in much the same position."

Poplollies and Bellibones: A Celebration of Lost Words. Susan Kelz Sperling. New York: Clarkson N. Potter, 1977.

Wonderful words that just don't get used much anymore:

Bellytimber—Food.

Murfles—Freckles, pimples.

One-Tongue—Tattle tale.

Porknell—Person as fat as a pig.

Snawk—To Smell.

To find other words out of fashion, or the history and origins of English words still being mercilessly bandied about, look up the twenty-volume *Oxford English Dictionary (OED)* (Oxford: Clarendon Press), the premiere etymological "dictionary" of the English language throughout time, and to the present. The *OED* tries to show the history of every English word, providing differences in meaning, spelling, pronunciation and usage of each word over an eight-hundred-year period. Using the *OED*, you will be able to match a word and its meaning(s) with a time period or time periods. Large academic and public libraries are home to the *OED*.

Profanity

Many "swear words" will also be found in collections of both slangs and regionalisms.

Dictionary of International Slurs. Abraham Aaron Roback. Cambridge: Sci-Art Publishers, 1944. [Reissued in 1979.]

A listing of what the author terms "ethnophaulisms," usually belittling, unflattering, or insulting words that refer to someone of a certain descent, or phrases that have some rude origins. Phrases are listed in English, in other languages, and as seen in proverbs and sayings. For example:

Irish Arms—"Thick legs."

Jewish Engineering—"Business Administration."

Nigger Roll—"A roll of single dollar bills."

Russian Proverb—"If anyone is born a German, God has sufficiently punished him."

To Get One's Indian Up—"To get riled or wrought up."

To Turn Turk—"To change completely for the worse."

Playboy's Book of Forbidden Words: A Liberated Dictionary of Improper English, Containing Over 700 Uninhibited Definitions of Erotic and Scatological Terms. Robert A. Wilson. Chicago: Playboy Press, 1972.

I am far too shy to list any but the *most* mild words in this book:

Charge—"Sexual excitation."

Cop a Cherry—"To deflower a virgin."

Wicked Words: A Treasury of Curses, Insults, Put-Downs and Other Formerly Unprintable Terms from Anglo-Saxon Times to the Present. Hugh Rawson. New York: Crown Publishers, 1989.

Profanity through the ages, such as:

Boot-Licker—"Someone who curries favor with those in power."

Pettifogger—"A quibbling, unscrupulous lawyer" (in use since the sixteenth century.)

Slang

Juba to Jive: A Dictionary of African-American Slang. Clarence Major, editor. New York: Penguin Books, 1994.

Griffe: (1780s-1920s) "The offspring of two mulattoes or the child of black and white parents."

Machine: (1950s-1960s) "An automobile; one's car."

Picking: (1990s) "Frantically searching for particles of rock cocaine on the ground."

Oxford Dictionary of Modern Slang. John Ayto and John Simpson. New York: Oxford University Press, 1992.

Slang words and phrases from throughout the English-speaking world.

The New Dictionary of American Slang. Robert L. Chapman. New York: Harper and Row, 1986.

Random House Thesaurus of Slang: 150,000 Uncensored Contemporary Slang Terms, Common Idioms and Colloquialisms Arranged for Quick and Easy Reference. Esther Lewin and Albert E. Lewin. New York: Random House, 1988.

Use this thesaurus to look up a commonly used word and find the slang equivalents.

Thesaurus of American Slang: 170,000 Zippy Synonyms for Thousands of Al-

phabetically Arranged Slang Words. Robert L. Chapman. New York: Harper and Row, 1989.

Street Talk—1: How to Speak and Understand American Slang. David Burke. Los Angeles: Optima Books, 1991.

This book looks at American argot as it would be heard:

In Schools: Dweeb—Simpleton

At Parties: Scarf Out—Eat a lot.

At the Movies: Noise—nonsense.

At the Mall: Rolling in it—Rich.

In a Car: Set of Skins—Set of tires.

At the Gym: Wiped out—Tired.

In the Home: Bottomless Pit—Insatiable appetite.

At Work: Zoned—Oblivious.

At the Market: Forget That Noise—That's an impossibility.

In Restaurants: Stiff a Waiter—Not leave a tip.

Clear examples are always provided on how to use the terms. The author has also written *Street Talk 2: Slang Used by Teens, Rappers, Surfers and Popular American Television Shows* (1992). There are cassette versions available of both of these books.

One way of learning some contemporary lingo of a certain area, especially among the younger crowd, is by reading the underground papers they produce. Just stop in the local trendy cafes and record stores to find them. A resource that lists many:

The World of Zines: A Guide to the Independent Magazine Revolution. Mike Gunderloy and Carl Goldberg Janice. New York: Penguin Books, 1992.

The editors of this guide are the editors of their own zine—*Factsheet*

Five—a zine that reviews other zines (P.O. Box 170099, San Francisco, CA 94117). Zines are basically independently produced small magazines covering every niche topic around. Some of the titles featured include *Dread Times* ("for Rasta's everywhere"), *Baby Split Bowling News* ("the Zeitgeist of Bowling") and *The Noise* (coverage of the Boston music scene).

Words for Writers

Allusions: Cultural, Literary, Biblical and Historical: A Thematic Dictionary. Laurence Urdang and Frederick G. Ruffner, Jr. Detroit: Gale, 1982.

You know the phrase "he's such a Scrooge." It's a way of saying someone is stingy by referring to a well-known stingy character in a book. This volume is a compilation of just such allusions that might be used in descriptive prose, such as:

Fastidiousness/Punctuality—Felix Unger, Phileas Fogg.

End—Armageddon, Checkmate.

Children's Writer's Word Book. Alijandra Mogilner. Cincinnati, OH: Writer's Digest Books, 1992.

You wouldn't want to use the line "she was disheveled and exhausted" in a book directed to first graders. What words do most first graders understand? This book tells you what words are most familiar to children from Kindergarten through the Sixth Grade. In addition to providing lists of words recommended for each grade category, the author also provides a thesaurus that shows a variety of synonyms for every word with its appropriate level noted. Tips on appropriate sentence lengths are also included.

The Describer's Dictionary: A Treasury of Terms and Literary Quotations for Readers and Writers. David Grambs. New York: W.W. Norton, 1993.

More than a thesaurus, the *Describer's Dictionary* provides examples of eloquent description of observable objects and shows many of them in use by well-known writers. There are four major categories covered: Things, Earth and Sky, Animals and People. Examples from the Patterns and Edges subsection in the Things category:

Having Spots—spotted, speckled, dappled, menald, macular, maculose, pardine, flecked.

Having Grooves—grooved, fluted, channeled, cannellated, chamfered, beveled, rutted.

Specialized Dictionaries in Major Topic Areas

Below are just examples of the hundreds of specialized dictionaries and samples of terms they contain (those containing only part of the definition listed in the dictionary are labeled as Excerpts. Those so labeled come from dictionaries with exceptionally long definitions.)

Many of these dictionaries define technical words and subject-specific meanings in certain topic areas. Remember that these resources exist when you look into a new area that you are not familiar with! If it's not in the unabridged dictionary it still might be in one of these. These dictionaries may be useful in conjunction with specialized encyclopedias of the type recommended

in chapter 8.

Remember, if your library does not have one of the titles listed below, they very well may have another dictionary on the topic. To locate specialized dictionaries in your library, try a subject search in your library's online catalog using a word describing your topic and the term DICTIONARIES. For example:

AERONAUTICS DICTIONARIES

FLOWERS DICTIONARIES

NUTRITION DICTIONARIES

You will sometimes need to try broader searches. For example, you may be using a small library that does not have a biology dictionary, but does have a general science dictionary that has the terms you are looking for. Some broader searches might be:

RELIGION DICTIONARIES (Instead of BUDDHIST DICTIONARIES)

SPORTS DICTIONARIES (Instead of FOOTBALL DICTIONARIES)

Abbreviations and Symbols

Something that almost every researchers runs across in their work: a bunch of letters with periods between them that stand for who-knows-what. Grab one of the books below to decipher them.

Acronyms, Initialisms and Abbreviations Dictionary. 5th edition. 3 Volumes. Detroit: Gale, 1994.

This set of three hefty volumes is the Mother of All Abbreviation Books and is commonly found in midsize to large public and academic libraries.

The contents for this set were culled from over one hundred sources, including other specialized abbreviation dictionaries, magazines, association directories and subject-specific dictionaries. Just look under an abbreviation (for example, STB) and see what it stands for (STB denotes a Bachelor of the Science of Theology degree). The companion set to this is the *Reverse Acronyms, Initialisms and Abbreviations Dictionary*, which enables the reader to look up the full name of an organization, or a full title or word, and find its abbreviation.

Abbreviations Dictionary. Ralph De Sola. 8th edition. Boca Raton: CRC Press, 1992.

The first nine hundred or so pages of this dictionary list abbreviations, acronyms, anonyms, contractions, signs, symbols and specialized terminology; the last few hundred pages show abbreviations/symbols for a wide range of places and things, including Airports of the World, Canadian Provinces, Chemical Element Symbols, International Vehicle License Letters, Proofreaders' Marks, Railroad Conductor's Cord Pull Signals and the Russian alphabet.

Symbol Sourcebook: An Authoritative Guide to International Graphic Symbols. Henry Dreyfuss. New York: Van Nostrand Reinhold, 1984.

A depiction of the symbols used in different countries for twenty-six categories, including Accommodations and Travel, Astronomy, Communications, Folklore, Mathematics, Recreation and Traffic.

Authorship, Literature

The Poet's Dictionary: A Handbook of Prosody and Poetic Devices. William Packard. New York: Harper and Row, 1989.

Enjambement—Excerpt—"Spillover of poetry from the end of one line to the beginning of the next line."

Pastiche—Excerpt—"A poem or poems written in deliberate imitation or parody of a previous author or work."

Writing A to Z: The Terms, Procedures and Facts of the Writing Business Defined, Explained and Put Within Reach. [Revised and Updated Edition of the *Writer's Encyclopedia*.] Kirk Polking, editor. Cincinnati, OH: Writer's Digest Books, 1990.

In addition to defining some buzzwords of writing and publishing, this resource shows examples of items such as news releases and radio scripts.

Kill—"This is a publishing term used to refer to the deletion of part or all of an article or book."

On Spec—Excerpt—"An editor may respond to a writer's query letter by offering to look at the proposed article "on speculation"; that is, the editor expresses interest in the article idea and agrees to consider the finished piece for publication."

Aviation

The Aviation/Space Dictionary. Larry Reithmaier. 7th edition. Blue Ridge Summit, PA: Tab Books, 1990.

Landing Mat—"A prefabricated, portable mat so designed that any number of planks (sections) may be rapidly fastened together to form surfacing for emergency runways, landing beaches, etc."

Quiet Sun—"The sun when it is free from unusual radio wave or thermal radiation such as that associated with sun spots."

Private Pilot's Dictionary and Handbook. 2d edition. Kirk Polking. New York: Arco, 1986.

Though there are no aircraft illustrations in this volume, it is filled with the jargon of pilots, and specifically the terms, operation procedures and rules for the VFR (Visual Flight Rules) pilot using a single engine aircraft. Symbols, signals and abbreviations that the pilot might need are illustrated and interpreted.

Business, Economics

Dictionary of Banking. Jerry M. Rosenberg. New York: John Wiley and Co., 1993.

Demand Draft—"A draft payable immediately upon sight or presentation to the drawee. Synonymous with *sight draft.*"

Pooled Income Fund—"A fund to which several donors transfer property, retaining an income interest, and giving the remainder to charity."

Dictionary of Investing. Jerry M. Rosenberg. New York: John Wiley and Sons, 1993.

Fundamentalist—"An individual who believes that the best investment results are obtained by studying the record of a firm and its industry, and the economy in general, as distinct from examining investment cycles."

Stag—"An individual speculator who rapidly buys and then sells shares for profit, having had no intention of retaining the securities for any length of time."

The Dictionary of Real Estate Appraisal. Chicago: American Institute of Real Estate Appraisers, 1984.

Chattels Personal—"Tangible, movable property items; e.g., furniture, refrigerators."

Speculative Building—"A structure that is built in the expectation that it will be sold or rented when completed."

Glossary of Insurance Terms: Over 2,500 Definitions of the Most Commonly Used Words in the Industry. Thomas E. Green and The Merritt Editors. 5th edition. Santa Monica, CA: Merritt Publishing, 1993.

Concurrent Causation—"A term referring to two or more perils acting concurrently to cause a loss. This created problems for property insurers when one of the perils was covered and one was not, and it led to recent revisions in policy language."

XCU—"Explosion, Collapse, and Underground Damage. This term is used in Business Liability Insurance to indicate that certain types of construction work involve these hazards. Many liability policies exclude them."

Handbook of Real Estate Terms. Dennis S. Tosh, Jr. Englewood Cliffs, NJ: Prentice Hall, 1992.

Earnest Money—Excerpt—"Money paid by a buyer at the time he or she enters into a contract to indicate both the ability and intent of carrying out the contract."

Pro Forma Statement—"A financial statement used to project anticipated revenues and expenses for a real estate project. The information is based upon assumptions regarding the operation of the property.

Human Resource Glossary: A Complete Desk Reference for HR Professionals. William R. Tracy. New York: AMACOM, 1991.

Deunionization—"The termination of union representation for a particular collective bargaining unit, accomplished by a decertification election in which workers vote to disband their union."

Persuasive Behavior—"The ability to present a product, service, argument or proposal in terms that others will respond to in a positive way. Persuasive behavior is a particularly important skill for salespersons, instructors and briefers."

International Business Dictionary and Reference. Lewis A. Presner. New York: John Wiley and Sons, 1991.

PLC—"The abbreviation of Private Limited Company, used in the U.K. instead of inc., the abbreviation for *incorporated* company or Ltd., the abbreviation for *limited* company.

Tatemae—Excerpt—"From the Japanese meaning 'official group stance,' refers to the impersonal, 'official,' group-oriented behavior of Japanese when in decision-making groups."

Link's International Dictionary of Business Economics. Albert N. Link. Chicago: Probus Publishing Co., 1993.

Demand Schedule—"A table or tabular representation of price and quantity demanded. The data from a demand schedule can be used to sketch a demand curve."

Monetization of Debt—"One way for a nation to pay its debts is for it to print money. Increasing the money supply for repayment of debt will result in inflation and, eventually, will result in higher interest rates."

The Marketing Glossary: Key Terms, Concepts and Applications in Marketing Management, Advertising, Sales Promotion, Public Relations, Direct Marketing, Market Research and Sales. Mark N. Clemente. New York: AMACOM, 1992.

Embargo—"The publicity practice of issuing a news release with the caveat that it not be used by the news media until after the date or time indicated on the release."

Flack—Excerpt—"Derogatory term for a public relations professional or press agent."

Computers

Computer Dictionary: Over 5,800 of the Most Important Computer Terms Defined in Easy to Understand Language. Donald D. Spencer. 3d edition. Ormond Beach, FL: Camelot Publishing Co., 1992.

Full-Screen Editing—"Ability to move the cursor over the entire screen to alter text."

Install Program—"A program that prepares a software program to run in the computer. It customizes elements of the new program so a specific computer system can use it."

The New Hackers Dictionary. Eric S. Raymond. 2d edition. Cambridge, MA: MIT Press, 1994.

Warning—if you are not a hacker yourself, you may need a computer dictionary to use this dictionary. It's a collection of slang terms used by computer hackers for "fun, social communication and technical debate."

Dec—Excerpt—"Verbal (and only rarely written) shorthand for decrement, i.e., 'decrease by one.'"

Feeper—"The device in a terminal or workstation (usually a loudspeaker of some kind), that makes the feep sound."

Crime

Crime Dictionary. Ralph De Sola. New York: Facts on File, 1988.

Blank—"Non-narcotic white powder sold to gullible drug users."

National Razor—"French nickname for the guillotine."

The Police Dictionary and Encyclopedia. John J. Fay. Springfield, IL: Charles C. Thomas Publishing, 1988.

Cocked Striker—"In bomb construction, a firing pin held under tension. Upon release of the tension, the pin initiates the bomb's firing train."

Spook—"A spy."

Foreign Language

Does your character need to say "That's not mine!" in Portuguese? (*Isso não e meu!*) Or "Hi!" in German? (*Hallo!*) Public and academic libraries are just brimming with foreign language dictionaries that translate words to English. To find them, do a subject search on your library's online catalog and combine the name of the language with the words LANGUAGE DICTIONARIES. For example:

FRENCH LANGUAGE DIC-
TIONARIES
SWAHILI LANGUAGE DIC-
TIONARIES

You can also throw the word ENGLISH in there for good measure, to be sure you are getting a dictionary that translates to English.

One all-in-one language dictionary is the *Harper Dictionary of Foreign Terms* (New York: Harper and Row, 1987). It lists more than 15,000 foreign expressions commonly used in English literature, conversation and media. Some examples:

Corragio!—Courage.

Pied-a-terre—A resting place; a temporary lodging.

History, Archaeology

Collins Dictionary of Archaeology. Paul Bahn, editor. Santa Barbara, CA: ABC-CLIO, 1993.

Broch—Excerpt—"A circular dry-stone defensive tower found in coastal parts of northern and western Scotland and the islands."

Shabti or Ushabti—"A figurine found in Egyptian tombs of the Middle Kingdom onwards, often in large numbers, and usually in the form of a mummy bearing agricultural implements. The shabti was intended to serve as a magical replacement should the deceased be called upon to perform tasks of manual labor in the netherworld."

Media, Communications

NTC's Mass Media Dictionary. R. Terry Ellmore. Lincolnwood, IL: National Textbook Co., 1990.

Bullet—"A large dot or other mark used as a decoration or to highlight important points in a story."

Impulse System—"A cable television interactive system that allows a subscriber to select pay-per-view programs by punching buttons on a control panel instead of calling the cable television system.

Webster's New World Dictionary of Media and Communications: The Most Comprehensive Source for Understanding the Language of Writers, Communicators, and the Media Industries. Richard Weiner. New York: Webster's New World, 1990.

Incipit—"From the Latin meaning 'here begins,' a word sometimes placed at the beginning of medieval manuscripts and early printed books."

Stipple—Excerpt—"To draw, engrave, paint or apply dots or points instead of lines or solid areas.

Dot and Tickle—Slang for use of the stipple technique."

Military

The Facts on File Dictionary of Military Science. Jay M. Shafritz, Todd J.A. Shafritz and David B. Robertson. New York: Facts on File, 1989.

Dirty Nuclear Weapon—Excerpt—"A nuclear weapon that causes damage (in addition to explosion and radiation emission) via radioactive by-products. It is intended to do more

harm to flesh than to inanimate objects."

Mae West—Excerpt—"A brightly colored inflatable lifejacket first worn for emergency use by American pilots during World War II flights over water."

The United States Navy: A Dictionary. Bruce W. Watson and Susan M. Watson.

Dual-Purpose Weapon—"a weapon that delivers effective fire against air or surface targets."

Scram—Excerpt—"In air intercept usage, a code meaning 'Am about to open fire. Friendly units keep clear of indicated contact, bogey or area.' "

Philosophy, Psychology, Sociology

The Concise Oxford Dictionary of Sociology. Gordon Marshall. New York: Oxford University Press, 1994.

Delinquent Drift—"David Matza, in his book *Delinquency and Drift* (1964), argues that delinquency did not emerge as a result of strongly deterministic forces, but rather through a gentle weakening of the moral ties of a society, which allowed some young people to drift into delinquency."

Solidarism—Excerpt—"This term refers to belief in the sharing of aims and interests. Solidarity is valued as a source of strength and resistance and, by implication, for its single-minded unity of purpose."

A Dictionary of Existentialism. Ralph Bubrich Winn. New York: Philosophical Library. 1960.

The definitions in this resource are quotations from the leaders in existentialist thought: Kierkegaard, Jaspers, Marcel, Heidegger, Sartre and De Beauvoir. They *don't* always agree.

Faith—"There is only one proof that the Eternal exists: Faith in it." Soren Kierkegaard, *Purity of Heart.*

Religion—"For man, to abandon and forget religion completely would be to end the philosophic quest itself. It would be replaced by unreasoning despair ignorant of itself." Karl Jaspers. *Tragedy is not enough.*

The International Dictionary of Psychology. Stuart Sutherland. New York: Continuum, 1989.

Dolorology—"The study of the nature, origins and treatment of pain."

Polydipsia—"The consumption of abnormally large amount of water."

The Oxford Dictionary of Philosophy. Simon Blackburn. NY: Oxford University Press, 1994.

Isolationism—Excerpt—"In aesthetics, the view that a work of art should be taken in isolation, understood entirely in its own terms and without reference to external factors such as its place in a tradition, or the social circumstances in which it is set, or the life or intentions of the artist. The opposing position is contextualism."

Tychism—"The view associated with (Charles Sanders) Peirce that chance is a real force in the universe; more recently, the view that chance mutations are the basis of evolutionary adaptation."

Politics

The Congress Dictionary: The Ways and Meanings of Capitol Hill. Paul Dickson and Paul Clancy. New York: John Wiley and Sons, 1993.

Beauty Contest—"A nonbinding primary election; a vote that does nothing more than measure popularity."

Float—"Put an idea into play by talking to key members, their staffs or the press to see how it is received. Floating has replaced 'sending up a trial balloon' as the term of preference."

The Dictionary of Marxist Thought. Tom Bottomore, editor. 2d edition. Cambridge, MA: Blackwell Publishers, 1991.

Dependency Theory—Excerpt—"A school of thought which explains the underdevelopment of poor countries and regions as a product of capitalist development in wealthy countries."

Social Democracy—Excerpt—"In their earlier writings Marx and Engels regarded social democracy 'a section of the Democratic or Republican Party more or less tinged with socialism.' "

The Dictionary of 20th Century World Politics. Jay M. Schafritz, Phil Willimas and Ronald S. Calinger. New York: Henry Holt and Co., 1993.

Little Red Book—"A red-covered book of quotations for the works of Chinese communist party chairman Mao Zedong. Virtually every Chinese citizen carried a copy of the red book during the cultural revolution as a symbol of loyalty to Mao and his ideas."

Saddle Point—"A concept from Game Theory to describe the point that neither side in a zero-sum situation can improve upon by independent movement."

Real Life Dictionary of American Politics: What They're Saying and What It Really Means. Kathleen Thompson Hill and Gerald N. Hill. Los Angeles: General Publishing Group, 1994.
Deficit-Neutral Spending—"Secretary of Health and Human Services Donna E. Shalala's term for new programs that will not increase or reduce national debt because they are covered by new taxes or use of other funds."
Feds—"Term for overbearing, intrusive federal government bureaucrats, usually with the implication that one cannot oppose or contradict their methods or power."

Science

Biotechnology from A to Z. William Bains. New York: Oxford University Press, 1993.
Cryopreservation—Excerpt—
Basically "the preservation of things by keeping them cold."
Cytokines—Excerpt—"Materials which stimulate cell migration."

The Harper Dictionary of Science in Everyday Language. Herman Schneider and Leo Schneider. New York: Harper and Row Publishers, 1988.
Central Processing Unit (CPU)—Excerpt—"Could be called the brain of a computer, if computers had brains. The CPU carries out the computer's arithmetic, logic and control operations."

Oncology—"The branch of medical science, named from the Greek *onkos,* 'mass bulk,' dealing with abnormal growths, called tumors.

A Modern Dictionary of Geography. John Small and Michael Witherick. Baltimore, MD: Edward Arnold, 1986.
Interglacial—Excerpt—"A period of relatively warm climate, separating two glacial periods within the Pleistocene."
Permafrost—Excerpt—"Perennially frozen ground in a periglacial environment."

Sports

The Encyclopedia of Sports Talk. Zander Hollander. New York: Corwin Books, 1976.
The words and lingo associated with fifteen sports are listed, including:
In Auto Competition: Tired Iron—"Out-of-Date Racing Car."
In Bowling: Clutch—"A pressure situation."
In Skiing: Mounting—"The process of attaching ski binding to skis."

The Illustrated Encyclopedia of Billiards. Mike Shamos. New York: Lyons and Burford, Publishers, 1993.
Jack-Up Pool—"Pocket Billiards in which one or both players shoot with one hand held in a trouser pocket and in which the cue stick may not be rested on a rail. An extreme handicap."
Sissy Stick—"A derogatory term for the mechanical bridge, wrongly implying that one who uses it must be frail in some way. One of a group of related synonyms that include

Crutch, Ladies' Aid and Old Man's Aid."

The Sailing Dictionary: A Comprehensive Reference Book of Sailing Terms. Joachim Schult. 2d edition. Dobbs Ferry, New York: Sheridan House, 1992.
Fend Off—"To push a boat clear of another boat or object, either by hand or with the boathook, etc.; similarly to push an object away from the boat."
Quant—"A long pole with a fork or disc at the lower end, used to propel a small boat (quanting) by pushing on the bottom; inland waters."

Visual and Performing Arts

The HarperCollins Dictionary of Art Terms and Techniques. Ralph Mayer. 2d edition. New York: HarperCollins, 1992.
Brownstone—"An American sandstone that contains iron. It is available in several shades, from pinkish to deep chocolate-brown. Connecticut, New Jersey and Pennsylvania brownstones are well known."
Floating Signature—Excerpt—"An artist's signature applied to a painting on top of the coating of varnish. Although an artist might conceivably sign his work after varnishing it, the discovery by test that a signature is floating is usually accepted as evidence that the signature is fraudulent."

Glossary of Art, Architecture and Design Since 1945. John A. Walker. 3d edition. Boston, MA: G.K. Hall and Co., 1992.
Habitat—Excerpt—"A vogue word

among architects and designers in the 1950s and 1960s. It means 'natural environment in which plants and animals develop,' hence 'place of abode.' "
Zeitgeist—Excerpt—"A German word meaning 'spirit of the age.' It was popularized by the idealist philosopher Georg Hegel and utilized by generations of art historians."

The New Harvard Dictionary of Music. Don Michael Randel. Cambridge, MA: The Belknap Press of Harvard University Press, 1986.
Aleatory Music—Excerpt—"Music in which deliberate use is made of chance or indeterminacy; the term chance music is preferred by many composers."
Lungo—"Long; *lunga pausa,* prolonged pause or rest."

NTC's Dictionary of Theatre and Drama Terms: A Comprehensive, Easy-to-Use Guide to Drama and Theatre. Jonnie Patricia Mobley.
Groundling—"In Elizabethan times, a spectator who stood in the pit immediately in front of the stage to see a performance. Since these were the cheapest of tickets, those who stood there were often unruly, and so, many low-comedy lines or gestures were thrown their way to keep them entertained."
Sense-memory—"An actor's device for summoning up emotion by recalling a previous real-life event."

Women

The Dictionary of Feminist Theory. Maggie Humm. Columbus: Ohio State

University Press, 1990.

Communal Research—Excerpt—"A feminist alternative to mainstream methods of social research. Communal research involves the techniques of uncontracted cooperation, non-linear patterning and a fusion of subject and object and ego boundary diffusion."

Womanculture—Excerpt—"Barbara Burris defines womanculture as a fourth world. Hypotheses of womanculture have been developed over the last decade by feminist anthropologists, sociologists and social historians to help theory move away from masculine systems and values, and to describe the primary nature of female cultural experience."

Womanwords: A Dictionary of Words

About Women. Jane Mills. New York: The Free Press, 1992.

The histories and meanings of more than three hundred words relating to women, such as:

Cheesecake—Excerpt—"For five hundred years cheesecake meant a cake or tart made of cheese or curdled milk, eggs, and sugar. During WWII it joined the long list of slang words for women as edible and sexually available to men."

Dog—Excerpts—"In distinguishing gender, a dog was once the male of the species, e.g.: 'The Dogge is though better than the Bitche' (1577). Dog is used pejoratively in many different contexts with connotations of inferiority or unattractiveness."

Chapter Fourteen

Choosing and Researching Names

When you need names of imaginary characters, places and gadgets, why not tap into lists that already exist? A gazetteer, like the eleven-volume *Omni Gazetteer of the United States of America*, reveals that there are eighty-one summits across the United States bearing the name "Sugarloaf," so using that name in a short story will stir the memories of many! *The Dictionary of Jewish Names and Their History* lists such original appellations as "Hamburger" and "Schmukler." Below are books brimming with names, waiting to bring personality and substance to the individuals, areas and items you have created in your writing.

Name Books

Animal Names

The Best Pet Name Book Ever. Wayne Bryant Eldridge. New York: Barron's, 1990.

The author, who is a veterinarian, has come up with reams of names to choose from to name your furry, feathery, leathery or scaled pet character. The names are listed alphabetically under categories such as Human Names (Elliot, Sheila), Religious Names (Amalek, Jehoshaphat), Screen and Television (Goofy, Pepe Le Pew), and Fashion and Cosmetics (Cashmere, Wrangler).

The Complete Book of Pet Names. Renee D. Cowing. San Mateo, CA: Fireplug Press, 1990.

The Complete Book of Pet Names lists the 50 Most Popular Cat Names (Kitty, Patches and Taffy are all on the list) and the Top 50 Dog Names (including Brandy, Muffin and Buffy). Of course, if you use such a popular name in a story, it would be one many could identify with. A few celebrity pet names are identified, such as Mel Brooks and his cat Marmalade, Bill Murray and his Golden Retriever named Bark, and Joe Namath with a kitty called Poppet. The A-to-Z listing of names is a mix of human names and "cute" animal names. There are short definitions for all the names, even ones like Frosty—"a soft ice-cream cone."

Nicknames

Baseball Nicknames: A Dictionary of Origins and Meanings. James K. Skipper, Jr. Jefferson, NC: McFarland and Co., Publishers, 1992.

The author identifies himself as a "sociologist and rabid baseball fan." He lists affectionate and perhaps not so affectionate nicknames identified with baseball players, umpires, managers, officials, sportswriters, broadcasters, owners and fans. Some are decidedly run of the mill, like Tex or Slim, but some are more interesting: Shortwave (nickname of shortstop Richard Bartell, who was also known as Rowdy Dick, Pepper Pot and Error Bartell), and the Round Man (for outfielder Ronald James Northy, who had a somewhat "roly-poly" frame). If you just want to browse the nicknames, head for the index of this book. Otherwise, the book is arranged in alphabetical order by the real names of the people.

The Dictionary of Historic Nicknames: A Treasury of More than 7,500 Famous and Infamous Nicknames From World History. Carl Sifakis. New York: Facts on File, 1984.

Most of the nicknames listed in this collection are not personal little pet names that their friends and colleagues might call them; they are more like grand titles by which they became known. For example, Guy Lombardo is said to have become known as The Man Who Owns New Year's or Mr. New Year's Eve, since he was so often on TV for New Year's; President James Garfield was known as the Teacher President as well as the Preacher President; and entertainer Dan Rice, who earned the title King of American Clowns in the nineteenth century.

Sobriquets and Nicknames. Albert R. Frey. Boston: Ticknor and Co., 1888. (Republished by Gale, Detroit, 1966.)

A listing of nicknames bestowed upon literary characters and famous people worldwide. Note that this reference book was originally published in 1888 (though this reprint is in many libraries), so the names referred to will be over a century old.

Person First Names and Last Names

Baby name books. Oh, there are so many. If you want to browse dozens of these, try the bookstore or public library. Some sample titles:

Beyond Jennifer & Jason: An Enlightened Guide to Naming Your Baby. Linda Rosenkrantz and Pamela Redmond Satran. New York: St. Martin's Press, 1994.

A modern, sometimes wise, sometimes silly, compilation of potential names for newborns. There are categories like Homestyle Names (Josie, Nat), Presidential Names (Carter, Jefferson), Neu Spellings (Cyndi, Barbra), and Handsome Names (Reed, Milo). There is actually an index to the names, which is helpful, since some names fall into more than one category. My name (Ellen) is described four ways: as the middle name of one of Tracy Ullman's daughters, as a "no-image" name and a "no-frill's" name, and as a sitcom mom name of the thirties and forties. Gosh, I feel exciting.

Dictionary of First Names. Alfred J. Kolatch. New York: Perigee Books, 1990.

A no-frills, noncategorized, A-to-Z listing of possible first names with their definition and often an example of someone who has the name. For example: "Evelyn—A variant spelling of the Celtic name Eveline, meaning 'pleasant.' Evelyn Pierrepont."

The Melting Pot Book of Baby Names. Connie Lockhart Ellefson. 2d edition. Cincinnati: Betterway Books, 1995.

Names are listed that come from

thirty-two countries and regions, with the definition of each name provided. One name from France is Alain, which means handsome, cheerful; Sonja, a name from Norway, translates as wisdom; and a pleasant Spanish appellation is Erasmo, which means amiable.

Some additional books to aid name searches:

The Book of African Names. Molefi Kete Asante. Trenton, NJ: African World Press, 1991.

A beautiful book to page through, printed on pinkish paper illustrated with African symbols and designs. Arranged by the different geographic areas of the African continent (Southern, Central, Eastern, Western and Northern), each name is briefly defined. There are many beautiful names listed, not yet common in the United States, including Birago, meaning down-to-earth, sensible, Patire, defined as "where we are," and Habiba, the beloved. The author actually purposefully omitted names with negative or demeaning meanings. The fact that there is no pronunciation assistance is a downfall of this volume.

A Dictionary of First Names. Patrick Hanks and Flavia Hodges. New York: Oxford University Press, 1990.

A different book than the baby book with the same title (and published the same year) listed above. This book provides, in a few sentences for each, the linguistic root of each name, historical background and the country in which it originated. Variations of each name are also provided.

A Dictionary of Jewish Names and Their History. Benzion C. Kaganoff. New York: Schocken Books, 1977.

The first half of the book discusses the origins and histories of naming in the Jewish religion. The second part is a dictionary of selected surnames. Names of note include the longest known Jewish family name, Katzenellenbogen, and Bernstein, a name commonly known in the United States, which means amber.

Dictionary of Surnames. Patrick Hanks and Flavia Hodges. New York: Oxford University Press, 1989.

A listing of European hereditary names of families handed down from father to children.

An Explanatory and Pronouncing Dictionary of the Noted Names of Fiction. Charles G. Wheeler. Boston: Houghton, Mifflin, and Co., 1865. (Reprinted in 1966 by Gale.)

This work strives to explain the allusions, in well-known literature, to places and persons both imagined and real. (Written over a hundred years ago, this book is fun to browse through and chock full of adjectives like Riotous, Licentious, Celebrated and Fabled. Also note the pointer illustration of the little pointing hand with the ruffled cuff.)

The First Name Reverse Dictionary. Yvonne Navarro. Jefferson, NC: McFarland and Co., 1993.

A particularly useful source for those writers who wish to give their characters a name with a specific meaning. Instead of needing to hunt through many likely sounding names, this volume allows you to look up a meaning and then see what name or names match. For example, there are many name choices listed under the word Heavenly including Celeste, Juno, Selena, Celene, Celesta and Celestina.

Hispanic First Names: A Comprehensive Dictionary of 250 Years of Mexican-American Usage. Richard D. Woods. Westport, CT: Greenwood Press, 1984.

This list of Hispanic first names does provide a word or two of description for names listed. However, there are, in place of a description, what seem like hundreds of cross-references to the original name that other names were derived from. For example, these are just some of the names followed by the instruction "See Crescencio" (which means "to grow"): Crescenciono, Crescensiana, Cresendo, Cresenio and Cresinta.

Irish Families: Their Names, Arms and Origins. Edward MacLysaght. 4th edition. Dublin: Irish Academic Press, 1985.

The author's intent is to present essential facts about Irish nomenclature and families. There are 243 color illustrations of coats of arms (but more than that many names described). Also by this author: *More Irish Families* (1981) and *The Surnames of Ireland* (1969).

New Dictionary of American Family Names. Elsdon C. Smith. New York: Harper and Row, 1973.

A straightforward alphabetic listing of last names used in America. The

country of origin and meaning are provided. For example, the name Hornik is identified as Czechoslavakian in origin and means "one who worked in a mine, a miner." Other books arranged in a similar manner include:

The New Name Dictionary: Modern English and Hebrew Names. Alfred J. Kolatch. Middle Village, New York: Jonathan David Publishers, 1989.

The author's purpose in writing this book was to assist parents in finding an appropriate Hebrew name to match an English one. For all the English names, Hebrew names that correspond in meaning are recommended. This dictionary lists over ten thousand first names (no last names), including several hundred Hebrew names that are currently in use in Israel.

The Origin and Significance of Scottish Surnames, With a Vocabulary of Christian Names. Clifford Stanley Sims. New York: Avenel Books. Originally published in 1862.

A slim A-to-Z volume of Scottish surnames, with some first names defined in a small section at the back of the book. Some of the names explained include Cameron, which means crooked nose, and Forester, which means just what it sounds like—a woodsman.

Our Italian Surnames. Joseph G. Fucilla. Baltimore: Genealogical Publishing Co., 1987.

The names in this collection are listed within textual explanations, in chapters that describe their origin. For example, some of the chapter titles, indicating the origin of surnames, are

Botanical Names, Topographical Names, Geographical Names, Bird Names, Occupative Names and Anatomical Names. The alphabetic listing in the back of the book allows the reader to locate the section a particular name appears in.

Spanish-Surnames in the Southwestern United States: A Dictionary. Richard D. Woods and Grace Alvarez-Altman. Boston: G.K. Hall and Co., 1978.

Names of Spanish origin are described with one or more meanings attached. Some of the melodic appelations include *Archibeque*, which means "captain of a ship," *Fuentes*, a spring, fountain, jet, or spray of water, and *Maestas*, which translates as "to teach."

The Writer's Digest Character Naming Sourcebook. Sherrilyn Kenyon. [With Naming Strategies by Hal Blythe and Charlie Sweet.] Cincinnati, OH: Writer's Digest Books, 1994.

The lists of names in this book are intended to assist the writer in naming characters, places and objects (for example, fictitious brand names). The name lists are in separate chapters, listed under the nations or civilizations that spawned them. The types of first and last names listed include those from ancient times (Greek, Norse), from many countries (France, Spain, Germany), different cultures (Hebrew, Native American), and the names of legends (Arthurian, and intermingled within the names of many lands, including Latin, Egyptian, and Welsh). Each name is defined in one or two words. The back-of-the-book alphabetic index allows you to quickly

trace names to their region and to see if the name is associated with more than one culture.

Phone book. Do remember that ultimate at-home reference source when trying to name your character? Just flip it open and browse. The names of those living in the United States represent peoples from all over the world so there is no lack of variety. For tips on finding phone books of different regions, see chapter 7, "Identifying Experts."

Place Names

African Placenames: Origins and Meaning of the Names for Over 2,000 Natural Features, Towns, Cities, Provinces and Countries. Adrian Room. Jefferson, NC: McFarland and Co., Publishers, 1994.

Many of these names sound quite exotic to English-speakers (Africa is home to over one thousand non-English languages). A few sentences of history and lore are provided for most entries. Some sample names include Caála, a town in west-central Angola, "one of the earliest European settlements in the country . . . named for a chief who had his base nearby," and Ndola, a town in north central Zambia; it means "clear spring."

A Dictionary of English Place-Names. A.D. Mills. New York: Oxford University Press, 1991.

A compilation of over twelve thousand names of cities, suburbs, towns, villages, counties, districts, rivers and coastal features of England. A few words of history, origin or description accompany each name. There are some perfect gothic-sounding names in this guide.

The Dictionary of Imaginary Places. Gianni Gaudalupi and Alberto Manguel. New York: Macmillan, 1980.

Co-author Alberto Manguel calls this the "traveller's guide to . . . places of literature." Limited to terrestrial destinations, this A-to-Z guide describes, based on the original author's story, intriguing places of fiction. Surely some of these places deserve to be visited again, in other stories? Places like the subterranean country of Nazar, the myopic Kingdom of the One-Eyed, and Pepperland, where the Blue Meanies reside.

The Illustrated Dictionary of Place Names: United States and Canada. Kelsie B. Harder. New York: Van Nostrand Reinhold Co., 1976.

The names of communities and geographical entities, many with either Native American or European origins, are listed along with brief explanations on how they came to be named. Some sample names include Cattaraugus (New York), which means "bad smelling shore," and Mauna Kea, the highest peak on Hawaii Island. Mauna Kea means "white mountain" in Hawaiian. Though this is supposedly an illustrated guide, the illustrations are few and far between.

Place-Names in Classical Mythology: Greece. Robert E. Bell. Santa Barbara, CA: ABC-CLIO, 1989.

A listing of mythological places (as well as real places that were named after them).

Space Names

A Concise Dictionary of Astronomy. Jacqueline Mitton. New York: Oxford University Press, 1991.

In addition to its use as a dictionary meant to define astronomical terms, this dictionary is also a goldmine for names from the skies. Try any dictionary of astronomy; do a subject search in your library's online catalog using the phrase ASTRONOMY DICTIONARIES.

The Dictionary of Astronomical Names. Adrian Room. New York: Routledge, 1988.

Celestial names of celestial places such as moons, planets, asteroids, satellites (of planets) and constellations are defined, along with details of when and by whom they were discovered. Also named in the appendices are craters of the moon and "minor" planets. Some of the haunting names—Himalia (Jupiter's sixth satellite), Adhara (a star) and Pavo (a constellation).

Gazeteers

Gazetteers list and describe geographical names; they are geographical dictionaries. For towns, cities, states, nations, counties, provinces and other organized, populated land areas with defined boundaries, gazetteers will usually provide population, square mileage, perhaps some information about the area's founding or creation, and notable geographic formations within its borders. Natural formations such as mountains, lakes and oceans are usually described in terms of height, depth and the like. I am telling you all this because I want you to be the one who succeeds in the next trivia game you play by being able to answer the question "What is a gazetteer?" Though all the information gazetteers provide may be of great interest, in this chapter I am suggesting you use gazetteers to find names of places. When searching for gazetteers in your library's online catalog, try a subject search using:

GAZETTEERS or
GEOGRAPHY DICTIONARIES
(*This search will sometimes get you actual dictionaries for the field of geography, but also will assist you in finding geographic dictionaries that are more or less gazetteers.*)

Sample gazetteers:

Omni Gazetteer of the United States of America: A Guide to 1,500,000 Place Names in the United States and Territories. 11 Volumes. Frank R. Abate, editor. Detroit: Omnigraphics, 1991.

A huge compilation of populated places, structures, facilities, locales, historic places and geographic features in the United States. Names galore!

The Times Index-Gazetteer of the World. Boston: Houghton Mifflin Co., 1966.

An alphabetic directory of 345,000 towns, villages, rivers, mountains and other geographical features, with longitude and latitude provided. This book also provides map locations that the reader can use to find the spot illustrated in another *Times* publication, the five-volume *Times Atlas of the World*, commonly found in large academic and public libraries. This is an exceedingly heavy volume; if you

are a small person ask someone to assist you in lifting this one.

Webster's New Geographical Dictionary. Springfield, MA: G and C Merriam Co., Publishers, 1988.

Detailed coverage of geographical areas of Canada and the United States; selected coverage for the rest of the world. Such elements as population, longitude and latitude, height and founding date are supplied. A historical summary of a sentence or two is also provided for some areas and geographical points.

I'll wind up this chapter with a sourcebook that is a veritable almanac of names:

All Those Wonderful Names: A Potpourri of People, Places and Things. J.N. Hook. New York: John Wiley and Sons, 1991.

A conglomeration of stories, jokes, histories and origins of names. There are also lists of names to choose from and lists of note, such as The Ten Most Common Italian American Surnames (Russo is number one). The top names for other backgrounds: Irish-American (Murphy is number one), Welsh-Americans (Williams), German-American (Myers), Scandinavian-American (Anderson) and Hispanic-American (Rodriguez). There are other "Top Ten" listings, such as the Most Common Surnames in Ten American Cities and London. The name "Smith" is the number-one-ranked name in Greater Atlanta, Boston, Denver, Greater Memphis, New York *and* London!

Chapter Fifteen

How to Kill Your Character

Conflict is a key element in an exciting story. This conflict may culminate in violence or even murder. There are a great many methods and instruments available to carry out your character's fatal fate. In order to kill your character realistically you need to know details—what types of weapons were available in a particular era? What are the precise effects of an industrial solvent on human skin? Realism is the key concept here. Nothing is more disappointing to the reader than to find that the method chosen to kill a character would in fact do no harm in real life. Check the resources included in this chapter for the facts.

Weapons

Armed and Dangerous: A Writer's Guide to Weapons. Michael Newton. Cincinnati, OH: Writer's Digest Books, 1990.

The author of this guide cautions the writer to be careful of making errors when describing weapons and their use; he warns that the publisher will know it's a mistake and that will be that as far as accepting your manuscript. *Armed and Dangerous* describes in detail the proper weapon for specific eras and situations. No illustrations.

The Art of Throwing Weapons. James W.

Madden. Las Vegas: Patrick Publications, 1991.

Photographs and descriptions lead you through techniques for throwing knives, tomahawks, axes, spears, shurikens and boomerangs.

Bows and Arrows of the Native Americans: A Complete Step-by-Step Guide to Wooden Bows, Sinew-Backed Bows, Composite Bows, Strings, Arrows and Quivers. Jim Hamm. New York: Lyons and Burford, Publishers, 1991.

A how-to book for creating bows and arrows.

CIA Special Weapons and Equipment: Spy Devices of the Cold War. H. Keith Melton. New York: Sterling Publishing Co., 1993.

Get Smart seems tame compared to some of the gadgets in this book! There's proof here that reality can sometimes be more interesting than TV. Some of the devices listed: The Combustible Notebook (will burn itself to bits to protect whatever secrets that were written in it), the briefcase recorder (à la *Mission Impossible*), the Tear Gas Pen (with a range of six feet it can "incapacitate the target long enough to allow an escape), and my favorite, the Dog Doo Transmitter (a homing beacon "camouflaged to resemble the excrement of a medium-size dog").

Everybody's Knife Bible: All New Ways to Use and Enjoy Your Knives in the Great Outdoors. Don Paul. 3d edition. Woodland, CA: Path Finder Publications, 1992.

The basics and beyond of knife use, wear, maintenance and production. Some photographs of knives and computer graphics illustrating concepts are included.

Guns of the Wild West: Firearms of the American Frontier, 1849-1917. George Markham. London: Arms and Armour Press, 1991.

This volume examines the great variety of handguns, longarms and shotguns during the time of the Gold Rush, the Civil War and the burgeoning American West. This publisher has also published:
Guns of the Elite
Guns of the Empire
Guns of the Reich

Jane's Directories.

The English publisher, Jane's Information Group, Inc. (founded by Fred T. Jane, not a woman named Jane), produces many directories that describe weapons, transportation systems and combinations thereof. Each directory supplies photos of the weapons/transport and supplies many details about each unit.

Sample Titles:
Jane's Air-Launched Weapons.

Looks at air-to-air missiles, air-to-surface missiles, cruise missiles, bombs, rockets and guns.

Jane's Fighting Ships.

Detailed information about specific naval ships and the strength of fleets in the navies of the world. Also names command personnel, diplomatic representatives, bases and shipyards.

Jane's Infantry Weapons.

A survey of infantry weapons in use by armed forces and paramilitary units worldwide. For each weapon, Jane's lists its name, history, specifications, function and performance.

Jane's Land-Based Air Defence.

Coverage of gun and missile mobile and air defense systems around the world.

Other Jane's:
Military Training Systems
Military Vehicles and Logistics
Naval Weapons Systems
Radar and EW (Electronic Warfare) Systems
Strategic Weapon Systems
Underwater Warfare Systems

Modern Combat Blades: The Best in Edged Weaponry. Duncan Long. Boulder, CO: Paladin Press, 1992.

A critical look at edged weaponry, including pocketknives, switchblades, bowie knives, daggers, stilettos, Samurai blades, kukris (knives with sloped blades created by the Nepalese), machetes, swords, battle-axes, meat cleavers, folding shovels and throwing blades. Each section describes the history, construction and use of each weapon, along with any pertinent laws pertaining to its use.

The New Illustrated Encyclopedia of Firearms. [Updated edition of the *Encyclopedia of Firearms*.] Ian V. Hogg. Secaucus, NJ: Wellfleet Press, 1992.

An alphabetic guide to nineteenth and twentieth century firearms, listed by manufacturer. The weapons shown were designed for both military use and sport. There are numerous illustrations.

The New Illustrated Guide to Modern Elite Forces: The Weapons, Uniforms and Tactics of the World's Secret Special Warfare Units. David Miller and Gerard Ridefort. London: Salamander Books Ltd., 1992.

The dress, trappings and arms used by such forces as the Alpini Troops of Italy, the Commandos of Taiwan, the U.K. Gurkhas and the U.S. Marines are described and illustrated. Other books from this publisher arranged like this one are:

The New Illustrated Guide to Modern Sub Hunters: The Weapons, Technology and Techniques Used in Today's Submarine Warfare (Miller, 1992).

The New Illustrated Guide to Modern Tanks and Fighting Vehicles: A Magnificent Directory of the Major Battle Tanks and Combat Vehicles in Service with the World's Armies Today (Miller, 1992).

One Hundred Great Guns: An Illustrated History of Firearms. Merrill Lindsay. New York: Walker, 1967.

Guns of many types are featured, including the Hand Cannon, Wheel Lock Guns, Breech-Loading Firearms, Revolvers and Semi-Automatics. The author visited many museums worldwide to collect his information, including England, Germany, Italy, Spain and Scotland.

The Shooter's Bible. South Hackensack, NJ: Stoeger Publishing Co. Annual.

Should the killer be holding a "gun" in your story, or should he be aiming an "Exemplar Hornet?" If only for pure inspiration, the "Bible" supplies names, prices, specifications and photos for foreign and domestic handguns, rifles, shotguns and black powder guns. There's also information on ammunition and scopes.

Weapon Systems: United States Army 1994. Washington, DC: The Pentagon, 1994.

A handbook of major weapon systems and support equipment that the Army has developed or is in the process of developing. For each weapon or device, color photographs and descriptions are provided. Foreign counterparts to the weapons and equipment are also named. One interesting system featured in this book is the Breacher, which looks like a cross between farm equipment and a monster, and is intended to provide an "instride breaching capability to overcome simple and complex obstacles . . . allowing mobility through minefields, rubble, tank ditches, wire and other obstructions."

Weapons: An International Encyclopedia - From 5,000 B.C. to 2,000 A.D. The Diagram Group. Updated Edition. New York: St. Martin's Press, 1990.

Twenty-five hundred illustrated entries are packed in this single volume, with each giving the history of the weapon and the principles by which it works. Pole-arms, torpedoes, chemical weapons . . . if it can hurt or defend it will probably be listed here.

Catalogs of Weapon Replicas

There are a number of companies that specialize in selling replicas of weapons from days gone by. Browsing through their catalogs may be useful. Or perhaps you want to buy the murder weapon that will be used in your story so that you will truly know it intimately. (Not to be used for actual murder and mayhem, please.) Two companies of note:

Arms and Armor. (800) 745-7345.

Arms and Armor is a company that specializes in making replicas of weaponry and protective clothing and devices that were in use between 1500 B.C. to A.D. 1700. Their stock includes rapiers, daggers, sword carriers, pole arms, helmets, shields and breastplates. Their catalog allows you to peruse their stock at leisure, happily imagining how to kill your character.

Museum Replicas Limited Catalog. (800) 883-8838.

Museum Replicas sells replicas of swords, daggers, axes, shields and helmets from the Roman Empire through the Renaissance. It is interesting to page through and see all the period (looking) pieces. This company has a good reputation for producing very accurate replicas. Also included in the catalog: period clothing, jewelry, coins, walking sticks, staffs and books.

Martial Arts

If Bruce Lee could knock off the bad guys with some expert chops and kicks,

your characters should be able to do the same!

Martial Arts: Traditions, History, Pioneers. John Corcoran, Emil Farkas and Stuart Sobel. Los Angeles: Pro-Action Publishing, 1993.

The authors review the traditions of thirty-three martial arts, including Aikido, Hapkido, Judo and Pukulan, as well as related arts, such as Thai Kick Boxing. Short biographies are provided of internationally known men and women involved in the martial arts, and a succinct chronology of the arts' evolution in Asia, Europe, the United States and other areas is provided.

Martial Arts of the Orient. Peter Lewis. London: MMB, 1993.

This book is filled with "action shots" of karate, jiu jitsu, judo, aikido, taekwon-do and other martial art forms. Many weapons of the martial artist are also pictured, including a chain whip, bo staff, tiger fork and rice flails. Some of these can be quite deadly.

Poisonous Creatures and Toxic Foliage

AMA Handbook of Poisonous and Injurious Plants. Kenneth F. Lampe and Mary Ann McCann. Chicago: American Medical Association, 1985.

A guide, geared to health practitioners, to plants that may cause harm to humans. Symptoms range from intense irritation of the mouth and lips (from the Caladium, also known as Angel Wings), to death (the

Water Hemlock, also known by several names: Beaver Poison, Children's Bane, Cicutaire, Death-of-Man, Musquash Poison, Musquash Root and Spotted Cowbane). Though the main portion of the guide is in alphabetical order by the plant's Latin name, the index includes both Latin and "trivial" names (i.e., Water Hemlock). The last third of the book is devoted to color pictures of the plants discussed.

A Colour Atlas of Poisonous Plants: A Handbook for Pharmacists, Doctors, Toxicologists and Biologists. Dietrich Frohne and Hans Jurgen Pfander. London: Wolfe Science Books, 1984.

Some of these nasty plants look exceedingly pretty in these color photographs. Easy to foist on a fictional victim!

Dangerous Reptilian Creatures. Missy Allen and Michel Peissel. New York: Chelsea House Publishers, 1993.

Geared to a younger crowd, but still full of great information, *Dangerous Reptilian Creatures* gives a four crossbone rating to almost all the creatures described (i.e., quite dangerous). For each reptile described, the author tells of its habitat, where it's likely to be found, how it gets and affects people, and methods of treatment and prevention. Among the scaly critters described: the Komodo Dragon (the world's largest lizard), the Coral Snake (known for its ability to cling to and chew on human fingers and toes), and Russell's Viper (renowned for its "tenacious" bite). Only drawings are provided. This book is part of the *Encyclopedia of Danger* series. Other titles in

the series include:
Dangerous Environments
Dangerous Flora
Dangerous Mammals
Dangerous Natural Phenomena
Dangerous Plants and Mushrooms
Dangerous Professions
Dangerous Sports
Dangerous Water Creatures

Deadly Bugs and Killer Insects. Hal Hellman. New York: M. Evans, 1978.

Some of the chapter headings should give you a feel for the contents of this book: Small and Dangerous, Stingers, Scratchers and Squirters, and Biters, Burrowers and Bloodsuckers. The "squirters" category caught my eye. Some of the pests in this grouping include the Formica Ant, whose abdomen is one-fifth full of choking formic acid, and a species of Assassin Bug that can squirt its venom up to a foot, capable of causing temporary blindness to a human whose eyeball happens to be in its path. There are photos and drawings of these dangerous bugs included.

Killer Animals. Edward R. Ricciuti. New York: Walker and Co., 1976.

The animals listed in this volume are not just of the "man-eating lion" variety. The author notes that there are some animals, such as attack dogs, which have been specifically bred and trained to inflict harm. Some of the dangerous animals described include snakes (including pit vipers and rattlesnakes), animals that are hunted by humans (antelope, bison), insects (bees, scorpions), animals held in zoos (elephants, wolves), and even animals on the farm (bulls, dogs). Black-and-white photographs of these potentially hazardous creatures are included.

Medical Guide to Hazardous Marine Life. Paul S. Auerbach. 2d edition. St. Louis: Mosby Year Book, 1991.

Most of the richly colored photographs in this handbook show lovely sea life that looks quite innocent. For example, the sea lion is known as quite mild-mannered . . . except during its mating season. If one of these darlings bites your character in the leg, this guide details methods of treatment.

Poisonous and Venomous Marine Animals of the World. 2d revised edition. Bruce W. Halstead. Princeton, NJ: Darwin Press, 1988.

This is not the book you want to read before you go scuba diving. (On the other hand, maybe it is!) A scholarly guide to the poisonous underwater vertebrates and invertebrates, along with the symptoms, treatment and prevention of poisoning. The many color plates allow the reader to see these toxic fellows close up.

Poisonous Dwellers of the Desert. [Popular Series #3] Natt N. Dodge. Globe, AZ: Southwestern Monuments Association, 1952.

A short volume featuring information and frightening photographs and drawings of such harmful creatures as the giant desert centipedes, conenose bugs and tarantulas.

Toxic Chemicals and Poisons

A time-honored way of doing away with characters: a little tea, a little poison.

Consolidated List of Products Whose Consumption and/or Sale Have Been Banned, Withdrawn, Severely Restricted or Not Approved by Governments. New York: United Nations, 1991.

For each unpleasant substance named, the names of those countries who have banned it (or restricted its use) are listed, with (in most cases) reasons for their actions. The types of substances included are agricultural chemicals, industrial chemicals and pharmaceuticals. For example, Chlordecone is banned in thirteen countries, including the United States, and is said to have "significant adverse effects on human health."

Deadly Doses: A Writer's Guide to Poisons. Serita Deborah Stevens with Anne Klarner. Cincinnati, OH: Writer's Digest Books, 1990.

Each chapter highlights a type of deadly substance, including Household poisons, Poisonous Plants, Medical Poisons, Snakes, Spiders and Other Living Things, and Street Drugs. For each toxin the author lists its common and scientific names, level of toxicity, where it can be found, which parts of it are deadly, its effects and the symptoms it causes, the amount of time that elapses before it takes effect, antidotes and treatments, and in some instances, actual case histories or additional notes. A superb all-in-one poison resource.

Handbook of Natural Toxins. Richard F. Keeler, and Anthony T. Tu. 7 Volumes. New York: Marcel Dekker, 1991.

A series of books geared to the scientist, covering the many toxic pitfalls in nature:

Volume 1—*Plant and Fungal Toxins*

Volume 2—*Insect Poisons, Allergens and Other Invertebrate Venoms*

Volume 3—*Marine Toxins and Venoms*

Volume 4—*Bacterial Toxins*

Volume 5—*Reptile Venoms and Toxins*

Volume 6—*Toxicology of Plant and Fungal Compounds*

Volume 7—*Food Poisoning*

Handbook of Poisoning: Prevention, Diagnosis and Treatment. Robert H. Dreisbach and William O. Robertson. 12th edition. Norwalk, CT: Appleton and Lange, 1987.

The authors describe the potential hazards of a wide variety of toxins, including poisons produced by plants and animals. Treatments are also outlined.

Hazardous Chemicals Desk Reference. Richard J. Lewis, Sr. 3d edition. New York: Van Nostrand Reinhold, 1993.

By hazardous, this reference is referring to chemicals that are explosive, highly flammable or highly reactive. For each chemical presented, the author provides a Hazard Rating of 1, 2 or 3 (Cedar Leaf Oil measures a moderate 2), the four-digit hazard code that the Department of Transportation calls for the display of during transport (and which determines the regulations for the shipping of the material), the molecular formula and weight, the properties, synonyms for the entry name and any cancer-causing suspicions surrounding the chemical. The Safety Profile lists how the chemical may be harmful (e.g., ingestion, skin contact) and reports what it does when heated to decomposition.

Many "emit acrid smoke and irritating fumes."

Poisoning: Toxicology, Symptoms, Treatments. Jay M. Arena, editor. 5th edition. Springfield, IL: Thomas, 1986.

A classic book on the toxicology, symptoms and treatments of a variety of poisons, including insecticides, rodenticides, fungicides, herbicides, fumigants, repellents, industrial hazards, soap, detergent, polishing and sanitizing agents, cosmetics and other toiletry, plants, reptiles, arthropods, insects and fish.

Killing the Environment

One way to wipe out a few people . . . or even mankind . . . is indirectly. For example, in Kurt Vonnegut's novel *Cat's Cradle* the fictional chemical Ice Nine is responsible for solidifying the earth and all that grows in it, making it uninhabitable. There are many diseases that may attack fauna. What if one of these went out of control?

Diseases of Trees and Shrubs. Wayne A. Sinclair, Howard H. Lyon and Warren T. Johnson. Ithaca, NY: Comstock Publishing Associates, 1987.

This scholarly guide describes the harm done to foliage by any number of diseases and mistreatment, including Mildews, Air Pollutants, Droughts and Freezing. The hundreds of color photographs included make it simple to see what the blighted plants and trees look like.

Insects That Feed on Trees and Shrubs. Warren T. Johnson and Howard H. Lyon. 2d edition. Ithaca, NY: Comstock Publishing Associates, 1988.

A highly illustrated volume, featuring insects that wreak havoc on foliage.

Westcott's Plant Disease Handbook. R. Kenneth Horst. 5th edition. New York: Van Nostrand Reinhold, 1990.

The author describes all sorts of nasty things that happen to plants and crops, including blights, leaf scorch, slime molds and wilt diseases. Descriptions of garden chemicals (fungicides, bactericides, nematicides, virocides) and methods of their application are also supplied.

Post-Mortem

After you're done killing your character, he's dead! If you want to use him even further, take a look at:

Cause of Death: A Writer's Guide to Death, Murder and Forensic Medicine. Keith D. Wilson. Cincinnati, OH: Writer's Digest Books, 1992.

This book is presented in three sections. Part I covers "Death and Dying," discussing the various stages one might go through when dying and the medical definitions of death. Part II, titled "Medical and Legal Procedures Related to Death," investigates the details of emergency room procedures, the specific steps involved in declaring someone legally deceased, what happens to the body after death, how the exact time of demise might be determined, what is involved in an autopsy, how to determine if a death might have been a murder or suicide, and where and how capital punishment is carried out. Part III looks at the many distressing possible causes of death, including electrocution, falling and chronic illnesses.

Death to Dust: What Happens to Dead Bodies? Kenneth V. Iverson. Tucson, AZ: Galen Press, Ltd., 1994.

This book was written by a doctor and has received favorable comment from others in the medical and forensic fields, but it is still accessible to the layman and written with a touch of humor, as evidenced by some of the chapter headings, including "Dying to Know" and "I'm Dead—Now What?" The book begins with the words "Death is a mutilating experience," and goes on to explain in detail just what that means. Some questions answered: How can a person be identified from partial or decomposed remains? How is a body prepared for embalming? and How is a shrunken head prepared?

Chapter Sixteen

Diseases and Mental Illness

After perusing the medical texts and reference books in this section you will see that there is no reason to invent a disease for your hapless character. There are thousands of ailments that our frail human bodies are susceptible to, many with unusual symptoms. For nonfiction writers, these resources supply facts and details on disorders that readers may be vulnerable to. This chapter also lists books that detail possible cures and therapies for both physical and mental ailments.

Medical Dictionaries

There are many words used in standard medical resources that will not mean a thing to those who are not health professionals (like me). While browsing the medical resources recommended in this section, you might want to have one of the following dictionaries nearby:

American Psychiatric Glossary. Jane E. Edgerton, editor. 7th edition. Washington, DC: American Psychiatric Press, 1994.

Definitions for psychiatric disorders, symptoms and situations are supplied. There are also tables listing commonly used abbreviations, drugs used in psychiatry, drugs that are commonly abused, and lists of legal terms, neurologic deficits, psychological tests and schools of psychiatry.

A Dictionary for Psychotherapists: Dynamic Concepts in Psychotherapy. Richard Chessick. Northvale, NJ: Jason Aronson, 1993.

Aimed at the clinician, this dictionary defines essential psychotherapy terms in entries ranging from a few paragraphs to a few pages. Some of the terms and concepts defined include: Acting Out, Curative Fantasy, Hysteria, Overdetermination, Shame and Working Through.

Dorland's Illustrated Medical Dictionary. 27th edition. Philadelphia: W.B. Saunders Co., 1988.

This book will help you look up terms you don't know when browsing through other books in this section. There are actually relatively few illustrations, despite the title.

Lexicon of Psychiatric and Mental Health Terms. 2d edition. Geneva: World Health Organization, 1994.

A skinny volume of terms used in conjunction with psychiatric and psychological health and treatment.

Melloni's Illustrated Medical Dictionary. Ida G. Dox, John B. Melloni and Gilbert M. Eisner. 3d edition. Pearl River, NY: The Parthenon Publishing Group, 1993.

The definitions are succinct but, for the most part, quite understandable to the layman. Unlike *Dorland's*, listed above, the illustrations are numerous and helpful for further imparting meaning to the words being defined.

Stedman's Medical Dictionary. 25th edition. Baltimore: Williams and Wilkins, 1990.

A standard medical dictionary with over one hundred thousand terms defined.

Here are two definitions I will supply right away, since they are used several times in this chapter: the *etiology* of a disease is its cause(s) or origin(s); looking into the *epidemiology* means to investigate the causes and controls of disease epidemics in a population.

Physical Diseases and Impairments

Allergies A-Z. Myron Lipkowitz. New York: Facts on File, 1994.

Each entry describes a substance that people are allergic to, a malady commonly brought on by specific sensitivities, or a treatment or therapy known to help with a specific allergy. If you dream of a character hacking, sniffling or developing rashes, then you will truly find this guide useful.

Complete Guide to Symptoms, Illness and Surgery. H. Winter Griffith. Los Angeles: The Body Press, 1989.

The "symptoms" section of this easy-to-use guide is a dream for those who enjoy self-diagnosis or hypochondria. Each major symptom is broken down into variations of the symptom, the possible problem causing it and what the sufferer should do. For example, excessive sweating and chest pain

might indicate a heart attack, and you should call a doctor now! The Surgery section details common operations, and includes illustrations of each procedure. Informative and not too unsettling. Also from this author:
Complete Guide to Pediatric Symptoms. 1989.
Complete Guide to Sports Injuries. 1986.
Complete Guide to Symptoms, Illness and Surgery for People Over 50. 1992.

Current Surgical Diagnosis and Treatment. Lawrence W. Way. Norwalk, CT: Appleton and Lange.

A compilation of chapters discussing current knowledge for a variety of medical problems that require surgery. This is definitely written for medical professionals. Other, similarly structured texts from this publisher include:
Current Pediatric Diagnosis and Treatment. 12th edition. 1994.
Current Obstetric and Gynecologic Diagnosis and Treatment. 1991.

Encyclopedia of Blindness and Vision Impairment. Jill Sardegna and T. Otis Paul. New York: Facts on File, 1991.

An alphabetically arranged compendium on blindness and related topics, including health issues, surgery, medications, social issues, myths, misconceptions, adaptive aids and organizations.

Gallaudet Encyclopedia of Deaf People and Deafness. 3 Volumes. John V. Van Cleve, editor-in-chief. New York: McGraw-Hill Book Co.

From the distinguished Gallaudet College, the institution of higher education specifically designed to teach deaf students and those with hearing impairments. The set looks at the social implications for deaf people in various settings, causes and diagnosis of audio disorders, sign languages and the way many nations of the world provide assistance, support, research and education in connection with audio impairments and deafness.

Health Information for International Travel. Atlanta: U.S. Dept. of Health and Human Services, Public Health Service, Centers for Disease Control and Prevention, National Center for Prevention Services. Annual.

The point of this book is to alert travelers of any vaccinations they may need, or precautions they might take when traveling abroad. One of the most interesting sections, however, which briefly describes exotic illnesses and the places they might be encountered, is under the unlikely heading Specific Recommendations for Vaccination and Prophylaxis (alphabetic by disease). The Geographic Distribution of Potential Health Hazards to Travelers section provides a very quick glimpse of diseases one would be likely to encounter at different points on the globe.

Merck Manual of Diagnosis and Therapy. Rahway, NJ: Merck, Sharp and Dohme Research Laboratories, 1992.

The Merck Manual editor claims that this reference is the "most widely used medical text in the world." Indeed, it covers a broad spectrum of health information, including descriptions of medical disorders and treatments, discussions of symptoms and paths to diagnosis. You can find some interesting

health problems to afflict your characters by looking up specific parts of the body. Looking under Elbow might lead you to tennis elbow or miner's elbow, a form of bursitis. Or simply pick an impressive Latin word from the index and see where it leads you.

Since the *Merck Manual* is geared to health professionals and students, parts of it may be incomprehensible to those of us who don't attend medical school. Other Merck manuals: *Merck Manual of Geriatrics.* 1990. *Merck Veterinary Manual: A Handbook of Diagnosis, Therapy and Disease Prevention and Control for the Veterinarian.* 1992.

Physicians' Guide to Rare Diseases. Jess G. Thoene, editor. Montvale, NJ: Dowden Publishing Co., 1992.

Prepared in association with the National Organization for Rare Disorders, this directory looks at the diseases that most sweet and well-loved characters tend to catch—the "rare" ones. For each uncommon malady, the editors provide a general description, signs and symptoms, the etiology, related disorders, standard remedies, treatments currently being investigated and resources for further reading.

The 1994 Red Book: Report of the Committee on Infectious Diseases. Committee on Infectious Diseases, American Academy of Pediatrics. Elk Grove Village, IL: American Academy of Pediatrics, 1994.

Geared to the physician, the *Red Book* is updated about every three years, and provides current recommendations for the prevention and management of pediatric infectious diseases (children's diseases). For each malady the committee lists the clinical manifestations, etiology, epidemiology, diagnostic tests for definitive diagnosis and treatments.

The Surgery Book: An Illustrated Guide to 73 of the Most Common Operations. Robert Youngson, with the Diagram Group. New York: St. Martin's Press, 1993.

If you are not a medical expert but want to make your character one, this book is really a winner. With diagrams and simple questions and answers, frequently performed operations are described. Some of the operations detailed include bone fracture treatment, leg amputation, removal of the appendix, hysterectomy, male sterilization, heart-lung transplants and sex-change surgery (common?). Some plastic surgery procedures are also explained, including hair transplants and implants, reshaping of the nose and face lifts.

Psychological Disorders

Diagnostic and Statistical Manual of Mental Disorders (DSM-IV). 4th edition. Washington, DC: American Psychiatric Association, 1994.

This is the standard source of official descriptions of psychological disorders. The *DSM-IV* identifies an impressive number of headings for potential disorders, including: disruptive behavior, eating, gender identity, psychoactive substance use, organic mental, psychotic, mood, anxiety, dissociative, sexual, sleep, factitious,

delusional, personal and impulse control. The Symptom Index links various symptoms with possible disorders. "Racing thoughts" might be related to Hallucinogen Mood Disorder, while "no close friends or confidants" could signal Avoidance Personality Disorder.

A companion to this book is the *DSM-IV Casebook: A Learning Companion to the DSM-IV*, which cites actual cases and the diagnosis for each case.

The Encyclopedia of Drug Abuse. Robert O'Brien, Sidney Cohen, Glen Evans, and James Fine. 2d edition. New York: Facts on File. 1992.

An A-to-Z look at drug abuse, including the history of specific drugs and descriptions of rehabilitation organizations. Appendix 1, Street Language, defines slang terms such as Jones, which means a drug habit, particularly a heroin habit, and Charlie, the street word for one dollar. Appendix 2, Slang Synonyms for Drugs, lists fifty terms for amphetamines alone, including Crystal, Eye Openers and Sparkle Plenties.

The Encyclopedia of Phobias, Fears and Anxieties. Ronald M. Doctor and Ada P. Kahn. New York: Facts on File, 1989.

Arranged in alphabetic order, this one-volume encyclopedia is an easy-to-read compilation of the terminology associated with phobias, fears and anxieties. Some entries include: Amnesiophobia, the fear of amnesia, Erythrophobia, fear of blushing, and Hypnophobia, the fear of sleep.

The Encyclopedia of Schizophrenia and the Psychotic Disorders. Richard M.A. Noll. New York: Facts on File, 1991.

An alphabetically arranged guide to types of psychological disorders, treatments, therapies and "lingo." Some of the disorders include *FaxenSyndrom* (also known as "Clown's Syndrome"), the reaction of childish, silly behavior of prisoners to being imprisoned; *Pica*, the eating of things that are not food, such as dirt or paint chips; and *Cheromania*, a term used in the Middle Ages that described an unnatural euphoric reaction to major disasters.

Tests: A Comprehensive Reference for Assessments in Psychology, Education and Business. Richard C. Sweetland and Daniel J. Keyser, editors. 3d edition. Kansas City, MO: Test Corporation of America, 1991.

Need to find out if one of your characters has a psychological disorder? Administer one of the tests recommended in this collection. This set describes tests that might be used in psychological testing and provides names and addresses of the publishers who produce them.

Medicinal and Therapeutic Cures

Traditional Medicine

Essential Guide to Prescription Drugs. James W. Long. New York: Harper and Row. Annual.

A guide to the most commonly prescribed drugs explained in terms geared to those of us who are not health professionals. Some of the in-formation supplied in each entry: Name of drug, the year it was introduced, whether it is prescription or over-the-counter, whether a generic equivalent is available, brand names it is sold under, the benefits of taking it versus the risks, the principal use of the medication, how the drug actually works in the human system and possible side or adverse effects.

Essential Guide to Psychiatric Drugs. Jack M. Gorman. New York: St. Martin's Press, 1992.

The author discusses drugs commonly used to treat such disorders as violence, anxiety, sleeping problems and depression. Explanations of the disorders and what the drugs prescribed are expected to accomplish are provided. The Drug Directory, following the general table of contents, is an index to those drugs, listed by both generic name and brand name, that are comprehensively described in this book.

Medical Instrumentation for Nurses and Allied Health-Care Professionals. Richard Aston and Katherine Kay Brown. London: Jones and Bartlett Publishers International, 1994.

This is definitely not a quick reference book; it is a book geared to practitioners. However, it does provide the nitty-gritty explanations on how to properly operate some modern medical devices, and so may be of interest to those with characters in the hospital. (For more on older and antique medical instrumentation, see chapter 4, "Architecture and Decor.")

Physicians' Desk Reference. Oradell, NJ.: Medical Economics Co. Annual, plus quarterly supplements.

The *PDR*, as it is commonly called, describes thousands of pharmaceutical and diagnostic products. Reading this can be slow going for the layman. However, passages dealing with "adverse reactions" and results of an "overdose" are both easily deciphered and great fodder for murder mysteries. The product identification section boasts glossy, colorful photos of pills, tablets and bottles. This publisher also puts out the *Physicians' Desk Reference for Non-Prescription Drugs.*

The publishers of *PDR* have also compiled some directories geared specifically to the layperson, both published in 1994:

The PDR Family Guide to Women's Health and Prescription Drugs.

The PDR Family Guide to Prescription Drugs.

Side Effect of Drugs—Annual: A Worldwide Yearly Survey of New Data and Trends. J.K. Aronson and C.J. Van Boxtel. New York: Elsevier. Annual.

This survey is arranged by chapters that focus on drugs meant for certain purposes (antidepressants or general anesthetics, for example) and, in some cases, a specific drug. Vitamins are also given a chapter. The two back-of-the-book indexes help the reader pinpoint specific drugs within the chapters or specific side-effect symptoms (for example, excitability, fatigue or persistent crying).

Treatments of Psychiatric Disorders: A Task Force Report of the American Psychiatric Association. 3 Volumes plus Index Volume. Washington, DC: American Psychiatric Association, 1989.

A compendium of essays that describe useful approaches for the treatment of mental disorders.

Alternative Medicine

Alternative Medicine: The Definitive Guide. The Burton Goldberg Group. Puyallup, WA: Future Medicine Publishing Group, 1993.

A lengthy (over one thousand pages) and clearly written survey of alternative therapies, such as Ayurvedic Medicine, Flower Remedies, Juice Therapy and Qigong. Descriptions of health conditions and how they might be treated "alternatively" are also furnished.

Alternative Healing: The Complete A-Z Guide to Over 160 Different Alternative Therapies. Mark Kastner and Hugh Burroughs. La Mesa, CA: Halcyon Publishing, 1993.

Some of the therapies listed: Dong Diet—a nutritional plan used to treat arthritis; Holotropic Breathwork—a technique of self-exploration; and SomatoEmotional Release—"a therapeutic process, the objective of which is to rid the mind and body of the residual effects of past injuries and negative experiences."

The Encyclopedia of Aromatherapy, Massage and Yoga. Carole McGilvery, Jimi Reed, Mira Mehta and Silva Mehta. London: Anness Books, 1993.

Seven hundred full-color photographs show the reader, step by step, how to perform massage (of babies, partners and self) and to properly execute yoga positions. The essences used in aromatherapy are also discussed.

Handbook of Hypnotic Suggestions and Metaphors. D. Corydon Hammond. New York: W.W. Norton and Co., 1990.

Geared to the clinical practitioner (including therapists, physicians and dentists), this book is a compilation of therapeutic suggestions that have been contributed by over one hundred hypnotherapists. Some of the areas for which suggestions are offered include Pain Management, Eating Disorders, Sexual Dysfunction and Academic Performance.

Health Plants of the World: Atlas of Medicinal Plants. Francesco Corbetta. New York: Newsweek Books, 1975.

Plants and herbs are described that are said to be beneficial to various physiological systems: digestive, cardiovascular, respiratory, nervous, genito-urinary and endocrine. Plants said to be beneficial to the skin are also mentioned, such as Solomon's seal, a root reputed to assist in the healing of wounds, and poplar buds, recommended for treating inflammations of all kinds. Realistic illustrations of the flowers, herbs and plants accompany the descriptions.

Natural Alternatives to Over-the-Counter and Prescription Drugs. Michael T. Murray. New York: William Morrow and Co., 1994.

Written by a naturopathic physician, this guide describes natural methods and medications for common ailments, including acne, arthritis, asthma, ulcers and sleeping problems.

There is also a chapter that provides tips for staying healthy.

Home Remedies

There are quite a few books that will teach you how to mix up your very own medications. If you do want your character to concoct his own medicinals, find some books by doing a subject search on your library's online catalog using the words FORMULAE and MEDICINE. Some sample titles I ran across using this method:

American Folk Medicine. Clarence Meyer. Glenwood, IL: Meyerbooks, 1985.

Chinese Herbal Remedies. Albert Y. Leung. New York: Universe Books, 1984.

Formulary of Tibetan Medicine. Vaidya Bhagwan Dash. Delhi, India: Classics India Publications, 1988.

Lifetime Encyclopedia of Natural Remedies. Myra Cameron. Englewood Cliffs, NJ: Prentice Hall, 1993.

Other Therapies

When looking for sources on other non-medicinal therapies using your library's online catalog, try these word combinations:

DANCE THERAPY
DRAMA THERAPEUTIC USE
MUSIC THERAPY
PHYSICAL THERAPY
PSYCHOANALYTIC THERAPY
PSYCHOTHERAPY

Illustrated Medical References

Though this is certainly not a pleasant task, it could be useful for the writer: Many medical journals picture those diseases that physically alter a person's appearance, e.g., skin rashes, bloating, discoloration and so on.

Unlike journals, many reference textbooks that discuss disease are not illustrated. And some of those that include graphics have only drawings. So, health magazines and journals will be a major source of illustrations. There are quite a few medical journals that do not feature photographs; those that do often feature photos on the microscopic or X-ray level only. Some examples of the specialized titles available in the medical field that tend to have illustrations featuring human beings with maladies or broken appendages:

Annals of Plastic Surgery
Archives of Dermatology
British Journal of Oral and Maxillo-
    facial Surgery
Burns: Journal of the International So-
    ciety for Burn Injuries
Dermatology: International Journal for
    Clinical and Investigative Dermatol-
    ogy
Emergency Medicine: Acute Medicine
    for the Primary Care Physician
Injury: International Journal of the
    Care of the Injured
International Journal of Oral and Max-
    illofacial Surgery
Journal of the American Academy of
    Dermatology
Journal of Foot and Ankle Surgery: Of-
    ficial Publication of the American
    College of Foot and Ankle Surgeons
Journal of Hand Surgery: An Interna-
    tional Journal Devoted to Surgery of

the Upper Extremity
Mayo Clinic Proceedings
Practitioner
Primary Care Bulletin

Often, your local hospital will maintain a library that is geared to doctors and nurses. Others mix the high-level professional material, for use by their staff, with layperson medical materials that patients and their family members may use. So if you want to "browse some diseases," check and see if your local hospital's library is open to the public.

Human Anatomy

If your character has a broken arm, you will want to know which bone has been shattered. And if a particular body part is supposed to splatter on the floor in your horror novel, best to know just what body part it is. Some resources that supply illustration of human anatomy:

Atlas of Human Anatomy. Frank Netter. New Jersey: Pharmaceuticals Division, CIBA-GEIGY Corporation, 1989.
    An elaborately illustrated atlas. Sections shown in detail include Head and Neck, Back and Spinal Chord, Thorax, Abdomen, Pelvis and Perineum, and Upper and Lower Limbs.

The Sourcebook of Medical Illustration: Over 900 Anatomical, Medical and Scientific Illustrations Available for General Re-use and Adaptation Free of Normal Copyright Restrictions. Peter Cull, editor. Park Ridge, NJ: The Parthenon Publishing Group, 1989.
    A compendium of simple black-and-white depictions of sections of the human body, including: the brain,

liver, bronchial tree and interior base of the skull. These undetailed pictures are intended to complement writings or speeches. Also included are drawings of bacteria, yeasts, protozoans, scientific symbols, animals and maps.

Most larger libraries will also own an edition of the well-known *Gray's Anatomy*.

Family Medical Books

There are a number of one-volume medical books, meant for family use and filled with advice on symptoms, cures and treatments. These can be one-stop-shopping for a writer who just needs a little information on a disorder. Some books that fill the bill:

The American Medical Association Family Medical Guide. Charles B. Clayman, medical editor. 3d edition. New York: Random House, 1994.

The New Good Housekeeping Family Health and Medical Guide. New York: Hearst Books, 1989.

Chapter Seventeen

Science and Invention

If you are planning to interview a scientist, inventor or someone in a technical profession, you will likely be in need of reference sources that explain the workings of machinery or systems. And of course your character may be called upon to build or repair an item in the course of your tale. How-to and discovery books abound in libraries.

For historical fiction or background for a nonfiction piece, the resources in this section also supply a time frame for when ideas, schools of thought and devices actually came into being.

How Do Things Work?

You will see, when reading my recommendations below, that science and engineering are not my strengths. Thus, I tend to recommend books that explain lofty concepts in as s-i-m-p-l-e a manner as possible. For those of you who are more advanced than I in these areas, I've allowed a few more sophisticated works to sneak in.

Dentistry: An Illustrated History. Malvin E. Ring. New York: Harry N. Abrams, Publishers, 1985.

A recounting of the practice of dentistry from the "primitive world" through twentieth-century practices. This is really a gorgeous volume, oversized with heavy paper and richly colored illustrations. Some of the fascinating photographs: the teeth of a

Mayan skull of the ninth century imbedded with round jade and turquoise stone (will this be the new fashion rage?), teeth bound together with gold wire (to form the equivalent of a modern-day bridge) found in Sidon, chief city of ancient Phoenicia, and the false teeth of the first president of the United States. Many historic tools of the trade are also pictured.

Eighteenth Century Inventions. K.T. Rowland. New York: Barnes and Noble Books, 1975.

Breakthroughs of the 1700s, the beginning of the industrial revolution, are examined under eighteen major headings, including Agriculture, Steam Power, Textiles, Civil Engineering and Domestic. Some noteworthy inventions of that time: the steamship, submarine, airplane and, less spectacularly but probably most importantly, the "water frame" for spinning cloth and yarn. There are many drawings (including many from that time period) and photographs included.

Electronic Inventions and Discoveries. G.W.A. Dummer. 3d revised and expanded edition. New York: Pergamon Press, 1983.

The first several chapters delve into the history of Audio and Sound Reproduction, Radio and Telecommunications, Radar, Television,

Computers, and Industrial and Other Applications of Electronics. The bulk of the book is comprised of brief descriptions of electrical devices, listed in order by year, beginning with 1642 and winding up with 1982. The original source the author used to write each description is listed with each entry; those can be useful pointers if you need to find more information. There are only a handful of illustrations in the whole book.

It can be interesting to see the originating dates of objects we are now so accustomed to using. For example, the beginnings of our first batteries were produced in Italy in 1775 by physicist Alessandro Giuseppe Antonio Anastasio Volta (Volta—voltage—aha!) and the first-time holographic images were seen was in 1948, by Dennis Gabor of the United Kingdom.

The Encyclopedia of How It Works: From Abacus to Zoom Lens. Donald Clarke, editor. New York: A&W Publishers, 1977.

This one-volume encyclopedia is a selective look at both simple inventions (like the boomerang) and more complex contrivances (such as an electron microscope). An explanation of at least a page is provided for each object or its properties, with at least one photograph and cross-sectional diagram provided for most entries. (This volume includes a photograph of a filling station pump with its outer casing removed—far more complex than you might imagine.)

Encyclopedia of Ideas That Changed the World: The Greatest Discoveries and Inventions of Human History. Robert Ing-pen and Philip Wilkinson. New York: Viking Studio Books, 1993.

Written in more of a narrative format, each chapter in this book focuses on a goal that humankind had and how that goal was brought into fruition through technology and the continued understanding of the physical world. For example, the chapter titled Utilizing the Earth's Resources has sections highlighting Natural Power, The Steam Engine, Electricity and the Battery, Internal Combustion, The Jet Engine, Rockets and Nuclear Power. Each essay is accompanied by nicely drawn illustrations.

Encyclopedia of Modern Technology. David Blackburn and Geoffrey Holister. Boston: G.K. Hall, 1987.

The editors have compiled descriptions of technology that assist mankind in nine tasks: Measuring, Seeing (i.e., Microscopes), Recording, Analyzing (using Computers, for example), Powering, Protecting (i.e., Shelter), Communicating, Moving (such as Space Transport) and Processing. Colorful, detailed photographs and diagrams assist the reader in understanding the workings of the many technological devices discussed.

Eureka! An Illustrated History of Inventions from the Wheel to the Computer. Edward De Bono, editor. New York: Holt, Rinehart and Winston, 1974.

Inventions are listed under fifteen major headings, including Transport, which discusses (among other things) balloons and traffic lights, Materials, of which two subheadings are Elastic and Stainless Steel, and Health, which mentions such items as False

Teeth and Limbs, and Aspirin. The volume has many colorful drawings and photos. Entries are brief but descriptive, ranging from a short paragraph to a page in length.

A History of Technology. 6 Volumes. Charles Singer, E.J. Holmyard, A.R. Hall and Trevor I. Williams, editors. (first five volumes); Trevor I. Williams, editor (Volume 6).

A well-known collection describing the origins of man's technological innovations in plain (and copious) words. The information ranges from food-collecting devices to the twentieth-century chemical industry. The line drawings were almost all specially created for each section (the latest edition also contains photographs). The volumes are:

Volume 1: *From Early Times to Fall of Ancient Empires.* 1954.

Volume 2: *The Mediterranean Civilizations and the Middle Ages, c. 700.* 1957.

Volume 3: *From the Renaissance to the Industrial Revolution, c. 1500-c. 1750.* 1964.

Volume 4: *The Industrial Revolution, c. 1750-c. 1850.* 1965.

Volume 5: *The Late Nineteenth Century, c. 1850-1900.* 1965.

Volume 6: *The Twentieth Century—c.1900-c.1950.* 1978.

The Illustrated Science and Invention Encyclopedia: How It Works. 26 Volumes. Westport, CT: H.S. Stuttman, Publishers, 1989.

This is a particular favorite of mine, since it covers such a wide range of apparatus and explains their workings simply, with lots of color illustration.

It is rare that I don't find what I'm looking for in here—a piano, an anchor, pistols and radios. Unfortunately, the collection is over a decade old, so don't look for CD players in this set.

Infoculture: The Smithsonian Book of Information Age Inventions. Steven Lubar. Boston: Houghton Mifflin Co., 1993.

Each section in this book is devoted to particular advances in the "information age," explaining their roots and looking ahead. The type of technology addressed includes high definition television, cellular phones and digital photography.

The MacMillan Visual Dictionary. Jean-Claude Corbeil and Ariane Archambault. New York: Macmillan Publishing Co., 1992.

The intent of this dictionary is to link words/concepts and illustrations together, to allow the drawing to help with the definition of the term or idea. The compilers succeed admirably. The brightly colored drawings look almost Technicolor and represent such diverse items as a weather satellite, vegetables, human blood circulation, household appliances, clothing, hairstyles, high-speed trains, space shuttles, musical instruments, pottery tools, games, first-aid equipment and stone age weapons. A cutaway view of many of the objects is provided.

The Major Achievements of Science. 2 Volumes. A.E.E. McKenzie. New York: Cambridge University Press, 1967.

In ten- to twenty-page articles, the

author explains, in fairly accessible terms, major scientific concepts like the Germ Theory of Disease, the Wave Theory of Light and the Structure of the Atom. Some chapters are also devoted to overviews of scientific progress in specific centuries.

Medical Discoveries: Who and When. J.E. Schmidt. Springfield, IL: Charles C. Thomas, 1959.

Thousands of medical and related scientific discoveries are listed, giving the date of the discovery, name of the discoverer and the founder's profession and nationality.

Medical Instruments. Elisabeth Bennion. London: Sotheby Parke Bernet Publications, 1979.

A survey of some fearsome-looking antique instruments of healing. There are devices and aids for all needs: knives, saws, toilet articles and ear, nose and throat needs, to name a few. A generous number of black-and-white photographs show such aids as wooden artificial limbs and one of the earliest anesthesia apparatuses from around 1846 (looks like an old Hoover vacuum cleaner).

Scientific Instruments in Art and History. Henri Michel. New York: The Viking Press, 1967.

A scholarly appraisal of antique instruments of measurement that were created to be both exact in their intended use and beautiful to behold. Many of the color photographs are full page, with the details of the engravings on the instruments easy to see. Some of the implements pictured include a water-level, sun dials, electro-static machines and calipers. Another book of this ilk, but with black-and-white photographs (and more interest in showing a wide spectrum of instruments rather than those that were also attractive) is the book *Scientific Instruments* by Harriet Wynter and Anthony Turner. (New York: Charles Scribner's Sons, 1975).

The Way Things Work: An Illustrated Encyclopedia of Technology. C. Van Amerongen. 2 Volumes. New York: Simon and Schuster, 1967. [The second volume was released in 1971.]

Two-color diagrams and lots and lots of little arrows help the reader understand the way things work and why things work. Over two thousand machines, principles and processes are explained.

The World of Invention: History's Most Significant Inventions and the People Behind Them. Bridget Travers. Detroit: Gale, 1994.

Among the significant inventions named: bottle tops, ferris wheels and pizza! Each section offers a nice history of the invention and how it's been used over time, but explanations on how they work/how they were created are exceedingly brief. (Not enough illustrations!) This volume does also supply biographical information on inventors.

How-To Compilations

Do you want your character to be working on a project? Tiling a floor? Building a deck? Is she a character who is absolutely fascinated with astronomy . . . as a hobbyist? Public libraries will be brimming with do-it-yourself books. Try the phrase MANUALS AMATEURS' in your online library catalog along with a particular project. For example:

> MANUALS AMATEURS' APPLI-
> ANCES
> MANUALS AMATEURS' CEIL-
> INGS

Some examples of do-it-yourself titles:

All Thumbs Guide to Repairing Major Home Appliances. Robert A. Wood. Blue Ridge Summit, PA: TAB Books, 1992.

The Complete Home Restoration Manual: An Authoritative Do-It-Yourself Guide to Restoring and Maintaining the Older House. Albert Jackson and David Day. New York: Simon and Schuster, 1992.

The How-To Book of Floors and Ceilings. Don Geary. Blue Ridge Summit, PA: Tab Books, 1978.

Star Ware: The Amateur Astronomer's Ultimate Guide to Choosing, Buying and Using Telescopes and Accessories. Philip S. Harrington. New York: Wiley, 1994.

"Mixing Stuff Together"

Any mad scientist worth his salt must know basic chemistry, and much science fiction is based on science fact. If you are truly a science novice and, like me, without a great science aptitude, then you might look for general library books that are geared to younger adults and children. Such books may teach complex concepts quite simply. Some examples of youth science book titles:

Janice VanCleave's 200 Gooey, Slippery, Slimy, Weird and Fun Experiments. Janice Pratt VanCleave. New York: Wiley, 1992.

Magic . . . Naturally! Science Entertainments and Amusements. Vicki Cobb. New York: HarperCollins Publishers, 1993.

Sink or Swim! The Science of Water. Barbara Taylor. New York: Random House, 1991.

An adult compilation on "mixing stuff together" is:

The Chemical Formulary. New York: Chemical Publishing Co. Irregular.
Each volume of this set (up to volume 32 in 1994) reproduces commercial formulas for a variety of substances, including beverages and food, paints, cosmetics, cleaners, drugs, adhesives, plastics and miscellaneous items such as mildewproofer for leather goods and dog shampoo. These formulas are intended as a starting point for chemists who want to tweak the formulas. There is currently a cumulative index to the first twenty-five volumes.

Chemical Properties

There are also reference sources for those of you who are science-literate. Two standards:

The CRC Handbook of Chemistry and Physics: A Ready-Reference Book of Chemical and Physical Data. David R. Lide, editor-in-chief. Boca Raton: CRC Press. Annual.
This source, which is widely used by

professionals in the various fields of science, is designed to also be handy for high school science students. It covers such information as Basic Constants, Units and Conversion Factors, Fluid Properties, Physical Constants of Organic Compounds and Properties of the Elements and Inorganic Compounds, and aspects of Nuclear and Particle Physics and Atomic, Molecular and Optical Physics.

The Merck Index: An Encyclopedia of Chemicals and Drugs. 11th edition. Rahway, NJ: Merck and Co., 1989.

An enyclopedia of chemicals, drugs and biological substances supplying descriptions of the preparation and properties of compounds, a listing of their "trivial," generic and chemical names, and explanations of their use, pharmacological properties and toxicity.

Ideas and Concepts: Textbooks and Specialized Encyclopedias

Just as you may wish to know when an invention surfaced, you may also want to know when a concept or school of thought became well known.

To find out the roots and beginnings literary movements, psychological theories, sociological conjectures and the like, I would recommend you use subject-specific encyclopedias. These are discussed at length in chapter 8, "Overviews on Any Subject: Encyclopedias and Handbooks." Also in that chapter, see the tips on finding textbooks. One collection of particular interest:

The Dictionary of the History of Ideas: Studies of Selected Pivotal Ideas. 4 Volumes. Philip P. Wiener, editor-in-chief. New York: Charles Scribner's Sons, 1973.

Heaven only knows why they named this monster a dictionary. The entries are all lengthy articles that look at critical and enduring ideas that have become part of the fabric of Western thought. Some of the essays: "Psychological Ideas in Antiquity," "Sin and Salvation," "Liberalism," "Metaphysical Imagination," the "Idea of God Since 1800," "Impressionism in Art," and "Infinity." The detailed index in the last volume of the series makes it simple to find specific ideas buried within the essays. You will find this book at almost all academic and larger public libraries.

Appendix A

Guide to Periodical Indexes

The indexes listed below represent those most commonly found at public and academic libraries. Extremely specialized and technical indexes are not included. Larger libraries will own quite a few of these sources, but almost none will own all!

Notice that you have many items to choose from under each heading. Check with your librarian to see which indexes are available and which they recommend you begin with for your topic. If your library does not own a particular source listed below, the librarian may recommend a similar one that is owned by the library.

The following information is supplied for each index:

- Name
- Who Publishes It
- The Year It Began
- What Kinds of Periodicals and Other Materials It Indexes
- Samples of the Titles It Indexes
- What Formats It Is Available In, Including:

  Print—That's the old-fashioned stuff made of paper and ink.

  CD-ROM—Available on disc through a terminal or personal computer.

  Online—Available through an online database through a vendor. (See chapter 2, "Exploring Articles," for a review of this concept.) The vendors who offer the database are listed in parenthesis. These vendors are described in Appendix B.

  Tape—Available through "tape-load," which means that your library might have the index loaded onto the library's online system.

A Note on the Formats: Remember, your library may have the index available in only one format, say print or CD-ROM. This list is simply meant to alert you to the possible formats you might find each index in.

Key:

- A (P) designates an index more often found in public libraries.
- An (A) designates an index more often found in academic libraries.
- An (A&P) designates an index commonly found in both public and academic libraries.

XV Sports, Physical Education, and Health . . . 305
Cumulative Index to Nursing and Allied Health Literature
Health Index
Index Medicus
Physical Education Index
Sport

Biography

Biography Index. (A&P) New York: H.W. Wilson Co., 1946-present.
The biographical material in this index is gathered from obituaries, collections of personal letters, diaries, memoirs, children's and young adult literature, book reviews, bibliographies, books and periodicals. Most of the people covered are American.
Sample Titles Indexed
Hispanic Review
Physics Today
Vanity Fair
The Review of Politics
Formats: Print, CD-ROM, Online (CDP, OCLC), Tape.

Business

ABI/INFORM. (A&P) New York: UMI, 1971-present.
Provides indexing and abstracts on all topics in business, including accounting, banking, computers, economics, health care, international trends, law, management, marketing, public administration, taxation and transportation.
Sample Titles Indexed
Economic Review
Computer Technology Review
Real Estate Issues
Marketing News

Formats: CD-ROM, Online (*Data-Star, DIALOG, DJNR, OCLC, NEXIS, ORBIT, STN* International and others), Tape.

Business Index. (A&P) Foster City, CA: Information Access Co., 1981-present.
An index to over eight hundred business journals, trade journals and newspapers. Newspaper coverage includes the business and financial sections and other articles relating to business from several national newspapers, including the *Wall Street Journal* and the *New York Times.*
Sample Titles Indexed
Byte
Aviation Week and Space Technology
Barron's
American Banker
Formats: Microform index, CD-ROM, Online (*America Online, CompuServe, DIALOG, LEXIS/NEXIS* and *Prodigy*), Tape.

Business NewsBank. (A&P) New Canaan, CT: NewsBank, 1985-present.
An index to business-related newspapers and the business sections of hundreds of newspapers across the country. This index concentrates on local newspaper, so you won't find the *New York Times* in this one. *Business Newsbank* is especially useful for exploring regional economic and industry information and gathering information on small, privately owned companies. Many of the current articles have the full text available on CD-ROM; older articles are reproduced on the *Business Newsbank Microfiche Collection.* Generally, libraries

own both the index and the full-text collection.

Sample Titles Indexed
Reuter Business Report
Washington Times
Florida Times-Union
Denver Business Journal
Formats: Print, CD-ROM.

Business Periodicals Index. (A&P) New York: H.W. Wilson Co., 1958-present. (Formerly titled *The Industrial Arts Index*, 1913-57.)

This has been the "standard" business index for almost a century now. BPI indexes journals covering accounting, advertising and marketing, banking, business personalities, communications, computer technology, economics, finance, insurance, international business, management, personnel, public relations, real estate, specific companies, taxation, transportation and other business-related topics.

Sample Titles Indexed
Labor History
Journal of Management
Personnel Psychology
Marketing News
Formats: Print, CD-ROM, Online (CDP, OCLC, Wilsonline), Tape.

Predicast's F&S Index: United States. (A&P) Foster City, CA: Information Access Co., 1960-present.

An index to company, product and industry information from trade publications, business-oriented newspapers and special reports. Because of the heavy trade journal emphasis, you will find marvelously specialized information. However, you may find that you need to interlibrary loan the material

because no local library actually owns the publication you need. There are citations to articles and announcements dealing with corporate acquisitions and mergers, new products, technological developments, and social and political factors affecting business. This is an excellent source to consult when trying to find the market share of an industry. There are non-U.S. versions of this index: *Predicast's F&S Index: Europe* (1978-present) and *Predicast's F&S Index: International* (1967-present).

Sample Titles Index
France Telecom
Plastics News
Swedish Economy
World Oil
Formats: Print, CD-ROM, Online (*Data-Star, DIALOG, NEXIS*).

Computers

Computer Literature Index. (Formerly titled *Quarterly Bibliography of Computers and Data Processing*.) (A&P) Phoenix: Applied Computer Research, 1971-present.

The citations in this index, relating to computers and data processing, are culled from articles, books and reports.

Sample Titles Indexed
Computer Design
Real-Time Systems: The International Journal of Time-Critical Computing Systems
Software World
Formats: Print, Microfiche.

Microcomputer Abstracts. (Formerly titles *Micro Computer Index*.) (A&P) Medford, New Jersey: Learned Information, 1980—present.

The magazine articles indexed and summarized in this set cover information in general articles concerned with microcomputing as well as reviews of microcomputer hardware, software and books.

Sample Titles Indexed
BYTE
Internet World
Macintosh Business Review
PC WEEK
Windows Magazine
Formats: Print, Online (*DIALOG*).

Criminal Justice, Law

Criminal Justice Abstracts. (A) Monsey, NY: Willow Tree Press, 1968-present.

A compilation of citations and abstracts of books, journal articles, dissertations, unpublished papers and governmental and nongovernmental agency reports on criminology and criminal justice worldwide.

Sample Titles Indexed
Criminal Behavior and Mental Health
Forensic Reports
Journal of Addictions and Offender
  Counseling
Law and Order
Trial
Violence and Victims
Formats: Print, CD-ROM, Online (*WESTLAW*).

Criminal Justice Periodical Index. (A&P) Louisville, KY: UMI, 1975-present.

An index to periodicals pertaining to corrections, criminal law, drug abuse, family law, juvenile justice, police studies, prison administration, rehabilitation and security systems.

Sample Titles Indexed
American Journal of Criminal Law

CJ International
Drugs and Society
Security Management
Law and Order
Formats: Print, CD-ROM, Online (*DIALOG*).

Current Law Index. (Law Libraries, A) Foster City, CA: Information Access Co., 1980-present.

CLI indexes 875 law journals from the United States, Canada, the United Kingdom, Ireland, Australia and New Zealand. Titles covered include academic reviews, bar association journals, specialty journals and selected journals treating related disciplines such as criminology and accounting.

Sample Titles Indexed
American University Law Review
High Technology Law Journal
Journal of Legal Medicine
National Black Law Journal
Formats: Print, CD-ROM—called LegalTrac, Online (*Data-Star, DIALOG, LEXIS, WESTLAW*).

Index to Legal Periodicals. (A&P) New York: H.W. Wilson Co., 1952-present.

Commonly found in academic libraries, this index provides indexing to articles discussing all aspects of law and legal research in periodicals from the United States, Canada, Great Britain, Ireland, Australia and New Zealand.

Sample Titles Indexed
Journal of Law and Social Policy
Journal of Law and Religion
Current Legal Problems
Trial Lawyers Quarterly
Formats: Print, CD-ROM, Online

(*CDP, OCLC, LEXIS, WESTLAW, Wilsonline*), Tape.

Education

Education Index. (A&P) New York: H.W. Wilson Co., 1929-present.

A standard indexing source covering journals dealing with preschool, elementary, secondary, higher and adult education. Topics covered include audiovisual education, health and physical education, computers in education, comparative and international education, language and linguistics, library and information sciences, multicultural/ethnic education, psychology and mental health, religious education, special education and rehabilitation and other related topics.

Sample Titles Indexed

Writing Instructor

TechTrends

Rural Educator

Phi Delta Kappan

Journal of Physical Education, Recreation and Dance

Journal of Alcohol and Drug Education

Formats: Print, CD-ROM, Online (*CDP, OCLC, Wilsonline*), Tape.

ERIC. (Educational Resources Information Center.) (A&P) Phoenix, AZ: The ORYX Press (*CIJE*); Washington, DC: Government Printing Office (*RIE*). *CIJE*: 1969-present; *RIE*: 1966-present.

Covering all topics in the field of education, *ERIC* is divided into two parts. The first part, *Resources in Education (RIE)*, contains current research findings, projects and technical reports, speeches, conference proceed-ings, unpublished manuscripts and books. The second part, *Current Index to Journals in Education (CIJE)*, covers hundreds of magazines and journals in the field of education. Some libraries, particularly academic libraries with large educational programs, purchase the huge *ERIC* Collection; a collection of the full text of all the documents in *RIE*. A fabulous educational resource.

Sample Journal Titles Indexed

Journal of Educational Psychology

Journal of Career Education

Bilingual Review

Formats: Print, CD-ROM, Online (*DIALOG, OCLC*), Tape.

Environment

Environment Abstracts Annual. (A) New Providence, NJ: R.R. Bowker (1971-1974), Congressional Information Service, (1975-present) 1971-present.

This index covers all aspects of environmental research, such as air, water and noise pollution; solid and toxic wastes; radiological contamination; toxicological effects; resource management; population; endangered species; and geophysical and climatic change.

Sample Titles Indexed

Agricultural Research

Audubon

Environmental Ethics

Outdoor America

Formats: Print, CD-ROM, Online—called Enviroline (*Data-Star, DIALOG, ORBIT* and others).

Wildlife Review. (A) Washington, DC: Government Printing Office. 1935-present.

Wildlife Review supplies indexing to the natural resource and wildlife literature in books, journals and symposia proceedings.

Sample Titles Indexed

Journal of Environmental Horticulture

Canadian Journal of Zoology

Wildlife Society Bulletin

Formats: Print, CD-ROM.

Folklore, Mythology, Philosophy, Religion

The Philosopher's Index. (A&P) Bowling Green, OH: Philosophy Documentation Center. 1940-present.

An index to all major philosophy journals in English, French, German, Spanish, Italian and other languages.

Sample Titles Indexed

Feminist Studies

Ethics

History of Political Thought

Journal of Religious Ethics

Philosophy of Science

Formats: Print, CD-ROM, Online (*CompuServe, DIALOG*).

Religion Index. (A) Evanston, IL: American Theological Library Association. 1953-present.

Indexes articles on the subject of religion. The index is primarily focused on Western religion and religious scholarship.

Sample Titles Indexed

The Christian Century

Harvard Theological Review

Journal of Feminist Studies in Religion

Japanese Journal of Religious Studies

Formats: Print, CD-ROM, Online (*DIALOG*).

General—All Topics

Access. (P) Evanston, IL: John Gordon Burke, 1975-present.

Access covers the magazines not presently covered by the *Readers' Guide to Periodical Literature*, as well as indexing regional and city magazines.

Sample Titles Indexed

Metropolis

Mirabella

On the Issues

Playboy

Village Voice

Formats: Print, CD-ROM.

Alternative Press Index. (A&P) Baltimore, MD: Alternative Press Center, 1969-present.

An index to "alternative press" publications.

Sample Titles Indexed

American Atheist

Earth First!

Interracial Books for Children

Lesbian Contradiction

Socialist Review

Formats: Print

Canadian Periodical Index. (Formerly titled *Canadian Index to Periodicals and Documentary Films.*) (A&P) Toronto, ON, Canada: Globe and Mail Publishing, 1938-present.

An index to over four hundred English- and French-language periodicals from the United States and Canada.

Sample Titles Indexed

The Beaver: Exploring Canada's History

Business Quarterly

Canadian Geographic

Financial Post

Format: Print, CD-ROM.

Children's Magazine Guide: Subject Index to Children's Literature. (P) New Providence, NJ: R.R. Bowker, 1948-present

Primarily an index to magazines whose audience is primarily children. There is also a limited index to professional magazines published for teachers and librarians.

Sample Titles Indexed
Highlights
Ladybug
Ranger Rick
Teacher K-8
Format: Print.

Expanded Academic Index. (A) Foster City, CA: Information Access Co., 1980-present.

EAI supplies indexing to fourteen hundred scholarly and general-interest journals in the areas of humanities, social sciences, political sciences and general sciences.

Sample Titles Indexed
PC Magazine
American Political Science Review
Animal Behavior
Chronicle of Higher Education
Social Problems
Women's Studies
Congressional Quarterly
Formats: Microform index, CD-ROM, Online (*Data-Star, DIALOG*), Tape.

Magazine Express. (P) Louisville, KY: UMI, 1986-present.

More than 130 general reference publications in a variety of fields are indexed: arts and entertainment, business and finance, computers, consumer issues, education, health and medicine, law, leisure, public policy, religion, science and technology, social sciences and sports and fitness.

The full text is available for articles from about 85 periodicals.

Sample Titles Indexed
Life
Parents
Popular Science
Time
World Health
Formats: CD-ROM

Magazine Index. (P) Foster City, CA: Information Access Co., 1959-1970, 1973-present.

An index to over four hundred popular and general-interest magazines on topics such as current affairs, leisure and travel, consumer affairs and products, people in the news, education, arts and science.

Sample Titles Indexed
Time
Fortune
People Weekly
Sports Illustrated
Ebony
Car and Driver
Datamation
Formats: Microfilm, Online: (*Data-Star, DIALOG*), Tape.

Poole's Index to Periodical Literature. (A&P) Gloucester, MA: Peter Smith, 1802-1906.

One of the earliest periodical indexes (note the years covered), Poole's covers periodicals on a wide variety of subjects.

Sample Titles Indexed
American Historical Review
Army and Navy Life
Bankers' Magazine
Catholic World
Folk-Lore

International Journal of Ethics
Popular Science Monthly
Format: Print.

Readers' Guide to Periodical Literature.
(A&P) New York: H.W. Wilson Co.,
1890-present.
Probably the best known of all
multisubject periodical indexes, *The
Reader's Guide* is likely to point you
to articles on almost any topic. The
magazines indexed are more popular,
newsstand-type magazines.
Sample Titles Indexed
Cosmopolitan
Forbes
National Geographic
Time
Formats: Print, CD-ROM, Online
(CDP, OCLC, Wilsonline), Tape.

UnCover. (A&P) Denver CO: Un-
Cover Co., 1988-present.
An index to articles from over ten
thousand scholarly journals and popu-
lar magazines published since October
1988 and is updated daily. A nice fea-
ture: You can look at each journal title
and browse the table of contents just
as if you had the magazine in your
hand and were flipping to the con-
tents page.
Sample Titles Indexed
Interior Design
Journal of Organic Chemistry
Modern Healthcare
Newsweek
PC Magazine
Studies in Short Fiction
Formats: Tape.

Vertical File Index. (A&P) New York:
H.W. Wilson Co., 1932-present.
A one-of-a-kind index! It's not an
index to periodicals, but you really
should know about it: the *Vertical File
Index* leads you to material published
in odd formats, such as pamphlets,
charts, posters, maps and other inex-
pensive paperbound items. Indexed by
subject. Ordering instructions for each
item are included.
Sample Titles Indexed
Acid; LSD Today (pamphlet)
*Vermont 1992 Official State Map and
Touring Guide*
*Tomorrow's Terrorists; Our Still
Dangerous World* (leaflet)
Formats: Print.

Government

*ABC POL SCI—A Bibliography of Con-
tents: Political Science and Government.*
(A) Santa Barbara, CA: ABC-CLIO,
1969-present.
An index to the international peri-
odical literature in the field of politi-
cal science and government as well as
the related disciplines of law, sociol-
ogy and economics.
Sample Titles Indexed
Africa Quarterly
International Affairs
Natural Resources Journal
Policy Studies Journal
Public Administration
Formats: Print, CD-ROM.

Public Affairs Information Service (PAIS).
(A&P) New York: Public Affairs Information Service, 1914-present.
PAIS is a unique index that indexes
literature covering contemporary public issues and the making and evaluat-
ing of public policy. Primarily, these
issues are in the areas of economics,
political science, public administra-

tion, international law and relations, the environment and demography. In addition to periodicals, *PAIS* also indexes government documents, books and other materials.

Sample Titles Indexed
Africa Today
Aging and Society
Economic and Social Review
Journal of Public Health Policy
Studies in Family Planning
Formats: Print, CD-ROM, Online (*Data-Star*, DIALOG, OCLC), Tape.

History, Anthropology

Abstracts in Anthropology. (A) Amityville, NY: Baywood Publishing Co., 1970-present.

Abstracts in Anthropology covers topics in the field of anthropology, such as man's speech, physiology, artifacts, history, environment and social relations.

Sample Titles Indexed
Asian Perspectives
Genetics
Journal of Health and Social Behavior
Journal of Sex Research
New England Journal of Medicine
Formats: Print.

America: History and Life. (A) Santa Barbara, CA: ABC-CLIO, 1964-present.

An index to the literature of the history and culture of the United States and Canada from prehistoric times to the present.

Sample Titles Indexed
Civil War History
Political Science Quarterly
Western Legal History
Technology and Culture

Formats: Print, CD-ROM, Online (*DIALOG*, *CompuServe*).

Historical Abstracts. (A) Santa Barbara, CA: ABC-CLIO, 1955-present.

This index covers all branches of world history from 1450 to the present for the world *except* for the United States and Canada. Examples of topics include: political, diplomatic, military, economic, social, cultural, religious and intellectual history.

Sample Titles Indexed
Journal of the History of Ideas
Twentieth Century British History
International History Review
History in Africa
Journal of Asian Studies
Formats: Print, CD-ROM, Online (*CompuServe*, DIALOG).

Humanities: Art, Architecture, Dance, Literature, Music, Theater

Architectural Periodicals Index and Books Cataloged by the British Architectural Library. (A) [Formerly titled *RIBA Library Review of Periodicals*, 1933-1945, *RIBA Library Bulletin*, 1946-1972, and the *RIBA Annual Review of Periodical Articles*, 1965-1972.] London: RIBA Publications, 1972-present.

This collection selectively indexes three hundred architecture journals from forty-five nations. There is an emphasis on literature, projects and designs in Great Britain. The fields covered in *API* include architecture and allied arts, constructional technology, design and environmental studies, landscape and planning.

Sample Titles Indexed
Architecture of Israel

Basa (Spain)
Habitat Pakistan
Old House Journal
Techniques and Architecture (France)
Formats: Print, Online (*DIALOG*).

Art Index. (A&P) New York: H.W. Wilson Co., 1929-present.

Found in most libraries, the *Art Index* covers all aspects of art and art research, including archaeology, architecture, art history, city planning, crafts, films, graphic arts, interior design, landscape architecture and photography.

Sample Titles Indexed
American Cinematographer
Art International
Film Comment
Folk Art
Sculpture Review
Interior Design
Formats: Print, CD-ROM, Online (*CDP, OCLC, Wilsonline*), Tape.

Avery Index to Architecture Periodicals. (A) Boston, MA: G.K. Hall & Co., (1973-1990), MacMillan Publishing Co. (1991-present), 1973-present.

Avery indexes periodicals in architecture, art history, archaeology and urban planning.

Sample Titles Indexed
The Architectural Forum
House and Garden
The American City
Formats: Print, CD-ROM.

Essay and General Literature Index. (A&P) New York: H.W. Wilson Co., 1900-present.

Okay, this one is not a periodical index either, but another handy and underused source. This is an index to es-

says published in books of collected essays, primarily in the fields of the humanities and social sciences. Examples of topics included are philosophy, religion, social and political science, economics, law, education, linguistics, science, the various arts, literature and history.

Sample Titles Indexed
Irish Writers and the Theater
The Political Re-Education of Germany and Her Allies After World War II
Formats: Print, CD-ROM, Online (*CDP, OCLC, Wilsonline*), Tape.

Film Literature Index. (A&P) Albany, NY: Film and Television Documentation Center, 1973-present.

An international index to articles about film, television and video.

Sample Titles Indexed
Art in America
Black Cinema
Film Comment
Premiere
Cinema Journal
Dance Magazine
Interview
Variety
Formats: Print.

Humanities Index. (A&P) New York: H.W. Wilson Co., 1974-present.

[Previously called *Social Sciences and Humanities Index* (1965-1974), *International Index* (1955-1965) and *International Index to Periodicals* (1907-1955).]

Another index found in almost any midsize to large academic or public library. The *Humanities Index* indexes topics in the humanities, such as archaeology, folklore, history, language and literature, performing arts, philosophy, religion and theology.

Sample Titles Indexed

Art in America
Film Quarterly
Essays in Literature
Journal of American Culture
Modern Drama
Philosophy Today

Formats: Print, CD-ROM, Online (*CDP, OCLC, Wilsonline*), Tape.

MLA International Bibliography of Books and Articles on the Modern Languages and Literatures. (A) New York: The Modern Language Association of America, 1921-present.

The premiere, scholarly index of languages and literature, the *MLA Bibliography* provides access to books and articles published on modern languages, literatures, folklore and linguistics.

Samples Titles Indexed

American Poetry
Critical Essays on World Literature
Comparative Drama
Journal of the Short Story in English

Formats: Print, CD-ROM, Online (*OCLC, Wilsonline*).

Music Index. (A) Warren, MI: Harmonie Park Press, 1949-present.

Topics covered in this specialized index include the history of music, different forms and types of music, musical instruments, historical and contemporary personalities in music, computer-produced music and reviews of recordings and performances.

Sample Titles Indexed

Choral Journal
Billboard
Black Music Research Journal

International Journal of Music Education

Formats: Print, CD-ROM.

Newspaper Indexes

The Christian Science Monitor Index. (A&P) Boston, MA: The Christian Science Publishing Society, 1945-present.

An index to the contents of the *Christian Science Monitor*, indexing news items, feature articles, editorials, editorial cartoons, commentaries, sports articles, business and financial news, reviews of books, art exhibitions, dance, movies, music, restaurants, theater and television programs.

Format: Print, CD-ROM, Online (*DIALOG*), Tape.

National Newspaper Index. (A&P) Foster City, CA: Information Access Co., 1989-present.

An index to the contents of five major newspapers.

Titles Indexed

The Wall Street Journal
The Christian Science Monitor
New York Times
The Los Angeles Times
Washington Post

Formats: CD-ROM, Online (*Data-Star, DIALOG*), Tape.

The New York Times Index. New York: The New York Times Co., 1851-present.

Indexes news items, editorial matter and special features published in the *New York Times.*

Format: Print, CD-ROM, Online (*DIALOG*), Tape.

NewsBank. (A&P) New Canaan, CT: NewsBank, 1970-present.

NewsBank indexes major headlines from local and regional newspapers from across the country. A variation of *NewsBank* called *CD NewsBank* also includes national and international news and some international wire services. The full text of the articles indexed on *NewsBank* is available on microfiche in the *NewsBank Microfiche Collection*.

Sample Titles Indexed
Anchorage Times
San Francisco Examiner
Boston Globe
Oregonian
Reuters
Formats: Print, CD-ROM.

The Wall Street Journal Index. (A&P) Ann Arbor, MI: UMI, 1955-present.

Indexes news items, columns, feature articles, editorials, letters to the editor, obituaries, certain tabular information, earnings reports, dividend reports and art reviews appearing in the *Wall Street Journal*.
Formats: Print, CD-ROM, Online (*DIALOG*), Tape.

The Washington Post Index. (A&P) Ann Arbor, MI: UMI, 1971-present.

An index to the contents of the *Washington Post*, covering news items, feature articles, editorials, editorial cartoons, obituaries, sports articles, business and financial news, and reviews of books, art exhibitions, dance, movies, music, restaurants, theater and television programs appearing in the newspaper.
Formats: Print, CD-ROM, Online (*DIALOG*), Tape.

Sociology, Psychology

Psychological Abstracts. (A) Washington, DC: The American Psychological Association, 1927-present.

The premiere scholarly index to the literature of psychology, *Psychological Abstracts* supplies coverage of approximately thirteen hundred periodicals in the areas of psychology and behavioral sciences. Electronic versions of this index also index books.

Sample Titles Indexed
Gender and Society
Gerontology
Journal of Chemical Dependency Treatment
Journal of Nonverbal Behavior
Formats: Print, CD-ROM—called *PsycLit*, Online—called *PsycInfo* (*DIALOG, CompuServe, Data-Star, CDP Online*).

Social Sciences Index. (A&P) New York: H.W. Wilson Co., 1974-present. [Previously called *Social Sciences and Humanities Index* (1965-1974), *International Index* (1955-1965) and *International Index to Periodicals* (1907-1955).]

Yet another of the classic indexes published by the H.W. Wilson Company. *SSI* provides indexing on a wide variety of social science topics, such as anthropology, community health and medical care, economics, geography, gerontology, international relations, law and criminology, minority studies, planning and public administration, police science and corrections, policy sciences, political science, psychiatry, psychology, social work and public welfare, sociology and urban studies.

Sample Titles Indexed
Latin American Perspectives

Journal of Memory and Language
Families in Society
Health and Social Work
Human Rights
Formats: Print, CD-ROM, Online (*CDP, OCLC, Wilsonline*), Tape.

Sociological Abstracts. (A) San Diego, CA: Sociological Abstracts, 1953-present.

A scholarly publication that provides citations and abstracts to journal articles in the broad discipline of sociology, which includes subjects such as anthropology, economics, education, medicine, community development, philosophy, statistics and political science.

Sample Titles Indexed
Feminist Studies
Human Ecology
Journal of Genetic Counseling
Law and Contemporary Problems
Rural History
Socialism and Democracy
Formats: Print, CD-ROM—called Sociofile, Online (*CDP, Data-Star, DIALOG, OCLC*), Tape.

Science: Biology, Chemistry, Electronics, Engineering, Mathematics, Physics

Applied Science and Technology Index. (A) New York: H.W. Wilson Co., 1958-present (Previously called *Industrial Arts Index*, 1913-1957).

This is a popular index, but since it indexes quite a number of scholarly, specialized journals, it is not as widely available as the *General Science Index* listed below. *The Applied Science and Technology Index* covers a wide variety

of applied science topics, including aeronautics and space science, atmospheric sciences, chemistry, computer technology, construction industry, energy resources and research, engineering, fire and fire prevention, food and food industry, geology, machinery, mathematics, metallurgy, mineralogy, oceanography, petroleum and gas, physics, plastics, textile industry and fabrics, and transportation.

Sample Titles Indexed
Marine Technology
Nuclear News
Journal of Rail and Rapid Transit
Recycling Today
Formats: Print, CD-ROM, Online (*CDP, OCLC, Wilsonline*), Tape.

General Science Index. (A&P) New York: H.W. Wilson Co., 1978-present.

A great first-stop science index. It provides indexing to a plethora of science topics, such as astronomy, atmospheric science, biology, botany, chemistry, earth science, environment and conservation, food and nutrition, genetics, mathematics, medicine and health, microbiology, oceanography, physics, physiology and zoology.

Sample Titles Indexed
Sky and Telescope
Wildlife Conservation
Food and Nutrition
Lancet
Formats: Print, CD-ROM, Online (*CDP, OCLC, Wilsonline*), Tape.

Biological and Agricultural Index. (A) New York: H.W. Wilson Co., 1964-present. [Previously called *The Agricultural Index*, (1916-1964).]

Scholarly coverage of the periodical literature on agricultural chemicals, agricultural economics, agricultural engineering, agricultural research, animal husbandry, biochemistry, biology, biotechnology, botany, ecology, environmental science, fishery sciences, food science, forestry, genetics, horticulture, marine biology, microbiology, nutrition, physiology, soil science, veterinary medicine and zoology.

Sample Titles Indexed
Advances in Human Genetics
Cell
Environment
Journal of Applied Nutrition
Tropical Agriculture
Format: Print, CD-ROM, Online (*CDP*, *OCLC*, *Wilsonline*), Tape.

Chemical Abstracts. (A) Columbus, OH: The American Chemical Society, 1907-present.

The standard index for chemists, *Chem Abs* (as it is often referred to) indexes and abstracts scientific and technical papers and journals containing new information of chemical or chemical engineering interest. Also reports chemical information from the patent literature. Information can be searched by topic or by name or formula of a particular chemical.
Sample Titles Indexed
Journal of Biological Chemistry
Journal of Neurochemistry
Parasite Immunology
Formats: Print, Online (*Data-Star*, *DIALOG*, *STN*).

Physics Abstracts. (A) Piscataway, NJ: The Institution of Electrical Engineers, 1897-present.

Like *Chemical Abstracts*, *Physics Abstracts* is the standard for physicists. It indexes conferences, book titles, bibliographies, dissertations and journal literature in the field of physics.
Sample Titles Indexed
Astrophysics Journal
Cryogenics
Nature
Formats: Print, CD-ROM.

Sports, Physical Education and Health

Cumulative Index to Nursing and Allied Health Literature (CINAHL). (A) Glendale, CA: CINAHL Information Systems, 1956-present.

An index to the literature from the nursing and allied health fields, covering topics such as health administration, biomedicine, consumer health, ethics, protocol, technology and psychology. *CINAHL* is often one of the first places I look for health information, since it is scholarly, but includes many journals that are more accessible than those found in *Index Medicus*. (See below.)
Sample Titles Indexed
Cancer Nursing
Child Welfare
Disability and Rehabilitation
Gerontologist
Hospice Journal
Formats: Print, CD-ROM, Online (*Data-Star*, *DIALOG*).

Health Index. (P) Foster City, CA: Information Access Co. Coverage is the most current 36 months.

This database provides indexing to professional journals, consumer-oriented magazines and newsletters on topics in health, fitness, nutrition and medicine. This database is simple to use and the literature indexed is (often) understandable to the layperson.

Sample Titles Indexed

American Journal of Cardiology

The Gerontologist

New England Journal of Medicine

The Physician and Sportsmedicine

Formats: CD-ROM, Online (*CompuServe, Data-Star, DIALOG*), Tape.

Index Medicus. (A) Washington, DC: Government Printing Office. 1960-present.

The standard medical index, geared to the medical professional, supplying indexing to over three thousand English- and foreign-language journals on biomedical subjects such as air pollution, dentistry, disease control, drugs, health education, history of medicine, infant mortality, legislation, nervous system, nutrition, public health and vital statistics.

Sample Titles Indexed

American Journal of Public Health

Current Problems in Surgery

Experimental Eye Research

Format: Print, CD-ROM, Online (*DIALOG*), Tape.

Physical Education Index. Cape Gerardeau, MO: BenOak Publishing Co., 1978-present.

An index to articles in the field of physical education, such as dance, health, physical therapy, recreation, sports and sports medicine.

Sample Titles Indexed

Runner's World

Sports Medicine

International Journal of Sport Psychology

Formats: Print.

Sport Bibliography. (A) Gloucester, ON, Canada: Sport Information Resource Centre, 1949-present.

An index to the worldwide literature on physical education, physical fitness, exercise physiology, sports medicine, coaching, officiating, sports administration, handicapped sport and recreation, sport injuries, health, and the administration of physical education programs and facilities.

Sample Titles Indexed

Journal of Adolescent Health

Journal of Biomechanics

Perceptual and Motor Skills

Formats: Print, CD-ROM—called SPORT Discus, Online—called Sport (*CDP, Data-Star, DIALOG*).

Appendix B

Online Service/Database Providers

This Appendix lists three types of online vendors:

I Online Interactive Service and Information Suppliers.

Those that provide access to information databases and interactive services, the latter including opportunities to shop, chat, correspond and make travel arrangements online. They also provide full or limited gateways to the Internet. (Note: Be aware that none of the providers in this category yet supply the full spectrum of Internet utilities and tools now available, and that they all offer *limited* access to Usenet. (Of course, many users have little need of the full spectrum of Internet utilities.)

II Internet Access Providers.

These are firms whose main objective is to connect you to the Internet. They do not lease or create information databases. However, each company has its own combination bag of utilities, software and so on to assist you in getting the most out of the Net.

III Online Information Vendors.

These vendors provide access to information databases that they create or lease. Their primary subscribers are businesses, libraries and other institutions. Interactive databases are minimal.

I Online Interactive Service and Information Database Suppliers

Note—Almost all these suppliers offer at least a few hours free of charge to try their service. So go ahead and experiment and find the service you best mesh with.

America Online—AOL
America Online, Inc.
8619 Westwood Center Drive
Vienna, VA 22182
(800) 827-6364.
E-Mail—YES.
Internet Connection—YES.
Bulletin Boards—YES, called Forums.
Usenet Access—YES.
Real Time Online Conversations Possible? YES.
Cost—*$9.95/month and $3.50/hour*

after 5 hours.

Notes, Sample Features and Databases:

Articles—Full-text access to more than fifty magazines, newspapers and news services, including *The Atlantic Monthly, Bicycling Magazine, Home Office Computing, Popular Photography, Wired* and *Woman's Day.*

Compton's Encyclopedia—Full-text access.

EAASY SABRE—Enables the user to make online reservations for airline flights, hotel accommodations and car rentals.

Easy to Use. In January 1995, *PC World* named *AOL* as the simplest service around for connecting to the Internet; *Delphi* was judged a close second.

Microsoft Small Business Center—Information and assistance of interest to small-business owners or individuals considering starting a small business.

Subject Areas—*AOL* databases and services appear under eight different headings: News and Finance, Entertainment, Travel and Shopping, People Connection, Computing and Software, Lifestyles and Interests, Learning and Reference, and What's New and Online Support.

CompuServe Information Service
5000 Arlington Centre Blvd.
P.O. Box 20212
Columbus, OH 43220
(800) 848-8199
E-Mail—YES.
Internet Connection—YES.
Bulletin Boards—YES, called Forums.
Usenet Access—YES.
Real Time Online Conversations Possible? YES.
Cost—$8.95/month and between $0.00 and $9.60/hour.

Notes, Sample Features and Databases:
Academic American Encyclopedia. Full-text access. (Also on *DJNR* described in section III.)

Bed and Breakfast Guide Online. Ratings of B&Bs in the United States and Canada.

Been Around. CompuServe is the largest and oldest commercial online service.

Business Database Plus. This database contains the full text of 450 regional, national and international business and trade publications.

Hardware and Software Forums. CompuServe has an impressive variety and amount of them. (All of the services in this section offer such forums.)

Low Fare Finder. For booking economical plane flights.

Periodical Access. CompuServe provides access to over 850 periodical databases, including the full text of over 700 professional journals, newspapers, consumer magazines and specialized newsletters.

Peterson's College Database—Descriptions of thousands of accredited or approved U.S. and Canadian undergraduate institutions. (Also on *CDP, DIALOG* and *Dow Jones*. The *Dow Jones* version is enhanced, supplying additional textual material written by college officials.)

*Phone*File.* A phone and address file that is composed of approximately eighty-three million households throughout the United States. (Our family used this database to successfully locate a long-lost relative.)

Subject Areas. The *CompuServe* databases and services are listed under ten areas: Communications/Bulletin Boards, News/Weather/Sports, Travel, The Electronic Mall/Shopping, Money Matters/Markets, Entertainment/Games, Home/Health/Education, Reference, Computers/Technology and Business/Other Interests.

Delphi Internet Services
Delphi Internet Services Corporation

1030 Massachusetts Avenue
Cambridge, MA 02138
(800) 695-4005
E-Mail—YES.
Internet Connection—YES.
Bulletin Boards—YES.
Usenet Access—YES.
Real Time Online Conversations Possible? YES.
Cost—$10/month, $4.00/hour after 4 hours, or $20/month, $1.80/hour after 20 hours. For Internet service add an additional $3.00 per month for either option.
Notes, Sample Features and Databases:
Chatting With the Stars. Users can have an online gab with TV personalities and fans of such shows as the *X-Files* and *Beverly Hills 90210*. More shows will be added in the future.
DIALOG Gateway—Delphi provides access to the many databases on the DIALOG information system (described in section III of this appendix).
Easiest Around. In January 1995, *PC World* named *AOL* as the *simplest* service around. *PC Magazine* judged *Delphi* as one of the easiest services to use (right after *AOL*, above).
The Federal Register. Full-text access to this U.S.-government-produced compilation of federal regulations.
Groliers Electronic Encyclopedia (Academic American). Full-text access.
*News Services—*Access to UPI, Reuters and BPI Entertainment newswires, providing up-to-the-minute coverage of sports, politics, national and international events and entertainment.
*Trendvest—*With *Trendvest*, users can custom analyze, rate and screen a selection of more than five thousand

stocks on various exchanges and maintain an updated portfolio. [Also available through *CompuServe, NewsNet* and *Trendvest Corporation* (412) 921-6900.]

GEnie—General Electric Network for Information Exchange
General Electric Information Services
P.O. Box 6403
Rockville, MD 20849
(800) 638-9636
E-Mail—YES.
Internet Connection—YES.
Bulletin Boards—YES, called Roundtables.
Usenet Access—YES.
Real Time Online Conversations Possible? YES.
Cost—$8.95/month and $3.00/hour U.S.—$4.00/hour Canada after 4 hours, off-peak. Prime Time $9.50/hour U.S.—$12.00 per hour Canada after 4 hours.
Notes, Sample Features and Databases:
*Adventure Atlas—*Helps users find trips that match personal criteria. (Also on *Delphi*.)
*Astro News and Events—*Provides daily guides for all signs from *American Astrology Magazine*, a schedule of astrological conferences, lectures and seminars, and a listing of astrological organizations.
College Aide Sources for Higher Education. A scholarship database listing financial aid opportunities for undergraduate and graduate schooling.
*DIALOG—*Like *Delphi, GEnie* provides access to *DIALOG* databases as one of their premium services. (*DIALOG* is described in section III of this appendix.)
Grolier's Electronic Encyclopedia.

(*Academic American.*) Full-text access.

Dow Jones News/Retrieval—Provides a link to *DJNR*, a premium service. (*DJNR* is described in section III of this appendix.)

Sports Network—Up-to-the-moment sports scores. (Also on *CompuServe.*)

Subject Areas: Computing Services, Finance and Investing Services, News-Sports and Features, Career/Professional Services, Leisure Pursuits and Hobbies, Entertainment Services, Research and Reference, Communications, Travel Services, Online Shopping, Multi-Player Games, Business Services, Education Services, Symposiums on Global Issues.

Prodigy
Prodigy Services Company
445 Hamilton Avenue
White Plains, NY 10601
(800) 776-3449
E-Mail—YES.
Internet Connection—YES.
Bulletin Boards—YES.
Usenet Access—YES.
Real Time Online Conversations Possible? YES.
Cost—$9.95/month for up to five hours of use, $2.95 per each additional hour.

Sample Features and Databases:

Academic American Encyclopedia. Full-text access.

America's Talking—*Prodigy* users can participate in on-air discussions and ask questions on the all-talk cable TV network *America's Talking.*

AP Online—Continually updated business, sports and news stories from the *Associated Press Newswire.* (Also on *CompuServe.*)

ESPNET Sports—Allows users to track the latest game scores and to find sports stats.

Subject Categories—News/Weather, Business/Finance, Sports-ESPN, Communications, Entertainment, Reference, Shopping, Computers, Travel, Home/Family/Kids.

The WELL
27 Gate Five Road.
Sausalito, CA 94965.
Phone (415) 332-4335.
Fax (415) 332-4927.
E-Mail—YES.
Internet Connection—YES.
Bulletin Boards—YES, called Conferences.
Usenet Access—YES.
Real Time Online Conversations Possible? YES.
Cost—$15/month, $2/hour WELL connect charge. (There may be other connect charges, depending on where you are calling from.)

Notes, Sample Features and Databases:

Conversation. The specialty of *The WELL* is online discussion. It is known as a particularly friendly network, counting some experts well known in their fields as members.

Join Online: To join *The WELL* online, call (415)332-6106 and type in NEWUSER at the login: prompt.

Subject Areas. The major conference sections are: Social Responsibility and Politics, Media and Communications, Business and Livelihood, Body/Mind/Health, Cultures, Place, Interactions, Arts and Letters, Recreation, Entertainment, Education and Planning, Grateful Dead and Computers.

II Internet Access Providers

There are at about two hundred Internet access providers in the United States—the number doubled in 1994, and is forecast to grow exponentially. Some providers work more with individuals, others specialize in connecting organizations and businesses to the Internet. Since many providers are regional, only a few national providers are being listed here.

One online method of finding providers: Send an e-mail to info-deli-server@net-com.com. In the subject or body of the message type send pdial. Pdial is a listing of Internet access providers. As mentioned in chapter 1, you can find firms who will provide Internet links listed in computer magazines. I recommend that you check with your computer store folks or local computer user groups to see if they have some tips on local providers or any others they have had good experience with.

When signing up for Internet access, be sure to quiz the provider long and hard about what they charge for. Do they charge for every e-mail you receive? Are there surcharges for peak usage? Don't be shocked by your first monthly bill by not being informed.

The Internet providers will also want to (justifiably) woo you with many extras that are not covered in this book. Listen to what they have to say; read their literature. Some of those options may be right for you.

Some providers:

AlterNet (UUNet Technologies)—
AlterDial Service
(800) 488-6384
Monthly Cost—$20, $3-$9/hour connection cost

Portal Information Network
(800) 433-6444
Setup Fee—$19.95
Monthly Cost—$19.95 plus .95-$2.95/hour.

Netcom (with *NetCruiser Interface*)
(800)501-8649
Setup Fee—$25.00
Monthly Cost—$19.95/month, $2/hour after 40 hours during peak-hour usage (9 A.M.—midnight); unlimited usage during off-peak hours.

Performance Systems International
(800) 774-3031
Setup Fee—$200, includes three free months and a copy of NetManage Chameleon.
Monthly Cost—$29/month and $2/hour after 29 hours.

III Online Information Vendors

The cost of searching databases offered by information vendors is usually a combination of paying for connect time, online or offline prints and royalty fees, varying greatly from database to database. Some will also charge a yearly or monthly fee in addition to those charges. Occasionally the subscriber (usually an institution or company) will pay a flat yearly fee for a certain amount of use or number of searches.

Rest assured that these searches are generally not cheap. It is easy to rack up $100 in charges in no time on some of these. Try to work with an experienced intermediary who will set up the search strategy beforehand and know shortcuts for keeping the price down.

An excellent source of online databases and the vendors that supply them is *The Gale Directory of Databases* (2 Volumes, Detroit: Gale). Volume 1 identifies online databases; Volume 2 lists and describes CD-ROM, diskette, magnetic tape, handheld and batch access database products.

CDP (CDP Online, CDP Colleague, CD PLUS)
CDP Technologies Inc.
333 Seventh Ave.
New York, NY 10001
(800) 950-2035

CDP provides access to a wide variety of databases, including biomedical databases, scientific databases and almost all *WILSONLINE* databases (described below), which cover business, the sciences, law and the humanities. Many of the *CDP* databases contain full-text information. To search *CDP* databases, you do have to learn their command language (but the company does provide training and the language is easy to learn). For those of you familiar with the *BRS* system (one of the older systems, as well known as *DIALOG*,)—these are the guys that bought them.

Sample *CDP* Databases:

Ageline—The citations and abstracts in these databases are all from information sources that discuss middle age and aging. (Also on *DIALOG* and *CompuServe's Knowledge Index*.)

BioethicsLine—Supplies coverage of materials devoted tomoral issues in biomedical research and clinical areas; citations and abstracts. (Also on *Data-Star, Orbit* and *Questel*.)

Comprehensive Core Medical Library

Full-Text. A full-text database of clinical medical information containing the complete texts of prominent medical journals.

Toxline—A collection of references to publications that comment on the effects of drugs and other chemicals.

DataTimes
14000 Quail Springs Parkway, Suite 450
Oklahoma City, OK 73134
(405) 751-6400

DataTimes provides access to over 3,500 national and international business, financial and news sources. Even if you don't have a computer, *DataTimes* will do a search for you if you give them the topic.

Sample *DataTimes* Databases:

Historic Stock, Bond and Mutual Fund Prices—Many are available dating back fifteen years.

Newspapers—A link to 120 U.S. and non-U.S. newspapers, including the *Wall Street Journal*, *The Asian Wall Street Journal*, *The European Wall Street Journal*, the *Washington Post*, *The Los Angeles Times* and *USA Today*.

Periodicals—Access to more than one thousand magazines, business journals, and trade publications, including *Forbes, Barron's* and *U.S. News and World Report*.

Real-Time Business Newswires—Spouting up-to-the-minute news from such services as *Dow Jones News*, *PR Newswire* and *Business Newswire*.

DIALOG
Knight-Ridder Information
Worldwide Headquarters
2440 El Camino Real
Mountain View, CA 94040
(800) 334-2564

DIALOG has been quite a mainstay at libraries and many organizations over the last twenty years. This vendor offers over 450 databases containing over 330 million articles, abstracts and citations. Approximately 2,500 of the journals, magazines and newspapers are offered online, full text. Subject areas covered include Agriculture, Food, Nutrition, Biosciences and Technology, Business News and Information, Chemistry, Computers and Software, Energy and Environment, Engineering, Government and Public Affairs, Law, Medicine, Patents, Trademarks and Copyrights, Social Sciences and Humanities and Travel. If you would like *DIALOG* to conduct a search for you, for a fee, on any of its databases, call *Dial-Search* at (800) 634-2564.

Unlike many of the other online databases listed in this appendix, *DIALOG* is not easy to use immediately because it requires the knowledge of a complex command language. The language actually allows for more accurate and efficient searching than other systems . . . once it is learned! Many major corporate and academic libraries, as well as some public libraries, offer *DIALOG* searches to their clients, with a librarian performing the search.

Sample *DIALOG* Databases:

AIDSLINE. 1980—present. AIDSLINE contains citations to articles, papers, symposia reports, dissertations, books, government reports and media dealing with the clinical and research aspects of AIDS, along with the epidemiology and health policy issues. (Also on *CDP*, *CompuServe's Knowledge Index* and *Data-Star*.)

CENDATA. Updated daily, CENDATA contains statistical data from censuses and surveys, press releases and product information from the (U.S.) Bureau of the Census. (Also on *CompuServe*.)

DMS/FI Contract Awards. 1981-present. This is a file of all nonclassified U.S. government prime contract actions of $25,000 or more. Some agencies covered: the Department of Defense, NASA, the Department of Transportation and the Department of Energy.

Financial Information. Through various databases, *DIALOG* provides access to financial profiles and background information on more than twelve million U.S. and one million international companies.

Mental Health Abstracts. 1969-present. A compilation of citations to information worldwide on the general topic of mental health. The citations are from journals from forty-one countries in twenty-one languages as well as books, technical reports and proceedings. (Also on *CompuServe's Knowledge Index*.)

Meteorological and Geoastrophysical Abstracts. 1972-present. Citations to research found in worldwide literature resources on the topics of meteorology, astrophysics, physical oceanography, hydrosphere/hydrology, environmental science and glaciology.

Occupational Safety and Health (NI-OSHTIC). Covering all aspects of occupational safety and health, *NI-OSHTIC* contains citations to more than two thousand journal titles and over seventy thousand books and technical reports. (Also on *ORBIT* and *QUESTEL.*)

DJNR—Dow Jones News/Retrieval
Dow Jones & Company, Inc.
P.O. Box 300
Princeton, NJ 08543-0300
(800) 815-5100

Dow Jones News/Retrieval provides access to approximately seventy unique databases, most of which address business and financial issues, investments, stock and mutual fund information, company information and current news. Subscribers also have the option of signing up with *Dow Jones Market Monitor,* a subset of *DJNR* available between 7:01 P.M. and 6 A.M.

Sample *DJNR* Database Information:

Dow Jones Business Newswires (WIRES)—WIRES supplies ninety days' worth of newswire information from press releases, analysts' reports and five Dow Jones newswire services, containing U.S. and international corporate and equities market news.

Dow Jones Enhanced Current Quotes— CQE provides quotes on common and preferred stocks, corporate and

foreign bonds, mutual funds, U.S. Treasury issues and options.

DowQuest—Access to five hundred business publications, including the *Wall Street Journal* and *Barron's.*

Innovest Technical Analysis Reports— This database furnishes price and volume analyses of more than 4,500 stocks trading on the New York and American exchanges and the OTC.

Media General Financial Services—Financial and statistical information on sixty-two hundred companies. (Also on *DIALOG.*)

Wall $treet Week Online—Full transcripts online of the PBS program *Wall $treet Week.*

LEXIS/NEXIS
A Division of Reed/Elsevier
9443 Springboro Pike
Dayton, OH 45401
(800) 227-4908

Though often referred to in the same breath, *LEXIS* and *NEXIS* are two systems, which can be subscribed to separately or together. *LEXIS* is an online service consisting primarily of legal information databases; *NEXIS* concentrates on business, news, government and current affairs. Each has dozens of "Libraries" of information, each representing many databases. Together, the holdings of *LEXIS/NEXIS* are nothing short of astounding. Many of the thousands of databases contain full-text information; some is abstracted.

Though law libraries and business libraries may subscribe to *LEXIS/NEXIS,* usage is strictly reserved for students and faculty of the institution the library serves. These libraries can actually lose their service if they allow nonauthorized people to use it. Law firms, media concerns and other businesses also subscribe to this service. Individuals may subscribe to *LEXIS/NEXIS* but will probably choose a limited option package to keep the cost reasonable. (This is not a cheap service.)

Individuals may have searches done for a fee by calling (800) 843-6476, Monday-Friday 8-6, EST. Some costs for this personalized searching: $6.00 per minute for search time (searches average 5 to 20 minutes), 5 to 8 cents per line print charges, $60 for rush service and $15 for overnight handling.

Sample *NEXIS* "Libraries" (Database Topic Areas):

The Asia/Pacific Rim Library (ASIA-PC)—This library contains detailed information about every country in Asia and the Pacific.

The Campaign News Library (CM-PGN)—Dedicated to the coverage of Presidential, Gubernatorial, Senatorial and Congressional political campaigns. CMPGN includes background on incumbents and challengers, political contributions and contributors, and news coverage of all elections.

The Europe Library—A wide variety of full-text sources in English, German, and French, covering Eastern and Western Europe business and political news, company information, country reports, case law and the *Official Journal of the European Community.*

Sample *LEXIS* Coverage:

Article Access—Articles from law reviews, bar association journals and other legal periodicals are available.

Federal and State Statutes—Full text.
Court Decisions—The full text of decisions from the U.S. Supreme Court, the U.S. Court of Appeals and district and state courts.
Code of Federal Regulations—Full text.
Federal Register—Full text.

OCLC (EPIC, FirstSearch)
Online Computer Library Center
6565 Frantz Road
Dublin, OH 43017
(800) 848-5878

OCLC produces both *EPIC* and *FirstSearch*; a subscription to *EPIC* is geared toward individuals while *FirstSearch* is designed for libraries and institutions. Both *EPIC* and *FirstSearch* provide access to a databases in all subject areas. Check with your local libraries to find out if they subscribe to *FirstSearch*. Searching is menu driven and fairly easy.

Sample Databases on Both *FirstSearch* and *EPIC*:

Arts and Humanities Search—Citations to items from more than eleven hundred arts and humanities journals. (Also on *DIALOG* and *Data-Star*.)

Encyclopedia of Associations—Descriptions and contact information for more than ninety-five thousand organizations worldwide. (Also on *DIALOG*.)

Library Literature—Want to become a librarian? (I recommend it.) This is one of the databases that contains references to literature of interest to library and information professionals. (Also on *CDP*, *DIALOG* and *Wilsonline*.)

Matter of Fact—Presents statistics found in magazines, newspapers and the *Congressional Record* on political, social, economic and environmental issues worldwide.

Microcomputer Abstracts—This database contains citations, with abstracts, to reviews and commentaries on the use and applications of microcomputers and software packages. (Also on *CompuServe's Knowledge Index* and *DIALOG*.)

WorldCat—Access to the holdings of library collections worldwide. (Yes—quite impressive and easy to use.)

Orbit/Questel
Orbit/Questel, Inc.
France Telecom Group
8000 Westpark Drive
McLean, VA 22102
(800) 456-7248

Orbit and *Questel*, are two systems with similar aims. Databases on the *Questel* system, focus on international trademark, patent, chemical, business and general news research. *Orbit* specializes in patent, scientific and technical information. Both are directed to those individuals interested in developing new products, wanting to trademark names or looking for competitive company intelligence data.

Sample *Questel* Databases:

BELGI—*Belgian Companies.* Detailed information on over 116,000 leading Belgian companies.

Danish Trademarks—A database containing all Danish trademarks valid since 1961.

International Database on Biomedical Ethics—Covers information on ethics and all aspects of health policy, reproduction, experiments and problems related to death and violence.

JAPIO—*Japanese Unexamined Appli-cations*—A collection of published, unexamined patent applications for all areas of technology from October 1976 on. (Also on *DIALOG*.)

Technology Transfer Proposals—This database is a window on technology innovations arising in all technological and scientific fields, submitted by those looking for a partner (i.e., licensee, associate, distributor, etc.).

Sample *Orbit* Databases:

Aqualine—Citations to the world's literature on water and wastewater technology and environmental protection. Subjects include: water quality, water treatment, low-cost technology, sewage and industrial effluents.

ChemQuest—A catalog of over 91,000 commercially available research chemicals and where they can be obtained.

Derwent World Patents Index. A file of data relating to patent specifications issued by patent offices of thirty-three major issuing authorities. (Also on *DIALOG* and STN.)

Food Science and Technology Abstracts. FSTA contains information from articles, patents, books, conference proceedings and legislative paper concerning food sciences, food safety, packaging and food products and processes. (Also on *CompuServe's Knowledge Index, Data-Star, DIALOG* and STN.

Who's Who in Technology. Biographic details and career histories, including publications and patents, for over 37,000 leaders of American technology.

STN International
Chemical Abstracts Service

2540 Olentangy River Road
P.O. Box 3012
Columbus, OH 43210

STN supplies access to more than 160 scientific and technical databases. STN is well known as the online supplier of Chemical Abstracts and other such monstrous scientific and technical indexes and abstracts that are unwieldy in paper format but quite tame online. Through the STNmail electronic mail service, users can stay in contact with others who share their scientific and technical interests.

Sample STN Databases:

BioBusiness/RN—Updated four times per month, BioBusiness/RN supplies citations to information on the business implications of technological advances in the life sciences, focusing on pharmaceuticals, health care and biotechnology. Information on product development, marketing, regulatory issues and user satisfaction is also included. (Also on CDP, Data-Star and DIALOG.)

EmBase—A database containing citations to articles, books, proceedings, dissertations and reports in the biomedical and pharmaceutical fields. (Also on CDP, CompuServe's Knowledge Index, Data-Star and DIALOG.)

Infor—Information on Research—Infor is a file containing information on research projects, in many fields, being conducted in Germany.

Inspec—The Information Service for Physics, Electronics and Computing—INSPEC contains citations with abstracts to world physics, electronics, electrical engineering, computers, control engineering and information

technology literature. (Also on CDP, CompuServe's Knowledge Index, Data-Star, DIALOG, EPIC, FirstSearch, ORBIT and Questel.)

Technology Assessment—An online file covering worldwide projects and publications on the potential economic, environmental and social impacts of the introduction of new or modified technologies.

WESTLAW
West Publishing Corporation
620 Opperman Drive
Eagan, MN 55123
(800) 937-8529

WESTLAW is comprised of more than five thousand law-related databases. Along with LEXIS, WESTLAW is commonly found in law libraries and any firms that need specialized or general up-to-date law information. WESTLAW is also a gateway to Dow Jones News/Retrieval.

Sample WESTLAW Databases:

Each of the following databases contains the complete text of U.S. federal court decisions, statutes and regulations, specialized files, and texts and periodicals dealing with a particular subject:

WESTLAW Bankruptcy Library—Bankruptcy topics, including the administration of debtor estates and insolvency.

WESTLAW Education Library—Educational issues, such as contracts, management of educational institutions and the rights and liabilities of teachers, administrators, students and elected officials.

WESTLAW Intellectual Property Library—Dealing with such issues as the rights of artists, authors, composers and designers of creative works and the significance of copyright, patent or trademark protection.

WILSONLINE
930 University Avenue
Bronx, NY 10452
(800) 367-6770

WILSONLINE offers access to over thirty specialized databases. *WILSONLINE* is also available through OCLC and *CDP Online*. Many libraries subscribe to some of the Wilson databases on CD-ROM; there is often a *WILSONLINE* connection available at those workstations. Thus, you can search a Wilson database such as

the *Art Index* on CD-ROM, and then search the same index on *WILSONLINE* for timelier information.

Sample *WILSONLINE* Databases.
(The print versions of these databases are described in Appendix A)

Biography Index
Business Abstracts
Education Index
General Science Index
Humanities Abstracts

Note: The databases listed as Abstracts are the same as their Index counterpart (i.e., *Business Index/Business Abstracts*) only they include summaries of the article.

Index